A Guide to Native Plants of the New York City Region

A Guide to Native Plants of the New York City Region

Margaret B. Gargiullo

Rivergate Books
An imprint of Rutgers University Press
New Brunswick, New Jersey, and London

First paperback printing, 2010

Library of Congress Cataloging-in-Publication Data

Gargiullo, Margaret B., 1942–
A guide to native plants of the New York City region / Margaret B. Gargiullo.
p. cm.
Includes bibliographical references and index.
ISBN–13: 978-0-8135-4042-9 (hardcover : alk. paper)
ISBN–13: 978-0-8135-4777-0 (pbk. : alk. paper)
1. Native plants for cultivation—New York Metropolitan Area. 2. Native plants for cultivation—New York Region. 3. Native plant gardening—New York Metropolitan Area. I. Title.
SB439.24.N5G37 2007
635.9'51—dc22

2006024984

A British Cataloging-in-Publication record for this book is available from the British Library.

This book was produced in association with "New York City Department of Parks & Recreation"

Illustrations on pp. 215–218 by Margaret B. Gargiullo. All other illustrations courtesy of Dover Publications, Mineola, New York.

Manufactured in the United States of America

Contents

Preface

MISSION

This book was compiled to aid landscape architects, designers, land managers, native plant growers, and restorationists in the New York City metropolitan area to realize the full scope of plant materials that are native to this region. I hope that this volume will help promote propagation and planting of a wider range of native plants and aid in the choice of appropriate plant materials for mitigation and restoration projects.

As more land is lost to development, there is less living space for natural populations of native plants. To prevent the loss of native species, we must return these plants to appropriate habitats in restoration projects. It is no longer likely that native plants will repopulate naturalizing sites on their own because seed sources are not available. It is incumbent upon those of us who are revegetating natural areas to restore not only the dominant plants but also the minor elements of the plant community so they will not become extinct in this region.

WHY USE NATIVE PLANTS?

Native species are plants that were growing in this region before Europeans came to North America. Plants native to the New York City metropolitan region come from seed that spread northward after the last glaciers melted thousands of years ago. These plants are adapted to the climate and soils of the New York City area. They have evolved relationships with birds, mammals, insects, and fungi and are integrated into the ecology of this region.

New York City has lost nearly 43 percent of its native plants. As more and more natural habitat is converted to buildings, pavement, or lawn, there are fewer and fewer places for native plants to live. "Common" native forest plants are becoming uncommon as more and more forest is destroyed. Use of native plants in gardens, restorations, landfills, and parks expands habitat and renews populations that are otherwise lost.

WHAT IS WRONG WITH EXOTIC PLANTS?

Exotic species are plants transported to this region by humans. These plants have been imported from parts of Europe and Asia that have climates similar to ours, or sometimes from other parts of North America. Many common exotics, such as lilacs (*Syringa* spp.) or *Zinnia* spp., do not reproduce well in our region and so make suitable plants for gardens. However, some exotic plants escape from cultivation and invade natural areas, displacing native plants.

Invasive plants decrease biodiversity by overwhelming and crowding out native species in natural areas. There is an ongoing controversy about the use of exotic plants. Many people trained in horticulture and landscape architecture promote the use of any plant that lives under the artificial conditions endured by trees in sidewalk pits, or in parks, where they are subjected to compaction, roadside salt, and other stresses. Ecologists and natural area managers, on the other hand, promote the use of plants native to the geographic location. They are concerned about invasion and proliferation of exotic species and the gradual disappearance of native plant populations.

The controversy is one of "plants as infrastructure" versus "plants as biological organisms." A tree in a sidewalk pit or a shrub in a manicured, mowed park or roadside edge is a piece of infrastructure, like a lamppost or bench; it serves the needs of people. A plant in a forest or meadow is a biological organism, free to reproduce itself.

Trouble occurs when the infrastructure plant is released to become a biological organism, free to reproduce in forests, meadows, and marshes. An exotic plant that is able to grow well and reproduce freely, without the biological constraints of its place of origin, can displace native flora and severely decrease diversity in natural areas where it invades. Nonnative plants that reproduce freely and displace native flora are generally referred to as invasive.

The northeastern United States has a number of notorious invasive exotic plants that have overwhelmed our local, native plants to the detriment of our natural heritage. Some of these exotics, including Norway maple, porcelainberry, Japanese honeysuckle, garlic mustard, purple loosestrife and oriental bittersweet, have completely replaced native plant communities. Lists of invasive exotics have been written by The Nature Conservancy, the New York State Natural Heritage Program and New York City Parks Natural Resources Group.

SOURCES OF NATIVE PLANTS

A search of the Web under "nurseries selling native plants, NY, NJ" and "native plant brokers" yields a number of sources. Another site is www.plantlocator.net, a subscription site. As more nurseries begin propagating more plants native to our region this list should grow. Nurseries and contractors also respond to demands for new native plants. If enough land managers, restorationists and landscape architects include more and different plants in their planting lists, eventually these will appear in the catalogs of native plant propagators. If you want specific plants you may need to have them custom grown. This will necessitate having a contract with a nursery that allows them the lead time necessary to collect seed and propagate and grow the plants to a size that can be put into the wild. For woody plants, this will require several years.

Acknowledgments

This project was funded by the New York State Natural Heritage Trust and by the City of New York Department of Parks & Recreation.

Plant illustrations are from the 1970 Dover Press edition of *An Illustrated Flora of the Northern United States and Canada,* 2nd edition (1913), by Nathaniel Lord Britton and Addison Brown.

I would like to thank Brooklyn Botanic Garden, New York Flora Project, for allowing us to use its map of the New York City metropolitan region. I would also like to thank Gerry Moore and Steven Glenn, taxonomists with BBG, for their continuing help with identification of plants species. I would also like to thank Robbin Bergfors, formerly of NYC Parks Natural Resources Group (NRG), for her generous contribution of time and expertise on salt marshes and brackish water habitats; Richard Kruzansky, former soil and water bodies manager of Central Park Conservancy, for his vital inputs on soils and aquatic vegetation; Tim Wenskus, Deputy Director, NYC Parks, NRG, for his contributions on forest restoration. For their time, expertise, and thoughtful evaluations of this project, I would like to thank Dean Cavallaro, NYC Department of Environmental Protection, Bluebelt Project; Gary Dearborne, Project Manager, Central Park Conservancy; and Marcha Johnson, Designer, NYC Parks Capital Projects. To Michael Feller, Chief Naturalist, Parks NRG, my gratitude for his amazing knowledge of obscure weeds. My thanks also to Marc Matsil, Chief of NRG, and to Bill Tai, Director of NRG, for allowing me to work on this long-term project and supporting its publication.

Introduction

THE BASICS OF PLANT COMMUNITY RESTORATION

Geological Units

The New York City Metropolitan Region can be divided into roughly three physiographic areas:

1. The coast itself, including salt marshes, beaches, dune, and back-dune habitats.
2. Coastal plain areas, comprised of the entire southeastern portion of New Jersey and, in New York, Staten Island and all of Long Island.
3. The Rocky New England Uplands, including the portion of NJ northwest of Route 1 (I am including here NJ Piedmont; the NY-NJ Highlands, and the NJ Ridge and Valley). The NY-NJ Highlands include the following counties: Fairfield, CT; Bergen, Morris, Passaic, Sussex, Warren, NJ; Dutchess, Orange, Putnam, Rockland, Westchester, upland formations of the Bronx and much of New York (Manhattan).

Physical Requirements of Plants

The four most critical factors dictating plant community composition are air, light, water, and soil chemistry (acidity/alkalinity).

Air

Plants require oxygen just as animals do. The primary way that most living organisms (anaerobic bacteria aside) obtain energy from sugar (the fundamental food) is to oxidize, i.e., burn it, with oxygen. The energy released from this oxidation is stored in the bonds of special chemicals (ATP). Water and carbon dioxide are the waste products of this process. Above ground plant parts are constantly exposed to air, but roots or other parts below ground must obtain air from porous, well-aerated soil.

Saturation: Soil in which all the spaces between soil particles are filled with water is saturated. Saturated soil does not contain enough oxygen to sustain

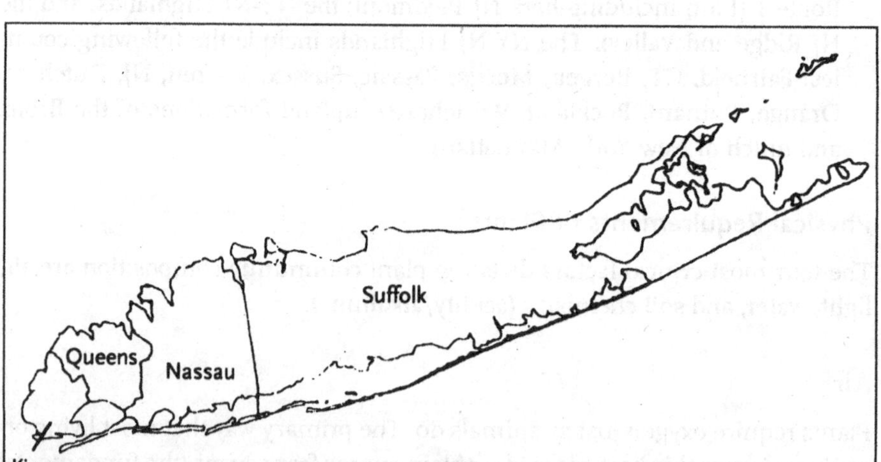

Map 1. New York City Metropolitan Area. Courtesy of Brooklyn Botanic Garden

most plants, and they will die. However, many wetland plants are adapted to living in saturated soils and have open "air ducts" of various kinds in their stems to bring oxygen to root tissues.

Compaction: Compaction is the result of weight compressing soil so that the air spaces between soil particles are decreased. Vehicle or foot traffic results in compression of air spaces in soil. Wet soil becomes compacted more easily than dry soil. Soil that is compacted loses pore spaces and also may contain too little oxygen to sustain many plant species. Compaction also results in poor soil drainage, which also decreases oxygen content. Uncompacted soil is roughly 50 percent soil particles, 20 percent air, and 30 percent water. It drains at a rate of 5 to 14 inches of water per day. Compacted soil drainage can be reduced to only 1.5 inches per day. The water collecting in wheel ruts and footpaths is the result of compaction, since water cannot infiltrate compacted soil. The term "bulk density" is defined as weight per volume. Uncompacted soil has a bulk density of less than one gram per cubic centimeter. Soil with bulk densities greater than one gram per cubic centimeter is compacted. In restoration work, soil compaction must either be remedied or plants should be chosen that tolerate soil compaction.

Light

Light provides the energy for plants to manufacture food (sugar, starch). The green pigment chlorophyll in plants captures light energy to make possible the combination of carbon dioxide and water into sugar with oxygen as the waste product. This is the process of photosynthesis. Plant parts that do not make sugar, such as roots and woody stems (and green plant parts in the absence of light), use the energy stored in sugar to live, as do virtually all living organisms (see Air). The following equation sums up the most fundamental processes of life on earth: $CO_2 + H_2O <\!\!-\!\!-\!\!> CH_2O + O_2$.

Different plant species are adapted to varying amounts of light. Some require full sun, while some forest understory plants can live on very low light levels. The term "succession" refers to the establishment of various types of plants with various light requirements, over time, in a previously disturbed site (such as a plowed field, burned over or bulldozed vacant lot, or new deposition of fill soil). When working on a restoration, it is critical to know the shade tolerance of the plants to be installed at a particular site. Here is the shade tolerance index from Hightshoe (1988):

Very tolerant: 8–10 (American beech, *Fagus grandifolia*)
Tolerant: 6–7.9 (northern red oak, *Quercus rubra*)
Moderate: 4–5.9 (white oak, *Quercus alba*)
Intolerant: 2–3.9 (pin oak, *Quercus palustris*)
Very intolerant 0–1.9 (pitch pine, *Pinus rigida*)

Water

All living things need water. The amount of soil water that a plant species needs can vary widely. In very dry soil it is difficult for plant roots to extract the little water that is present. In soil saturated with water, plant roots must live in an oxygen-deprived environment because all the air is displaced by water. Matching a plant to the moisture regime of a site is vital to the success of a restoration. It is important to remember that the majority of plants need a soil that has both air and water in it. They do best in habitats that are neither wetlands nor dry uplands.

Definition of wetlands: A wetland is legally defined by the U.S. Army Corps of Engineers as an area that is "inundated or saturated by surface water or ground water at a frequency and duration sufficient to support vegetation typically adapted for life in saturated soil. Wetlands generally include swamps, marshes, bogs and similar areas." The defining characteristic of wetland plants is that they can tolerate soil that has little oxygen because the air spaces are filled with water (saturated).

Non-wetlands are defined as "uplands or lowlands that are seldom or never inundated or, if inundated, have saturated soils for only brief periods during the growing season." In other words, non-wetlands are areas that have well aerated soil, with plenty of oxygen, almost all the time.

Wetland status: In order to delineate wetlands in a relatively predictable way, the Corps of Engineers has developed categories to classify the wetland status of plants found in a given area (both native and nonnative). Use of these categories enables the designer to communicate better with those involved in natural resource work. It gives everyone a common language that is legally acceptable. The abbreviated terms OBL (obligate wetland plant), FACW (facultative wetland plant), FAC (facultative plant), FACU (facultative upland plant), and UPL (upland plant), are used to indicate the tolerance of a plant for anaerobic soil, saturated with water. Conversely, these terms indicate a plant's need for moisture. An "obligate" wetland plant, such as buttonbush, is very intolerant of dry soil, whereas an upland plant, such as scarlet oak, is intolerant of saturated soil. The term "facultative" indicates latitude in a plant's tolerance. For instance, red maple and sweet gum, both listed as FAC, are often dominants in the swamp forests in New York City and regions to the immediate south, yet both of these trees are also often found in uplands. In some cases this may be caused by differences in the plants' genetic makeup but may also indicate a wide tolerance for different moisture regimes.

The abbreviations are standards used by the U.S. Army Corps of Engineers. They are defined as the percentage of instances (probability) a plant species might be found in a wetland:

OBL = >99%, plants always found in wet soil or standing water. The plant needs, or tolerates, soil saturated with water and, therefore, having little oxygen.
FACW = 67–99%, plants usually found in wet to moist soil. Tolerates periods of saturated soil (flooding) during the growing season but usually not permanent, standing water. Often tolerant of compacted or heavy clay soils with low oxygen content.
FAC = 34–66%, plants occurring in both wetlands and moist upland soil. Most will tolerate short periods of saturated soil, brief flooding, especially during the winter when dormant. They generally do not tolerate very dry soil for prolonged periods.
FACU = 1–33%, plants sometimes occur in wetlands. They tolerate moist to dry soil; many will tolerate brief flooding but not for more than a day or two. All plants tolerate flooding better when they are dormant.
UPL = 0%, plants that almost never occur in wetlands. Plants that do not tolerate oxygen-poor, saturated soils. Most of these plants also will not tolerate soil compaction. Not all of these plants tolerate very dry soils, such as those of pine barrens. Most require moist soil with an occasional period of drought. Even plants that tolerate dry soils will generally not grow during prolonged dry periods.

A plus (+) following the acronym indicates the plant is slightly more tolerant of saturated soil, a minus (−) indicates it is slightly less tolerant of saturated soil.

Wetland status has as much, or more, to do with a plant's need for oxygen around its roots as with its need for water around its roots.

Maritime wetlands (plants of high marsh habitats unless noted otherwise): When restoring or mitigating for salt marsh habitats, the most critical factor for success is elevation. Salt marsh, brackish, and freshwater tidal elevations are site specific. You will need to consult local tide information sources for the tidal elevations of your site. Grading must be done with extreme precision. Salinity levels for tidal wetlands are as follows:

Freshwater = 0–0.5 parts per thousand (ppt) salt
Brackish water = 0.6–10 ppt salt
Saline tidal water = 10–35 ppt.

Water quality and use of floating and submerged aquatic plants: A major summer problem for land and park managers is the growth of algae in shallow ponds, especially where water is overloaded with nutrients from lawn fertilizers, goose droppings, and dog waste.

Planting submerged or floating leaved aquatics can alleviate algal growth, diminish mosquito populations, and improve habitat for fish and frogs. Rooted aquatic plants such as water lilies and pondweeds stabilize sediments and may improve water clarity after rainstorms, which normally stir up bottom sediment. Aquatic plants keep water cooler and help shade out algae. They provide shelter from direct sunlight for fish and frogs, which cannot tolerate the high ultraviolet light in shallow water bodies. Plants also provide surfaces for egg-laying invertebrates that become food for fish and frogs. Fish, frogs, and predatory insect larvae, such as those of dragonflies, eat mosquito larvae. The oxygen produced by aquatic plants dissolves in the water and helps prevent leeching of phosphates trapped in bottom sediments. Floating, unrooted plants such as duckweeds take up soluble nitrogen and phosphorus directly from water and trap inorganic compounds that are stored in sediments, making them unavailable for algal growth. Wetland plants listed as tolerating acid, or low nutrient water, probably cannot compete with plants inhabiting high-nutrient, circumneutral or alkaline waters.

A dense buffer of wetland vegetation around pond margins helps prevent eroded soil and high nutrient runoff from reaching the water body. Dense vegetation slows runoff and gives water a chance to be absorbed into soil. In addition Canada geese will not readily colonize a water body that is closely surrounded by vegetation because they cannot see over it or easily walk through it and so may not feel as safe as when the landscape is open.

Soil

Mineral constituents of soil: Soil qualities are tightly interwoven with the availability of water and oxygen. Mineral soils, the portion derived from weathered rock, vary greatly in texture depending on the proportion of sand, silt, and clay they contain. Sand consists of mineral particles 0.05–2 millimeters (mm) in diameter, large enough to be seen with the naked eye. Sandy soils feel rough and gritty. These soils are loose and do not stick together when pressed, even when wet. Silt-sized particles are 0.002–0.05 mm in diameter and cannot be seen without a microscope. Silty soils feel smooth but are not sticky. Clay-sized particles are less than 0.002 mm in diameter and are only visible with a microscope or electron microscope. Clay soils feel slick and sticky when wet and can become very hard when dry. The finer the particles, the smaller the spaces between them. These spaces hold air and water that are available to plant roots. Coarse, sandy soils drain quickly, hold little water and few nutrients, but are well aerated. At the opposite extreme, heavy clay soils are very fine and tend to become waterlogged, compacted, and anaerobic. Loam refers to soils that contain a mixture of all three particle sizes from loamy sand with less than 20 percent clay, to silty clay loam with less than 30 percent sand. The total volume of a loamy soil may consist of 50 percent pore spaces filled with water and air. Soil texture is a fundamental quality that should be known before a planting plan is written.

Organic soil constituents: Living and dead plants and animals, animal wastes, fungi, bacteria, woody debris, and leaf litter contribute to the organic matter in soils. Organic materials are often referred to as "carbon" since they are tissues derived from living organisms and so are based on carbon compounds. A typical mineral soil contains about 5 percent organic matter by weight. That may not seem great, but a temperate forest soil stores about 100 tons of carbon per hectare (2.5 acres). Soils store large amounts of carbon that slowly combine with oxygen to become carbon dioxide, which diffuses into the atmosphere. In waterlogged or other anaerobic soils, carbon does not break down easily and accumulates as peat. Organic matter increases the water-holding capacity in soils and is a major source of nitrogen, phosphorus, and sulfur, essential plant nutrients.

Humus: Insoluble, partially decayed organic materials form a blackish, soft, crumbly substance that collects as a layer between mineral soil and the surface layer of undecayed leaf litter and woody debris. This layer of humus is typical of undisturbed, healthy temperate forest soils. It is critical as a habitat for mycorrhizal fungi and fine plant roots to take up water and nutrients. Soil invertebrates and fungi slowly decompose humus, releasing nutrients and organic chemicals that promote plant growth. The value of natural accumulations of leaf litter and woody debris on a forest floor cannot be emphasized too much. One acre in a 56-year-old forest stand may accumulate over 11 tons of dead wood on the forest floor and almost 2 tons of standing dead wood. All this is essential to nutrient recycling, water-holding capacity, continuing forest regeneration, and wildlife habitat.

Soil pH, mycorrhizas, and nutrient status (soil pH is given where the information is available): The acidity or alkalinity of soil is critical to the survival and health of plants. Many native plants require acid soil with pH 4.5–6.5 (some native plants can tolerate very acid soils down to pH 3.5). Soils with pH above 6.5 are considered neutral and soils with pH above 7.5 are alkaline (pH above 8.5 is strongly alkaline and must be modified). Acid soils favor the growth of mycorrhizal fungi that form symbiotic relationships with the roots of most native trees, shrubs, and herbs. Evergreens, oaks, and plants in the heath family (Ericaceae: *Vaccinium, Rhododendron,* etc.) are especially dependant upon low pH soils that support adequate populations of appropriate mycorrhizal species. Mycorrhizal fungi increase uptake of both moisture and nutrients by roots.

Except for plants adapted to limestone-derived soils, native plants generally are adapted to low-nutrient, acid soils. Lime or fertilizer should not be added to soils in urban natural areas unless the pH is extremely low (<4.5) because such additions will encourage competition from nonnative invasive plants that require high-nutrient, circumneutral soils. High-nutrient, circumneutral soils also often harbor large populations of European and Asian earthworms that inhibit or prevent establishment of some native plants (see Pouyat et al. 1994 and Gundale 2002). In addition, uptake of nitrogen and other nutrients requires energy and will further weaken stressed plants.

Plants adapted to alkaline soils are specifically noted in this list, as they are likely to tolerate concrete debris present in many urban fill soils. Alkaline soils are difficult to acidify on more than a temporary basis. Addition of sulfur decreases the pH for a time, but will not permanently acidify soil, since it is soluble. In addition, contractors may apply sulfur in such a way that it burns the soil by temporarily overacidifying. Addition of acid organic material such as wood chips, acidic compost, ground hardwood bark, old Christmas-trees, pine bark, or pine needles may help acidify soil over a longer period. Once established, plants that produce acidic litter can permanently acidify soils at least locally. Urban soils, especially fill soil containing demolition debris, generally contains a lot of concrete, which is alkaline. The wear of sidewalks, streets, curbs, and other concrete structures falls out as concrete dust that finds its way even into native soils. It is necessary, therefore, to give thought to the use of acidifying soil amendments if evergreens, oaks, heath family plants, or other acidophiles are to be used in a project. In rural areas of the region, some soils may be excessively acidic due to acid rain. Soils with pH 4.5 or below may need some amendment.

Alkaline fill should also be tested for salt content. The test for this is EC (electrical conductivity), which gives an indirect measure of salt content. The EC should not be higher than 2 mMhos/cm (millimhos) or 2000 microMhos/cm. EC is also sometimes reported in milli Siemans (mS), in which case the number should not exceed 2 mS.

A good discussion of soils in restoration projects may be found in Sauer et al. (1998). A Web search will probably also yield useful information on other restoration techniques.

Vegetation of Open Sites: Plant Community Succession

It is crucial to keep a few basic principles in mind when a restoration project is undertaken in this region. First, the normal plant community in the New York City region is forest. The New York metropolitan region receives an average annual rainfall of roughly 44 inches, distributed throughout the year. This means that woody vegetation will become established in undisturbed sites on virtually any soil type, given sufficient time (including dry, sandy soils of back dunes and pine barrens). Periodic disturbance of storms, fires, or clearing are the reasons that some sites remain open (not including toxic waste sites, contaminated with heavy metals). Without human interference, fire is a very infrequent cause of disturbance in this part of the country. Unlike the western United States, we rarely have dry lightning, the regular cause of fires in the West. In the Northeast, according to NOAA, lightning is almost always accompanied by rain. With few exceptions (some pine barrens species), our native plants are not adapted to fire. In an undisturbed forest, succession and renewal usually occur as periodic wind or ice storms cause blowdowns and otherwise open the tree canopy. Beaver meadows and back-dune grasslands are probably our only naturally occurring meadow habitats. These also are created by major periodic disturbances.

All open restoration sites will become wooded over time unless they are mowed at least every year or two (burning in usually not an option). Even then, habitats intended to be meadows often develop a low, woody stubble of vines and shrub stumps over time. Continual human disturbance caused by trampling, vehicle traffic, dumping, and arson not only sets back succession but often destroys mature forest understories by causing loss of vegetation, humus, mineral soil, and entry to invasive plants. In recent decades deer populations have also destroyed many native plants and prevented forest regeneration.

The development of forest from open, abandoned farm fields is one of the most intensively studied ecological phenomena in the northeastern United States. This sequence is generally as follows:

1. Annual herbs and grasses, from seeds already in the soil (ragweed, horseweed).
2. Perennial herbs, from soil seeds or from surrounding vegetation (goldenrods, asters).
3. Shrubs and trees from seeds carried by birds or wind (poplars, eastern red cedar, ash, sumac).

Fast-growing "pioneer" species that need full sun are usually the first to attain full size, followed by slower-growing, longer-lived, and more shade-tolerant species (oaks, hickories, sugar maple, beech).

The first plants to become established on open soil are referred to as *pioneer species*. They are often annual weeds or perennials that require full sunlight. They include plants such as ragweed, horseweed, some asters, goldenrods, and exotics such as mugwort. Woody pioneer species become established within another few years. These include plants that require full sunlight, grow very rapidly, and are tolerant of a wide range of conditions. Some of our most common pioneer species are eastern cottonwood and other poplars, wild black cherry, and sumacs. Unfortunately, many aggressive exotics fall into this category and can rapidly dominate open sites (multiflora rose, porcelainberry, oriental bittersweet, autumn or Russian olive, white mulberry, black locust, and ailanthus). While the site still enjoys full sun, slower-growing, shade-intolerant species such as scarlet oak become established. Once tree canopy cover is established, slower-growing, more shade-tolerant trees and shrubs start to become established. Common shade-tolerant species in this region include beech, sugar maple, and maple-leaved viburnum. There are a number of shade-tolerant invasives such as Norway and sycamore maple, Japanese honeysuckle, and several species of exotic bush honeysuckles that can take over woodlands and exclude native plants.

When vegetating an open site, the goal is to establish cover appropriate to the site conditions that will help exclude invasives. Plan ahead for succession. Get native plants established before the invasives take over the site. A cover of aggressive native "old field" herbs such as Canada goldenrod, rough goldenrod, indian hemp, and common milkweed may be effective in competing with mugwort. At the same time, establishment of many small-sized, fast-growing native trees and shrubs, along with a scattering of slower-growing species, will help develop shade quickly, while letting the slower-growing species become established. As short-lived, shade-intolerant species gradually die out, slower-growing trees and shrubs are there to take over. There must still be management of the site to remove invasives as native plants are becoming established. It is unfortunate that in our small, fragmented, natural areas, nature can no longer heal itself as it once was able to do.

Forest restoration: When restoring understories of established woodlands, it is important to use plants that are shade tolerant. Unless it is necessary to fill in large open areas within the forest, the plants used should be mostly shrubs, herbs, and graminoids.

It should be noted that evergreen plants such as *Mitchella repens* and *Kalmia* spp. probably do a major amount of photosynthesis during the spring and autumn when the tree canopy is bare and they receive almost full sunlight. Most forest understory plants are probably not as shade tolerant as they appear to be in midsummer. Therefore, these plants should probably not be planted under the permanent shade of evergreen trees or other perpetually shady situations. The reason almost no plants can grow under Norway maple is that it leafs out early and drops leaves late, denying light to plants below its canopy.

Planting trees under an already established, closed canopy is liable to be unsuccessful because the newly planted trees have no opening in which to grow up. The tree canopy forms a "ceiling" that blocks light and will prevent growth of most newly planted trees. In addition, digging in the understory will damage roots of resident trees. When restoring forest understories, it is best to plant small, containerized shrubs and 2-inch plugs of herbs and graminoids. When replacing exotic trees with natives, do not remove too many trees at one time. Large open areas will quickly become overrun with exotic vines and trees. It is probably best to kill exotic trees in situ and plant native saplings under them. Dead standing trees make excellent habitat and food resources for woodland birds and other wildlife. They should not be removed unless they are a threat to pedestrians in a developed park.

If soil stabilization of slopes is necessary, jute or coconut fiber (coir) matting should be laid down and pinned into the soil over appropriate soil amendments (compost, leaf litter, etc.) The matting can then be planted into. If erosion control matting cannot be used, a layer of sticks, dry shrub and tree cuttings, and leaf litter can be used. This must be loose and light enough to allow plants to grow up through it. The essential thing is to prevent further soil erosion and to keep foot, dog, bicycle, and other traffic off the site. Small sites should be fenced off for a year or two when possible. Residents who regularly use an area will want to know what is being done and why someone is making changes in their natural area. Good signage that explains the project and encourages the image of care and healing can engage local residents with a sense of ownership and participation. This approach can often help prevent vandalism.

A complete discussion of restoration techniques is beyond the scope of this book and the expertise of the author. However, the book by Leslie Sauer and Andropogon Associates, *The Once and Future Forest, a Guide to Forest Restoration Strategies* (Island Press, Washington, D.C., 1998), will answer many questions on forest restorations. In addition, a search of the Web, under "Northeastern Forest Restorations," yields information from many other sources, including the Society for Ecological Restorations and a number of particular restoration projects.

Adaptation to Environmental Stress

To select the right plants for a given habitat, it is critical to understand the stresses imposed by that habitat and the stresses to which a given plant is adapted. Plants adapted to dry, acid, low-nutrient soils are usually unable to compete with more aggressive plants in moist, higher-quality soils. Spring ephemerals are not adapted to permanent shade. Plants adapted to shady habitats will not tolerate full sun and competition from plants adapted to open habitats. Plants adapted to various stressful environments have most often "traded-off" the ability to grow rapidly for the ability to live where faster-growing plants cannot find enough water or nutrients to live or where it is too wet or too salty for most plants to tolerate.

Use of Local Genotypes

Many of the plants listed in this book are currently extinct in New York City. Most, however, exist somewhere within the metropolitan region. Many of these species have wide ranges in eastern North America and may be sold by growers from Wisconsin to Tennessee to northern New York State. However, local populations of a given plant species are adapted to local climate conditions and will do better than individuals from more distant populations. A red maple from Georgia may not tolerate New York City winters, whereas a red maple from Canada may not tolerate our hot summers. In addition, it is important to maintain local gene pools of different plants so that variation and adaptability are maintained. It is, therefore, strongly recommended that plants be grown locally, from populations within 150 miles of the site where they will be established.

Protecting Wild Populations

When growing or purchasing native plants that are not regularly cultivated, it is extremely important to ensure that plants are *not* taken from wild populations. Plants should be propagated from modest amounts of seed or cuttings collected from a number of different local sources to ensure regional genetic diversity. Never take all the seed from any one source since continued reproduction of wild populations is critical to the survival of each species.

Plants Not Included

This book does not include plants with highly specialized ecological needs, such as ground pines (*Lycopodium* spp., *Selaginella* spp.), orchids (Orchidaceae), and Pyrolaceae (*Pyrola* and *Chimaphila* spp.). These plants are symbiotic with specialized fungi and are extremely difficult to propagate and establish. Ferns in the genus *Botrychium* also fall into this category. More research needs to be done to determine the soil requirements of these plants. Rescued plants transplanted to similar habitats, in humus supplemented with partially decayed oak and pine leaf litter, may have a chance at success in some cases. Habitat conservation is currently the only method for preventing extinction of these plants. Other plants that have been excluded from the book are parasites and hemiparasites, such as *Cuscuta* and *Agalinis* spp., because their specialized ecological needs may make them very difficult to cultivate.

Rare Plants

A plant may be rare because it is at the limit of its range (as are blackjack and willow oaks), and is abundant elsewhere. Or it may be rare throughout its range due to loss of habitat, microsite requirements, or infrequent reproduction (*Helonias bullata*, swamp pink). In any case, if a rare plant is to be used in a restoration project, understanding of the plant's ecological needs and consultation with a conservation organization is strongly recommended.

Be aware that rare plant lists and designations are updated frequently. For the latest information on the status of a particular plant, go to one of the following Web sites:

Connecticut: www.ct-botanical-society.org/galleries/rareindex.html
New Jersey: www.natureserve.org/nhp/us/nj/
New York State: http://www.dec.state.ny.us/website/dfwmr/heritage/

Plant Characteristics

Sexes on different plants (dioecious): Plant one male tree for every four to five females.

Nitrogen fixers: Many legumes, and other nitrogen fixers, form root nodules containing bacteria that take nitrogen from the atmosphere and transform it into compounds that plants can use. These plants should improve sterile soil.

Shade tolerant: Even shade-tolerant plants usually need dappled light. Very few plants can grow in deep shade.

Fruit type: Fleshy fruits are usually eaten, and seeds dispersed, by birds and/or mammals. Many spring ephemerals have seeds with small fleshy attachments and are dispersed by ants. Unless noted otherwise, herbs have dry fruits.

Annuals: All plants listed are perennials, unless noted as annual.

Plant Names

Scientific names of plants have two parts: the first word is the "genus" a proper noun, and is always capitalized. The second word is the "species," an adjective, describing the proper noun, and is never capitalized, even when it is derived from a proper noun (e.g., *Solidago canadensis*). Scientific names are usually italicized.

Many plants listed here have more than one scientific name. My source for the primary scientific name is *Manual of Vascular Plants of Northeastern United States and Adjacent Canada* by Gleason and Cronquist (2nd ed., 1991). This book is currently the most widely used plant manual for this region. However, many plant catalogs and field guides list older names, many of which I have included here. On the other hand, the USDA plant information database (http://plants.usda.gov/index.html) uses nomenclature developed by John Kartesz at the Biota of North America Program (BONAP). I have included these synonyms anticipating that the reader may need this information.

The changing scientific plant names used by taxonomists are a sore point for many plant enthusiasts (e.g., is it *Solidago graminifolia* or *Euthamia* g.?). However, taxonomy, like other science, is about discovery, and new information often dictates a change in the names used for a species. This is especially true now that DNA analysis is possible and relationships among plants can be determined at the genetic level. Although I have included common names, I strongly urge use of scientific names. The same common name is often used for more than one plant, and one plant species may have several common names. Scientific names are unique for each plant: one name is never used for more than one plant species (even through one species may have several scientific names). Use of scientific names is particularly important in contract specifications for restoration and mitigation work so there can be no mistake about what plants the contractor must supply.

How to Use This Book

The plants in Part I are arranged by habit: that is, woody versus nonwoody; trees versus shrubs, etc. Part II lists plants by habitat and particular conditions. For instance, if your site is covered with high pH fill soil and has a lot of low, wet areas, you would look at plants listed for "Freshwater wetlands—alkaline soils."

Always go back to Part I and look at the individual plant summaries to make sure you choose the plants that are likely to grow and reproduce best on your site. Although the range of native plants available from nurseries in our region has been steadily increasing, many plants discussed in this book may currently be difficult to obtain. However, some nurseries may grow plants to order if they have sufficient notice. In any case, increased demand should encourage native plant growers to expand their stock. One of my primary goals for this book is to increase the number of native plants available for restoration projects.

Keys to Plant Status, Characteristics, and Requirements

NEW YORK STATE RARE PLANT STATUS

S1 = critically imperiled
S2 = imperiled
S3 = rare in New York State
E = endangered
T = threatened
R = rare
V = vulnerable
U = unprotected

GLOBAL RANK

G1 = critically imperiled
G2 = imperiled
G3 = very rare
G4 = apparently secure

PLANT CHARACTERISTICS

A = needs or tolerates acid soil (pH below 6.5)
B = attractive to butterflies or their larvae; larvae of many species eat sedges and grasses in wet areas
C = colonial
D = dioecious (sexes on different plants); plant one male tree for every four to five female trees
E = evergreen
F = good fall color
G = ground cover
H = attractive to hummingbirds
K = needs limestone (calcareous) soil; should tolerate high pH of concrete debris

N = many legumes and other nitrogen fixers form root nodes containing bacteria that take nitrogen from the atmosphere and transform it into compounds that plants can use. These plants should improve sterile soil.
S = shade tolerant. Even shade tolerant plants usually need dappled light. Very few plants can grow in deep shade.
s = at least moderately tolerant of salt
* = usually available, or common in New York City, good urban plant

WETLAND STATUS

OBL >99%, plants always found in standing water or wet soil
FACW 67–99%, plants usually found in wet to moist soil
FAC 34–66%, plants occurring in both wetlands and moist upland soil
FACU 1–33%, plants sometimes occur in wetlands, tolerate moist to dry soil
UPL 0%, plants that almost never occur in wetlands and tolerate dry soil

SHADE TOLERANCE INDEX (FROM HIGHTSHOE 1988)

Very tolerant: 8–10 (American beech, *Fagus grandifolia*)
Tolerant: 6–7.9 (northern red oak, *Quercus rubra*)
Moderate: 4–5.9 (white oak, *Quercus alba*)
Intolerant: 2–3.9 (pin oak, *Quercus palustris*)
Very intolerant: 0–1.9 (pitch pine, *Pinus rigida*)

pH ACIDITY/ALKALINITY OF SOIL OR WATER

Strongly acid: pH below 4.5
Acid soil/water: pH 4.5–6
Neutral: pH 6.5–7.5
Alkaline: pH 7.5–8.5
Strongly alkaline: pH 8.6 and above

[ ] Bracketed species are those not recommended due to severe diseases or other problems.

Part 1

Plants of New York City and Vicinity

Chapter 1

Trees

Trees are usually defined as woody plants with a single trunk, that reach a height of over 20 feet at reproductive maturity. The majority of common trees in our region lose their leaves in autumn (deciduous), and hence our woodlands are part of "the eastern deciduous forest." The tree community on a particular site varies with soil chemistry, moisture regime, age, and random factors such as the seeds present when the forest began to grow. Once the canopy closes, the opportunity for addition of new species decreases considerably. Many tree species can begin their growth in shade, but most will eventually die at sapling size if no canopy opening (gap) appears overhead. In general, seedlings are more shade tolerant than older trees. A few species tend to seed into open sites rapidly and dominate forest communities of various types.

Along the coastal plain, swamp forests and sites that flood regularly are generally dominated by red maple (*Acer rubrum*) and sweet gum (*Liquidambar styraciflua*). In the piedmont, in rocky, glaciated regions, and in the uplands to the north and west, swamp forests may be dominated by green ash (*Fraxinus pensylvanica*) or red maple. Pin oak (*Quercus palustris*) is often a codominant or subdominant tree in wet to moist forests throughout our region. Other common trees in wet forests are black tupelo (*Nyssa sylvatica*), swamp white oak (*Quercus bicolor*), and American elm (*Ulmus americana*).

Trees in floodplain forests, along river margins, must tolerate currents and periodic scouring in times of flooding, as well as saturated soil. Common trees in these forests tend to be fast-growing pioneer species that tolerate disturbance well but are very intolerant of shade. These include black willow (*Salix nigra*), American sycamore (*Platanus occidentalis*), eastern cottonwood (*Populus deltoides*), box elder (*Acer negundo*), and river birch (*Betula nigra*). These two tree communities are not mutually exclusive, and all species may be found in both forest communities depending on environmental circumstances.

At the opposite end of the moisture-regime spectrum, forests on dry, sandy, or rocky soil and ridge tops must be able to withstand prolonged dry periods. Common trees adapted to dry conditions include black oak (*Quercus velutina*), chestnut oak (*Q. prinus*), scarlet oak (*Q. coccinea*), white oak (*Q. alba*), and black birch (*Betula lenta*).

In sites with moderate soil moisture that does not dry out except during prolonged droughts, tree species are less limited by environmental factors. A typical "mesic" tree community may include a rather wide range of species, including tulip tree (*Liriodendron tulipifera*), red maple, red oak (*Quercus rubra*), white oak, white ash (*Fraxinus americana*), sweet gum, black tupelo, beech (*Fagus grandifolia*), wild black cherry (*Prunus serotina*), and various species of hickory (*Carya ovata, C. cordiformis, C. glabra,* and *C. tomentosa*).

When planning a forest restoration, it is critical to understand the soil and basic water dynamics of the site in order to choose species that will live, grow, and, ultimately, reproduce.

TREE SPECIES

Flowers small, dull; fruit dry unless otherwise indicated.

*Acer negundo (box elder, ash-leaf maple)

Acer negundo

To 60 ft., usually less, often shrubby, leaning, rather weedy, fast growing. Blooms April–May; seeds wind dispersed Sept.–Oct. into winter. Wildlife value high. Seeds, buds, flowers eaten by birds and mammals. **Habitat requirements:** Floodplains, moist to wet, disturbed soil (FAC+). Soil pH 5–8. Tolerant of flooding, saturated soil up to 75 percent growing season; tolerant of drought; compaction, demolition debris, concrete rubble, old blacktop. Moderately tolerant of salt. Intolerant of shade, index 1.8. **Note:** A sturdy, widely tolerant tree for wetland restorations but sloppy looking, not decorative. Common. Available. **Uses:** Primary or secondary species for restoration of flood plains and in moist fill soils in open sites.

*Acer pensylvanicum (moosewood, striped maple)

To 36 ft., bark often green, striped with white. Flowers yellow May–June; fruit May–Aug. **Habitat requirements:** Moist, rich, cool, rocky woods (FACU). Tolerates soil pH 4.4–6.5. Tolerant of shade. **Notes:** Native to northwestern NJ and NYS north of NYC. Not a coastal plain or piedmont species. **Uses:** Minor species for restoration of upland forests north and west of NYC.

*Acer rubrum (red maple)

To 100 ft., growth rate medium to fast. Fall color yellow to red. Blooms March, masses of tiny red flowers; seeds wind dispersed May–June. Wildlife value high. Seeds, buds, flowers eaten by birds and mammals. **Habitat requirements:** Swamp forests, freshwater tidal and nontidal wetlands, floodplains, moist and sometimes upland woods (FAC). Soil pH 4.5–7. Tolerant of flooding, saturated soil up to 25% growing season; tolerates ozone; soil compaction; shade, index 6–8. Moderately tolerant of drought. Intolerant of salt. **Notes:** Common in NYC. Available. Variation in habitat tolerance is both genetic and probably also environmental. Trees adapted to dry soil may not be tolerant of wet or compacted soil. Many cultivars available, try to get local stock. **Uses:** Primary species for restoration of swamp forests, flood plains, wetland mitigation. Street tree, horticultural.

**Acer saccharinum* (silver maple)

To 90 ft., fast growing, but older trees tend to fall apart in storms. Blooms Feb.–March; seeds wind dispersed April–May. Wildlife value high. Seeds, buds, flowers eaten by birds and mammals. **Habitat requirements:** Typically found in moist to wet soil of floodplains (FACW). Soil pH 4–7. Tolerates flooding or saturated soil up to 25% of growing season. Tolerates soil compaction, drought. Moderately salt tolerant. Shade tolerance medium, index 5.8. **Notes:** Common. Available. **Uses:** Primary species for restoration of swamp forests, flood plains, wetland mitigation. A fast growing tree to establish light shade and shelter while slower growing species, such as swamp white oak, become established.

Acer saccharum (sugar maple)

To 100 ft., long lived, slow growing, famous for vivid red to orange fall color. Blooms April–May; seeds wind dispersed Sept.–Oct. **Habitat requirements:** Upland forests, rocky New England province areas, piedmont (FACU). Not usually a coastal plain species in this region. Tolerates soil pH 5.5–7.3. Very shade tolerant, index 10. Moderately drought tolerant. Intolerant of salt, soil compaction, flooding. **Notes:** *Warning!* There are numerous species of Acer. Avoid substitution with nonnative *Acer* spp. (*A. platanoides* and *A. pseudoplatanus* are extremely invasive). Many cultivars available. Try to get local stock. **Uses:** Secondary species in forest restoration in rocky upland areas. Park tree, suburban street tree.

Acer spicatum (mountain maple)

To 30 ft., stems often clumped. Flowers green June–Aug.; fruit July–Oct. Seeds wind dispersed. **Habitat requirements:** Moist to dry, cool, rocky woods (FACU−). Tolerates soil pH 5.8–7. Tolerant of shade. **Notes:** Uncommon. Native to northern NJ and NYS north of NYC. Not a coastal plain species. **Uses:** Minor species for restoration of upland forests north and west of NYC.

Betula alleghaniensis (yellow birch)

To 80 ft., bark, yellowish silvery, peeling. Blooms April–May; seeds ripe Aug.–Oct., wind dispersed through winter. Host to larvae of some butterfly species.

Habitat requirements: Moist, well-drained, fertile loam soils (FAC). Moderately acid soil pH 4.6–6.9. Intolerant of shade, flooding. **Notes:** Avoid substitutions! Many species and cultivars of birch are grown. Try to get local stock. A northern forest tree. Southern limit, NW shore of Long Island. **Uses:** Minor element in forest restoration, especially north of NYC. Park tree.

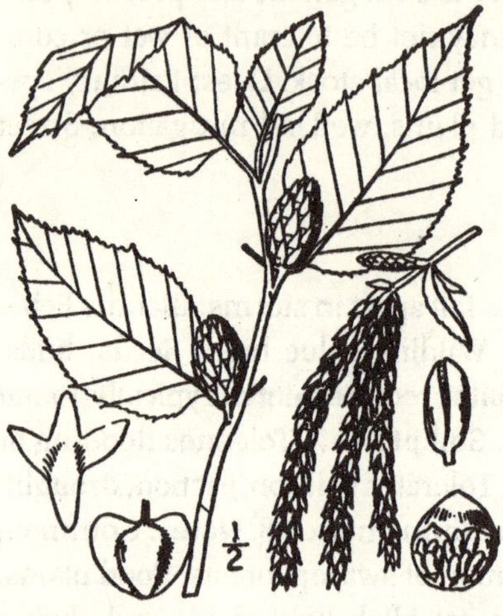

Betula lenta

Betula lenta (black birch, sweet birch)

To 70 ft., fast growing, fall foliage yellow. Blooms April–May; seeds wind dispersed Sept.–Nov. High wildlife value. Seeds eaten by birds; host to larvae of some butterfly species. **Habitat requirements:** Moist to dry, well-drained, upland, acid, forest soils, pH 4.0–6.8 (FACU). Moderately tolerant of salt and drought, shade index 4–6. Sensitive to soil compaction. **Notes:** Common. Available. **Uses:** Secondary species for increased diversity and aesthetics in forest restoration. Park tree.

Betula nigra (river birch)

Rare (NYS S3, U, watch list); to 75 ft., growth rate fast, bark attractive shreddy, pinkish brown on young trees. Blooms April–May; seeds wind dispersed May–June. Wildlife value high. Seeds, buds, and catkins eaten by birds and mammals. **Habitat requirements:** Swamp forests, floodplains, river and stream banks (FACW). Soil pH 4–6.5. Tolerant of drought, flooding, or saturated soil up to 25% of growing season. Intolerant of shade, index 2–4. Intolerant of salt. **Notes:** Very infrequent in NYC natural areas but relatively common in central NJ. Available. **Uses:** Secondary species for restoration of swamp forests, flood plains, stream and river bank stabilization, wetland mitigation. An attractive horticultural tree.

Betula papyrifera (paper birch)

To 80 ft., bark white, fall color yellow. Blooms April–June; seeds dispersed Aug.–spring. High wildlife value. Host to larvae of some butterfly species. **Habitat requirements:** Cold adapted, best in deep, well-drained, moist soils, pH 5–8.5 (FACU). Should tolerate concrete debris. Tolerant of salt. Moderately drought tolerant. Sensitive to compaction, flooding, shade index 1. **Notes:** Very infrequent. The north part of our region is the southern limit of this tree. **Uses:** Minor element in forest restoration, especially north of NYC. Park tree.

*Betula populifolia (gray birch)

To 30 ft., often multistemmed, forms thickets, fast growing, short lived, bark white, fall color yellow. Blooms April–May; seeds wind dispersed from Oct. into winter. High wildlife value. Host to larvae of some butterfly species. **Habitat requirements:** Pioneer species on open, nutrient poor, acid to circumneutral soils, pH 3.5–7.5 (FAC). Tolerant of salt, sterile, sandy fill, compaction, drought, intermittent flooding, or saturated soil up to 75% of growing season. Intolerant of shade, index 1. **Notes:** Very common. Available. Try to get local stock. **Uses:** Primary species for restoration of vegetation on open, bare mineral soil. Goes well with eastern red cedar and little bluestem or broom sedge in successional habitats. Park tree.

Carpinus caroliniana

Carpinus caroliniana (American hornbeam, ironwood)

To 40 ft., often multistemmed, bark dark gray, trunks sinuous, fall color yellow. Growth rate slow. Blooms April. Seed dispersal Oct.–spring. Host to larvae of some butterfly species. **Habitat requirements:** Usually an understory tree of well-established forests, in moist, well-drained soils (FAC), pH 4.0–7.5. Tolerant of shade, index 8–10. Intolerant of flooding, salt, compaction, drought. **Notes:** Common in the region but not on L.I. Available. *Warning!* Do not allow substitution with nonnative *C. betulus* (European hornbeam). **Uses:** Secondary or minor species for increased diversity and aesthetics in restoration of forest understories. Park tree in moist, well-drained soil.

Carya cordiformis

Carya cordiformis (bitternut hickory)

To 90 ft., slow growing, long lived, fall color deep yellow. Blooms April–May; nuts ripe Sept.–Nov. Moderate wildlife value; nuts bitter; host to larvae of some butterfly species. **Habitat requirements:** Wet to dry forest soil

(FACU+), pH 5.5–8.5. Should tolerate concrete debris. Moderately tolerant of brief flooding, drought, soil compaction and shade, index 5.8. Intolerant of salt. **Notes:** Common in the region north and west of NYC, not found on southeastern Long Island. *Carya* spp. are slow growing and difficult to grow due to their long tap roots. Increased demand may encourage greater availability. **Uses:** Secondary species for increased diversity and aesthetics in upland forest restoration. Park tree, street tree.

Carya glabra (pignut hickory)

To 90 ft., slow growing, long lived, fall color deep yellow. Blooms April–May. Nuts ripe Sept.–Nov. Nuts edible. Host to larvae of some butterfly species. **Habitat requirements:** Dry woods and slopes (FACU−), soil pH 4.8–7.5. Tolerant of drought. Moderately shade tolerant, index 4–6. Intolerant of salt, flooding, soil compaction. **Notes:** Common. **Uses:** Secondary species for increased diversity and aesthetics in upland forest restoration. Park tree, street tree.

Carya ovalis (sweet pignut-hickory, false shagbark)

To 80 ft. Nuts edible, ripe Sept.–Nov. Host to larvae of some butterfly species. **Habitat requirements:** Dry woods (UPL). **Notes:** Not found in NYC, infrequent in the region. **Uses:** Secondary species for increased diversity and aesthetics in upland forest restoration. Park tree, street tree.

Carya ovata (shagbark hickory)

To 90 ft., slow growing, long lived, fall color deep yellow. Blooms April–June. Nuts ripe Sept.–Nov. Nuts edible, eaten by birds and mammals. Moderate wildlife value; host to larvae of some butterfly species. **Habitat requirements:** Rich, moist forest soil (FACU−), pH 4–6.7. Tolerant of drought. Moderately tolerant of shade, index 5.4, moderately tolerant of salt. Intolerant of flooding, soil compaction. **Notes:** Common north and west of NYC, infrequent on coastal plain. **Uses:** Secondary species for increased diversity and aesthetics in upland forest restoration. Park tree, street tree.

Carya tomentosa (mockernut hickory)

To 80 ft., slow growing, long lived, fall color deep yellow. Blooms April–May. Nuts ripe Sept.–Nov. Nuts edible, eaten by birds and mammals. Moderate wildlife value. Host to larvae of some butterfly species. **Habitat requirements:** Dry to moist forest soil (UPL), pH 5–7.4. Tolerant of drought. Intolerant of salt, flooding, soil compaction, shade, index 2–4. **Notes:** Common, but may be hard to find. See *C. cordiformis*. **Uses:** Secondary species for increased diversity and aesthetics in upland forest restoration. Park tree, street tree.

**Celtis occidentalis* (common hackberry)

To 70 ft. Blooms April–May; fruit fleshy, black, Sept.–Oct., fruits eaten and seeds dispersed Sept.–Winter. Wildlife value high. Host to larvae of some butterfly species. Fruit eaten by birds. Moderately fast growing. Dry rocky areas, limestone soils, coastal back dune forests (FACU). Tolerant of salt, drought, alkaline soil, concrete debris, soil pH 6.0–8.5 (found in soil pH 5.2). Moderately tolerant of flooding or saturated soil, for up to 25% growing season; shade, index 4–6. **Notes:** Fairly common. Available. Susceptible to a nonlethal "witches' broom" disease, of only aesthetic concern. Otherwise a widely tolerant tree for difficult, urban soils. **Uses:** Primary species for vegetation of fill soils with concrete debris or high pH. Street tree, park tree.

Chamaecyparis thyoides (Atlantic white cedar)

Rare (NYS S3, R); to 75 ft., evergreen; growth rate moderate, foliage attractive, feathery. Cones small, bluish, turning brown. Seed dispersal Oct.–March. Wildlife value moderate. **Habitat requirements:** Normally grows on hummocks in acid bogs (OBL). Prefers moist, acid soils, pH 3–5.5, but tolerant of muck soils once established. Tolerant of flooding or saturated soil for almost 100% of growing season. Intolerant of shade, especially for seed germination and seedling stages; older trees supposedly of intermediate shade and drought tolerance. **Notes:** Formerly common, now infrequent in our region due to loss of wetlands and beavers. It is relatively easy to establish but is unlikely to reproduce in NYC under present high pH, high nutrient environmental conditions. Use regional stock. Available. *Warning!* Do not substitute nonnative *Chamaecyparis* species. **Uses:** Minor element for restoration of outer edges of marshes and acid bogs. Park tree or evergreen screen in full sun, moist to wet soil. Use local stock.

Cornus florida (flowering dogwood)

To 40 ft., fall color red. Flowers white, showy, April–June, fruit fleshy, red, ripe Oct.–Nov. Wildlife value high; host to larvae of some butterfly species; high fat fruit valuable to fall migrating birds. **Habitat requirements:** Forest understories and edges, in moist, well-drained soil (FACU−), pH 5.5–7. Tolerant of shade, index 8–10. Moderately tolerant of drought. Intolerant of salt, soil compaction. **Notes:** Recent high mortality from an Anthracnose fungus (*Discula destructiva*), especially in shady habitats, calls for caution in use of this tree. Common throughout region. Available. Use local stock. *Warning!* Do not substitute *C. kousa, C. mas,* or other nonnative species. **Uses:** Secondary or minor species for increased diversity and aesthetics in restoration of forest understories. Park tree.

Diospyros virginiana (persimmon)

Rare (NYS S2, T); to 40 ft., growth rate moderate in good, moist soil. Aggressively colonial from root sprouts. Blooms May–June, sexes sometimes separate (some plants female); fruit fleshy, orange, edible after frost, Oct.–Nov. Wildlife value high; fruit eaten by birds and mammals. **Habitat requirements:** Moist, open woodlands, often grows on wetland edges (FAC−). Prefers pH 5–7 but is probably more tolerant. Tolerant of drought. Moderately tolerant of flooding, soil compaction. Intolerant of shade, index 2–4. **Notes:** Infrequent in NYC. Available. NYC is about the northern limit. More common along coastal plain than inland. Use only local stock. Some trees have only male flowers. Plant both sexes. **Uses:** Minor element for increased wildlife value, diversity, and aesthetics in forest restoration, slope stabilization.

Fagus grandifolia

Fagus grandifolia (American beech)

To 90 ft., slow growing, handsome silver bark, often colonial from root sprouts. Blooms April–May; seeds ripe Oct.–Nov. High wildlife value. Nuts edible; eaten and dispersed by birds and mammals. **Habitat requirements:** Maturing or mature forests (FACU), in moist, acid soil, pH 4.1–6.5. Very shade tolerant, index 9.3. Intolerant of flooding, drought, salt, compaction. Beech bark disease is sometimes a problem. **Notes:** Common in mature forests. *Warning!* Be alert for substitution of *F. sylvatica* (European beech). **Uses:** Secondary species for forest restoration. This is a late successional tree that comes into maturing forests.

Fraxinus americana (white ash)

To 80 ft., fall color clear yellow to purplish. Sexes separate (dioecious); seeds ripe/dispersed Sept.–Dec. Fast growing. **Habitat requirements:** Moist, fertile soil pH 5–7.5 (FACU). Moderately tolerant of shade, index 6–8, salt, drought, flooding, soil compaction. The disease "ash yellows" may be a problem. Drought and other environmental stresses increase this susceptibility. **Notes:** Frequent in NYC. Available. Plant both sexes. **Uses:** Secondary species for forest restoration, should tolerate some fill soils. Park tree.

Fraxinus nigra (black ash)

To 75 ft., fast growing. Blooms May–June; sexes sometimes separate (dioecious to polygamous), seeds wind dispersed Aug.–Oct. Wildlife value low. Seeds eaten by birds and mammals. **Habitat requirements:** Swamp forests (FACW).

Soil pH 4.4–8.2. Tolerant of flooding, drought, soil compaction. Moderately tolerant of salt. Intolerant of shade, index 2–4. Infrequent in NYC. **Notes:** Susceptibility to "ash yellows" is not known. **Uses:** Secondary species for increasing diversity in swamp forest restoration and wetland mitigation.

Fraxinus pennsylvanica (green ash)

To 75 ft., fast growing; fall color yellow to purplish. Blooms May; sexes separate (dioecious); seeds wind dispersed Oct. into winter. **Habitat requirements:** Freshwater tidal and nontidal forested wetlands (FACW). Prefers moist to wet soil, pH 6–8. Tolerates compaction, flooding, or saturated soil up to 75% of growing season; should tolerate concrete debris. Moderately salt tolerant. Intolerant of shade, index 2–4. Susceptible to "ash yellows." Drought increases this susceptibility. **Notes:** Common in NYC. Available. Plant both sexes. **Uses:** Secondary species for swamp forest and floodplain restoration and wetland mitigation.

Ilex opaca (American holly)

To 40 ft., evergreen. Flowers white, small. Sexes on separate plants, blooms May–June. Fruit fleshy, red, Oct.–Nov., persists all winter. Eaten and dispersed by birds, particularly early spring migrants. **Habitat requirements:** Coastal in our region. Sterile, sandy soil, back-dune forests (FACU+). Tolerates acid soil, pH 4.0–7.5, salt, shade (part). **Notes:** Warning! Do not allow substitution of *I. aquifolia* (English holly). **Uses:** Primary species in back-dune holly forests and scrub along with eastern red cedar.

[*Juglans cinerea* (butternut)

To 80 ft. Not recommended due to Sirococcus canker until resistant varieties are found. (FACU+), soil pH 6–7.]

Juglans nigra (black walnut)

To 100 ft., fast growing. Inhibits growth of some other plant species (allelopathic). Blooms April–June. Nuts ripe Oct.–Nov., edible. Host to larvae of some butterfly species. A pioneer species in open areas. **Habitat requirements:** Prefers deep, well-drained soils (UPL), pH 4.6–8.2. Seems to do well on fill soils with concrete debris. Tolerant of drought. Moderately tolerant of salt, soil compaction, flooding. Intolerant of shade, index 4. **Notes:** Occasional in NYC. Easily grown from nuts. **Uses:** Secondary species for vegetation of open fill sites. Park tree.

**Juniperus virginiana* (eastern red cedar)

To 60 ft., evergreen, slow growing. Sexes separate (dioecious). Cones small, fleshy, blue, seeds ripe Oct., dispersed Oct.–March by birds. Very high wildlife value. Host to larvae of some butterfly species. **Habitat requirements:**

2/3

Juniperus virginiana

Typical successional species of old fields and back-dune coastal woodlands (FACU). Well-drained soil pH 4.7–8.5. Tolerant of salt, drought, pollution. Also should be tolerant of concrete debris. Intolerant of flooding, soil compaction, shade, index 0–2. **Notes:** Infrequent in NYC. Available. Combine with gray birch and little bluestem. An occasional host of cedar-apple rust fungus (*Gymnosporangium juniperi-virginianae*). **Uses:** Primary species for vegetation of open fill, sandy dredge spoils. Plant both sexes (4–5 females for each male).

Larix laricina (tamarack, American larch)

To 60 ft., deciduous conifer. Seeds dispersed Sept. through winter. Fast growing. Moderate wildlife value. **Habitat requirements:** Bogs, wet, acid soil (NYC near southern limit), swamp forests (FACW). Soil pH 4.5–7.5. Tolerant of flooding, soil compaction, salt. Very intolerant of shade, index 0.8. Intolerant of drought. **Notes:** Unlikely to reproduce in urban and suburban areas. A northern bog tree. **Uses:** Secondary species or minor element for swamp forest restoration and wetland mitigation.

**Liquidambar styraciflua* (sweetgum)

To 100 ft., growth rate slow to moderate. Fall color yellow-red. Blooms April–May; seeds wind dispersed Sept.–Nov. Prickly fruits deciduous in spring. Wildlife value low. **Habitat requirements:** Swamp forests and moist uplands (FAC). Prefers soil pH 6–7, but found in soils pH 4.4–5.6. Also seen growing in concrete rubble. Tolerates poorly drained soil, flooding, up to 75% of growing season. Tolerant of compaction. Moderately tolerant of salt. Intolerant of shade, index 2–4. NYC northern limit. **Notes:** Common in NYC, at least south and east of Manhattan. Available. **Uses:** Primary component of swamp forests, floodplain forests. Wetland mitigation. Street or park tree.

**Liriodendron tulipifera* (tulip tree)

To 120 ft., fast growing, fall color clear yellow. Flowers green and orange, showy, May–June; seeds wind dispersed Nov.–Dec. Host to larvae of some butterfly species. Attractive to hummingbirds. **Habitat requirements:** A pioneer species of old fields and large forest gaps, on moist, well-drained, loose soils (FACU), pH 4.0–6.5. Moderately shade tolerant, index 4–6. Intolerant of salt, flooding, drought, soil compaction. Common in NYC. Available. **Uses:** Primary species for reforestation of sites with good-quality moist soil. Park tree.

Magnolia virginiana (sweet-bay magnolia)

Rare (NYS S1, U); to 60 ft., growth rate moderate. Flowers white, showy, fragrant, May–July. Fruit fleshy, red, eaten by birds, Aug.–Oct. Wildlife value high. **Habitat requirements:** Understories of coastal plain red maple swamp forests and Atlantic white cedar bogs (FACW+), soil pH 5–6 (probably tolerates lower). Tolerant of partial shade, salt, soil compaction, flooding. Intolerant of drought. **Notes:** A southern tree; coastal plain NJ and southern NYS, Long Island. Plant in cooperation with conservation organization restoration specialist. Use only local stock. **Uses:** Minor species for swamp forest restoration and wetland mitigation in appropriate locations.

Morus rubra (red mulberry)

To 60 ft., fast growing. Blooms May–June, sexes sometimes separate (dioecious to monoecious). Fruit fleshy, edible June–July. Wildlife value high. Fruit eaten by birds and mammals, which disperse the seeds. **Habitat requirements:** Rich, moist woods and upper floodplains (FACU), soil pH 6.3–8. Tolerant of salt, drought. Moderately tolerant of flooding, soil compaction, tolerant of part shade, index 4–6. **Notes:** Infrequent in NYC. Some trees are male only. Plant both sexes. *Warning!* Asian mulberry (*Morus alba*) is a weedy invasive from Asia that may also have purple fruit and is very common. **Uses:** Secondary species for forest restoration. Should tolerate concrete debris.

Nyssa sylvatica var. *sylvatica* (black tupelo)

To 90 ft., growth rate slow. Fall color red. Blooms May–June, sexes separate (dioecious). Fruit fleshy, dark blue (females only), ripens Sept.–Oct. Wildlife value high. **Habitat requirements:** Swamp forests, moist uplands (FAC), prefers soil pH 4.5–6. Tolerant of salt, drought, flooding. Tolerant of partial shade, index 2–4, very persistent and growing slowly in forest understories with dappled shade. **Notes:** Common in NYC. Available. (*N.S.* var. *sylvatica* is the northern variety.) **Uses:** Secondary species for swamp forest restoration, floodplains, and wetland mitigation. Street and park tree (use females for specimen trees, males root sprout).

Nyssa sylvatica

Ostrya virginiana (hophornbeam)

To 30 ft., slow growing. Blooms April–May; seeds wind dispersed Sept.–Nov. Host to larvae of some butterfly species. **Habitat requirements:** Forest subcanopy tree, soil pH 4.2–8. Often found on limestone soils (FACU−), should tolerate concrete debris. Tolerant of shade, index 8–10. Moderately tolerant of drought. Intolerant of flooding, soil compaction, salt. **Notes:** Very infrequent in NYC. **Uses:** Understory tree for increased diversity and aesthetics in forest restoration. Park tree. Street tree, possibly a good substitute for *Zelkova*.

Picea rubens (red spruce)

To 90 ft., evergreen. Seeds dispersed Sept.–March. **Habitat requirements:** Moist rocky woods, hillsides, uplands (FACU), soil pH 4–5.5. Prefers cool temperatures. Intolerant of shade. **Notes:** Marginally native to the northern part of the region, mainly a northern New England species. Not a component of our local coastal-plain forests. **Uses:** Secondary species for reforestation of rocky or northern pine barrens habitats, northern NYC metro region. Park tree in northern suburbs.

Pinus echinata (shortleaf pine)

Rare (NYS S1, E); to 90 ft., evergreen. Seeds wind dispersed Oct.–Nov. **Habitat requirements:** Dry, sandy, or rocky soil, a pine barrens tree (UPL). Requires acid soil, pH 4–6. Prefers deep, well-drained sandy soil. **Notes:** A southern species. NYC is near its northern limit. **Uses:** Minor element in forest restoration in sandy soil of south Staten Island, Long Island, New Jersey coastal plain. Plant in cooperation with conservation organization restoration specialist. Use only local stock.

Pinus resinosa (red pine)

To 100 ft., evergreen. Seeds wind dispersed Oct.–Nov. **Habitat requirements:** Dry, sandy, or rocky soil, uplands (FACU), acid soil pH 4–6.5. Moderately tolerant of drought. Intolerant of soil compaction, flooding, salt, shade, index 2.4. **Notes:** A northern species, southern limit in northwestern NJ and NYC. **Uses:** Secondary species for reforestation of rocky or pine barrens habitats, northern NYC metro region. Park tree in northern suburbs.

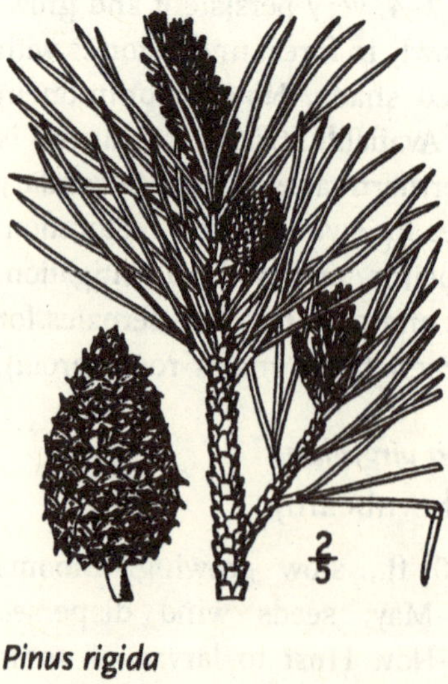

Pinus rigida

**Pinus rigida* (pitch pine)

To 60 ft., evergreen, fast growing, trunk often crooked, trunk and stump sprouts if burned. Seeds dispersed Sept.–Dec. Wildlife value very high. **Habitat requirements:** Open, sterile sandy, acid soil (FACU), pH

3.5–6.5. Tolerant of drought, salt. Intolerant of flooding or saturated soil for more than 25% of growing season; intolerant of soil compaction; shade index 0–2. **Notes:** Dominant species in NJ and Long Island pine barrens. Do *not* plant in alkaline fill, unless heavily amended with acid mulch or low organic sand (less than 30% silt). Rare in NYC. Available. **Uses:** Primary species for reforestation of vegetation on sandy, coastal plains and back dunes. Also should work for gravelly or sandy bare mineral soil in burned-over areas.

Pinus strobus (eastern white pine)

To 110 ft., fast growing, evergreen, rather brittle, tends to lose limbs in storms. Cones ripe Aug.–Oct. Wildlife value very high, providing both food and shelter for birds. Favored for roosting by owls. **Habitat requirements:** Moist, well-drained acid soil (FACU), pH 3.8–6.5. Moderately shade tolerant, index 4.4. Intolerant of salt, flooding, drought. **Notes:** Natural range south to central NJ. Commonly planted in NYC. Available. **Uses:** Secondary or minor element for increased diversity and aesthetics in upland forest restoration. Does well on somewhat acid fill soils. Park tree.

Pinus virginiana (Virginia pine)

Rare (NYS S1, E); to 30 ft., evergreen. Seeds dispersed Oct.–winter. **Habitat requirements:** A pine barrens species, pioneer on bare mineral sandy, sterile soil (UPL), pH 4.6–7.9. Drought tolerant. Very intolerant of shade. **Notes:** Eastern Long Island and north-central NJ is about the natural northern limit. **Uses:** Minor element for increased diversity and aesthetics in forestation of sandy, acid soils along with pitch pine. Long Island and south. In NY plant in cooperation with conservation organization restoration specialist. Use only local stock.

**Platanus occidentalis* (American sycamore)

To 150 ft., growth rate very fast, bark handsome, mottled brown and chalky white. Blooms April–May; seeds ripe Nov., wind dispersed Feb.–April. Wildlife value low. **Habitat requirements:** A tree of flood plains, also a pioneer on moist fill (FACW), soil pH 6.5–8.5. Tolerates concrete debris. Moderately shade tolerant, index 4. Tolerant of flooding or saturated soil for up to 25% of growing season. Tolerant of compaction. Intolerant of salt. **Notes:** Occasional in NYC. Available. *Warning!* Be alert for substitution of London plane tree (*P.* x *hybrida*) when planting this species. **Uses:** Primary species for floodplain forest restoration, river and stream banks. Secondary species for wetland mitigation. Park tree.

Populus balsamifera (balsam poplar)

To 80 ft., fast growing. Blooms March–April; seeds wind dispersed. **Habitat requirements:** River banks, shores (FACW). Tolerates soil pH 4.5–7. **Notes:** A northern species. NYC is near southern limit. Sometimes used in phytoremediation projects. Very uncommon in our region. **Uses:** Secondary species for floodplain restoration, river and stream banks. Wetland mitigation.

**Populus deltoides* var. *deltoides* (eastern cottonwood)

To 150 ft., very fast growing. Blooms March–April; seeds wind dispersed May–Aug. Host to larvae of some butterfly species. **Habitat requirements:** Pioneer tree on moist fill soils (FAC); considered weedy. Tolerant of salt, drought, pollutants, compaction, poor soil, and flooding or saturated soil to 25% of growing season. Common in disturbed sites on bare soil, pH 5.5–7.5. Intolerant of shade, index 2.2. **Notes:** Common in NYC. Easily grown from seeds or cuttings (var. *deltoides* is the eastern variety). **Uses:** Primary species for floodplain restoration, vegetation of moist to wet fill soils. **Bioengineering:** Roots very well from cuttings. Vegetation and aforestation of fill, from sandy dredge spoils to old garbage or demolition debris. Provides light shade and shelter, adds organic material to improve soil for less tolerant, longer-lived species.

**Populus grandidentata* (big-toothed aspen)

To 60 ft., fast growing, short lived, often colonial from root sprouts. Produces dappled, open shade. Blooms in April, sexes separate (dioecious); seeds wind dispersed May–June. Wildlife value high. Host to larvae of some butterfly species. **Habitat requirements:** Pioneer on poor, sandy soil, well-drained acid soil (FACU−), pH 4.8–7.2. Moderately tolerant of salt, drought. Intolerant of flooding, soil compaction, shade, index 1. **Notes:** Occasional in NYC. **Uses:** Primary species for vegetation of well-drained burned-over mineral soil. May be of use as a "nurse tree" for sheltering slower-growing species.

Populus heterophylla (swamp cottonwood)

Rare (NYS S2, T); to 60 ft. (less this far north), colonial from root sprouts. Blooms early spring, sexes separate (dioecious); seeds wind dispersed May–June. Host to larvae of some butterfly species. **Habitat requirements:** Swamp forests, in shallow water or wet to moist soil (FACW+). Tolerates soil pH 4.6–5.9. Tolerant of flooding, drought, salt, compaction. Intolerant of shade, index 2.2. **Notes:** Northern limit of this species is Long Island and coastal CT. **Uses:** Minor element in swamp forest restoration or wetland mitigation in appropriate parts of the region. Plant both sexes. Plant in cooperation with conservation organization restoration specialist.

**Populus tremuloides* (quaking aspen)

To 50 ft., fast growing, short lived, often colonial from root sprouts. Blooms March–April, sexes separate (dioecious); seeds wind dispersed May–June. Wildlife value high. Host to larvae of some butterfly species. **Habitat requirements:** Well-drained sandy or rocky soil (UPL), pH 4.5–6.5. Moderately tolerant of drought, salt. Very intolerant of shade, index 0.7. Intolerant of flooding, soil compaction, competition. **Notes:** Occasional in NYC. **Uses:** Primary species for vegetation of well-drained bare soil, burn sites. May be of use as a "nurse tree" for sheltering slower-growing species.

Prunus americana (hedge plum)

To 24 ft., often multistemmed, colonial. Flowers white, showy, fragrant, April; fruit red-yellow, edible, bird and mammal dispersed, Aug.–Sept. Host to larvae of some butterfly species. **Habitat requirements:** Moist edges, open sites (FACU−), prefers soil pH 5–7.5. Tolerant of drought. Intolerant of shade, index 2–4; intolerant of flooding, soil compaction. **Notes:** Infrequent in NYC. **Uses:** Minor element for increased diversity; aesthetics and wildlife value in revegetation of old fields or open areas. May tolerate well-drained fill soils. Park tree.

Prunus pensylvanica (pin cherry)

To 45 ft., colonial. Flowers white, fragrant, April–June; fruit amber to yellow, Aug.–Sept., eaten and dispersed by birds. Host to larvae of some butterfly species. Fast growing, aggressive. **Habitat requirements:** Pioneer cover in disturbed areas (FACU−) on dry, open soil pH 4.3–7.5. Tolerant of drought, salt. Intolerant of flooding, soil compaction, shade, index 0.7. **Notes:** Infrequent in NY. A northern species, range limit around Long Island, central NJ. **Uses:** Secondary or minor species for erosion control; increased diversity and wildlife value in revegetation of old fields, eroded open slopes. May tolerate well-drained fill soils.

Prunus serotina (wild black cherry)

To 75 ft., fall foliage orange-yellow. Flowers white, May–June; fruit black, semiedible, July–Aug. Wildlife value high. Fruit eaten and dispersed by birds. **Habitat requirements:** Found in almost any soil type, from infertile, sandy, acid, back-dune soil to concrete debris, well-drained forest soils (FACU), soil pH 3.9–8, often a pioneer species on fill. Tolerant of drought, salt. Intolerant of flooding, soil compaction, shade, index 2.4; but saplings are common in forest understories. **Notes:** The most common species of woody plant in the NYC metro region. *Warning!* Fruits at the same time as Asian white mulberry (*Morus alba*), may attract birds dispersing those seeds. **Uses:** Secondary species in aforestation of fill, open areas, eroded, open slopes, burns, wildlife corridors. Concrete rubble-demolition debris.

Prunus virginiana (chokecherry)

To 30 ft., multiple trunks, colonial, fast growing, forming thickets; fall foliage yellow-orange. Flowers white, fragrant, April–June; fruit fleshy red-black, edible, Aug.–Oct. Eaten and dispersed by birds. **Habitat requirements:** Prefers moist, well-drained soil, pH 5.2–8.4 (FACU). Tolerant of salt, drought.

Moderately tolerant of shade, index 4–6. Intolerant of flooding, soil compaction. **Uses:** Secondary species for vegetation of open areas, slope stabilization, wildlife corridors. Should tolerate well-drained fill soils.

**Quercus alba* (white oak)

To 75 ft., slow-growing, long-lived, fall foliage often red. Blooms May; acorns ripe Sept.–Nov. Wildlife value very high. Acorns eaten by birds and mammals. Host to larvae of some butterfly species. **Habitat requirements:** Does best with full sun in deep, undisturbed native soils (FACU–). Tolerates soil pH 3.5–7.5, often in sandy, rocky, acid, low-nutrient soil. Tolerant of salt. Moderately tolerant of drought and shade, index 5.7. Intolerant of flooding. Very intolerant of compaction and filling over roots. **Notes:** Common in NYC forests. Available. *Warning!* Be alert for substitution of English oak (*Quercus robur*). **Uses:** Primary or secondary species for reforestation of large gaps (clear-cuts and vine removals), old fields. Park tree.

Quercus bicolor (swamp white oak)

To 70 ft., growth rate moderate to fast. Blooms May; seeds (acorns) ripe Sept.–Oct. Wildlife value very high. Host to larvae of some butterfly species. Acorns eaten by birds and mammals. **Habitat requirements:** Swamp forests, floodplain forests (FACW). Tolerant of flooding or saturated soil for up to 25% of growing season, prefers moist soil pH 5–7.5. Tolerant of salt, drought, soil compaction. Moderately shade tolerant, index 4–6. **Notes:** Occasional in NYC. Available. **Uses:** Secondary species for increased diversity, aesthetics, and wildlife value in restoration of swamp forests, floodplain forest, stream banks. Wetland mitigation.

**Quercus coccinea* (scarlet oak)

To 75 ft., medium to fast growing, long lived, fall foliage red. Blooms May; acorns ripe Sept.–Nov. the following year. Wildlife value high. Acorns eaten by birds and mammals. Host to larvae of some butterfly species. **Habitat requirements:** Dry uplands, sandy soil, prefers well-drained soil pH 4.5–6.9, but typically found growing in sandy or rocky, acid, low-nutrient soils (UPL). Tolerant of drought, salt. Intolerant of soil compaction, flooding, shade, index 2–4. **Notes:** Occasional in NYC upland forests. Available. **Uses:** Primary or secondary species for reforestation of large gaps (clear-cuts and vine removals), old fields, rocky slopes, in well-drained native soils. Park or street tree.

Quercus marilandica (blackjack oak)

Rare (NYS S3, R); to 50 ft., usually smaller in NYS, small, slow growing. Acorns ripe Sept.–Oct. of the following year. Wildlife value very high. Acorns eaten by birds and mammals. Host to larvae of some butterfly species. **Habitat requirements:** Dry, sandy, well-drained sterile soil (UPL), pH 4–5.6. Pine barrens and oak barrens of coastal plain. Tolerant of salt, drought. Intolerant of flooding, soil compaction, shade, index 2–4. **Notes:** A southern tree. Long Island is northern limit for this species. **Uses:** Primary or secondary species for increased diversity and aesthetics in restoration of oak barrens, pine barrens, and back-dune coastal woodlands in appropriate locations. Plant in cooperation with conservation organization restoration specialist. Use only local stock.

Quercus muehlenbergii (chinquapin, yellow oak)

To 50 ft., growth rate slow. Blooms May; acorns ripe Sept.–Oct. of the following year. Wildlife value very high. **Habitat requirements:** Dry rocky rich soils, slopes, oak barrens (UPL), soil pH 5–8.5. Should tolerate concrete debris. Tolerant of drought. Intolerant of shade, flooding, soil compaction. **Notes:** Native mostly north and west of NYC, Hudson Valley, northwestern NJ, southwestern CT. Not found in NYC, eastern NJ. Very infrequent on eastern Long Island. **Uses:** Secondary species for increased diversity and aesthetics in aforestation of fill with concrete debris.

**Quercus palustris* (pin oak)

To 80 ft., growth rate fast. Blooms April–May; seeds ripe Oct.–Nov. of the following year. Wildlife value very high. Host to larvae of some butterfly species. Acorns eaten by birds and mammals. **Habitat requirements:** Swamp forests, moist upland forests (FACW). Tolerant of flooding or saturated soil up to 25% of growing season. Tolerant of nutrient-poor, poorly drained acid soil and fill pH 4.5–6.5. Tolerant of drought, salt. Sensitive to compaction. Intolerant of shade, index 0–2. **Notes:** Common in NYC. Available. **Uses:** Primary species in swamp forest restoration, floodplains. Wetland mitigation. Street and park tree.

Quercus phellos (willow oak)

Rare (NYS S1, E); to 80 ft., growth rate moderate. Blooms May; seeds ripe Sept.–Nov. of the following year. Wildlife value very high. Host to larvae of some butterfly species. Acorns eaten by birds and mammals. **Habitat requirements:** Swamp forests (FAC+), soil pH 4.5–6. Tolerant of flooding or saturated soil up to 25% of growing season. Intolerant of shade, salt. **Notes:** Not native north of Long Island (but planted all over NYC). **Uses:** Secondary species for restoration of swamp forests and wetland mitigation, south Staten Island, central NJ. Use only wild, local stock.

**Quercus prinus* (*Q. montana*) (chestnut oak)

To 70 ft., slow growing (but faster than white oak), long lived. Blooms May; acorns ripe Sept.–Nov. Wildlife value high. Host to larvae of some butterfly species. Acorns eaten by birds and mammals. **Habitat requirements:** Dry uplands, sandy soil, rocky slopes, tolerates soil pH 3.5–6.5 (UPL). Very drought tolerant, but prefers well-drained moist soils. Tolerant of salt, drought. Moderately shade tolerant, index 4–6. Intolerant of flooding, soil compaction. **Notes:** Occasional in NYC upland forests. Available. **Uses:** Primary or secondary species for reforestation of large gaps (clear-cuts of exotic trees and vine removals), old fields, rocky slopes, in well-drained native soils. Park or suburban street tree.

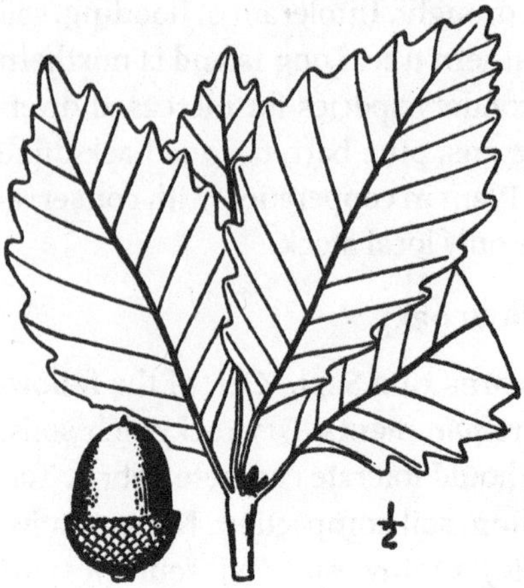

Quercus prinus

**Quercus rubra* (*Q. borealis*) (red oak)

To 90 ft., rather slow growing, long lived, fall foliage usually red. Blooms May; acorns ripe Sept.–Oct. of the following year. Wildlife value high. Host to larvae of some butterfly species. Acorns eaten by birds and mammals. **Habitat requirements:** Does best in deep, moist, well-drained soils (FACU−), commonly found with white oak, soil pH 3.8–6.5. Tolerant of salt. Moderately tolerant of drought, shade, index 7.8 (the most shade-tolerant oak). Intolerant of flooding. Common in NYC forests. Available. **Uses:** primary species for restoration of upland, deciduous forests, in gaps created by clear-cuts, removal of vines or invasive trees. Park or street tree.

Quercus stellata (post oak)

To 60 ft. (usually smaller in NY), northern limit NYC and Long Island, slow growing. Blooms May; acorns ripe Sept.–Nov. Wildlife value high. Host to larvae of some butterfly species. Acorns eaten by birds and mammals. **Habitat requirements:** Usually a small, slow-growing tree of dry, sandy, or rocky soil, often found with blackjack oak in oak barrens, pine barrens (UPL), acid soil pH 4.6–6.5. Tolerant of salt, drought. Intolerant of flooding, soil compaction, shade, index 2–4. Infrequent in NYC. **Notes:** Basically a southern tree, but common on Long Island and NJ outer coastal plain. **Uses:** Secondary or primary species for restoration of woodlands in sandy soil of coastal, back dune, oak barren habitats or rocky uplands, with pitch pine and blackjack oak.

Quercus velutina (black oak)

To 80 ft. Growth rate slow. Blooms May. Acorns ripe Sept–Oct. Wildlife value high. Host to larvae of some butterfly species. Acorns eaten by birds and mammals. **Habitat requirements:** Sandy or rocky, acid, low nutrient soils of upland forests. Tolerates soil pH 3.5–6.5, (UPL). Tolerant of salt, drought. Moderately tolerant of shade, index 6–8. **Notes:** Occasional in NYC upland forests. Available. **Uses:** Primary or secondary species for reforestation of large gaps in upland forests, park, or suburban street tree.

*_Salix nigra_ (black willow)

To 40 ft., growth rate very fast, short lived, often leaning and irregular in shape. Blooms May, sexes separate; seeds wind dispersed June–July. Wildlife value high. Host to larvae of some butterfly species. **Habitat requirements:** Freshwater tidal, and nontidal wetlands (FACW+), tolerates soil pH 6–8. Tolerant of flooding or saturated soil up to 75% of growing season. Tolerates fill soils, concrete debris, drought, and compaction. Intolerant of salt; shade, index 1.4. **Notes:** Common in NYC and the region. Available. *Warning!* Be alert for substitution of nonnative *Salix* spp. **Uses:** Primary species for floodplain and river bank restoration. Wetland mitigation. **Bioengineering:** Roots extremely well from cuttings. Provides light shade and shelter, adds organic material to improve soil for less-tolerant, longer-lived species.

*_Sassafras albidum_ (sassafras)

To 50 ft. (usually smaller), fast growing, colonial from root sprouts, fall color yellow to orange, eventually shaded out by taller trees. Flowers greenish yellow, blooms April–May, sexes separate (dioecious); fruit fleshy, black, eaten and dispersed by birds, July–Sept. Wildlife value high. Oily fruit important for migrating birds. Host to larvae of some butterfly species. **Habitat requirements:** Pioneers of disturbed areas (FACU−), common in frequently burned open sites. Shallow ground fires leave roots intact. Tolerates soil pH 3.8–7. Intolerant of soil compaction, shade, index 2–4. **Notes:** Common in the entire region. Available. **Uses:** Primary or secondary species for revegetation of open, disturbed areas, mineral soil, eroded slopes.

Thuja occidentalis (northern white cedar)

To 45 ft., evergreen, growth rate medium-fast. Seeds ripe Aug.–Nov. Wildlife value low. **Habitat requirements:** Moist to wet soil, northern bogs and swamps (FACW), soil pH 6–8.5. Tolerant of flooding or saturated soil up to 75% of growing season; soil compaction, drought; should tolerate concrete debris. Shade tolerance moderate, index 4–6. Intolerant of salt. **Notes:** A northern tree. Formerly more common but does not reproduce under urban and horticultural conditions. **Uses:** Minor element in wetland mitigation. Evergreen screens. Horticultural uses in concrete fill.

Tilia americana (American linden, basswood)

To 80 ft., growth rate medium, foliage very dense, shady. Flowers pale yellow, fragrant, June–July; fruit ripe Sept.–Oct. **Habitat requirements:** Prefers rich, moist soil, pH 5.6–7.5 in relatively sheltered areas, north- or east-facing slopes (FACU). Tolerant of concrete, shade, index 8. Intolerant of flooding, drought, salt, soil compaction. **Notes:** Infrequent in NYC but fairly common north and west. *Warning!* Numerous exotic species are sold, *T. americana* has larger leaves than most. **Uses:** Minor element for increased diversity and aesthetics in reforestation of moist, sheltered, or partly shaded sites. Park tree. Suburban street tree.

[*Tsuga canadensis* (Canadian hemlock)

Not recommended until woolly adelgid problem is under control (FACU).]

[*Ulmus americana* (American elm)

To 100 ft. Seeds ripe March–April. Subject to Dutch elm disease, probably should not be planted until resistant strains developed (FACW−), soil pH 5.5–8. *Warning!* Do not plant invasive Siberian elm (*U. pumila*).]

[*Ulmus rubra* (slippery elm)

To 70 ft. Subject to Dutch elm disease, probably should not be planted until resistant strains developed (FAC).]

Chapter 2

Shrubs

Shrubs are generally defined as woody plants, less than 20 feet tall at reproductive maturity, often with multiple stems. Individual stems may die off but are replaced by new ones growing from the base of the shrub. There is no hard line between a large shrub and a small tree. Some plants may be either, depending on environmental circumstances, and are put into one category or the other rather arbitrarily. Some shrubs tend to have a single main trunk (*Viburnum prunifolium*), while others may send up leafy, flowering stems from underground stems (rhizomes), e.g., *Cornus racemosa.*

As with trees in our region, the vast majority are deciduous. Shrubs vary in their tolerance for shade, soil moisture, and chemistry, so that shrubs for a restoration site must be selected keeping site conditions in mind. Very few shrubs can grow and flower well in deep shade. *Lindera benzoin* and *Viburnum acerifolium* are two of the most shade-tolerant native shrubs, but even they do best under a high forest canopy with bright, dappled shade. Some plants may live and grow very slowly in dense shade but are weakened by lack of light. They will not flower well, and will be more susceptible to fungal diseases or predation. It is critical to understand the ecological needs of plants to be installed in a restoration so that they are able to grow and reproduce. I have outlined the major needs and tolerances of each plant to the limits of the information available to me at this time. More and more plants are being entered into databases available on-line, and it is generally fruitful to simply type the plant name into a search engine (Google, etc.) to see what comes up.

SHRUB SPECIES

Alnus incana (*A. rugosa*) (speckled alder)

To 35 ft., colonial. Flowers yellow catkins, March–April; fruit dry, conelike, Aug.–Oct., persistent. Wildlife value high. Host to larvae of some butterfly species. **Habitat requirements:** Moist to wet soil, freshwater tidal and nontidal marshes, pond edges, open stream banks (FACW), pH 6.5–7.5. Nitrogen fixer, may improve soil nutrients. Tolerant of poor soil, flooding, and soil

Alnus incana

compaction. Moderately tolerant of salt. Intolerant of drought, shade, index 0–2. **Notes:** Available. *Warning! Alnus glutinosa* (European alder), a highly invasive, exotic tree, is often substituted. Do not accept plants if top of leaf is notched, or present in late autumn. **Uses:** Secondary species for increased diversity and aesthetics in wetland restoration or mitigation in open habitats. Pond edges, river or stream banks, shrub swamps.

Alnus serrulata (smooth alder)

To 20 ft., growth rate fast, colonial, forms thickets. Flowers catkins, March–April; fruit dry, conelike, Aug.–Oct., persistent. Wildlife value high. Host to larvae of some butterfly species. **Habitat requirements:** Wet soil, pond or lake edges, open swamp or marshes, stream banks (OBL), soil pH 5.5–7.5. Nitrogen fixer, may improve soil nutrients. Tolerant of flooding, soil compaction, drought, low-nutrient soils. Intolerant of salt, shade. **Notes:** Available. *Warning! A. glutinosa* (European alder) highly invasive exotic tree, often substituted for native shrubs (see above). **Uses:** Secondary species for increased diversity and aesthetics in wetland restoration or mitigation in open habitats.

Amelanchier arborea (serviceberry)

To 40 ft., fall foliage red-orange. Flowers white, April–May; fruit fleshy, red-purple, edible, June. Wildlife value high. Host to larvae of some butterfly species. Fruit eaten by birds and mammals. **Habitat requirements:** Upland woods, rich limestone soils (FAC). Soil pH 5.5–7.5. Tolerant of partial shade. Should tolerate concrete debris. **Notes:** Not found in NYC. Mostly north and west in the region, some on Long Island. **Uses:** Secondary species for increased diversity and aesthetics in restoration of forest understories, successional shrub lands in moist soil.

**Amelanchier canadensis* (shadbush)

To 25 ft., growth rate moderate, fall foliage red-orange. Flowers white, April–May; fruit fleshy, purple, edible, June–July. Wildlife value high. Fruit eaten and seeds dispersed by many birds. Host to larvae of some butterfly species. **Habitat requirements:** Moist to dry soil, shrub swamps, moist, sterile sandy soil of back-dune thickets (FAC), prefers acid soil pH 5–7.5. Tolerant of shade, index 8–10. Moderately tolerant of salt; flooding or saturated soil for up to 25% of growing season. Intolerant of drought, soil compaction. **Notes:** Occasional in

NYC. Available. Mostly on the outer coastal plain, Long Island and NJ. **Uses:** Primary or secondary species for restoration of back-dune woodlands, shrub swamps, moist woodlands, swamp forests, wetland mitigation.

Amelanchier spicata (*A. stolonifera*) (dwarf serviceberry)

To 3 ft., colonial. Flowers white, May–June; fruit fleshy, purple, edible, July–Aug. Fruit eaten and seeds dispersed by many birds. Host to larvae of some butterfly species. **Habitat requirements:** Dry, rocky, or sandy sterile, acid soil, open woods, edges, fields (FACU). Tolerates partial shade. **Notes:** Infrequent in NYC. **Uses:** Secondary species for increased diversity and aesthetics in restoration of open forest understories, successional areas, slope stabilization, in shade or part shade.

**Aronia arbutifolia (Photinia pyrifolia)* (red chokeberry)

To 12 ft., colonial, fall foliage red. Flowers white, showy, April–May; fruit fleshy, red, Sept.–Oct., persistent. Wildlife value moderate. Fruit eaten and dispersed by birds. Host to larvae of some butterfly species. **Habitat requirements:** Swamps and moist to wet woods, salt marsh edges, and back-dune swales (FACW), soil pH 5–7.5. Tolerant of flooding (saturated soil 25% growing season), tolerant of salt, soil compaction. Moderately tolerant of shade, drought. **Notes:** Especially common on the coastal plain, NJ, and Long Island. Available. **Uses:** Primary species for shrub layer of swamp forest and marsh restoration, pond edges, stream banks, moist to wet fill. Wetland mitigation. Upper edges of brackish or freshwater tidal marshes.

Aronia melanocarpa (Photinia m.) (black chokeberry)

To 6 ft., colonization rate slow, fall foliage red. Flowers white, showy, April–May; fruit fleshy, black, July–Oct., persistent. Wildlife value moderate. Fruit eaten and dispersed by birds. Host to larvae of some butterfly species. **Habitat requirements:** Swamps and moist to wet woods (FAC), soil pH 5–7.5. Tolerant of flooding, drought, salt, soil compaction. Moderately tolerant of shade. **Notes:** Scattered throughout the region. Available. **Uses:** Secondary species for increased wildlife value, diversity, and aesthetics restoration of swamp forest, shrub swamps edges, and marsh restoration, pond edges, stream banks. Wetland mitigation. Moist back-dune shrub lands.

Aronia prunifolia (*Photinia floribunda*) (purple fruit chokeberry)

To 12 ft., somewhat colonial, fall foliage red. Flowers white, showy, April–May; fruit fleshy, dark purple Aug.–Sept., persistent. Wildlife value moderate. Host to larvae of some butterfly species. **Habitat requirements:** Swamps and wet woods (FACW), soil pH 5–7.5. Tolerant of flooding, salt, soil compaction. Moderately tolerant of shade, drought. **Notes:** Probably a hybrid between *A. arbutifolia* and

A. melanocarpa. **Uses:** Minor element for swamp forest and marsh restoration, pond edges, stream banks. Wetland mitigation.

**Baccharis halimifolia* (groundsel bush)

To 12 ft., semievergreen. Blooms and fruits Sept.–Oct.; white seed plumes (sexes separate). Wildlife value low, nesting and cover. **Habitat requirements:** Coastal. Salt marsh edges, usually upland of *Iva* (FACW). Soil pH 5.5–8.5. Tolerant of brackish to salt water; flooding (to 0.5 ft. or saturated soil for 75% growing season); tolerant of drought; soil compaction; concrete debris. Very intolerant of shade. Tidal elevation: above mean high high water (same elevation as *Panicum virgatum*). **Notes:** Common along coast. Available. **Uses:** Primary species for shrub layer of salt marsh restoration and mitigation. Vegetation of moist to wet fill on former salt marsh. **Bioengineering:** Roots fairly well from cuttings.

Ceanothus americanus (New Jersey tea)

To 4 ft., colonial, growth rate slow to medium. Flowers white, June–July; fruit dry (seeds ejected from capsule, may be fire adapted), Aug.–Oct. Host to larvae of some butterfly species. **Habitat requirements:** Open, dry, oak woods, acid soil (UPL), pH 4.5–6. Nitrogen fixer, may improve soil nutrients. Tolerant of drought, salt. Moderately tolerant of shade. Intolerant of soil compaction, flooding. **Notes:** Formerly much more common in the region. **Uses:** Minor component for dry areas, pine barrens, erosion control on dry slopes.

**Cephalanthus occidentalis* (buttonbush)

To 12 ft., colonial. Flowers white, ball-shaped clusters, July–Aug.; fruit dry, Sept.–Jan., dispersed by water. **Habitat requirements:** Open, saturated soil, freshwater tidal and nontidal marshes, pond edges (OBL), soil pH 6–8.5. Tolerates concrete debris, soil compaction, flooding (temporary inundation for up to 75% of growing season), often grows in shallow standing water. Very intolerant of shade, drought. **Notes:** Common in the region. Available. **Uses:** Primary species for shrub swamp and marsh restoration, open pond edges, stream banks. Wetland mitigation.

Cephalanthus occidentalis

Chamaedaphne calyculata (leatherleaf)

To 3 ft., evergreen, colonial. Flowers white, April–May; fruit dry, Sept.–Oct. Wildlife value low. **Habitat requirements:** Acid bogs, marshes, pond edges (OBL), acid soil pH 4.5–6. Tolerant of flooding, salt, soil compaction. Intolerant of drought, shade. **Uses:** Minor element for increased diversity and aesthetics in restoration of open bog or swamp habitats in sandy, or peaty, acid, low-nutrient soils.

Clethra alnifolia (sweet pepperbush)

To 8 ft., colonial. Flowers white, fragrant, July–Aug.; fruit dry, Sept.–Oct., persistent. Wildlife value low; cover. Host to larvae of some butterfly species. **Habitat requirements:** Moist to wet woods, pond edges (FAC+), tolerant of acid soil, pH 4.5–6.5. Often a dominant shrub of understories in moist forests. Tolerant of salt, soil compaction, shade, flooding (brief), saturated soil for up to 25% of growing season. Intolerant of drought and permanently saturated soil. **Notes:** Common understory shrub. Available. **Uses:** Secondary or primary understory shrub for increased erosion control, diversity, and aesthetics in swamp forest and marsh restoration or mitigation. Pond edges, upland of buttonbush.

Comptonia peregrina (sweet fern)

To 4 ft., colonial, growth rate slow, plant aromatic. Flowers dull, catkins May–June, sexes separate; fruit dry. Wildlife value low. **Habitat requirements:** Open, dry, sterile soil (UPL), pH 4.5–6.5. Tolerant of salt, drought. Intolerant of soil compaction, shade. Nitrogen fixer, may improve soil nutrients. **Notes:** Plant both sexes. **Uses:** Minor component for increased diversity and aesthetics in restoration of open, sandy soil, rocky sites, slope stabilization, roadside banks.

Cornus alternifolia (pagoda dogwood)

To 25 ft., slow growing, often a small tree. Flowers white, clusters showy, May–June; fleshy fruit, blue-black with red stems, July–Sept. Wildlife value very high. Fruit eaten by birds. **Habitat requirements:** Rich woods, stream and pond banks; prefers moist soil (UPL), pH 5.8–7.5. Very tolerant of shade, index 8–10. Moderately tolerant of flooding and soil compaction. Intolerant of drought. **Notes:** Formerly more common along NYC to Philadelphia corridor. **Uses:** Minor element for increased diversity and aesthetics in restoration of forest understories. Park tree, shrub for moist shade.

**Cornus amomum* (silky dogwood)

To 9 ft., sprawling, colonial, branch tips rooting. Flowers white, clusters showy, May–July; fruit fleshy, blue-white, Aug.–Sept., eaten and dispersed by birds. Wildlife value very high. Host to larvae of some butterfly species. **Habitat**

requirements: Open freshwater tidal and nontidal marshes, pond edges, flood plain forests, wet to moist (FACW), slightly acid to alkaline soils, pH 6–8.5. Tolerant of concrete debris, flooding, saturated soil for up to 25% of growing season. Moderately tolerant of drought. Intolerant of shade, salt. **Notes:** Very common, reproduces very well spontaneously from seed. Available. **Uses:** Primary or secondary shrub for restoration of open pond edges, stream bank stabilization, erosion control, marshes, wetland mitigation in fill, demolition debris, and other urban conditions. **Bioengineering:** Roots very well from cuttings.

**Cornus racemosa* (*C. foemina*) (red-panicle dogwood; gray dogwood)

To 15 ft., colonial, medium growth rate. Flowers white, clusters showy, May–July; fruit fleshy, white with red stems, Aug.–Sept. Wildlife value very high. Fruit eaten by many migrating and resident birds. **Habitat requirements:** Moist soil (FAC), pH 5–8.5, should tolerate concrete debris, alkaline fill. Moderately tolerant of flooding; saturated soil for up to 25% of growing season; drought; soil compaction; shade (does not bloom or fruit well in full shade). Intolerant of salt. **Notes:** Most common inland but occasional on the coastal plain. Available. **Uses:** Primary or secondary species for erosion control and slope stabilization in part shade or open sites, successional habitats, vegetation of alkaline fill or upland edges of wetland mitigation. Maintenance of low vegetation in power-line cuts. Park shrub for naturalization of open moist woodlands and wetland edges. **Bioengineering:** Roots fairly well from cuttings.

Cornus rugosa (roundleaf dogwood)

To 9 ft., growth rate medium. Twigs green, with purple mottles. Flowers white, fragrant, clusters showy, May–June; fruit blue, with red stems, Aug.–Oct. Wildlife value very high. Fruit eaten by many migrating and resident birds. **Habitat requirements:** Dry to moist sandy or rocky soil in forest understory (UPL), acid to alkaline soil, pH 6–8.5. Should tolerate concrete debris. Tolerant of shade. Intolerant of salt, drought, flooding, soil compaction. **Notes:** Infrequent north and west of NYC. Never frequent along coastal plain. **Uses:** Minor element for increased diversity and aesthetics in restoration of forest understories in moist, well-drained soil. Park shrub for naturalization of shady woodland and wetland edges. **Bioengineering:** Roots well from cuttings.

Cornus sericea (*C. stolonifera*) (red-osier dogwood)

To 8 ft. Flowers white, clusters showy, May–Aug.; fruit fleshy, white, Aug.–Oct., eaten and dispersed by birds. Wildlife value very high. Host to larvae of some butterfly species. **Habitat requirements:** Pond and marsh edges, moist open woods (FACW), acid to alkaline soils pH 6–8.5. Tolerant of partial shade, concrete debris. **Notes:** Used extensively in horticulture but does not reproduce well in the region south of CT and Warren County, NJ. Available. NYC is near the southern limit on the East Coast. **Uses:** Minor species for wetland restoration and mitigation. Horticultural shrub. **Bioengineering:** Roots very well from cuttings.

Corylus americana (American hazelnut)

To 9 ft., growth rate medium-fast. Flowers yellow catkins, March–April; fruit Sept. Nuts edible. Wildlife value moderate. Nuts eaten by birds and mammals. **Habitat requirements:** Moist to dry woods, thickets (FACU–), soil pH 5–7.5. Tolerant of partial shade. Moderately tolerant of drought, soil compaction. Intolerant of salt, flooding. **Notes:** Fairly common in our entire region. **Uses:** Minor element for increased diversity and aesthetics in forest restoration, vegetation of shady woodland edges, slopes.

Corylus cornuta (beaked hazelnut)

To 9 ft., growth rate medium. Flowers yellow catkins, March–April; fruit Sept. Nuts edible. Wildlife value moderate. Nuts eaten by birds and mammals. **Habitat requirements:** Moist to dry woods, edges (FACU–), soil pH 5–7.5. Tolerant of partial shade. Moderately tolerant of drought, soil compaction. Intolerant of salt, flooding. **Notes:** Found north and west of NYC. Not a coastal-plains plant. **Uses:** Minor element for increased diversity and aesthetics in forest restoration, vegetation of shady woodland edges, slopes.

Crataegus crus-galli (cockspur hawthorn)

To 30 ft., usually a small tree, growth rate slow, thorns to 3 in. long. Flowers white, showy May–June; fruit fleshy, red, Oct.–Nov. Wildlife value moderate. Fruit eaten by birds and mammals. **Habitat requirements:** Open rocky uplands, sandy or rocky acid to alkaline soil (FACU), pH 4.5–8.5. Should tolerate concrete debris. Tolerant of drought. Moderately tolerant of soil compaction. Intolerant of flooding, salt, shade, index 2–4. **Notes:** Do not use in high-maintenance areas due to thorniness. Never common in our region. **Uses:** Minor element for increased diversity and aesthetics in vegetation of concrete rubble, erosion control, deterrent to trampling or vehicle use in open, naturalizing areas.

Crataegus intricata (Biltmore hawthorn)

To 24 ft., sometimes a small tree, growth rate slow, thorns 1–2 in. Flowers white, showy, May; fruit fleshy, green to red, Oct. Wildlife value moderate. Fruit eaten by birds and mammals. **Habitat requirements:** Thickets, rocky, open woods (UPL). Tolerant of partial shade. **Notes:** Do not use in high maintenance areas due to thorniness. Very infrequent in our region. **Uses:** Minor element for increased diversity and aesthetics in vegetation of open areas for erosion control, deterrent to trampling or vehicle use in open, naturalizing areas.

Crataegus pruinosa (frosted hawthorn)

To 24 ft., usually a small tree, growth rate slow, very thorny. Flowers white, May; fruit fleshy, red, Oct. Wildlife value moderate. Fruit eaten by birds and mammals. **Habitat requirements:** Open woods, uplands, rocky soil (UPL), pH 6–8.5, should tolerate concrete debris. Tolerant of drought. Moderately tolerant of soil compaction. Intolerant of flooding, salt, shade, index 2–4. **Notes:** Do not use in high-maintenance areas due to thorniness. Very infrequent in our region. **Uses:** Minor element for vegetation of concrete rubble, erosion control, deterrent to trampling or vehicle use in open, naturalizing areas.

Crataegus uniflora (one flower hawthorn)

Rare (NYS SH, U); to 6 ft. Flowers white, May; fruit fleshy, greenish yellow, Aug.–Oct. Thorny. Wildlife value moderate. Fruit eaten by birds and mammals. **Habitat requirements:** Sandy or rocky, open woods, often on limestone soils (UPL). Should tolerate concrete debris. Tolerant of partial shade. **Notes:** Do not use in high-maintenance areas due to thorniness. Always rare in our region. **Uses:** Minor element for erosion control in open areas, deterrent to trampling or vehicle use in open, naturalizing areas.

Diervilla lonicera

Diervilla lonicera (dwarf-bush honeysuckle)

To 3 ft., colonial, growth rate fast, short lived. Flowers yellow to red, June–July; fruit dry, Aug.–Oct. Wildlife value low. Flowers attractive to hummingbirds. **Habitat requirements:** Dry, upland woods, rocky soil (UPL), pH 4.8–7.0. Very tolerant of shade. Tolerant of drought, soil compaction. Intolerant of flooding. **Notes:** Mostly inland, piedmont, highlands, rocky New England province. Not coastal. **Uses:** Secondary species for increased diversity and aesthetics in slope stabilization in dry shade. Restoration of forest understories, successional habitats. Park shrub for shady, dry edges.

Dirca palustris (leatherwood)

To 6 ft., slow growing. Flowers pale yellow, April–May; fruit fleshy, yellow-green, June–July. Wildlife value low. Fruit eaten by birds. **Habitat requirements:** Rich, moist woods, often in limestone soil (FAC), pH 6–8.5. Should tolerate concrete debris. Very tolerant of shade. Tolerant of salt, soil compaction. Intolerant of flooding, drought. **Notes:** Very infrequent in our region. Formerly more frequent. **Uses:** Secondary species for increased diversity and aesthetics in restoration of forest understories, slope stabilization in moist shade. Park shrub for shady edges.

Eubotrys racemosa (*Leucothoe r.*) (fetterbush)

To 12 ft. Flowers white, small, May–June; fruit dry, Sept.–Oct., persistent. Wildlife value low. Eaten by deer. **Habitat requirements:** Swamp forests, margins of woodland ponds and vernal pools, moist to wet understories of oak woodlands (FACW), needs acid soil, pH 4.4–6. Tolerant of shade, saturated soil up to 75% of growing season. Intolerant of salt. **Notes:** Occasional in NYC. More common on the coastal plain than inland. **Uses:** Secondary species for increased diversity and aesthetics in restoration of swamp forest understories, pond edges, forested shrub-swamp edges in acid soils.

Euonymus americanus (strawberry bush)

Rare (NYS S1, T); to 7 ft., growth rate medium. Flowers greenish purple, May–June; fruit a warty capsule, seeds with red, fleshy coat. Wildlife value low. **Habitat requirements:** Moist woods, shady edges (FAC), soil pH 5–7.5. Very tolerant of shade. Moderately tolerant of flooding, soil compaction. Intolerant of salt, drought. **Notes:** Susceptible to Euonymus scale. NYC is the northeastern limit. **Uses:** Minor element in stabilization of moist, shady forest slopes, forest understories at wetland edges.

Gaylussacia baccata (black huckleberry)

To 3 ft., colonial, very slow growing. Flowers white, May–June; fruit fleshy, black, edible, Aug.–Sept. Wildlife value high. Fruit eaten by birds and mammals. Host to larvae of some butterfly species. **Habitat requirements:** Dry, sandy, or rocky oak woods, pine barrens (FACU). Acid soil pH 4.5–6.5, but tolerates soil acidity down to pH 3.9. Tolerates partial shade of high forest canopy or open woods. **Notes:** Common throughout our region. **Uses:** Secondary species for increased wildlife value, diversity and aesthetics in restoration of mixed oak woodlands, pine barren forest understories, in acid soil.

Gaylussacia dumosa (dwarf huckleberry)

To 20 in., colonial, very slow growing. Flowers white, May–June; fruit fleshy, black, edible, Aug.–Sept. Wildlife value high. Fruit eaten by birds and mammals. Host to larvae of some butterfly species. **Habitat requirements:** Moist to dry sandy soil (FAC), oak forests, pineland bogs, acid soil, pH 4.3–6.5. Tolerant of partial shade. **Notes:** Quite uncommon now, formerly frequent along NJ outer coastal plain and on Long Island. **Uses:** Secondary species for increased wildlife value, diversity and aesthetics in restoration of oak woodlands, pine barren forest understories, in acid soil.

Gaylussacia frondosa

Gaylussacia frondosa (tall huckleberry)

To 6 ft., colonial, very slow growing. Flowers white, May–June; fruit fleshy, blue, edible, Aug.–Sept. Wildlife value high. Fruit eaten by birds and mammals. Host to larvae of some butterfly species. **Habitat requirements:** Moist to dry (FAC), open oak or pine woods, very acid soil, pH 3.8–5.5. Tolerant of partial shade. **Notes:** More common on the coastal plain than inland. **Uses:** Secondary species for increased wildlife value, diversity and aesthetics in restoration of oak woodlands, pine barren forest understories, in acid soil.

Hamamelis virginiana (witch hazel)

To 25 ft., slow growing. Flowers yellow Sept.–Nov.; fruit dry, autumn of the following year, persistent. **Habitat requirements:** Moist, rich, open woods (FAC–). Soil pH 4.5–6.5. Very tolerant of shade, index 8–10. Intolerant of salt, flooding, drought, soil compaction. **Notes:** Common throughout our region. **Uses:** Secondary species for increased diversity and aesthetics in restoration of forest understories in moist, moderately acid soil. Park shrub for shady edges.

Hudsonia ericoides (Pine-barren false heather, golden heather)

About 1 ft. or less, mound or mat forming, evergreen. Flowers yellow, showy, May–June; fruit dry, July–Aug. **Habitat requirements:** Dry, sandy soil of pine barrens, acid, rocky outcrops (UPL). Intolerant of shade. Cannot compete with weedy vegetation in good-quality soil. **Notes:** Apparently confined to sites along NJ outer coastal plain and Long Island. **Uses:** Secondary or minor element for increased diversity and aesthetics in restoration in rocky or sandy barrens.

Hudsonia tomentosa (false heather)

Less than 1 ft., shrubby, mat forming, evergreen. Flowers yellow, May–June; fruit June–Aug. **Habitat requirements:** Coastal. Open sandy soil, blow-outs, back dunes (UPL). Soil pH 5.5–6.9. **Uses:** Secondary or minor species for holding sand, increased diversity, and aesthetics in back-dune restoration.

Hypericum hypericoides (*Ascyrum h.*) (St. Andrew's Cross)

To 4 ft. Flowers yellow, showy, July–Sept.; fruit dry, reddish to maroon, Sept.–Oct. **Habitat requirements:** Dry, sandy, or rocky soil, open woods, edges, pine barrens (UPL). Tolerant of partial, light shade. Probably easily shaded out by competing vegetation. **Notes:** Long Island, northern limit. Outer coastal plain of NJ and Long Island. Very infrequent. **Uses:** Minor element for increased diversity and aesthetics in restoration in rocky or sandy open sites. Early successional vegetation of open habitats.

Hypericum prolificum (shrubby St.-John's-wort)

To 3 ft. Flowers yellow, showy, June–Aug.; fruit dry. Wildlife value moderate. **Habitat requirements:** Moist soil of swamp margins, to cliffs, sandy or rocky soil, pastures (FACU), soil pH 6–8.5. Tolerant of salt, brief flooding, drought, soil compaction. Should tolerate concrete debris. Very intolerant of shade. Easily shaded out by competing vegetation. **Notes:** Very infrequent in our region. **Uses:** Minor element for increased diversity and aesthetics in early successional vegetation of open areas, concrete debris, wetland edges.

Hypericum stans (*H. crux-andreae; Ascyrum* s.) (St.-Peter's-wort)

To 32 in. Flowers yellow, July–Aug.; fruit dry, Oct.–Nov. **Habitat requirements:** Dry, sandy soil of barrens (UPL). Soil pH 5.4–7. **Notes:** Northern limit is NJ and Long Island. Not listed as occurring in our region by some sources. **Uses:** Minor element for increased diversity and aesthetics in restoration in rocky or sandy open sites. Pine or oak barrens along coast.

Ilex glabra (inkberry)

To 6 ft., evergreen, eventually colonial, growth rate slow. Flowers white, small, June–July, sexes separate (dioecious); fruit fleshy, black (females), Sept.–Nov., persistent. Wildlife value high. Fruit eaten and seeds dispersed by birds. Good winter cover for small birds. **Habitat requirements:** Margins of bogs and swamps of coastal plain and pine barrens, Atlantic white cedar swamps (FACW), sandy, acid soil, pH 4.5–7. Tolerant of shade, flooding, saturated soil to 25% of growing season; tolerant of salt, soil compaction. Intolerant of drought. Available (plant both sexes). **Notes:** Cultivar commonly available is female only, will not produce fruit. **Uses:** Secondary species for increased diversity and aesthetics in restoration of wetlands in pine barrens or oak barrens, wet forest understory or shrubby edge. Back-dune marshes and swales. Horticultural as foundation planting in appropriately prepared, acid soils.

Ilex laevigata (smooth winterberry)

To 9 ft. Flowers white, small, May–June, sexes separate (dioecious); fruit fleshy, red (females), Sept.–Oct., persistent. **Habitat requirements:** Margins of swamp forests, acid soil (OBL). **Notes:** This species virtually identical to *Ilex verticillata* but very uncommon in our region. **Uses:** Minor element for swamp forest restoration. Wetland mitigation.

***Ilex verticillata* (winterberry)**

To 15 ft., growth rate slow, males often colonial. Flowers white, small, June–July, sexes separate (dioecious); fruit fleshy, red (female plants), Sept.–Oct., persistent into winter. Wildlife value high. Fruit eaten by birds in winter. **Habitat requirements:** Freshwater tidal marshes, shrub swamps, swamp forest, floodplain forests (FACW), in acid soil, pH 4.5–7.5, but apparently tolerates alkaline soil to pH 8. Tolerant of flooding or saturated soil for up to 25% of growing season; tolerates soil compaction. Moderately tolerant of drought, shade. Intolerant of salt. **Notes:** Common throughout our region. Available. **Uses:** Primary or secondary species for shrub layer in restoration of shrub swamps, swamp forests, stream banks, pond edges. Wetland mitigation.

***Iva frutescens* (marsh elder)**

To 9 ft., usually dying back in winter. Flowers greenish, blooms and fruits Aug.–Oct. **Habitat requirements:** Coastal. High salt marsh and salt marsh edges (FACW+), soil pH 5–7.5. Tolerant of brackish to saltwater, flooding, concrete debris, drought. Very intolerant of shade. Tidal elevation: mean high water, at the margin of high and low marsh elevations. **Notes:** Common along coast. Available. **Uses:** Primary species for restoration of high salt marsh shrub layer, below *Baccharis*.

***Juniperus communis* (common juniper)**

To 6 ft., evergreen, growth rate slow. No true flowers; sexes on separate plants; fruit a berrylike cone, blue-black, Oct., persistent. Wildlife value very high. Evergreen cover and food for small birds. Fruit eaten by overwintering birds and fall migrants. **Habitat requirements:** Sterile, dry, open rocky soil (UPL), pH 5–8.5. Should tolerate concrete debris. Tolerant of drought. Moderately tolerant of salt. Intolerant of shade, flooding, competition from weedy vegetation. **Notes:** Very infrequent throughout region. **Uses:** Secondary species for increased diversity and aesthetics in slope stabilization of open areas. Vegetation of rocky sites, concrete demolition debris, sandy fill.

Kalmia angustifolia

***Kalmia angustifolia* (sheep laurel)**

To 3 ft., evergreen, gradually colonial. Flowers pink, showy, May–June; fruit dry, Aug.–Oct. Growth rate slow. Wildlife value low. **Habitat requirements:** Dry to moist, acid, sterile sandy soil (FAC), pH 4.5–6, oak or pine woods, barrens, bog edges. Tolerant of open shade, flooding, drought, soil compaction. Probably intolerant of salt. **Uses:** Secondary or minor species for increased diversity and aesthetics in restoration of upland edges of swamp forests. Restoration of pine or oak barren forests.

Kalmia latifolia (mountain laurel)

To 9 ft., evergreen, grows slowly. Flowers white, showy, May–July; fruit dry, Aug.–Oct. Wildlife value low. **Habitat requirements:** Sandy or rocky, oak or pine woods, north-facing slopes (FACU), acid soil pH 4.5–6. Oak forests, pine barrens. Tolerant of open dappled shade. Moderately tolerant of salt, drought. Intolerant of flooding and compaction. **Uses:** Secondary species for increased diversity and aesthetics in restoration of forest understories in sandy or rocky acid soil, oak or pine barrens. Horticultural in acid soil, woodland edges.

Kalmia polifolia (pale laurel, bog laurel)

To 3 ft., evergreen. Flowers rose-purple, May–July; fruit dry. **Habitat requirements:** In peaty, wet soil of northern bogs (OBL). Soil pH 6–7.3. **Notes:** Long Island and Morris County, NJ, southern limit but apparently now extinct in our region. **Uses:** Minor species for shrub layer in restoration of northern bogs.

Ledum groenlandicum (*Rhododendron g.*) (Labrador tea)

To 3 ft., evergreen. Flowers white, May–June; fruit dry, Aug. (probably persistent). **Habitat requirements:** Acid, sphagnum bogs, pond shores (OBL). Soil pH 5–7. **Notes:** Southern limit Morris County, NJ (old record). Recently rediscovered in Sussex County, NJ. **Uses:** Minor species for shrub layer in restoration of acid, northern bogs, peaty pond shores.

**Lindera benzoin* (spicebush)

To 15 ft., grows slowly, fall foliage clear yellow. Flowers yellow, small, March–April, sexes separate (dioecious); fruit fleshy, red (females), Sept.–Oct. Wildlife value very high. Oily fruit important for migrating birds. Host to larvae of some butterfly species. **Habitat requirements:** Swamp forests, understory of moist to wet forests (FACW), soil pH 4.5–7.7. Tolerant of shade. Moderately tolerant of salt, flooding, saturated soil, up to 25% of growing season. Intolerant of drought. Does not grow well in heavy clay soils. **Notes:** Available. Common in our region. **Uses:** Primary species for restoration of moist to wet or seasonally flooded forest understories. Floodplain forests.

Lonicera canadensis (fly-honeysuckle)

To 6 ft., grows fast. Flowers yellowish, May–June; fruit fleshy, red, July–Aug. Wildlife value low. Fruit eaten by birds. Flowers attractive to hummingbirds. **Habitat requirements:** Dry to moist woods (FACU). NYC southern limit along East Coast. Tolerant of shade, salt, drought, soil compaction. Intolerant of flooding. **Notes:** Very infrequent in our region. Formerly common north of NYC. **Uses:** Minor species for increased diversity and aesthetics in restoration of forest understories, especially northwards.

Lyonia ligustrina

Lyonia ligustrina (male-berry)

To 12 ft., growth rate moderate. Flowers white, small, May–July; fruit dry, Sept.–Oct. into winter. Wildlife value low. **Habitat requirements:** Swamps, moist to wet open woods, pond edges (FACW), acid soil, pH 4–6. Tolerant of flooding, salt, drought, soil compaction. Moderately shade tolerant. **Notes:** Formerly more common throughout our region. **Uses:** Secondary to minor species for increased diversity and aesthetics in restoration of forest understories in moist, acid soil, bogs, pine barren or oak forest swamp, or pond margins.

Lyonia mariana (staggerbush)

To 6 ft., gradually colonial. Flowers white, May–June; fruit dry, Sept.–Oct. into winter. **Habitat requirements:** Moist to dry, sandy soil, open oak or pine woods, needs acid soil (FAC–). Found in soil pH 5.3. Tolerant of partial shade. **Notes:** Formerly more common. A coastal-plains plant. Mostly on the outer coastal plain. **Uses:** Secondary species for increased diversity and aesthetics in restoration of forest understories in sandy or rocky acid soil, oak or pine barrens.

Myrica gale (sweet gale)

To 5 ft., plant aromatic, colonial. Flowers small catkins, April–June, sexes on separate plants; fruit small nuts, July, eaten by birds. **Habitat requirements:** Swamps and shores (OBL). Soil pH 5–7.8. **Notes:** An uncommon, northern species, NYC, Long Island, and northern NJ near southern limit. **Uses:** Secondary to minor species for increased diversity and aesthetics in restoration of open wetlands; wetland mitigation.

**Myrica pensylvanica* (northern bayberry)

To 6 ft., gradually colonial, growth rate moderate, often semievergreen. Flowers dull, May–June; sexes separate; fruit (females) waxy, gray-white persistent, July–Aug., persisting through fall–winter. Wildlife value high. Fruit eaten by migrating and winter resident birds. **Habitat requirements:** Open, dry to moist, sandy soil, pH 5–7.8. Back-dune scrub, coastal areas with switchgrass, freshwater and brackish tidal marshes (FAC). Tolerant of salt (brackish water to 20 ppt salt), drought, soil compaction. Tolerant of saturated soil for 25% growing season. Intolerant of shade. **Notes:** Nitrogen fixer, may improve soil nutrients. Most common along coastal plain. **Uses:** Primary species for vegetation of sandy, open soil or fill. Revegetation of back dunes, sandy soil along highway banks, slope stabilization.

Nemopanthus mucronatus (mountain holly)

To 9 ft. Flowers white, May–June, sexes separate (dioecious); fruit fleshy, red (females), Aug.–Sept. **Habitat requirements:** Moist to wet woods, deep shade of swamp forests (OBL). Probably prefers acid soil. **Notes:** Very infrequent. May be difficult to find. **Uses:** Minor element for increased diversity and aesthetics in restoration of swamp forest understories, shrub swamps.

Physocarpus opulifolius (ninebark)

To 10 ft., colonial, growth rate fast. Flowers white, May–June; fruit dry, reddish, June–July, persistent. Wildlife value moderate. **Habitat requirements:** Open shores, swamp margins, streamsides, wet shrub lands (FACW), sandy or rocky moist soil pH 6–8.5. Should tolerate concrete debris. Tolerant of flooding, drought, soil compaction. Moderately tolerant of shade, salt. **Notes:** Very infrequent. Found occasionally in northwestern NJ. Rarely on the coastal plain. **Uses:** Secondary species for vegetation of wet to moist fill, concrete debris. Wetland mitigation, open pond and swamp margins. **Bioengineering:** Roots fairly well from cuttings.

Potentilla fruticosa (shrubby cinquefoil)

To 3 ft., growth rate medium. Flowers yellow, showy, June–Sept.; fruit dry. Wildlife value low. **Habitat requirements:** Open areas, wet to moist soil (FACW), pH 6–8.5. Should tolerate concrete debris. Tolerant of salt, flooding, drought. Intolerant of shade. **Notes:** Mostly northern. NYC is about the southern limit for this plant. **Uses:** Minor species for increased diversity and aesthetics in restoration of calcareous bogs. Wet concrete fill. Horticultural.

**Prunus maritima* (beach plum)

To 6 ft. Flowers white April–June; fruit fleshy, dark blue, edible, Sept.–Oct. **Habitat requirements:** Coastal. Back-dune scrub, dry sand (UPL). Soil pH 5.8–7.7. **Uses:** Primary species for holding sand, increased diversity and aesthetics in back-dune shrub-land restoration.

Prunus pumila var. *cuneata* (*P. susquehanae*) (sand cherry)

3 ft.; branches ascending. Flowers white, May–June; fruit fleshy, black, July–Sept. **Habitat requirements:** Dry, rocky woods, acid soil (UPL). Tolerant of partial, light shade. **Notes:** Very infrequent in our region. Soil pH 5.9–7 (probably wider than this). **Uses:** Secondary or minor species for increased diversity and aesthetics in vegetation of dry, rocky woodlands.

Prunus pumila var. *depressa* (sand cherry)

To 1 ft., prostrate, mat forming. Flowers white, May–June; fruit fleshy, black, July–Sept. **Habitat requirements:** Rocky or sandy soil of beaches and shores (UPL), especially in calcareous areas, should tolerate concrete debris. Soil pH 5.9–7 (probably wider than this). **Uses:** Secondary or minor species for increased diversity and aesthetics in vegetation of sandy, open soil, concrete fill.

Quercus ilicifolia (bear oak)

To 15 ft., growth rate medium. Blooms May; acorns ripe Sept. of the following year, persistent. Wildlife value very high. Acorns eaten by birds and mammals. **Habitat requirements:** Dry rocky or sandy, sterile acid soil (UPL) in oak and pine barrens, coastal scrub, pH 4–7.5. Tolerant of drought. Moderately tolerant of salt. Intolerant of flooding, shade. **Uses:** Common along the outer coastal plain, scattered inland. Available. **Uses:** Secondary species for increased diversity and aesthetics in restoration of coastal scrublands, pine or oak barrens.

Quercus ilicifolia

Rhododendron canadense (rhodora)

Rare (NYS S2, T); to 3 ft. Flowers pink-purple to white, April–June; fruit dry. **Habitat requirements:** Shady edges of acid bogs, rocky, wooded slopes, wet barrens (FACW). Soil pH 4–5.3. **Notes:** Extinct in our region. A northern species, south to Middlesex County, NJ, but not on Long Island after 1800. Probably never common. **Uses:** Minor element in restoration of acid bogs or wet barren habitats. Plant in cooperation with conservation organization restoration specialist. Use only local stock.

Rhododendron maximum (white laurel)

To 30 ft., evergreen, gradually colonial. Flowers white, showy, June–July; fruit dry, Sept.–Nov. Wildlife value low. Winter cover for birds. **Habitat requirements:** Wet to moist woods, Atlantic white cedar bogs, soil pH 4.5–6 (FAC). Prefers cool, moist, high shade. Tolerant of flooding, shade index 6–8. Intolerant of drought, compaction, disturbance, salt (very intolerant). **Notes:** Damaged by various fungi and insects (stem borers). Mostly inland of coastal plain. **Uses:** Minor element for increased diversity and aesthetics in restoration of moist forest understories, north-facing slopes, edges of acid bogs. In undisturbed sites.

Rhododendron periclymenoides (*R. nudiflorum*) (pinkster azalea)

To 6 ft., gradually colonial, growth rate slow. Flowers pink, showy, April–May (before leaves); fruit dry, Sept., persistent into late fall. Wildlife value low. **Habitat requirements:** Moist oak woods (FAC), acid soil, pH 4.5–5.5. Tolerant of shade, soil compaction, flooding (saturated soil for up to 25% growing season). Moderately tolerant of drought. Intolerant of salt. **Notes:** Common in our region. Available. **Uses:** Secondary species for increased diversity and aesthetics in restoration of forest understory in acid soils, oak and pine barrens, upland edges of forested wetlands. Park shrub in shady edges.

Rhododendron prinophyllum (*R. roseum*) (early azalea)

To 9 ft., growth rate slow. Flowers pink to purple, fragrant, spicy, May–July; fruit dry, Aug.–Oct. Wildlife value low. **Habitat requirements:** Moist oak woods, rocky areas (FAC), soil pH 5–8. Tolerant of shade. Moderately drought tolerant. Intolerant of salt, flooding, soil compaction. **Notes:** Extinct in our region. Infrequent before 1800. **Uses:** Minor element for increased diversity and aesthetics in restoration of piedmont oak forest understories, in moist, well-drained soil Horticultural.

**Rhododendron viscosum* (swamp azalea)

To 6 ft., growth rate moderate, colonization rate slow. Flowers white, showy, fragrant, spicy, June–July; fruit dry, Sept.–Oct. Wildlife value low. **Habitat requirements:** Open swamp forests, bogs (OBL), acid soil pH 4–6. Tolerant of saturated soil for up to 75% of growing season; tolerates soil compaction. Moderately tolerant of drought, shade. Intolerant of salt. **Notes:** Common throughout our region. Available. **Uses:** Primary or secondary species for restoration of swamp forests, pond edges, acid bogs. Wetland mitigation in partially shaded sites, acid soil. Horticultural, pond or stream edges.

Rhus aromatica (fragrant sumac)

To 12 ft., colonial, forming thickets, short lived, fall foliage red. Flowers pale yellow, sexes on separate plants, April–May; fruit red (females), hairy, May–July, persistent. Wildlife value high. Fruit eaten by many birds. **Habitat requirements:** Open sites, moist to dry, sandy, rocky soil, open upland woods (UPL), limestone cliffs to oak barrens, soil pH 6–8.5. Tolerant of drought, salt. Intolerant of shade, soil compaction, flooding. **Notes:** Mostly a Midwestern plant. Very infrequent in our region. Plant both sexes. **Uses:** Minor species in open sites with other shade-intolerant plants, eroded slopes, roadside banks, landfills.

**Rhus copallina* (winged sumac, shining sumac)

To 25 ft., colonial, grows fast, fall foliage bright red. Flowers greenish, sexes on separate plants, July–Sept.; fruit red (females), clusters showy, Aug.–Oct.

through winter. Wildlife value high. Fruit eaten by some overwintering birds. **Habitat requirements:** Open, sandy, sterile soil, fill, back-dune shrub lands (UPL), soil pH 5.3–7.5. Tolerant of salt, drought. Tolerates weedy vegetation. Intolerant of soil compaction, flooding, shade, index 0–2. **Notes:** Common in NYC. Mostly along the coastal plain. Available. **Uses:** Primary species for initial vegetation of eroded slopes, fill, landfills, disturbed back-dune habitats, roadside banks.

Rhus glabra (smooth sumac)

To 15 ft. Colonial, fall foliage red-orange. Flowers greenish, sexes on separate plants, June–July; fruit red (females), clusters showy, July–Oct., persistent through winter. Fruit eaten by some overwintering birds. **Habitat requirements:** Open areas, rich soils, fill soils (UPL), pH 5.3–7.5. Tolerant of salt, drought. Tolerates weedy vegetation. Intolerant of soil compaction, flooding, shade, index 0–2. **Notes:** Common throughout our region. Available. **Uses:** Primary or secondary species for initial vegetation of eroded slopes, fill, landfills, roadside banks.

Rhus typhina (*R. hirta*) (staghorn sumac)

To 15 ft., colonial, fall foliage red-orange. Flowers greenish, sexes on separate plants, June–July; fruit red (females), clusters showy, July–Sept., persistent through winter. **Habitat requirements:** Open, rocky areas, edges, fill (UPL), pH 4.5–7.2. Tolerant of salt, drought. Tolerates weedy vegetation. Intolerant of soil compaction, flooding, shade, index 0–2. **Notes:** Common throughout our region. Available. **Uses:** Primary or secondary species for initial vegetation of eroded slopes, fill, landfills, roadside banks.

Ribes americanum

Ribes americanum (wild black currant)

To 6 ft., growth rate moderate. Flowers pale yellow, April–June; fruit fleshy, black, June–Sept. Wildlife value high, fruit eaten by birds. **Habitat requirements:** Rich, moist woods, swamp forests, stream banks (FACW), soil pH 6–8.5. Tolerant of concrete debris, flooding, soil compaction. Moderately tolerant of shade, drought. Intolerant of salt. **Notes:** *Warning!* An occasional carrier of white pine blister rust if previously exposed. Uncommon on the coastal plain. Do not accept

R. sativum or other nonnative species. **Uses:** Minor element for increased diversity and aesthetics in wetland restoration, swamp forests. Wetland mitigation in sites with concrete debris.

Ribes cynosbati (dogberry)

To 5 ft., stems often prickly and spiny, growth rate moderate to fast; fall color yellow to purple. Flowers greenish, May–June, fruit fleshy, pale red, prickly, July–Sept. Wildlife value high. Fruit eaten by birds and mammals. **Habitat requirements:** Rich, moist, open woods, rocky soil (UPL), pH 6–8.5. Tolerant of shade, drought. Should tolerate concrete debris. Moderately tolerant of flooding, soil compaction. **Notes:** Apparently not a carrier of white-pine blister rust. Very infrequent in our region. *Warning!* Do not accept nonnatives such as *R. sativum*. **Uses:** Minor element for increased diversity and aesthetics in restoration of forest understories, rocky slopes, vegetation of fill with concrete debris.

Ribes hirtellum (smooth gooseberry)

To 3 ft. Flowers greenish yellow, April–July, fruit fleshy, black, June–Sept. Fruit eaten by birds and mammals. **Habitat requirements:** Wet, rocky, or swampy woods, bogs (FAC). Tolerant of partial shade. **Notes:** Apparently not a carrier of white-pine blister rust. Infrequent in our region. *Warning!* Do not accept nonnatives such as *R. sativum*. **Uses:** Minor element in restoration of moist to wet forest understories, rocky slopes, vegetation of fill.

Ribes rotundifolium (Appalachian gooseberry)

To 5 ft., spiny. Flowers greenish, April–May; fruit fleshy, green-purple, June–Sept. Fruit eaten by birds and mammals. **Habitat requirements:** Rich, open, rocky woods, thickets, cliffs (UPL). Tolerant of partial shade. **Notes:** Apparently not a carrier of white-pine blister rust. Northwest section of our region. *Warning!* Do not accept nonnatives such as *R. sativum*. **Uses:** Minor element in restoration of forest understories, rocky slopes, vegetation of fill.

Ribes triste (swamp red current)

To 2.5 ft., reclining. Flowers dull pink, April–July; fruit fleshy, red, June–Aug. **Habitat requirements:** Acid bogs, cool wet woods, ravines (OBL). Tolerant of shade. **Notes:** *Warning!* Possible carrier of white-pine blister rust but only if previously exposed. Very uncommon in our region. Not a coastal-plain plant. **Uses:** Minor element for wetland restoration, swamp forests. Wetland mitigation.

Rosa blanda (smooth rose)

To 6 ft., prickly, colonial. Flowers pink, showy, June–July; fruit fleshy, red Aug.–Nov., probably persistent. Fruit eaten by birds and mammals. **Habitat requirements:** Rocky, open sites, often in calcareous soils (FACU). Should tolerate concrete. Probably intolerant of shade. **Notes:** Apparently extinct (or nearly so) in our region. Formerly common in the Delaware valley, northern NY State, central CT. **Uses:** Minor species for increased diversity and aesthetics in vegetation of fill with concrete debris, vegetation barrier to intrusions, slope stabilization, vegetation of roadside banks. Horticultural, protective hedges.

**Rosa carolina* (pasture rose)

To 3 ft., prickly, colonial, growth rate fast. Flowers pink, showy, June; fruit fleshy, red, probably persistent. Wildlife value moderate. Fruit eaten by birds and mammals. **Habitat requirements:** Dry, open areas, sandy or rocky soil (UPL), pH 6–8.5. Tolerant of drought. Should tolerate concrete debris. Moderately tolerant of soil compaction. Intolerant of shade, flooding, salt. **Uses:** Primary or secondary species for vegetation of fill with concrete debris, vegetation barrier to intrusions, slope stabilization, vegetation of roadside banks. Horticultural, protective hedges.

Rosa palustris (swamp rose)

To 6 ft., stems prickly; aggressively colonial. Flowers pink, showy, June–July; fruit fleshy, red, Sept.–Oct. Wildlife value high. Fruit eaten by birds. **Habitat requirements:** Freshwater tidal and nontidal marshes, pond edges (OBL). Soil pH 4–7. Tolerant of flooding or saturated soil up to 75% of growing season. Intolerant of salt, shade. **Notes:** Frequent in the entire region. **Uses:** Secondary species for increased diversity and aesthetics in restoration of shrub swamps, marshes, pond edges. Wetland mitigation. Protection of sensitive wetlands from foot traffic.

Rosa virginiana

**Rosa virginiana* (Virginia rose)

To 6 ft., prickly, colonial. Flowers pink, showy, June–Aug.; fruit fleshy, red, Sept.–Oct, persistent. Fruit eaten by birds and mammals. **Habitat requirements:** Dry to wet open areas, moist swales in back-dune scrub (FAC), usually in acid soils, pH 5–7. **Uses:** Primary or secondary species for vegetation of sandy soil, back-dune scrub, vegetation barrier to intrusions, slope stabilization, vegetation of roadside banks. Horticultural, protective hedges.

**Rubus allegheniensis* (common blackberry)

Stems to 6 ft., armed with stout, curved, sharp prickles; growth rate fast, colonial.

Flowers white, May–July; fruit fleshy, black, edible, Aug.–Sept. Wildlife value very high. Fruit eaten by birds and mammals. **Habitat requirements:** Wide tolerance of soil and moisture, grows in fill soils (FACU), pH 4.5–7.5. Moderately tolerant of flooding, drought, soil compaction. Tolerates open, partial shade. Intolerant of salt. **Notes:** Very common throughout our region. **Uses:** Primary species for use as protective barriers, vegetation of fill soils, stabilization of slopes and roadside banks, protection of slower growing reforestation plantings, upper edges of wetland restoration and mitigation, enhanced wildlife habitat. **Bioengineering:** Roots well from cuttings.

Rubus enslenii (southern dewberry)

Stems slender, to 3 ft. tall, arching to prostrate, to about 9 ft. long, colonial, rooting at tips, prickles sparse. Flowers white, June–Aug.; fruit fleshy, black, edible, July–Aug. Fruit eaten by birds and mammals. **Habitat requirements:** Open woodlands, thickets (FACU). Tolerant of partial shade, soil pH 5–7. **Uses:** Secondary species for slope stabilization of open woodland slopes or roadside banks, erosion control. Increased diversity and aesthetics of open woodland or successional understories.

Rubus flagellaris (dewberry)

To about 3 ft., stems arching to prostrate, colonial; prickles stout, sharp. Flowers white, June–July; fruit fleshy, black, edible, July–Aug. Fruit eaten and seeds dispersed by birds and small mammals. **Habitat requirements:** Open soil, fill, weedy sites (UPL). Soil pH 5–7 but appears tolerant of concrete debris. Intolerant of shade. **Notes:** Common throughout our region. **Uses:** Secondary species for slope stabilization and protection of open sites, roadside banks, fill, erosion control.

Rubus occidentalis (black raspberry)

To 4 ft., colonial; stems prickly, bluish, good winter color, growth rate fast. Flowers white, May–June; fruit fleshy, black, edible, June–July. Wildlife value very high. Fruit eaten by birds and mammals. Not as widely tolerant or as prickly as *R. allegheniensis*. **Habitat requirements:** Open areas, edges, part shade, open woodlands, rich acid soil (UPL), pH 4.5–6.5. Tolerant of drought. Moderately tolerant of flooding, soil compaction, shade (grows poorly in full shade). **Notes:** Common throughout our region. **Uses:** Secondary or primary species for stabilization of slopes and roadside banks, protective barriers, vegetation enhancement for wildlife in open areas, woodland edges, enhanced wildlife habitat. Horticultural-edible fruit.

Rubus odoratus (flowering raspberry)

To 6 ft., unarmed, colonial, growth rate fast. Flowers purple, showy, July–Aug.; fruit fleshy, red, edible (barely), Aug.–Sept. Wildlife value very high. Fruit eaten by birds and mammals. **Habitat requirements:** Moist part shade, rocky woodland edges (UPL), soil pH 4.5–6.5. Tolerant of partial shade. Moderately tolerant of drought, soil compaction. Intolerant of flooding. **Notes:** Mostly in the northwest part of the region. Not a coastal-plain plant. **Uses:** Secondary species for increased diversity and aesthetics in restoration of open forest understories, slope stabilization in light shade. Horticultural.

Rubus pensilvanicus (Pennsylvania blackberry)

Canes to 10 ft. long, purple, armed with stout prickles. Flowers white, May–June; fruit fleshy, black, July–Aug., edible. Fruit eaten by birds and mammals. **Habitat requirements:** Thickets, woodland edges, successional habitats (UPL). **Notes:** Very uncommon in our region. **Uses:** Secondary species for use as protective barriers, vegetation of fill soils, stabilization of slopes and roadside banks, protection of slower-growing reforestation plantings, enhanced wildlife habitat.

Rubus setosus (bog blackberry)

To about 3 ft., densely bristly. Flowers white, July–Aug.; fruit fleshy black, Aug.–Sept. Wildlife value high. Fruit eaten by birds and mammals. **Habitat requirements:** Swamps, moist to wet soil (FACW+). **Notes:** Mostly north of our region. **Uses:** Secondary species for increased diversity and aesthetics in restoration of wetlands.

Salix bebbiana

Salix bebbiana (beaked willow)

To 15 ft., grows fast. Catkins March–April, sexes on separate plants; fruit May–June. Wildlife value high. Host to larvae of some butterfly species. **Habitat requirements:** Swamp and pond edges, open, wet to moist soil (FACW), pH 5.5–7.5. Tolerant of flooding, salt, drought, soil compaction. Intolerant of shade, index 0–2. **Notes:** Susceptible to various insects and fungal diseases. Plant both sexes. Very infrequent throughout region. **Uses:** Secondary species for increased diversity and aesthetics in wetland restoration and mitigation.

Salix candida (sage-leaved willow)

To 3 ft. Catkins April–June, sexes on separate plants; fruit July–Aug. Host to larvae of some butterfly species. **Habitat requirements:** Cold, limestone soils, calcareous bogs (OBL). Soil pH 5.7–7.6. Should tolerate concrete debris. **Notes:** Southern limit, Morris County, NJ. Plant both sexes. Apparently extinct in the region. **Uses:** Secondary species for increased diversity and aesthetics in wetland restoration and mitigation.

**Salix discolor* (pussy willow)

To 15 ft., grows fast. Silvery catkins (males only) March–April, sexes on separate plants; fruit May; seeds wind dispersed. Wildlife value high. Host to larvae of some butterfly species. Twigs and buds eaten by some mammals. **Habitat requirements:** Successional species in open wetlands, moist to wet soil, fill (FACW). Soil pH 4–7.5. Tolerant of flooding, drought, salt, soil compaction. Intolerant of shade, index 0–2. **Notes:** Plant both sexes. Common throughout the region. **Uses:** Primary woody species for wetland restoration and mitigation in open habitats, pond edges, stream banks, flood plains. **Bioengineering:** Roots very well from cuttings. Pond and stream edges in parks.

Salix eriocephala (*S. rigida*) (stiff willow, heart-leaved willow)

To 12 ft., grows fast. Catkins April–May, sexes on separate plants; fruit May–June. Host to larvae of some butterfly species. **Habitat requirements:** Open, wet soil, pond edges, ditches (FACW). Soil pH 4–7. **Notes:** Plant both sexes. Uncommon, found only on Long Island and north. **Uses:** Secondary or minor species for wetland restoration and mitigation in open habitats, pond edges, stream banks, floodplains.

* *Salix exigua* var. *interior* (*S. interior*) (sandbar willow)

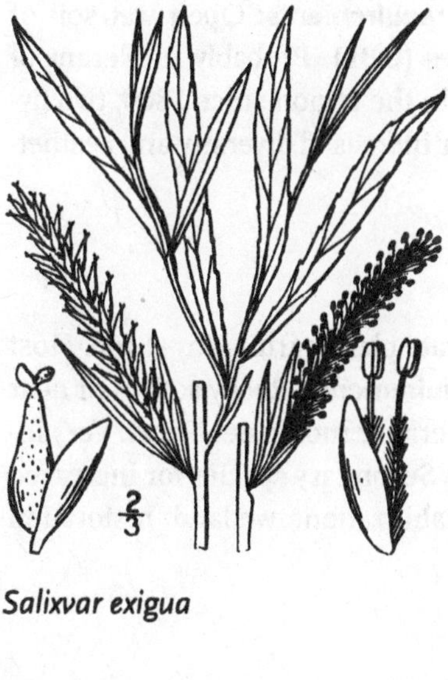

Salixvar exigua

To 9 ft., extensively colonial. Catkins April–May, sexes on separate plants; fruit May–June. Host to larvae of some butterfly species. **Habitat requirements:** Open mud, wet sand, or fill, floodplains (OBL). Tolerant of flooding, salt. Intolerant of drought, shade. **Notes:** Only four records of this plant in the region since 1800, one living. Plant both sexes. USDA maps on line show many more records. **Uses:** Primary or secondary species for stream bank stabilization, erosion control. Good substitute for the exotic *S. purpurea*. **Bioengineering:** Roots well from cuttings.

Salix humilis (upland willow)

To 9 ft., colonial, growth rate slow to moderate. Flowers in catkins, anthers red, sexes separate, March–April. Wildlife value high. **Habitat requirements:** Dry, open, barrens (FACU), soil pH 6–7.5. Tolerant of drought, flooding, soil compaction, salt. Intolerant of shade. **Notes:** Mostly on Long Island, very infrequent elsewhere. **Uses:** Minor species for vegetation of fill, slopes, wetland edges, open areas. **Bioengineering:** Roots well from cuttings.

Salix lucida (shining willow)

To 18 ft., growth rate fast. Flowers, catkins, April–June, sexes on separate plants; fruit July–Aug. Wildlife value high. Host to larvae of some butterfly species. **Habitat requirements:** Open moist to wet soil, shores, marshes (FACW), soil pH 5.8–7.5. Tolerant of flooding, drought, soil compaction, salt. Intolerant of shade. **Notes:** Only five records of this plant in the region since 1800, one living. Plant both sexes. **Uses:** Secondary species for increased diversity and aesthetics in wetland restoration, mitigation, stream bank stabilization. Pond edges. **Bioengineering:** Roots well from cuttings.

Salix occidentalis (*S. tristis*) (dwarf upland willow)

To 3 ft., colonial. Flowers in catkins, sexes separate, March–April; fruit May. Host to larvae of some butterfly species. **Habitat requirements:** Dry, exposed, sandy barrens, open woodlands, roadsides (UPL). **Uses:** Minor species for increased diversity in vegetation of fill, slopes, successional habitats.

Salix petiolaris (meadow willow)

To 20 ft. Catkins May–June, sexes on separate plants; fruit June–July. Host to larvae of some butterfly species. **Habitat requirements:** Open wet soil of stream banks, pond and lake shores, marshes (OBL). Probably intolerant of shade. **Notes:** Only four records of this plant in the region since 1800, two living. Plant both sexes. **Uses:** Minor element for increased diversity and aesthetics in wetland restoration and mitigation.

Salix sericea (silky willow)

To 12 ft. Catkins March–April, sexes on separate plants; fruit May–June. Host to larvae of some butterfly species. **Habitat requirements:** Rocky soil, in or near running water (OBL). Soil pH 5.2–7. Shade tolerance moderate. **Notes:** Very infrequent in our region. Plant both sexes. **Uses:** Secondary species for increased diversity and aesthetics in stream bank stabilization, wetland restoration and mitigation.

*_Sambucus canadensis_ (elderberry)

To 12 ft., colonial, growth rate fast. Flowers white, clusters showy, June–July; fruit fleshy, black, July–Sept. Wildlife value very high. Fruit eaten by birds and mammals, which disperse seeds. **Habitat requirements:** Freshwater tidal and nontidal marshes, wet edges, shrub swamps, forms thickets (FACW), soil pH 5–8. Tolerant of flooding or saturated soil for up to 25% growing season. Tolerant of drought, soil compaction. Probably tolerant of concrete debris. Moderately tolerant of part shade (will not bloom or fruit in dense shade). Intolerant of salt. **Notes:** Very common throughout the region. **Uses:** Primary species for restoration of open wetlands, shrub swamps, stabilization of pond edges, floodplains, marsh edges. Wetland mitigation, stream bank stabilization. **Bioengineering:** Roots well from cuttings.

*_Spiraea alba_ var. _latifolia_ (meadowsweet)

To 6 ft., colonial, growth rate fast. Flowers white, clusters showy, June–Aug.; fruit dry, Sept.–Oct. Wildlife value moderate. Host to larvae of some butterfly species. **Habitat requirements:** Moist to wet open uplands, rocky slopes, meadows (FAC+), soil pH 6.6–7.5. Tolerant of flooding, drought, soil compaction. Intolerant of salt, shade. **Notes:** Available (var. _latifolia_ is the native, northeastern variety). Frequent in our region. **Uses:** Primary species for vegetation of wet fill, wetland edges, shrub swamp margins, pond edges. Wetland mitigation, stream bank stabilization. **Bioengineering:** Roots fairly well from cuttings.

*_Spiraea tomentosa_ (hardhack)

To 5 ft., colonial, growth rate fast. Flowers pink, clusters showy, July–Sept.; fruit dry, Sept.–Oct. Wildlife value moderate. Host to larvae of some butterfly species. **Habitat requirements:** Open swamps, wet meadows (FACW), rocky, acid, sterile soil, pH 5–6. Tolerant of flooding, drought, soil compaction. Intolerant of salt, shade. **Notes:** Occasional throughout the region. Available. **Uses:** Primary species for restoration of bogs, shrub swamps, pond edges, in moderately acid soil. Wetland mitigation, stream bank stabilization, pond edges. **Bioengineering:** Roots fairly well from cuttings.

Staphylea trifolia (bladdernut)

To 15 ft., growth rate moderate; bark striped. Flowers white, May; fruit dry, inflated, Sept.–Oct. Wildlife value low. **Habitat requirements:** Forest understories and edges in moist, often rocky soil (FAC), pH 6–8. Tolerant of shade. Moderately tolerant of drought, flooding. **Notes:** Uncommon on the coastal plain. **Uses:** Secondary or minor species for increased diversity and aesthetics in restoration of understories of moist forest.

Taxus canadensis (Canada yew)

To 6 ft., evergreen, growth rate slow. No flowers; fruit (seed coat) fleshy, red, bird dispersed. Wildlife value moderate. **Habitat requirements:** Rocky or sandy upland forest understories (FAC). Soil pH 5–7.5. Tolerant of shade, salt. Intolerant of flooding, drought, soil compaction. **Notes:** A northern plant. Long Island is about the southern limit on the East Coast. **Uses:** Minor species for forest understory restoration. Horticultural evergreen for shady or open sites.

**Vaccinium angustifolium* (lowbush blueberry)

To 2 ft., eventually colonial, growth rate slow. Flowers white, May–July; fruit fleshy, blue, edible, Aug.–Sept. Wildlife value very high. Fruit eaten by birds and mammals. Host to larvae of some butterfly species. **Habitat requirements:** Sandy or rocky soil, open oak woods, needs acid soil (FACU), pH 4–6. Tolerant of partial, light shade, drought, salt. Intolerant of soil compaction, flooding. **Notes:** Most common on the coastal plain, scattered inland. Available. **Uses:** Primary species for restoration of open oak forest and pine barrens forest understories.

**Vaccinium corymbosum* (highbush blueberry)

To 9 ft., growth rate slow, fall foliage red. Flowers white, small, May–June; fruit fleshy, blue, edible, July–Aug. Wildlife value very high. Host to larvae of some butterfly species. Fruit eaten by birds and mammals. **Habitat requirements:** Swamp edges, moist upland forests, shrub swamps (FACW), moist acid soil pH 3.5–6.5. Tolerant of flooding or saturated soil for up to 25% of growing season; tolerant of partial shade, tolerant of soil compaction. Moderately tolerant of salt, drought. **Notes:** Common throughout our region. Available. **Uses:** Primary species for restoration of moist to wet oak forest understories, shrub swamps or bogs, pine barrens wetlands. Wetland mitigation. Horticultural and agricultural.

**Vaccinium pallidum* (*V. vacillans*) (early low blueberry)

To 3 ft., colonial, growth rate slow. Flowers white, May–June; fruit fleshy, blue, edible, July–Aug. Wildlife value very high. Fruit eaten by birds and mammals. Host to larvae of some butterfly species. **Habitat requirements:** Open oak woods, sandy, acid soil (UPL), pH 3.9–5.0, prefers deep humus. **Notes:** More common in NYC than *V. angustifolium* in woodlands. Appears more shade tolerant. Often found with *Viburnum acerifolium*. **Uses:** Primary species for restoration of mixed oak forest understories.

Vaccinium stamineum (deerberry)

To 5 ft., eventually colonial, growth rate slow. Flowers greenish white, May–June; fruit fleshy, yellowish to blue, July–Sept., edible (sour). Wildlife value

Vaccinium stamineum

high. Host to larvae of some butterfly species. Fruit eaten by birds. **Habitat requirements:** Dry to moist open oak woods, pine barrens (FACU–), in acid soil pH 4–6.5. Tolerant of partial shade, drought, salt. Moderately tolerant of soil compaction. Intolerant of flooding. **Notes:** Most common inland. Infrequent on the coastal plain. **Uses:** Secondary species for increased diversity and aesthetics in restoration of oak forests and pine barrens.

**Viburnum acerifolium* (maple-leaved viburnum)

To 7 ft. (usually about 3–4 ft.), eventually colonial, growth rate slow to moderate, fall foliage pinkish purple. Flowers white, clusters showy, May–June; fruit fleshy, black, Aug.–Sept. persistent into winter. Wildlife value high. Fruit eaten by overwintering birds. Host to larvae of some butterfly species. **Habitat requirements:** Understory of moist to moderately dry forests, with oak, beech, hickory, maple (UPL). Acid soil pH 3.9–6. Prefers deep humus. Tolerant of shade. Moderately tolerant of drought, soil compaction. Intolerant of flooding, salt. Often found with *Vaccinium pallidum* in beech-oak woodlands. **Notes:** Common throughout the region in suitable sites. **Uses:** Primary or secondary species for restoration of moist to dry forest understories.

Viburnum alnifolium

Viburnum alnifolium (*V. lantanoides*) (hobblebush)

To 6 ft., colonial, growth rate moderate. Flowers white, clusters showy, May–June; fruit fleshy, red turning purple, Aug.–Oct. Wildlife value high. Fruit eaten by birds. Host to larvae of some butterfly species. **Habitat**

requirements: Understories of moist forests (UPL), soil pH 5.5–6.5. Tolerant of shade. Moderately tolerant of soil compaction. Intolerant of flooding, drought, salt. **Notes:** A northern species. Southern limit on the East Coast, around Sussex County, NJ, Westchester County, NY. Essentially extinct in our region. Never common. **Uses:** Secondary species for increased diversity and aesthetics in restoration of forest understories, slope stabilization. **Bioengineering:** Roots well from cuttings.

Viburnum cassinoides (*V. nudum* var. *c.*) (witherod)

To 12 ft., growth rate moderate, fall foliage often red. Flowers white, clusters showy, May–June; fruit fleshy, pink turning blue-black, Aug.–Oct. Wildlife value high. Fruit eaten by migrating birds. **Habitat requirements:** Understories of wet to moist woods (FACW), acid soil pH 5–6.5. Tolerant of shade, flooding, salt, soil compaction. Moderately tolerant of drought. **Uses:** Secondary species for increased diversity and aesthetics in restoration of wet forest understory, swamp and bog edges. Wetland mitigation.

**Viburnum dentatum* (*V. recognitum*), (*V. d.* var. *lucidum*) (arrowwood)

To 10 ft., colonial, growth rate moderate. Flowers white, clusters showy, June–July; fruit fleshy, dark blue, Aug.–Oct. Wildlife value high. Fruit eaten by mammals and by migrating and resident birds. Host to larvae of some butterfly species. **Habitat requirements:** Swamps, freshwater tidal and nontidal marshes, pond edges, swamp forest gaps, moist to wet soil (FAC), pH 3.9–7. Tolerant of flooding or saturated soil up to 25% growing season, tolerant of drought, moist fill soils. Moderately tolerant of shade; salt, soil compaction. **Notes:** Very common throughout the region. Available. **Uses:** Primary species for restoration of wetlands, stream bank stabilization, pond edges, shrub swamps, wetland mitigation. **Bioengineering:** Roots well from cuttings.

Viburnum lentago (nannyberry)

To 30 ft., colonial, forms thickets, often a small tree, growth rate fast. Flowers white, fragrant, clusters showy, May–June; fruit fleshy, black, Aug.–Oct. Wildlife value high. Host to larvae of some butterfly species. Fruit eaten by birds. **Habitat requirements:** Open woods, edges, rich, moist soil (FAC), pH 6–8.5, should tolerate concrete debris. Tolerant of drought. Moderately tolerant of shade, index 5–6. Tolerant of flooding or saturated soil up to 25% of growing season. Intolerant of salt, soil compaction. **Notes:** Mostly inland, north and west. Infrequent along coastal plain. **Uses:** Secondary species for increased diversity and aesthetics in restoration of moist forest understories, swamp forests, slope and soil stabilization, wetland edges. Wetland mitigation. **Bioengineering:** Roots fairly well from cuttings.

Viburnum nudum (*V. cassinoides*) (possum-haw)

Rare (NYS S1, T); to 12 ft., growth rate moderate. Flowers white, clusters showy, May–June; fruit fleshy, pinkish becoming blue-black Aug.–Oct. Wildlife value high. Fruit eaten by birds and mammals. Host to larvae of some butterfly species. **Habitat requirements:** Swamps, moist woods, pond edges (OBL), acid soil pH 5–6. Tolerant of partial shade, flooding, soil compaction. Moderately tolerant of drought. Intolerant of salt. **Notes:** Most frequent along coastal plain. *V. cassinoides* sometimes listed as a separate species or a variation of *V. nudum*. **Uses:** Secondary species for increased diversity and aesthetics in wetland restoration and mitigation, shrub swamps. Horticultural for pond edges.

[*Viburnum opulus* var. *americanum* (*V. trilobum*) (highbush cranberry)

To 15 ft. Flowers white June–July; fruit fleshy, red, Sept.–Oct. Cool, moist woods (FACW). *Not Recommended.* Native only as far south as Putnam County, NY, and Warren County, NJ. The plant often sold as highbush cranberry is the Eurasian guelder rose (*V. opulus* var. *opulus*). The American variety has leaf stalk glands that are round-topped and stalked. The exotic has unstalked concave-topped glands and is not a wetland plant.]

**Viburnum prunifolium* (black-haw)

To 15 ft., a small tree, grows rather slowly. Flowers white, clusters showy, April-May; fruit fleshy, black, Sept.–Oct. Wildlife value high. Host to larvae of some butterfly species. Fruit eaten by birds and mammals. **Habitat requirements:** Open woods, open habitats, edges (FACU), soil pH 5–8.5, should tolerate concrete debris. Tolerates drought. Somewhat tolerant of partial, open shade, index 2–4. Intolerant of salt, flooding, soil compaction. **Notes:** Common. Not as frequent east of NYC in our region but scattered. **Uses:** Primary or secondary species for vegetation of woodland edges, fill, landfills, open areas. Horticultural. Good substitute for exotic flowering trees. Park tree or shrub.

Viburnum rafinesquianum (downy arrowwood)

To 7 ft., growth rate moderate. Flowers white, clusters showy, May–June; fruit fleshy, black, July–Sept. Wildlife value high. Host to larvae of some butterfly species. Fruit eaten by birds. **Habitat requirements:** Dry woodlands, calcareous soil (UPL), pH 6–8.5, should tolerate concrete debris. Tolerant of shade, drought. Moderately tolerant of salt, soil compaction. Intolerant of flooding. **Notes:** Not a coastal-plain plant. **Uses:** Secondary species for increased diversity and aesthetics in restoration of upland forest understories, slope stabilization, vegetation of fill with concrete debris.

Zanthoxylum americanum (prickly ash)

To 25 ft., rarely a small tree, stems prickly, bark and foliage aromatic. Grows fast. Flowers yellow-green, sexes separate, April–May; fruit dry, July–Sept. Wildlife value high. **Habitat requirements:** Moist to dry woods (UPL), soil pH 6–8.5, should tolerate concrete debris. Tolerant of drought. Moderately tolerant of flooding. Intolerant of soil compaction, shade, index 2–4. **Notes:** Northwest part of our region, infrequent. Not along coastal plain. **Uses:** Secondary species for increased diversity in restoration of forest understories, slope stabilization, site protection, vegetation of fill with concrete debris. Plant both sexes.

Chapter 3

Vines

Vines are woody or herbaceous plants with stems that cannot support themselves but are adapted for climbing other plants or objects. Some, such as grapes, climb with the aid of tendrils, others twine their stems around their host plant's stems. Very aggressive vines can cover and shade out their host plant. However, with native vines, this tends to happen more often in very disturbed sites. Some vines provide good ground cover and soil holding capabilities (Virginia creeper and poison ivy). Other vines can only be used under selected conditions due to their aggressive tendencies (grape). The majority of native vines seem to strike a balance with their host plant and do not cause major damage to mature trees and shrubs (wild bean). Many vines provide food and shelter for native insects, birds, and mammals (Virginia creeper, poison ivy, greenbrier). There are a number of nonnative vines that do cause major damage (Asian bittersweet, Japanese honeysuckle, wisteria, and porcelainberry).

VINE SPECIES

Apios americana (wild bean)

Herbaceous, twining, colonial. Flowers brownish purple-pink, July–Sept.; fruit pods dry, Sept.–Oct. Host for some butterfly species. **Habitat requirements:** Marshes, rich, moist soil (FACW). Soil pH 6–7.5 (probably more acid tolerant than this). Potentially a nitrogen fixer, may improve soil nutrients. Tolerant of partial shade. **Uses:** Minor species for addition of diversity and soil improvement in wetland restoration and mitigation.

Celastrus scandens (American bittersweet)

Aggressive woody climber to 20 ft., growth rate very fast. Flowers greenish, small, May–June; fruit a yellow capsule, seed coats fleshy, bright orange, dispersed by birds, Oct. into winter. Wildlife value moderate. **Habitat requirements:** Sandy or rocky soil, pH 6–7.5 (FACU−). Tolerant of shade, drought, salt. Moderately tolerant of flooding, soil compaction. **Notes:** Can be aggressive, may damage shrubs and trees. (Asian bittersweet, a very destructive invasive vine, is *C. orbiculatus.*) **Uses:** Minor element for soil stabilization on slopes. Horticultural.

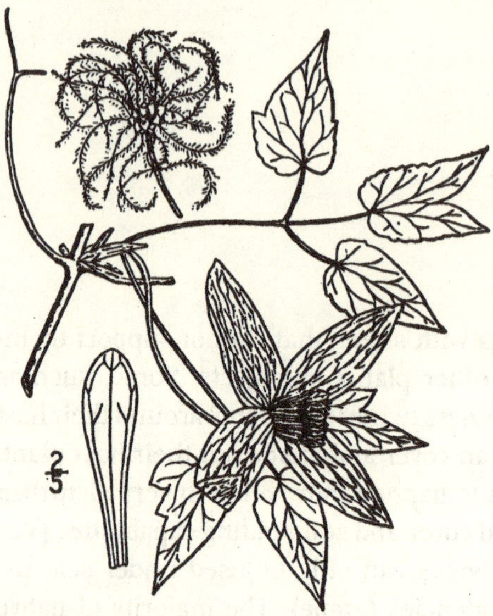

2/5

Clematis occidentalis

Clematis occidentalis (purple clematis)

Scarcely woody climber, to 6 ft., colonial, growth rate moderate to fast. Leaves poisonous. Flowers violet, showy, May–June; fruit dry, July–Sept. **Habitat requirements:** Rocky, limestone woods, slopes, soil pH 6–8.5 (UPL). Tolerant of concrete debris and shade. Moderately tolerant of drought. Intolerant of flooding, soil compaction. **Notes:** Northwest part of region only. Now nearly extinct here. **Uses:** Minor element for increased diversity and aesthetics in slope stabilization, especially in alkaline soil. Horticultural.

Clematis virginiana (virgin's bower)

Scarcely woody climber, to 9 ft., growth rate very fast. Leaves may be irritating. Flowers white, showy en masse, July–Aug.; fruit dry, Sept.–Oct. **Habitat requirements:** Low woods, moist soil, pH 6–8.5 (FAC). Tolerant of concrete debris, partial shade, flooding, drought, soil compaction. **Note:** *Warning! Clematis terniflora* is an invasive Asian species with similar flowers. **Uses:** Minor element for increased diversity and aesthetics in vegetation of fill with concrete debris, slope stabilization. Horticultural.

Clitoria mariana (butterfly pea)

Herbaceous, to 3 ft. Flowers blue, showy, July–Aug.; fruit pods dry, Aug.–Sept. Host for some butterfly species. **Habitat requirements:** Upland woods, sandy barrens (UPL). Potentially a nitrogen fixer, may improve soil nutrients. **Notes:** Mostly a southern plant. Long Island is northern limit. **Uses:** Minor element for increased diversity and aesthetics in soil stabilization on slopes. Horticultural.

Dioscorea villosa (wild yam)

Slender, herbaceous, twining vine, to 15 ft. Flowers small, green, May–July; fruit dry, July–Sept., persistent. **Habitat requirements:** Understory of moist or wet forests and edges (FAC+). Tolerant of shade. **Uses:** Minor element for addition of diversity, soil stabilization on shady slopes, edges of wetlands.

Echinocystis lobata (balsam apple)

Annual, herbaceous, high-climbing vine. Flowers whitish, July–Sept.; fruit bladderlike, prickly, about 2 in. long, Sept.–Oct. **Habitat requirements:** Open or partly shady floodplains, rich, moist soil (FAC). Tolerant of partial shade. **Notes:** Rather aggressive. **Uses:** Minor element for addition of diversity, edges of wetlands.

Galactia regularis (milk pea)

Herbaceous, prostrate, to 3 ft. long. Flowers reddish purple, June–Aug.; fruit pods dry, Aug.–Oct. Host for some butterfly species. **Habitat requirements:** Dry, sandy open woods and barrens (UPL). Potentially a nitrogen fixer, may improve soil nutrients. Tolerant of partial shade. **Uses:** Minor element for addition of diversity, butterfly gardens, soil improvement in open, dry habitats.

Galactia volubilis (downy milk pea)

Herbaceous, twining vine, to 4 ft. Flowers reddish purple, July–Aug.; fruit pods, Aug.–Oct. Host for some butterfly species. **Habitat requirements:** Dry woods and barrens (UPL). Potentially a nitrogen fixer, may improve soil nutrients. Tolerant of partial shade. **Uses:** Minor element for addition of diversity and aesthetics in butterfly gardens, soil improvement in dry, open woodland habitats.

Ipomoea pandurata (wild potato vine)

Herbaceous, trailing or twining vine, to 15 ft. Flowers white and red, showy, July–Oct.; fruit dry. Attractive to hummingbirds. **Habitat requirements:** Dry woods, old fields, edges (FACU). Tolerant of partial shade. **Uses:** Minor element for addition of diversity and aesthetics in open woodlands. Horticultural.

Lathyrus palustris (marsh pea)

Herbaceous, twining vine, to 3 ft., colonial. Flowers red-purple, showy, June–Aug.; fruit pods, Aug.–Sept. Host for some butterfly species. **Habitat requirements:** Wet meadows, wooded swamps (FACW+). Potentially a nitrogen fixer, may improve soil nutrients. Tolerant of partial shade. **Uses:** Minor element for addition of diversity and aesthetics in butterfly gardens, soil improvement in wetlands, swamps, mitigation.

Lonicera dioica (limber honeysuckle)

Shrub or woody climber, to 9 ft., growth rate moderate to fast. Flowers bright yellow, May–June; fruit fleshy, red, July–Sept. Wildlife value moderate. Fruit eaten and seeds dispersed by birds. **Habitat requirements:** Moist rocky woods, soil pH 6–8.5 (FACU). Tolerant of concrete debris, shade, drought, salt.

Lonicera dioica

Moderately tolerant of flooding and soil compaction. **Notes:** Nearly extinct in our region. Not a coastal-plain plant. *Warning! Lonicera japonica* is a very invasive exotic vine. **Uses:** Minor element for diversity and aesthetics in slope stabilization, vegetation of concrete fill soils. Horticultural.

Lonicera sempervirens (trumpet honeysuckle)

Woody, twining vine, to 20 ft., colonial, growth rate moderate. Flowers red-yellow, showy, May–Aug.; fruit fleshy, red, Aug.–Oct. Eaten by birds, which disperse the seeds. Wildlife value moderate. Attractive to hummingbirds. **Habitat requirements:** Open woods edges (FACU), soil pH 6–7.5. Tolerant of shade, drought. Moderately tolerant of soil compaction. Intolerant of flooding. **Notes:** Formerly more frequent but never abundant. Available. *Warning!* Do not allow substitution of *L. japonica.* **Uses:** Minor element for diversity and aesthetics in stabilization of slopes in woodlands. Horticultural.

Menispermum canadense (moon seed)

Woody climber or ground cover, to 12 ft., colonial, growth rate very fast. Flowers whitish, June–July; fruit fleshy, blue-black, poisonous, Sept. Wildlife value high. **Habitat requirements:** Moist rich woods, edges (UPL), soil pH 5–7.5. Tolerant of shade, flooding, soil compaction. Moderately tolerant of drought. **Notes:** Frequent in our region but less so along the coastal plain. **Uses:** Secondary element for slope stabilization in woods or open areas. Vegetation of concrete debris fill.

Mikania scandens (climbing hempweed)

Herbaceous twining vine, stems to 17 ft. long. Can be aggressive in high-nutrient soils. Flowers dull purple, July–Oct. **Habitat requirements:** Wet soil, swamps, stream margins, climbing over shrubs (FACW+). Soil pH 5.7–7.5. **Uses:** Minor species for increased diversity and aesthetics in wetland restoration and mitigation.

**Parthenocissus quinquefolia* (Virginia creeper)

Woody climber or ground cover, to 35 ft., tendrils with adhesive disks at tips; colonial, growth rate very fast. Fall foliage red. Flowers tiny, dull yellowish,

June–July; fruit fleshy, blue-black with red stems, Sept.–Oct. Wildlife value high. Fruit eaten by birds, which disperse seeds. **Habitat requirements:** Woods, edges, back-dunes, scrub, soil pH 3.8–7.5 (FACU). Tolerant of shade, flooding, drought, soil compaction. Moderately tolerant of salt. Found in many habitats. **Notes:** Common throughout our region. Available. **Uses:** Primary species for slope stabilization in forests and open areas, sterile back dunes to rich forest soil. Vegetation of fill, landfills.

Parthenocissus vitacea (grape-woodbine, thicket creeper)

Woody climber or ground cover, to 35 ft., colonial, growth rate very fast. Fall foliage red. Virtually identical to *P. quinquefolia* but no adhesive disks on tendril tips. Flowers tiny, dull yellowish, June–July; fruit fleshy, blue-black with red stems, Sept.–Oct. Wildlife value high. Fruit eaten by birds which disperse seeds. **Habitat requirements:** Woods, edges, back-dune scrub, soil pH 3.8–7.5 (FACU). Tolerant of shade, flooding, drought, soil compaction. **Notes:** Very infrequent in our region. **Uses:** Primary species for slope stabilization in forests and open areas, sterile back dunes to rich forest soil. Vegetation of fill, landfills.

Polygonum cilinode (fringed bindweed)

Herbaceous, climbing or reclining vine, stem to 6 ft. Flowers small, white, June–Aug. **Habitat requirements:** Dry to moist open woods, rocky or sandy soils, thickets (UPL). Tolerant of partial shade. **Uses:** Minor element for increasing diversity in vegetation of edges, open rocky or sandy soils.

Sicyos angulatus (bur-cucumber)

Annual, herbaceous climber, to 9 ft. Flowers whitish, July–Sept.; fruit 1 in., hairy-spiny, Sept.–Oct. **Habitat requirements:** Moist soil of floodplains, marsh edges (FACU). **Uses:** Minor element for increasing diversity in vegetation of edges. Possibly useful for addition to initial seed mix in vegetation of open soil in new restoration.

Smilax glauca (glaucous greenbrier)

Slender, thorny, woody, high climber, to 20 ft., semievergreen, colonial, growth rate fast. Flowers yellowish, May–June; fruit fleshy, blue, Aug. into winter. Wildlife value moderate. Fruit eaten by birds in fall and winter. **Habitat requirements:** Dry to moist sandy soil, pH 6–8.5 (probably tolerates more acid soil), open woods, scrub (FACU). Tolerant of shade, salt, drought, soil compaction. Moderately tolerant of flooding. **Notes:** Most common along the coastal plain. **Uses:** Secondary species for vegetation of concrete fill, back-dune scrub, dry open or partly shaded slopes, low maintenance roadside banks. Protection of sensitive areas from intrusion.

Smilax herbacea (carrion flower)

Herbaceous, unarmed climber to 7 ft. Flowers yellowish, May–June; fruit fleshy, blue, July–Sept. Eaten by birds. **Habitat requirements:** Moist, rich woods, floodplains (FAC). Tolerant of shade. **Uses:** Secondary or minor species for increasing diversity, aesthetics, and wildlife value in forest understory restoration.

Smilax pulverulenta (downy carrion flower)

Rare (NYS S1, E); herbaceous, unarmed climber to 7 ft. Flowers yellowish, May–June; fruit fleshy, blue, July–Sept. Eaten by birds. **Habitat requirements:** Moist to dry, upland woods (FACU). Tolerant of shade. **Uses:** Secondary species for increasing diversity in forest understory restoration. Plant only in coordination with a conservation organization restoration specialist.

Smilax pseudochina (false China-root)

Rare (NYS S1, E); herbaceous, unarmed climber to 6 ft. Flowers yellowish, May–June; fruit fleshy, black, July–Sept. Eaten by birds. **Habitat requirements:** Sphagnum bogs, low woods, moist sandy soil, coastal plain, NJ and south (FAC+). Tolerant of shade. Probably needs acid soil. **Uses:** Minor species for increasing diversity in bog and wet forest understory restoration. Plant only in coordination with a conservation organization restoration specialist.

**Smilax rotundifolia* (common greenbrier)

Woody, thorny, slender, high climber, to 35 ft., stems evergreen; growth rate moderate, but aggressively colonial in high light habitats. Flowers yellowish, May–June; fruit fleshy, blue black, Aug.–winter. Wildlife value moderate. Eaten by birds, which disperse seeds through winter. **Habitat requirements:** Moist, open woods, back-dune scrub (FAC), soil pH 4.4–8.5. Tolerant of concrete debris, tolerant of acid soil, drought, shade, flooding, salt, soil compaction. **Notes:** Very common, especially along the coastal plain. **Uses:** Primary species for vegetation of alkaline to acid, sandy fill, landfills, demolition debris, slope stabilization in woodlands, edges, or open habitats. Low maintenance roadside banks. Edge planting for protection of sensitive areas from intrusion.

Strophostyles helvola

Strophostyles helvola (trailing wild bean)

Annual, herbaceous, twining, to 3 ft. Flowers pink-purple, becoming greenish, July–Sept.; fruit dry, Aug.–Oct. Host for some butterfly species. **Habitat requirements:** Dry to moist, sandy soil, often on cinders (FACU−). Potentially a nitrogen fixer; may improve soil nutrients. **Uses:** Minor species for addition of diversity and aesthetics of restoration, initial seed mix for slope stabilization, open habitats. Possibly useful for addition to initial seed mix in vegetation of open soil in new restoration.

Toxicodendron radicans (poison ivy)

Woody ground cover or stout, woody climber, to 35 ft. (or more), growth rate fast, aggressively colonial. Fall foliage orange-red. *All parts poisonous on contact.* Flowers greenish, May–June; fruit a waxy berry, Sept. into winter. Wildlife value high. Fruit eaten by birds in winter. **Habitat requirements:** Ubiquitous. Moist woods, open areas, back-dune scrub, wetland edges (FAC), soil pH 5–6.5 (probably more tolerant of alkaline soil). Tolerant of concrete debris, fill, shade, flooding, drought, soil compaction. **Uses:** Secondary species for soil stabilization and revegetation of slopes, landfills, fill, back dunes. Use away from foot traffic.

Vicia caroliniana (wood vetch)

Herbaceous trailing or climbing to 3 ft. Flowers white, May–June, fruit pods June–July. Host for some butterfly species. **Habitat requirements:** Moist edges, open woods on limestone soils (FACU−). Should tolerate concrete debris. Tolerant of shade. Potentially a nitrogen fixer; may improve soil nutrients. **Uses:** Minor species for addition of diversity and aesthetics to restoration, slopes, open habitats.

Vitis aestivalis (summer grape)

Vitis aestivalis

Woody, high climber. Flowers greenish, June–July; fruit fleshy, small, dark purple, Sept.–Oct., eaten by birds and mammals. **Habitat requirements:** Moist woods, edges, thickets, stream banks (FACU). Soil pH 5.3–7. Tolerant of partial shade. **Uses:** Secondary species for wildlife food and shelter along roadsides, edges; vegetation of fill.

Vitis labrusca (fox grape)

Woody, high climber, to 35 ft., colonial, growth rate very fast. Flowers greenish, June–July; fruit fleshy, dark purple, edible, Sept.–Oct. Wildlife value very high. Eaten by birds and mammals. **Habitat requirements:** Edges, thickets, moist soil (FACU), pH 5.5–7.5. Tolerant of flooding, salt, soil compaction. Moderately tolerant of drought. **Uses:** Secondary species for wildlife food and shelter along roadsides, edges; vegetation of fill.

Vitis riparia (river grape)

Woody, high climber, to 35 ft., growth rate very fast. Flowers greenish, June; fruit fleshy, black, Aug.–Sept. Wildlife value very high. Eaten by birds and mammals. **Habitat requirements:** Moist to wet rich soil of edges, stream margins, floodplains (FACW), soil pH 6–8.5. Tolerant of shade, flooding, salt, soil compaction, drought, concrete debris. **Uses:** Secondary species for stream bank stabilization, vegetation of moist of wet fill, concrete debris. Wildlife food and shelter.

Chapter 4

Herbs

This chapter includes annual, biennial, and perennial plants. Herbs have a wide range of moisture requirements and tolerances. They include five general categories among which there is a great deal of overlap.

1. *Floating-leaved and submerged aquatics:* These plants are adapted to bodies of open water such as ponds or lakes. Some of them are rooted in the saturated soil at the bottom of the water body and some are not rooted, but merely float on, or just below, the surface of the water. These plants function to keep water temperatures cooler and provide shade, thereby decreasing algal growth. They also provide shelter and shade for fish, frogs and invertebrates that consume mosquito larvae.

2. *Emergent herbs requiring/tolerating shallow water or saturated soil:* Emergent plants stand with their leaves above the water line. They are rooted in mud at the bottom of shallow ponds or lake margins, or in saturated soil of seasonal ponds and pond edges. Most require full sun or nearly so. These plants are adapted to rooting in soil with very little oxygen but cannot tolerate dry soil. They need to be planted in or around permanent water bodies or other wetlands that do not dry out completely during the summer. They are important for holding soil in place and providing habitat for numerous animals.

3. *Herbs requiring moist or wet soil:* These plants require soil that does not become completely dry. Some are adapted to soil that becomes saturated with water periodically and remains moist in dry periods. Obligate wetland plants are intolerant of dry soil. However, most are not found in standing water for more than short periods of time, such as a day or so after a heavy rain or a few hours during tidal cycles (freshwater or brackish tidal zones).

4. *Herbs requiring moderately moist soil:* These herbs require "average" soil moisture. They are not generally found in wetlands but neither are they adapted to very dry soil of rocky ledges and sand barrens.

5. *Herbs tolerant of drier soil:* These herbs are adapted to soils that are well drained and often become dry. Not all are tolerant of very dry soils of sand barrens or thin soils over rocky sites and cliffs. Most tolerate periods of drought in average-well drained soil.

HERB SPECIES

Acalypha gracilens (three-seeded mercury)

Annual, to 20 in. Flowers green, July–Sept.; fruit Aug.–Oct. **Habitat requirements:** Open woods, meadows, fields, in sandy, sterile soil (UPL). **Uses:** Minor species for addition to seed mix for initial erosion control and increased diversity on open soil of new restoration.

Acalypha rhomboidea (*A. virginica* var. *r.*) (three-seeded mercury, copper-leaf)

Annual, to 2 ft. Flowers greenish, July–Oct. **Habitat requirements:** Open woods, roadsides, edges, disturbed moist to dry soil (FACU−). **Uses:** Minor species for addition to seed mix for initial erosion control and increased diversity on open soil of new restoration.

Acorus calamus (sweet flag)

Emergent, to 4 ft., colonial from rhizomes. Growth rate moderate. Plant sweetly scented. Flowers yellowish brown, May–July; fruit to Sept. (rarely fruits). Wildlife value high. **Habitat requirements:** Saturated soil, pH 5.2–7.2, water depth to 0.5 ft. Open swamps, pond edges, freshwater and brackish tidal marshes from mean high water to spring tide elevation (OBL). Tolerates brackish water to 10 ppt salt. Tolerates partial shade, acid soil. **Notes:** Eaten by muskrats. **Uses:** Secondary species for increased diversity and aesthetics in wetland restoration and mitigation. Erosion control of pond edges.

Actaea alba

Actaea alba (*A. pachypoda*) (doll's eyes, baneberry)

To 32 in. Flowers white, May–June; fruit fleshy, white, fruiting stem pink, July–Sept. **Habitat requirements:** Rich woods, moist to dry soils (UPL). Tolerant of shade and acid soils. **Uses:** Minor species for increased diversity and aesthetics in restoration of deciduous forest understories with moist to dry, good-quality soil.

Actaea rubra (*A. spicata*) (red baneberry)

To 32 in. Flowers white, May–July; fruit fleshy, red, Aug.–Oct. **Habitat requirements:** Rich woods in moist to dry soils

(UPL). Tolerant of shade and acid soils. **Uses:** Minor species for increased diversity and aesthetics in restoration of deciduous forest understories with moist to dry, good-quality soil.

Agastache nepetoides (giant yellow hyssop)

Rare (NYS S2S3, T); to 5 ft. Flowers yellow, July–Sept. **Habitat requirements:** Open woods, upland meadows, edges, moist to dry, disturbed soil (FACU). Seems to tolerate partial shade. **Notes:** Apparently a poor competitor with more vigorous plants. Plant in coordination with conservation organization restoration specialist. Use only local stock. **Uses:** Minor species for increased diversity and aesthetics in restoration of successional habitats.

Agastache scrophulariaefolia (*A. scrophulariifolia*) (purple giant hyssop)

To 4 ft. Flowers purplish, July–Sept.; fruit Oct. **Habitat requirements:** Rich woods (UPL). Tolerant of shade. **Uses:** Minor species for increased diversity and aesthetics in restoration of deciduous forest understories with moist to dry, good-quality soil.

Agrimonia gryposepala (common agrimony)

To 4 ft., colonial. Flowers yellow, July–Aug.; fruit dry, Aug.–Oct. **Habitat requirements:** Moist, open woods (FACU). Soil pH 4.5–7.0. Tolerant of shade. **Uses:** Minor species for increased diversity in restoration of deciduous forest understories with moist, good-quality soil.

Agrimonia pubescens (downy agrimony)

To 3 ft., colonial. Flowers yellow, July–Sept.; fruit dry, Aug.–Oct. **Habitat requirements:** Thickets, rich, upland woods (UPL), calcareous soils. Should tolerate concrete debris. Tolerant of shade. **Uses:** Minor species for increased diversity in restoration of deciduous forest understories with moist to dry, average to good-quality soil.

Aletris farinosa (colic root)

Rare (NYS S2, T); to 3 ft. Flowers white, June–July; fruit July–Aug. **Habitat requirements:** Sand barrens, moist to moderately dry, open oak or pine woods (FAC). Tolerant of partial shade. **Notes:** Plant in coordination with a conservation organization restoration specialist. **Uses:** Minor species for increased diversity and aesthetics in restoration of open or edge habitats in pine or oak barrens habitats with moist soil.

**Alisma subcordatum* (southern water plantain)

Emergent, about 1 ft., colonial, growth rate moderate. Flowers white, July–Aug.; fruit Aug.–Oct. Wildlife value moderate. **Habitat requirements:** Pond edges, slow stream banks, freshwater tidal marshes (OBL). Water depth to 1 ft., or saturated soil, pH 5–7. Freshwater, less than 0.5 ppt salt. Appears to tolerate moderate disturbance in urban areas. Intolerant of shade. **Notes:** Available. **Uses:** Primary species for wetland restoration and mitigation. Vegetation and erosion control of pond edges.

Alisma triviale (A. plantago-aquatica) (southern water plantain)

Emergent, to 3 ft. (usually less); colonial. Flowers white, July–Aug. **Habitat requirements:** Open wetlands, marshes, wet ditches (OBL). Very tolerant, sturdy. **Notes:** Available. **Uses:** Secondary species for wetland restoration and mitigation. Vegetation of pond edges.

Allium tricoccum

Allium canadense (meadow onion)

To 2 ft. Flowers usually replaced by bulblets, blooms, and fruits, May–June. **Habitat requirements:** Open woods, fields, meadows (FACU). *Allium vineale* (field garlic) is a European agricultural and lawn weed. **Uses:** Minor species for increased diversity and aesthetics in restoration of open or edge habitats.

Allium tricoccum (wild leek)

1 ft., leaves ephemeral, before flowers. Flowers white, April–Aug.; fruit July–Sept. **Habitat requirements:** Rich, moist woods (FACU+). Tolerant of shade. **Uses:** Minor species for increased diversity and aesthetics in restoration of woodland habitats.

Amaranthus cannabinus (Acnida c.) (salt marsh hemp)

To 8 ft., stems fleshy. Flowers dull, blooms and fruits, July–Oct. Dioecious, plant both sexes. **Habitat requirements:** Salt marshes, freshwater and brackish tidal shores (OBL). **Uses:** Secondary or minor species for increased diversity in salt marsh restoration and mitigation.

Ambrosia artemisiifolia (ragweed)

Annual, to 40 in. Flowers green; blooms and fruits, July–Oct. Wildlife value very high. Seeds eaten by numerous songbirds. **Habitat requirements:** Open, disturbed moist to somewhat dry soil (FACU). **Notes:** Plants soon crowded out by perennials. Pollen notoriously allergenic. **Uses:** Addition to annual seed mix for initial soil stabilization and increased wildlife value in newly restored open sites.

Ambrosia trifida (great ragweed)

Annual, to 6 ft. Flowers green; blooms and fruits, July–Sept. Wildlife value very high. Seeds eaten by numerous songbirds. **Habitat requirements:** Open, disturbed moist soil, freshwater tidal marshes (FAC). **Notes:** Plants soon crowded out by perennials. Pollen notoriously allergenic. **Uses:** Addition to annual seed mix for initial soil stabilization and increased wildlife value in newly restored open sites.

Amianthium muscaetoxicum (*A. muscitoxicum*) (fly poison)

Rare (NYS SX, U); to 4 ft. Bulb poisonous. Flowers white; seeds with red fleshy coat; blooms and fruits June–July (Sept.). **Habitat requirements:** Open woods, moist to wet sandy soil, bogs, meadows (FAC). Tolerant of partial shade. NYC is northern limit. **Notes:** Plant in coordination with conservation organization restoration specialist. Stock should be from source closest to NYC. **Uses:** Minor species for increased diversity and aesthetics in restoration of open woodland habitats.

Amphicarpaea bracteata (American hog peanut)

Annual, twining herb, to 40 in. long. Flowers pale purple to white; bloom July–Sept.; fruits Sept.–Oct. **Habitat requirements:** Moist woods, thickets, bogs, flood plains (FAC). Potentially a nitrogen fixer; may improve soil nutrients. Tolerant of partial shade. **Uses:** Secondary or minor species for increased diversity and aesthetics in restoration of open woodland habitats. Addition to seed mix for initial erosion control in new woodland restoration.

Anaphalis margaritacea (pearly everlasting)

To 3 ft. (rarely), colonial. Flowers white, July–Sept. Host for some butterfly species. **Habitat requirements:** Dry open sites, old fields; often in sandy or gravelly soils (UPL). Soil pH 6.0–7.5. **Notes:** May not compete well in moist soil. **Uses:** Minor species for increased diversity and aesthetics in restoration of open habitats, dry grasslands, meadows, sandy fill.

Anemone canadensis (Canadian anemone)

To 2 ft., colonial. Flowers white, May–July. **Habitat requirements:** Open, sandy shores, wet meadows (FACW). **Uses:** Secondary species for increased diversity and aesthetics in wetland restoration and mitigation.

Anemone cylindrica (thimbleweed)

To 3 ft. Flowers greenish white; blooms and fruits June–Sept. **Habitat requirements:** Dry open woods, gaps, limestone soils (UPL). Should tolerate concrete debris. Tolerant of partial shade. **Uses:** Minor species for increased diversity and aesthetics in restoration of moist to dry open woodland habitats.

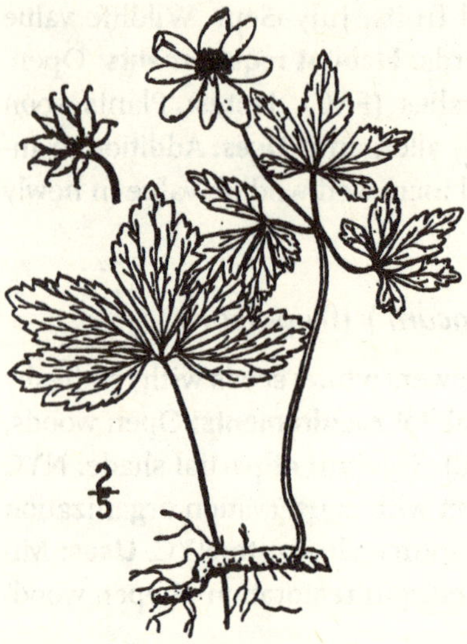

Anemone quinquefolia

Anemone quinquefolia (wood anemone)

Spring ephemeral to 8 in., colonial. Flowers white, April–May; fruit May–June. **Habitat requirements:** Moist, rich open woods, often near vernal ponds or swamp forest edges (FACU). **Uses:** Minor species for increased diversity and aesthetics in restoration of moist woodland habitats.

Anemone virginiana (tall anemone)

To 3 ft. Flowers greenish white, June–Aug.; fruit July–Sept. **Habitat requirements:** Rich, moist to dry open woods, pond banks (UPL). Tolerant of partial shade. **Uses:** Minor species for increased diversity and aesthetics in restoration of moist to dry open woodland habitats.

Anemonella thalictroides (rue anemone)

Spring ephemeral to 8 in. Flowers white, April–May; fruit May–June. **Habitat requirements:** Dry to moist woods (UPL). **Uses:** Minor species for increased diversity and aesthetics in restoration of moist woodland habitats.

Angelica atropurpurea (purplestem angelica)

To 6 ft. Flowers whitish, June–July; fruit July–Oct. Host for some butterfly species. **Habitat requirements:** Marshes, wet woods on limestone soils (OBL). Tolerant of partial shade. Should tolerate concrete debris. **Uses:** Secondary species for increased diversity and aesthetics in wetland restoration and mitigation.

Angelica venenosa (hairy angelica)

To 6 ft., plant poisonous. Flowers whitish, July–Aug.; fruit Sept.–Oct. Host for some butterfly species. **Habitat requirements:** Dry, open woods (UPL). Tolerant of partial shade. **Uses:** Minor species for increased diversity and aesthetics in restoration of moist woodland habitats. Butterfly gardens.

Antennaria neglecta (field pussytoes)

To 16 in., colonial. Flowers white, May–July. **Habitat requirements:** Dry fields, rocky slopes, tolerates sterile soil (UPL). Soil pH 5.5–7.5. **Uses:** Minor species for increased diversity and aesthetics in restoration of dry, open habitats, dry grasslands, meadows, sandy fill.

Antennaria plantaginifolia (plantain-leaved pussytoes)

To 16 in. Flowers white, April–June; fruit June–Aug. **Habitat requirements:** Dry, open areas (UPL). **Uses:** Minor species for increased diversity and aesthetics in restoration of dry, open habitats, dry grasslands, meadows.

Apocynum androsaemifolium (spreading dogbane)

to 30 in. Flowers pink, June–Aug. Host for some butterfly species. **Habitat requirements:** Dry thickets, edges of woods (UPL). Tolerant of partial shade. **Uses:** Minor species for increased diversity and aesthetics in restoration of dry woodland and edge habitats. Butterfly gardens.

Apocynum cannabinum

**Apocynum cannabinum* (Indian hemp)

To 4 ft., colonial. Flowers white, June–Aug.; fruit Sept.–Oct. Attractive to butterflies, host for some butterfly species larvae. **Habitat requirements:** Open fields, moist to dry soils, widely tolerant of fill soils, disturbance (FACU). Soil pH 4.5–7.0, but seems to tolerate concrete debris. **Notes:** Typically found with *Asclepias syriaca* (common milkweed) and *Aster pilosus* along roadsides, and urban "meadows." A tough, urban-tolerant plant. Should be propagated. **Uses:** Primary or secondary species for addition to erosion control plantings, vegetation of fill, increased diversity and aesthetics in restoration of dry, open habitats, grasslands, meadows, open slopes.

Aquilegia canadensis (wild columbine)

To 18 in. Flowers red-yellow, April–June; fruit June–July. Attractive to hummingbirds. **Habitat requirements:** Rich, moist to dry rocky woods (FAC); tolerates a wide range of pH. Tolerant of shade. **Notes:** Usually available, grows easily from seed. **Uses:** Secondary or minor species for increased diversity and aesthetics in restoration of moist to dry woodlands, especially rocky habitats. Hummingbird gardens.

Arabis canadensis (sickle-pod)

Biennial, to 40 in., winter rosette evergreen. Flowers (second year) cream-white, May–July; fruit Aug.–Sept. Stem stout. **Habitat requirements:** Rocky banks, rich woods, thickets (UPL). Tolerant of shade. **Uses:** Secondary or minor species for increased diversity and aesthetics in seed mix for initial erosion control on open soil of new woodland restoration.

Arabis hirsuta var. *pycnocarpa* (hairy rock cress)

Biennial or short-lived perennial, to 32 in., winter rosette evergreen. Flowers white, May–June; fruit June–July. **Habitat requirements:** Calcareous rocky banks, ledges, moist to dry woods (FACU). Tolerant of shade. **Uses:** Secondary or minor species for increased diversity and aesthetics, in seed mix for initial erosion control on new restoration, especially on soils with concrete debris.

Arabis laevigata (smooth rock cress)

Biennial, to 40 in., winter rosette evergreen. Flowers white, April–June; fruit May–June. **Habitat requirements:** Rich woods, shady, calcareous ledges and slopes (UPL). Tolerant of shade. **Uses:** Secondary or minor species for increased diversity and aesthetics, in seed mix for initial erosion control on new woodland restoration, especially on soils with concrete debris.

Arabis lyrata (lyre-leaved rock cress)

Biennial or short-lived perennial, to 16 in., winter rosette evergreen. Flowers white, April–June; fruit May–July. **Habitat requirements:** Ledges, calcareous cliffs, gravelly or sandy soils, open moist to dry woods (FACU). Tolerant of partial shade. **Uses:** Secondary or minor species for increased diversity and aesthetics in seed mix for initial erosion control on open soil of new restoration.

Aralia hispida (bristly sarsaparilla)

To 4 ft., colonial. Flowers whitish, June–July; fruit July–Aug. Fruit fleshy, black. Eaten by birds, possibly by mammals. **Habitat requirements:** Dry, open woods (UPL), tolerates sterile, sandy soil. Tolerant of shade. **Uses:** Secondary or minor species for increased diversity and aesthetics in restoration of moist to dry woodlands.

Aralia nudicaulis (wild sarsaparilla)

To 15 in., colonial (very slowly at first). Flowers dull white, May–June; fruit fleshy, black, June–July. Eaten by birds, possibly by mammals. **Habitat requirements:** Moist to moderately dry rich woods (FACU). Common in mixed oak

Aralia nudicaulis

forests. Forest soils pH 4.4–7.2. Tolerant of shade. **Notes:** Often with Canada mayflower, bellwort, and Solomon's seal. **Uses:** Secondary species for increased diversity and aesthetics in restoration of moist to dry woodlands. Some soil-holding capacity as colony grows.

Aralia racemosa (spikenard)

To 6 ft., colonial. Flowers white, June–Aug.; fruit fleshy, dark purple, Sept.–Oct. Eaten by birds and probably mammals. **Habitat requirements:** Rich, moist to dry woods (UPL). Tolerant of shade. **Uses:** Secondary or minor species for increased diversity and aesthetics in restoration of moist to dry woodlands.

Arctostaphylos uva-ursi (bearberry)

To 6 in., evergreen, trailing, colonial, woody at base. Flowers white, May–June; fruit fleshy, dull red, Aug.–Sept., persistent into winter. Host for some butterfly species. **Habitat requirements:** Open rocky areas, ridge tops, dry, sterile, sandy soil, barrens and back dunes, soil pH 4.5–6 (UPL). Tolerant of salt, drought. Intolerant of flooding, soil compaction, shade. Poor competitor in good soils (high nutrient, circumneutral) or dense vegetation. **Uses:** Secondary or minor species for increased diversity and aesthetics in restoration of open rock outcrops, pine or oak barrens, sandy back-dune scrub, in dry, low-pH, low-nutrient soils.

Arenaria lateriflora (*Moehringia l.*) (grove sandwort)

Stems to 16 in. long, colonial, creeping. Flowers white, May–June; fruit June–Aug. **Habitat requirements:** Moist, open woods, edges, shores, gravelly soils (FAC). Tolerant of partial shade. **Uses:** Minor species for increased diversity and possibly soil-holding capacity, in restoration of woodlands, moist banks.

Arisaema triphyllum (jack-in-the-pulpit)

To 2 ft., growth rate slow. Flowers green-purple spike, May–July; fruit fleshy red, Aug.–Oct. Wildlife value moderate. **Habitat requirements:** Wet woods (FACW−). Tolerant of shade, tolerates acid soil, pH 4.0–7.0, tolerates saturated soil for up to 25% of growing season. Intolerant of salt. **Uses:** Secondary or minor species for increased diversity and aesthetics in restoration of swamp forests and wet woodlands.

Aristolochia serpentaria (Virginia snakeroot)

Rare (NYS S1, E); to 18 in. Flowers purple-brown, May–July; fruit July–Aug. Host for some butterfly species. **Habitat requirements:** Rich rocky woods, often on limestone soils (UPL). Tolerant of shade. **Uses:** Secondary or minor species for increased diversity and aesthetics in restoration of moist to dry woodlands. Use only local stock. Plant in coordination with conservation organization restoration specialist.

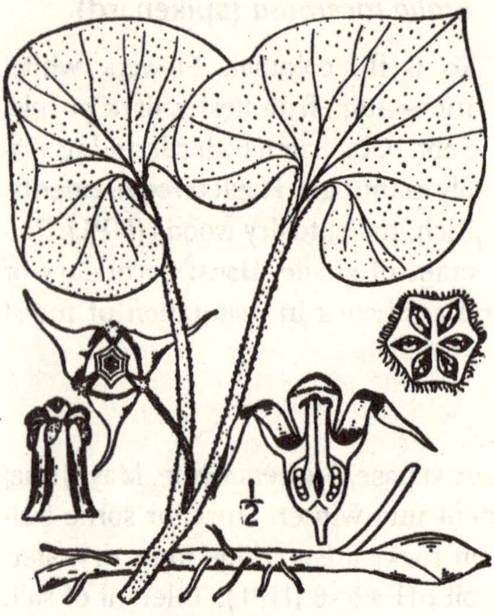

Asarum canadense

Asarum canadense (wild ginger)

About 8 in., colonial, spreads very slowly. Flowers dull purple, April–May. **Habitat requirements:** Rich, moist woods, often on limestone soils (UPL). Tolerant of shade. Rather intolerant of drought. **Uses:** Secondary or minor species for increased diversity and aesthetics in restoration of moist woodlands. Some soil-holding capacity as colony grows.

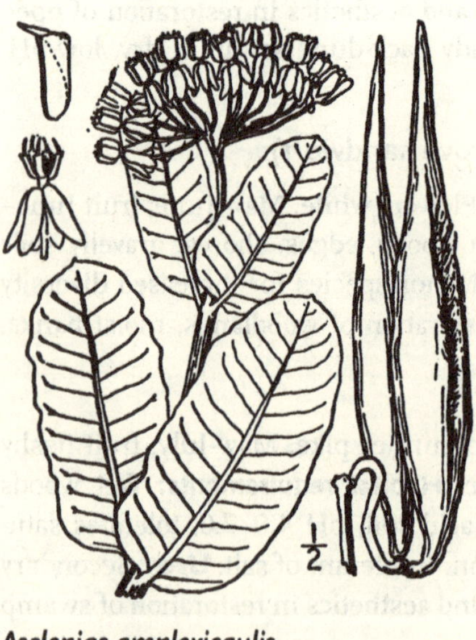

Asclepias amplexicaulis

Asclepias amplexicaulis (clasping milkweed)

To 32 in. Flowers pink-purple, June–July; fruit June–Aug. Host for some butterfly species. **Habitat requirements:** Dry fields, well-drained, sandy soil, open woods (UPL). Tolerant of partial shade. **Uses:** Secondary or minor species for increased diversity and aesthetics in restoration of dry, open woodlands, meadows. Butterfly gardens.

Asclepias exaltata (poke milkweed)

To 5 ft. Flowers white to pink, June–July; fruit Aug.–Sept. Host for some butterfly species. **Habitat requirements:** Moist woods, rich soil (FACU). Tolerant of shade. **Uses:** Secondary or minor species for increased diversity and aesthetics in restoration of moist woodlands. Butterfly gardens.

Asclepias incarnata

*Asclepias incarnata (swamp milkweed)

To 4 ft., colonial, growth rate slow. Flowers pink, showy, July–Aug.; fruit Sept.–Oct. Wildlife value high. Host for some butterfly species. **Habitat requirements:** Open swamps, wet meadows, pond edges (OBL). Soil pH 5–8. Tolerates periodic flooding, freshwater tidal areas, saturated soil up to 75% of growing season; tolerates drought. Intolerant of salt or shade. **Notes:** Regenerates well from seed in disturbed soil. Available. **Uses:** Primary to secondary species for increased diversity and aesthetics in wetland restoration and mitigation. Butterfly gardens.

Asclepias purpurascens (purple milkweed)

Rare (NYS S3, U); to 3 ft. Flowers purple, showy, June–July. Host for some butterfly species. **Habitat requirements:** Dry to moist woods and shady edges (FACU). **Uses:** Secondary or minor species for increased diversity and aesthetics in restoration of moist to dry woodlands. Coordinate plantings with a conservation organization restoration specialist.

Asclepias quadrifolia (four-leaved milkweed)

To 20 in. Flowers pink to white, May–June; fruit Aug.–Sept. Host for some butterfly species. **Habitat requirements:** Dry to moist woods (UPL). Tolerant of shade. **Uses:** Secondary or minor species for increased diversity and aesthetics in restoration of dry woodlands. Butterfly gardens.

Asclepias rubra (red milkweed)

Globally rare (G4G5, NYS SX, U); to 2 ft. Flowers red, showy, June–July; fruit July. Host for some butterfly species. **Habitat requirements:** Swamps, wet soil (OBL). Intolerant of shade. **Notes:** Long Island is the northern limit of range. **Uses:** secondary species for increased diversity and aesthetics in wetland restoration and mitigation in wet meadows, marshes, swamps. Butterfly gardens. Use only local stock. Plant in coordination with a conservation organization restoration specialist.

**Asclepias syriaca* (common milkweed)

To 6 ft., colonial. Flowers dull lavender, fragrant, June–Aug.; fruit July–Sept. Host for some butterfly species. **Habitat requirements:** Open fields, sunny roadsides (UPL). Widely tolerant of fill soils, disturbance. Seems to tolerate concrete debris. **Notes:** Typically found with Indian hemp and *Aster pilosus* along roadsides, and urban "meadows." A tough, urban-tolerant plant. Intolerant of shade. **Uses:** Primary or secondary species for addition to erosion control plantings, increased diversity and aesthetics in vegetation of fill and restoration of dry, open habitats, grasslands, meadows, open slopes. Butterfly gardens.

Asclepias tuberosa (butterfly weed)

To 2 ft., emerges late. Flowers orange, showy, July–Aug.; fruit Aug.–Oct. Host for some butterfly species. **Habitat requirements:** Dry, fields, roadsides, well-drained, sandy, acid soil (UPL). Soil pH 4.8–6.8. **Notes:** Not very persistent, apparently easily shaded out by other plants. Not a good competitor in dense vegetation. **Uses:** Secondary or minor species for increased diversity and aesthetics in restoration of moist to dry open areas, meadows. Butterfly gardens.

Asclepias variegata (white milkweed)

Rare (NYS S1, E); to 3 ft. Flowers white, June–July; fruit July–Sept. Host for some butterfly species. **Habitat requirements:** Woods, thickets, dry, open, sandy or gravelly soil (UPL). Tolerant of shade. **Uses:** Minor species for increased diversity and aesthetics in restoration of moist to dry woodlands. Coordinate plantings with a conservation organization restoration specialist.

Asclepias verticillata (whorled milkweed)

To 18 in. Flowers greenish white, July–Aug.; fruit Sept.–Oct. Host for some butterfly species. **Habitat requirements:** Open woods, fields, dry, circumneutral, nonacid, sterile soil (UPL). Tolerant of partial shade. **Uses:** Minor species for increased diversity and aesthetics in restoration of moist to dry, open areas, meadows, thin woods, warm season grasslands. Butterfly gardens.

Asclepias viridiflora (green milkweed)

Rare (NYS S2, R); to 3 ft. Flowers pale green, July–Aug. Host for some butterfly species. Limestone cliffs, dry soil, shady edges, open woods, fields, barrens (UPL). Apparently prefers circumneutral to alkaline soils. Tolerant of partial shade. **Uses:** Minor species for increased diversity and aesthetics in restoration of dry, open barrens, woods, serpentine soils. Coordinate plantings with a conservation organization restoration specialist.

Aster acuminatus (*Oclemena acuminata*) (whorled aster)

To 32 in., colonial. Flowers white, June–Sept. Host for some butterfly species. **Habitat requirements:** Rich, northern woods (UPL). Tolerant of shade. **Uses:** Minor species for increased diversity and aesthetics in restoration of moist to dry woodlands.

Aster concolor (*Symphyotrichum c.*) (silvery aster)

Rare (G4?; NYS S1, E), to 3 ft., colonial. Flowers blue, Sept.–Oct. Host for some butterfly species. **Habitat requirements:** Dry, sandy soil, pine barrens and coastal plains (UPL). **Uses:** Secondary or minor species for increased diversity and aesthetics in restoration of moist to dry woodlands. Coordinate plantings with a conservation organization restoration specialist.

**Aster cordifolius* (*Symphyotrichum cordifolium*) (heart-leaved aster)

To 5 ft. Flowers blue, showy, Aug.–Oct.; fruit Sept.–Nov. Host for some butterfly species. **Habitat requirements:** Rich woods, gaps, edges (UPL). Soil pH 5.7–7.5. Tolerant of shade. **Notes:** Not as common or as tough as *A. divaricatus*. Also seems to be less tolerant of shade. **Uses:** Primary or secondary species for restoration of open forest understories, slope stabilization in dry mixed, deciduous woods.

**Aster divaricatus* (*Eurybia divaricata*) (white wood aster)

To 3 ft. (rarely), usually about 2 ft. in bloom, colonial, foliage dark green, attractive. Flowers white, inflorescences showy, Aug.–Oct.; fruit Oct.–Nov. Host for some butterfly species. **Habitat requirements:** Moist to dry, rich woods (UPL). Very tough, widely tolerant, urban forest understory plant. Found even in weedy, disturbed, degraded woodlands. Tolerates acid soil down to pH 3.8. Very shade tolerant. **Uses:** Primary species for revegetation and restoration of forest understories, slope stabilization, in dry mixed, deciduous woods.

Aster dumosus (*Symphyotrichum dumosum* var. *strictior*) (bushy aster, rice button aster)

To 34 in., colonial. Flowers bluish, Aug.–Oct. Host for some butterfly species. **Habitat requirements:** Dry to moist open areas, sandy soil, woods, shady edges, bog edges (FAC). Tolerant of partial shade. **Uses:** Minor species for increased diversity and aesthetics in restoration of moist to dry open areas, meadows, warm-season grasslands. Butterfly gardens.

**Aster ericoides* (*Symphyotrichum ericoides*) (many-flowered aster, white heath aster)

To about 3 ft. Flowers white, Aug.–Oct. Host for some butterfly species. **Habitat requirements:** Dry, open areas, frequent on sandy soil in NYC coastal habitats, successional scrub (FACU). Available. **Uses:** Primary species for vegetation of open, sandy soil, fill, in restoration of moist to dry open areas, meadows, warm-season grasslands, coastal back-dune successional habitats. Butterfly gardens.

Aster infirmus (*Doellingeria infirma*) (Appalachian flat-topped white aster)

To 44 in. Flowers white, July–Sept. Host for some butterfly species. **Habitat requirements:** Dry woods, rocky slopes (UPL). Tolerant of shade. **Uses:** Minor species for increased diversity and aesthetics in restoration of woodland understories.

Aster laevis

**Aster laevis* (*Symphyotrichum laeve*) (smooth blue aster)

To 3 ft., leaves waxy, dark green. Flowers blue, showy, Aug.–Oct. Host for some butterfly species. **Habitat requirements:** Dry open woods, sandy soil (UPL). Soil pH 5.8–7.8. Coastal plain and sand barrens. Tolerant of partial shade. **Notes:** Available. **Uses:** Primary or secondary species for vegetation of open sandy soil, fill in restoration of moist to dry open areas, meadows, increased diversity and aesthetics for warm-season grasslands, coastal back-dune successional habitats. Butterfly gardens.

Aster lanceolatus

**Aster lanceolatus* (*A. simplex*, *Symphyotrichum lanceolatum*) (lined aster)

To 4 ft., aggressively colonial. Flowers white to bluish, Aug.–Oct.; fruit Sept.–Nov. Host for some butterfly species. **Habitat requirements:** Moist to wet woods, edges, often found along moist, shady roadsides (FACW). Soil pH 5.8–7.4. Very tolerant of disturbance, urban habitats. Tolerant of shade. **Notes:** Sometimes available. **Uses:** Primary or secondary species for restoration of swamp forests, shady wet edges, wet woodlands, roadsides and wetland mitigation, erosion control on moist, shady slopes.

Aster lateriflorus

***Aster lateriflorus* (*Symphyotrichum lateriflorum*) (calico aster)**

To 3 ft., white to bluish, Aug.–Oct.; fruit Oct.–Nov. **Habitat requirements:** Moist meadows, open edges (FACW−). **Uses:** Secondary species for increased diversity and aesthetics in wetland restoration and mitigation in wet meadows, marshes.

***Aster linariifolius* (*Ionactis linariifolius*) (stiff aster)**

To 2 ft. Flowers violet, showy, Aug.–Oct. Host for some butterfly species. **Habitat requirements:** Dry, open areas, sandy soil, open woods, pine or oak barrens (UPL). Tolerant of partial shade. **Uses:** Minor species for increased diversity and aesthetics in restoration of dry open areas, meadows, warm-season grasslands. Butterfly gardens.

***Aster lowrieanus* (*Symphyotrichum lowrieanum*) (smooth heart-leaved aster, Lowrie's blue wood aster)**

To 3 ft. Flowers blue, Sept.–Oct. Host for some butterfly species. **Habitat requirements:** Rich woods (UPL). Tolerant of shade. **Uses:** Minor species for increased diversity and aesthetics in restoration of moist to dry to moist mixed deciduous woodland understories. Butterfly gardens.

***Aster macrophyllus* (*Eurybia macrophylla*) (big-leaved aster)**

To 3 ft., colonial. Flowers white to pale blue, clusters showy, July–Sept. Host for some butterfly species. **Habitat requirements:** Rich, dry to moist woods (UPL). Soil pH 4.9–6.9. Tolerant of shade. **Uses:** Minor species for increased diversity and aesthetics in restoration of moist to dry to moist mixed deciduous woodland understories. Butterfly gardens.

***_Aster novae-angliae_ (*Symphyotrichum novae-angliae*) (New England aster)**

To 6 ft., eventually colonial growth rate slow. Flowers blue-purple, showy, Aug.–Oct.; fruit Oct.–Nov. Wildlife value low. Host for some butterfly species. **Habitat requirements:** Moist meadows, swamps, pond edges (FACW−). Tolerant of flooding (25% growing season); tolerant of moderate drought. Intolerant of shade, salt. **Notes:** Available. **Uses:** Primary species for open wetland restoration and mitigation. Butterfly gardens.

**Aster novi-belgii* (*Symphyotrichum novi-belgii*) (New York aster)

To 4 ft., colonial. Flowers blue, showy, Aug.–Oct. Host for some butterfly species. **Habitat requirements:** Moist to wet open areas (FACW+). Tolerant of salt. Soil pH 5.5–7. Available. **Uses:** Primary species for increased diversity and aesthetics in open wetland restoration and mitigation. Butterfly gardens.

Aster patens (*Symphyotrichum p.*) (late purple aster)

To 5 ft. Flowers violet, showy, Aug.–Oct. Host for some butterfly species. **Habitat requirements:** Dry, open areas, open woods (UPL). Soil pH 4.9–6.9. **Uses:** Minor species for increased diversity and aesthetics in restoration of moist to dry open areas, meadows, warm-season grasslands. Butterfly gardens.

Aster paternus (*Sericocarpus asteroides*) (toothed white-topped aster)

To 2 ft. Flowers white, June–Aug. Host for some butterfly species. **Habitat requirements:** Dry woods (UPL). Tolerant of shade. **Uses:** Minor species for increased diversity and aesthetics in restoration of moist to dry to moist mixed deciduous woodland understories. Butterfly gardens.

Aster pilosus

**Aster pilosus* (*Symphyotrichum pilosum*) (awl aster)

To 5 ft. Flowers white, Aug.–Nov. Host for some butterfly species. **Habitat requirements:** Moist to dry, open areas, sandy soil. Widely tolerant of fill soils, disturbance (UPL). Soil pH 5.4–7.0. Seems to tolerate concrete debris but also acid soils. Typically found with Indian hemp and common milkweed along roadsides, and urban "meadows." **Notes:** A tough, urban tolerant plant. Available. **Uses:** Primary or secondary species for vegetation of fill, addition to erosion control plantings, and restoration of dry to moist open habitats, meadows, slopes. Butterfly gardens.

Aster puniceus (*Symphyotrichum puniceum*) (bristly aster)

To 8 ft. Flowers blue to rose, Aug.–Oct. Host for some butterfly species. **Habitat requirements:** Marshes, wet meadows (OBL). Wet soil, pH 4.5–7.5. **Uses:**

Secondary or minor species for increasing diversity and aesthetics in wetland restoration and mitigation.

Aster racemosus (*Aster vimineus, Symphyotrichum racemosum*) (small white aster)

To 5 ft. Flowers white, Aug.–Nov. Host for some butterfly species. **Habitat requirements:** Moist, open areas, floodplains, marsh edges (FAC). **Uses:** Minor species for increased diversity and aesthetics in restoration of moist, open areas, meadows. Butterfly gardens.

Aster radula (*Eurybia r.*) (rough low aster)

Rare (NYS SH, U); to 4 ft., colonial. Flowers violet, July–Sept. Host for some butterfly species. **Habitat requirements:** Sandy soil of bogs, stream banks, moist to wet woodlands (OBL). Tolerant of shade. **Uses:** Secondary or minor species for increasing diversity and aesthetics in wetland restoration and mitigation. Plant only in coordination with conservation organization restoration specialist.

Aster sagittifolius (*Symphyotrichum urophyllum*) (arrow-leaved aster)

To 4 ft. Flowers pale blue, Aug.–Oct. Host for some butterfly species. **Habitat requirements:** Dry, open woods, gaps (UPL). Tolerant of partial shade. **Uses:** Minor species for increased diversity and aesthetics in restoration of moist to dry open woods.

Aster solidagineus (*Sericocarpus linifolius*) (narrow-leaved white-topped aster)

Rare (NYS S2 T); to 2 ft. Flowers white, June–Sept. Host for some butterfly species. **Habitat requirements:** Dry, sandy, open to partly shady areas (UPL). A pine barrens species. Found in southern NJ. **Uses:** Minor species for increased diversity and aesthetics in restoration of moist to dry areas, pine or oak barrens. Use only local stock. Coordinate planting with a conservation organization restoration specialist.

Aster spectabilis (*Eurybia s.*) (showy aster)

Rare (NYS S2 T); to 3 ft. Flowers violet, showy, Aug.–Oct. Host for some butterfly species. **Habitat requirements:** Tolerates acid, dry sandy soil (UPL). A pine barrens species. **Uses:** Minor species for increased diversity and aesthetics in restoration of dry, sandy soil of pine or oak barrens. Plant only in coordination with conservation organization restoration specialist. Use only stock from NYC metro region.

Aster subulatus (*Symphyotrichum subulatum*) (annual salt-marsh aster)

Rare (NYS S2, T); to 3 ft. tall. Flowers purplish, blooms and fruits late July–Oct. **Habitat requirements:** Coastal. Salt marshes (OBL). Soil pH 5.6–7.0. Intolerant of shade. **Uses:** Secondary or minor species for increased diversity and aesthetics in high salt-marsh restoration and mitigation. Plant only in coordination with a conservation organization restoration specialist.

Aster tenuifolius (*Symphyotrichum tenuifolium*) (perennial salt-marsh aster)

To 18 in. Flowers blue, blooms and fruits Sept.–Oct. **Habitat requirements:** Coastal. Wet salt-marsh borders (OBL). Intolerant of shade. **Uses:** Secondary or minor species for increased diversity and aesthetics in high salt-marsh restoration and mitigation.

Aster tradescantii (*Symphyotrichum t.*) (shore aster)

To 2 ft., colonial. Flowers white, July–Sept. Host for some butterfly species. **Habitat requirements:** Damp rocky or gravelly shores, seasonally inundated stream banks (FACW). **Uses:** Secondary or minor species for increasing diversity and aesthetics in wetland restoration and mitigation, especially on pond and lake shores, stream banks.

Aster umbellatus (*Doellingeria umbellata*) (flat-topped aster)

To 5 ft., colonial. Flowers white, Aug.–Sept.; fruit prob. Oct.–Nov. Host for some butterfly species. **Habitat requirements:** Moist to wet meadows, woods, edges (FACW). Tolerant of partial shade. **Uses:** Secondary or minor species for increasing diversity in wetland restoration and mitigation.

Astragalus canadensis

Aster undulatus (*Symphyotrichum undulatum*) (clasping heart-leaved aster)

To 4 ft. Flowers blue, Aug.–Oct. Host for some butterfly species. **Habitat requirements:** Dry to moist, open woods, edges (UPL). Tolerant of partial shade. **Uses:** Minor species for increased diversity and aesthetics in restoration of dry, open woodlands.

Astragalus canadensis (milk vetch)

To 4 ft., colonial. Flowers yellowish, June–Aug. Host for some butterfly species. **Habitat**

requirements: Moist, open areas (FAC). Soil pH 6–8. Potentially a nitrogen fixer; may improve soil nutrients. **Uses:** Minor species for increased diversity and aesthetics in restoration of moist, open areas, meadows.

Atriplex arenaria (sea-beach orach)

Annual, to 20 in., often prostrate. Flowers inconspicuous, blooms July–Sept.; fruit Aug.–Oct. Plant silvery green. **Habitat requirements:** Coastal. Beaches, salt-marsh edges (FAC−). **Uses:** Secondary or minor species for holding sand, increased diversity and aesthetics in beach dune and salt-marsh upland restoration.

Baptisia tinctoria (wild indigo)

To 3 ft. Flowers yellow, June–July; fruit Aug.–Sept. Host for some butterfly species. **Habitat requirements:** Open, dry, acid, sterile, sandy soil, open woods (UPL). Soil pH 5.8–7.0.Tolerant of partial shade. Potentially a nitrogen fixer; may improve soil nutrients. **Uses:** Minor species for increased diversity and aesthetics in restoration of dry, open areas, meadows, warm-season grasslands.

Bidens cernua (bur-marigold)

Annual, to 40 in. Flowers yellow, Aug.–Oct. **Habitat requirements:** Wet habitats, shores, ditches, freshwater tidal marshes (OBL). Soil pH 5.1–7. **Uses:** Secondary or minor species for increasing diversity in wetland restoration and mitigation. Addition to seed mix for initial erosion control on new restoration/mitigation.

Bidens coronata (tick-seeded sunflower)

Annual, to 4 ft. Flowers yellow, showy, Sept.–Oct. **Habitat requirements:** Wet, open areas, meadows, ditches (OBL). Soil pH 5.2–7.1. **Notes:** Reproduces very well from seed year to year. **Uses:** Secondary or minor species for increasing diversity and aesthetics in wetland restoration and mitigation. Addition to seed mix for initial erosion control on new restoration/mitigation.

Bidens frondosa (devil's beggar-ticks)

Annual, to 4 ft. Flowers yellow, often dull, Aug.–Oct. **Habitat requirements:** Wet soil, open wet areas (FACW). Soil pH 5.2–7.2. Grows easily. **Uses:** Minor species for addition to seed mix for initial erosion control on new wetland restoration/mitigation.

Boehmeria cylindrica (false nettle)

To 40 in. Flowers green, sexes separate (dioecios), July–Sept.; fruit Aug.–Oct. **Habitat requirements:** Swamp forests, wet soil (FACW+). Soil pH 5.1–7.

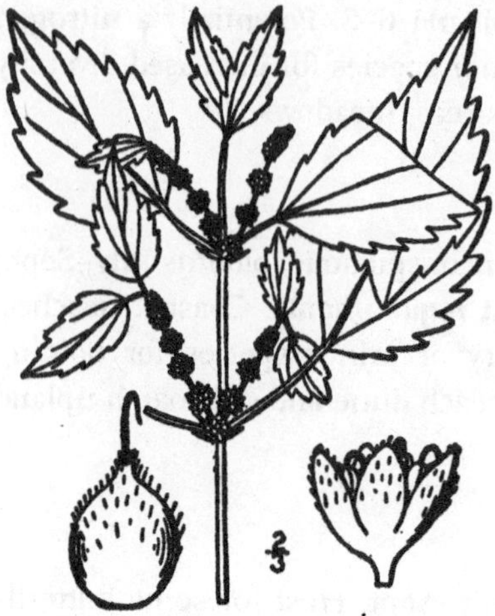

Boehmeria cylindrica

Tolerant of shade. Frequent in NYC. **Uses:** Secondary or minor species for increasing diversity in restoration of swamp forests and in mitigation.

Brasenia schreberi (water-shield)

Rooted, floating-leaved aquatic, to about 7 ft. long, colonial. Flowers dull purple, small; blooms June–Sept. **Habitat requirements:** Quiet water, shallow ponds (OBL). **Uses:** Cover and shade for fish and invertebrates that help control mosquito populations in artificial ponds.

Cakile edentula (American sea rocket)

Annual, to 32 in., plant succulent. Flowers pale purple to white, June–Oct.; fruit Aug.–Nov. **Habitat requirements:** Coastal. Primary dunes, upland of high high-tide line (FACU). **Uses:** Secondary or minor species for holding sand, increased diversity and aesthetics in back-dune restoration. Usually with *Ammophila breviligulata, Solidago sempervirens.*

Calla palustris (*C. verna*) (water arum)

Emergent, to 12 in., colonial. Flowers white, June–July; fruit July–Aug. **Habitat requirements:** Open shallow water, sphagnum bogs, fens, acid Atlantic white cedar swamps (OBL). Tolerant of partial shade. **Uses:** Secondary or minor species for increasing diversity and aesthetics in acid bog restoration.

Callitriche heterophylla (two-headed water starwort)

Annual, rooted, submerged aquatic, stems, to 8 in. long. Flowers inconspicuous, April–July; fruit May–Oct. **Habitat requirements:** Quiet water, shallow ponds (OBL). **Uses:** Cover and shade for fish and invertebrates that help control mosquito populations in artificial ponds.

Callitriche palustris (vernal water starwort)

Annual, rooted, submerged aquatic, stems to 8 in. long. Flowers inconspicuous, April–Nov. **Habitat requirements:** Quiet water, shallow ponds (OBL). **Uses:** Cover and shade for fish and invertebrates that help control mosquito populations in artificial ponds.

Callitriche terrestris (*C. deflexa*) (starwort)

Annual, to 2 in., tufted. Flowers inconspicuous, May–July; fruit June–Aug. **Habitat requirements:** Moist to wet shady soil (FACW+). Tolerant of shade.

Uses: Minor species for addition to soil stabilization seed mix for shady open soil.

Caltha palustris (marsh marigold)

Emergent, to 2 ft., eventually colonial, growth rate slow. Flowers yellow, showy, April–May; fruit June. Wildlife value low. **Habitat requirements:** Open stream banks, bright swamps (OBL). Soil pH 4.9–6.8. Cannot compete with weedy, aggressive vegetation. Tolerates partial shade. Intolerant of salt. **Notes:** Available. *Warning!* Often confused with the very invasive exotic *Ranunculus ficaria*. **Uses:** Minor element for increasing diversity and aesthetics in restoration of stream banks with clean, low-nutrient water. Water gardens.

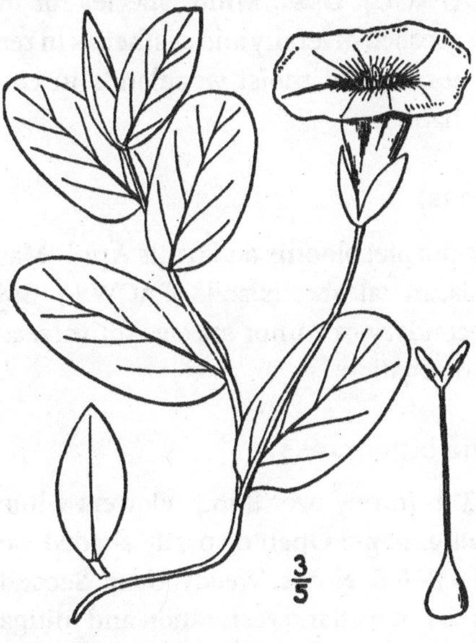

Calystegia spithamaea

Calystegia spithamaea (*Convolvulus spithameus*) (low bindweed)

To 18 in. Flowers white, showy, May–June; fruit June–Aug. Attractive to hummingbirds. **Habitat requirements:** Dry, rocky or sandy soil, open woods (UPL). Tolerant of partial shade. **Uses:** Minor species for increased diversity and aesthetics in restoration of dry, open woodlands, dry open areas. Hummingbird gardens.

Campanula americana (*Campanulastrum americanum*) (tall bellflower)

Winter annual, or biennial, to 5 ft. Flowers blue, June–Aug. **Habitat requirements:** Moist edges, open woods (FAC). Soil pH 5.5–7.5. Tolerant of partial shade. **Uses:** Minor species for increased diversity and aesthetics in restoration of moist open woodlands and edges. Addition to erosion control seed mix for new restoration.

Campanula aparinoides (marsh bellflower)

To 2 ft., colonial, reclining on other plants. Flowers whitish, June–Aug. **Habitat requirements:** Open, wet meadows (OBL). Soil pH 6.0–7.5. **Uses:** Secondary or minor species for increasing diversity in wetland restoration and mitigation.

Cardamine concatenata (*Dentaria laciniata*) (toothwort)

Spring ephemeral, to 16 in., colonial. Flowers pale lavender, April–May; fruit May–June. **Habitat requirements:** Rich moist woods, shady edges (FACU).

Uses: Minor species for increased diversity and aesthetics in restoration of moist, open woodlands and edges.

Cardamine diphylla (*Dentaria d.*) (broad-leaved toothwort)

Spring ephemeral, to 16 in., colonial. Flowers dull purple, April–June; fruit June–July. **Habitat requirements:** Upland, rich woods, west-facing ravines (FACU). **Uses:** Minor species for increased diversity and aesthetics in restoration of moist woodlands in cool habitats.

Cardamine concatenata

Cardamine douglassii (pink spring cress)

Rare (NYS, S3, U); to 10 in. Flowers pink-purple; blooms and fruits April–May. **Habitat requirements:** Rich, moist woods, in calcareous soils (FACW+). Soil pH 6.0–7.7. Tolerant of shade. **Uses:** Secondary or minor species for increasing diversity in wetland restoration and mitigation.

Cardamine pensylvanica (Pennsylvania bitter cress)

Annual, winter annual, or biennial, to 2 ft. (rarely over 8 in.). Flowers white, April–July; fruit May–Sept. **Habitat requirements:** Open or partly shaded wet soil, swamps, wet woods (OBL). Soil pH 4.8–6.8. **Notes:** Weedy. **Uses:** Secondary or minor species for increasing diversity in wetland restoration and mitigation. Addition to seed mix for initial erosion control on open, wet soil.

Cardamine rhomboidea (*C. bulbosa*) (spring cress)

To 16 in. Flowers white, April–June; fruit July–Sept. **Habitat requirements:** Open, wet woods or meadows (OBL). Soil pH 5.0–6.8. **Uses:** Secondary or minor species for increasing diversity in wetland restoration and mitigation.

Caulophyllum thalictroides (blue cohosh)

To 32 in. Plant poisonous. Flowers greenish yellow, April–June; seeds fruitlike, blue, July–Aug. **Habitat requirements:** Rich woods, often on limestone or rocky areas (UPL). Soil pH 4.5–7. Tolerant of shade. **Uses:** Minor species for increased diversity and aesthetics in restoration of upland forest understories on good soils.

Cerastium nutans (nodding chickweed)

Annual, to 2 ft. Flowers white, April–June. **Habitat requirements:** Rich woods, slopes, calcareous rocky habitats, floodplains (FAC). Tolerant of shade. **Uses:** Minor species for addition to seed mix for initial erosion control in woodland restoration.

[*Ceratophyllum demersum* and *C. echinatum* (coontail, hornwort)
Submerged, rootless aquatics of quiet ponds, slow streams, freshwater tidal zone (OBL).Water pH 6.2–8.3. Very aggressive native plants. Probably should not be planted. Use less aggressive plants.]

Chamaecrista fasciculata (*Cassia chamaecrista*) (partridge pea)

Annual, to 30 in. Flowers yellow, showy, July–Sept.; fruit Aug.–Nov. **Habitat requirements:** Open, disturbed sites, dry, sandy soil, open, dry woods (UPL). Soil pH 6.5–7.5. Potentially a nitrogen fixer; may improve soil nutrients. Tolerant of light, partial shade. Reseeds well in open areas. **Uses:** Minor species for increased diversity and aesthetics in restoration of dry open areas, meadows, warm-season grasslands on sandy soil, back dunes, pine and oak barrens. Addition to seed mix for initial erosion control.

Chamaecrista nictitans (*Cassia n.*) (dwarf partridge pea)

Annual, to 20 in. Flowers yellow, July–Oct.; fruit Sept.–Nov. **Habitat requirements:** Dry, sandy soil, open woods, dunes (FACU−). Potentially a nitrogen fixer, may improve soil nutrients. **Uses:** Minor species for increased diversity and aesthetics in restoration of dry open woodlands, warm-season grasslands on sandy soil, back dunes, pine and oak barrens. Addition to seed mix for initial erosion control.

Chamaelirium luteum (blazing star)

Rare (NYS S2, T; NJ S3); to 4 ft. Flowers white, sexes separate, May–June; fruit July–Sept. **Habitat requirements:** Bogs, moist woods, shady edges (FAC). Plant both sexes. **Notes:** Plant in cooperation with conservation organization restoration specialist. Use only local stock. **Uses:** Minor species for increased diversity and aesthetics in restoration of moist woodlands.

Chelone glabra (turtlehead)

To 3 ft. Flowers white, Aug.–Sept.; fruit Sept.–Nov. Host for some butterfly species. **Habitat requirements:** Open, wet woods, meadows (OBL). Tolerant of partial shade. Available. **Uses:** Secondary or minor species for increasing diversity and aesthetics in wetland restoration and mitigation.

Chenopodium berlandieri (pitseed goosefoot)

Annual, to 5 ft. Flowers greenish, July–Nov. **Habitat requirements:** A weed on open soil (UPL). Use local seed only. **Uses:** Minor species for addition to erosion control seed mix for open soil of new restoration.

Chenopodium capitatum (strawberry-blite)

Annual to 2 ft. Persistent flower parts becoming red in fruit, May–Aug. **Habitat requirements:** Fire scars, roadsides, open areas (UPL). **Uses:** Minor species for addition to diversity, aesthetics in erosion control seed mix for open soil of new restoration.

Chrysopsis falcata (*Pityopsis f.*) (Atlantic golden aster)

Chrysopsis falcata

To 14 in. Flowers yellow, showy, blooms and fruits June–Sept. **Habitat requirements:** Dry, sandy soil of coastal plain (UPL). **Uses:** Minor species for increased diversity and aesthetics in restoration of coastal back dunes and grasslands.

Chrysopsis mariana (golden aster)

To 32 in. Flowers yellow, showy, blooms and fruits Aug.–Nov. **Habitat requirements:** Pine barrens plant, sandy soil, open woods (UPL). Tolerant of partial shade. **Uses:** Minor species for increased diversity and aesthetics in restoration of sandy back-dune scrub, oak or pine barrens.

Chrysosplenium americanum (water mat)

Reclining, ground cover. Flowers greenish yellow, April–May; fruit June–July. **Habitat requirements:** On muddy soil (OBL). Tolerant of shade. **Uses:** Secondary or minor species for increasing diversity in wetland restoration and mitigation.

Cicuta bulbifera (water hemlock)

To 3 ft. Plants very poisonous. Flowers white, July–Sept. **Habitat requirements:** Marshes (OBL). Host for some butterfly species. **Uses:** Secondary or minor species for increasing diversity in wetland restoration and mitigation.

Cicuta maculata (common water hemlock)

To 6 ft. Plants very poisonous. Flowers white, June–Aug.; fruit Aug.–Oct. **Habitat requirements:** Marshes (OBL). Host for some butterfly species. **Uses:** Secondary or minor species for increasing diversity in wetland restoration and mitigation.

Cimicifuga racemosa (black snakeroot)

To 7 ft. Flowers white, June–July; fruit Sept.–Oct. Host for some butterfly species. **Habitat requirements:** Rich, moist woods (UPL). Tolerant of shade. **Uses:** Secondary or minor species for increased diversity and aesthetics in restoration of forest understory in mixed deciduous forests.

Circaea lutetiana (*C. quadrisulcata*) (enchanter's nightshade)

To 2 ft., colonial. Tolerant of shade. Flowers white, June–Aug.; fruit July–Sept. **Habitat requirements:** Moist, rich woods, forested floodplains, and disturbed woodlands (FACU). Tolerates soil acidity down to pH 4.1. Found in forest, soil pH 5.6. Frequent in NYC in moist to wet woodlands. **Uses:** Secondary or minor species for addition to erosion control species, increased diversity and aesthetics in restoration of forest understory in rich, moist soil of mixed deciduous forests.

Cirsium discolor (field thistle)

To 6 ft., very spiny. Flowers purple, July–Oct. Host for some butterfly species. Attractive to hummingbirds. Seeds eaten by small birds. **Habitat requirements:** Fields, disturbed sites, usually in moist soil, wetlands margins, woods (UPL). Tolerant of partial shade. **Note:** *Warning! Cirsium arvense* (Canada thistle) is a very aggressive Eurasian weed. **Uses:** Minor species for increased diversity and aesthetics in restoration of open, moist soil, protection of sensitive restoration areas.

Cirsium muticum (swamp thistle)

To 6 ft., very spiny. Flowers purple, July–Sept.; fruit Sept.–Nov. Host for some butterfly species. Attractive to hummingbirds. **Habitat requirements:** Marshes (OBL). **Uses:** Secondary or minor species for increasing diversity in wetland restoration and mitigation. Protection of sensitive areas.

Cirsium pumilum (pasture thistle)

Biennial, to 32 in. Flowers purple (second year); fragrant, July–Aug.; fruit Aug.–Oct. Seeds eaten by small birds. **Habitat requirements:** Dry fields, on neutral or alkaline soils (UPL). **Uses:** Minor species for addition to seed mix for initial erosion control on newly restored areas, increased diversity, and aesthetics.

Claytonia caroliniana (Carolina spring beauty)

Spring ephemeral, about 4 in. Flowers pinkish, showy, April–June. **Habitat requirements:** Moist woods (FACU). **Uses:** Minor species for increased diversity and aesthetics in restoration of open moist soil of woodlands.

**Claytonia virginica* (spring beauty)

Claytonia virginica

Spring ephemeral, to 7 in., colonial. Flowers pinkish white, showy, March–May; fruit May–June. Seeds dispersed by ants. **Habitat requirements:** Moist, rich woods, floodplain forests, lawns (FACU). Occasional in NYC. Colony spreading slowly. Often found with trout lily. Found in soil pH 6. **Uses:** Primary or secondary species for increased diversity and aesthetics in restoration of moist woodland understories and forested floodplains.

Collinsonia canadensis (horse balm)

To 3 ft., colonial. Flowers pale yellow, Aug.–Sept.; fruit Sept.–Oct. **Habitat requirements:** Rich, moist woods (FAC). Tolerant of shade. **Uses:** Secondary or minor species for increased diversity and aesthetics in restoration of moist mixed deciduous forest understories.

Conyza canadensis (*Erigeron c.*) (horseweed)

Annual, to 5 ft. Flowers tiny, white, July–Oct. **Habitat requirements:** Open dry, sandy soil. A field and roadside weed (UPL). Soil pH 4.8–7.2. Soon outcompeted by perennials. **Uses:** Minor species for addition to seed mix for initial erosion control on newly restored areas.

Coptis trifolia (goldthread)

To 6 in., evergreen, colonial. Flowers white, May–July. **Habitat requirements:** Wet woods, bogs, mossy ground (FACW). Tolerant of shade. **Uses:** Secondary or minor species for increasing diversity and aesthetics in wetland restoration and mitigation.

Corydalis aurea (golden Corydalis)

Annual or biennial, to 2 ft. Flowers yellow, showy, May–June. **Habitat requirements:** Calcareous rocky, sandy soil, woodlands (UPL). Tolerant of partial shade. Should tolerate concrete debris. **Uses:** Secondary or minor species for increased diversity and aesthetics in restoration of woodlands with concrete debris fill soils. Addition to appropriate annual seed mixes.

Corydalis sempervirens (pink Corydalis)

Wintergreen, annual or biennial, to 2 ft. Foliage pale, waxy green. Flowers pink and yellow, May–June; fruit June–Sept. **Habitat requirements:** Dry, rocky woodlands (UPL). **Uses:** Secondary or minor species for increased diversity and aesthetics in restoration of dry, rocky, open woodlands. Addition to appropriate annual seed mixes.

Cryptotaenia canadensis (Canada honewort)

To 3 ft. Flowers white, June–July; fruit Aug.–Sept. Host for some butterfly species. **Habitat requirements:** Rich, moist woods (FAC). Tolerant of shade. Occasional in NYC woodlands. **Uses:** Secondary or minor species for increased diversity and aesthetics in restoration of moist, mixed deciduous forest understories.

Cunila origanoides (dittany, stone-mint)

To 18 in. Flowers pink-purple, July–Oct. **Habitat requirements:** Dry, open, rocky woods (UPL). **Uses:** Secondary or minor species for increased diversity and aesthetics in restoration of open woodlands. Tolerant of shade.

Cuphea viscosissima

Cuphea viscosissima (*C. petiolata*) (blue wax-weed)

Annual, to 2 ft. Flowers red-purple, July–Oct.; fruit Sept.–Nov. **Habitat requirements:** Dry, open soil (FAC−). **Uses:** Secondary or minor species for increased diversity and aesthetics in restoration of dry meadows, grasslands, open areas. Addition to appropriate annual seed mixes.

Cynoglossum virginianum (wild comfrey)

To 3 ft. Flowers blue, April–June. **Habitat requirements:** Dry to moist woods (UPL). Tolerant of shade. **Uses:** Secondary or minor species for increased diversity and aesthetics in restoration of open woodlands.

**Decodon verticillatus* (swamp loosestrife)

To 4 ft., stems arching, emergent, colonial. Old stems persistent into winter. Flowers purple, July–Aug.; fruit Sept.–Oct. **Habitat requirements:** Open, shallow water, pond edges, marshes (OBL). Soil pH 5.2–7.2. Common around pond edges in NYC. Available. Appears to tolerate partial or dappled shade. **Uses:** Primary or secondary species for stabilization of pond and lake edges, increasing diversity and aesthetics in wetland restoration and mitigation. Protection of herbaceous edge plantings from Canada geese.

Desmodium canadense (showy tick-trefoil)

To 6 ft. Flowers pink-purple, showy, June–Aug.; fruit July–Sept. Host for some butterfly species. **Habitat requirements:** Moist, open woods, edges (FAC). Tolerant of partial shade. **Notes:** Potentially a nitrogen fixer; may improve soil nutrients. Available. **Uses:** Secondary or minor species for increased diversity and aesthetics in restoration of open woodlands, edges.

Desmodium canescens (hoary tick-clover)

To 4.5 ft. Flowers white, July–Aug.; fruit Aug.–Oct. Host for some butterfly species. **Habitat requirements:** Dry, sandy or rich open woods, fields (UPL). Tolerant of partial shade. **Notes:** Potentially a nitrogen fixer; may improve soil nutrients. **Uses:** Secondary or minor species for increased diversity and aesthetics in restoration of open woodlands, edges.

Desmodium ciliare (little-leaf tick-trefoil)

Rare (NYS S2S3, T); to 40 in. Flowers pink-purple, July–Sept.; fruit Aug.–Oct. Host for some butterfly species. **Habitat requirements:** Dry, sandy soil, open woods, fields, clearings (UPL). Tolerant of partial shade. **Notes:** Potentially a nitrogen fixer; may improve soil nutrients. Plant in coordination with conservation organization restoration specialist. Use only local stock. **Uses:** Secondary or minor species for increased diversity and aesthetics in restoration of open woodlands, edges.

Desmodium cuspidatum (tick-clover)

To 6 ft. Flowers pink, July–Sept.; fruit Aug.–Oct. Host for some butterfly species. **Habitat requirements:** Rich, rocky woods (UPL). Tolerant of partial shade. **Notes:** Potentially a nitrogen fixer; may improve soil nutrients. **Uses:** Secondary or minor species for increased diversity and aesthetics in restoration of open woodlands, edges.

Desmodium glabellum (tall tick-clover)

To 4 ft. Flowers pink-purple, July–Sept.; fruit Aug.–Oct. Host for some butterfly species. **Habitat requirements:** Dry, open woods, sandy soil (UPL). Tolerant of partial shade. **Notes:** Potentially a nitrogen fixer; may improve soil nutrients. **Uses:** Secondary or minor species for increased diversity and aesthetics in restoration of dry, open woodlands. Plant in coordination with conservation organization restoration specialist. Use only local stock.

Desmodium glutinosum

Desmodium glutinosum (cluster-leaf tick-trefoil)

To 16 in. Flowers pink-purple, July–Aug.; fruit Aug.–Sept. Host for some butterfly species. **Habitat requirements:** Dry, rocky, or rich woods (UPL). Tolerant of shade. **Notes:** Potentially a nitrogen fixer; may improve soil nutrients. **Uses:** Secondary or minor species for increased diversity and aesthetics in restoration of woodlands.

Desmodium laevigatum (smooth tick-trefoil)

Rare (NYS SH, E); to 4 ft. Flowers rose to purple, July–Aug.; fruit Aug.–Sept. Host for some butterfly species. **Habitat requirements:** Dry, sandy woods, clearings (UPL). Tolerant of partial shade. **Notes:** Potentially a nitrogen fixer; may improve soil nutrients. **Uses:** Secondary or minor species for increased diversity and aesthetics in restoration of dry, sandy woodlands. Plant in coordination with conservation organization restoration specialist. Use only local stock.

Desmodium marilandicum (Maryland tick-trefoil)

To 4 ft. Flowers pink to purple, Aug.–Sept.; fruit Sept.–Oct. Host for some butterfly species. **Habitat requirements:** Dry, sandy, open woods, fields (UPL). Tolerant of partial shade. **Notes:** Potentially a nitrogen fixer; may improve soil nutrients. **Uses:** Secondary or minor species for increased diversity and aesthetics in restoration of dry, open woodlands.

Desmodium nudiflorum (naked-flowered tick-clover)

To 3 ft. Flowers pink, July–Sept.; fruit Aug.–Oct. Host for some butterfly species. **Habitat requirements:** Rich, dry woods (UPL). Tolerant of shade. **Notes:** Potentially a nitrogen fixer; may improve soil nutrients. **Uses:** Secondary or minor species for increased diversity and aesthetics in restoration of open woodlands, edges.

Desmodium paniculatum (panicled tick-clover)

To 3 ft. Flowers pink-purple, July–Sept.; fruit Aug.–Oct. Host for some butterfly species. **Habitat requirements:** Dry, open woods, fields (UPL). Soil pH 6–7 (range probably wider than this). Tolerant of partial shade. **Notes:** Potentially a nitrogen fixer, may improve soil nutrients. **Uses:** Secondary or minor species for increased diversity and aesthetics in restoration of open woodlands, edges, meadows.

Desmodium rotundifolium (round-leaf tick-trefoil)

To 5 ft. long, stems prostrate. Flowers pink-purple, July–Sept.; fruit Aug.–Oct. Host for some butterfly species. **Habitat requirements:** Dry, open woods, barrens (UPL). Tolerant of partial shade. **Notes:** Potentially a nitrogen fixer; may improve soil nutrients. **Uses:** Secondary or minor species for increased diversity and aesthetics in restoration of dry woodlands, oak and sand barrens.

Desmodium viridiflorum (velvety tick-trefoil)

To 6 ft. Flowers pink, turning green, July–Sept.; fruit Aug.–Oct. Host for some butterfly species. **Habitat requirements:** Dry, sandy, open woods, clearings (UPL). Tolerant of shade. **Notes:** Potentially a nitrogen fixer; may improve soil nutrients. **Uses:** Secondary or minor species for increased diversity and aesthetics in restoration of dry, open woodlands, edges.

Dicentra canadensis (squirrel corn)

Spring ephemeral, to 6 in. Flowers white, April–May; fruit June. **Habitat requirements:** Rich, moist to dry woods (UPL). **Uses:** Secondary or minor species for increased diversity and aesthetics in restoration of forest understories.

Dicentra cucullaria (Dutchman's breeches)

Spring ephemeral, to 6 in. Flowers white and yellow, April; fruit May–June. **Habitat requirements:** Rich, moist to dry woods (UPL). **Uses:** Secondary or minor species for increased diversity and aesthetics in restoration of forest understories.

Diodia teres (buttonweed, poorjoe)

Annual, stems to 32 in. long, prostrate, spreading or reclining. Flowers small, white to pale purple, July–Sept.; fruit Aug.–Oct. **Habitat requirements:** Dry, sandy soil, open woods, pine barrens, fields, fill (UPL). Tolerant of partial shade. **Uses:** Minor species for addition to seed mix for open sandy soil of newly restored sandy grasslands or open sand barrens or vegetation of sandy fill.

3/5

Diodia teres

Draba reptans (Carolina Whitlow-grass)

Annual, or winter annual, to 8 in. Flowers white, April–May. **Habitat requirements:** Dry, sterile sand and edges (UPL). **Uses:** Minor species for addition to seed mix for open sandy soil of newly restored sandy grasslands or open sand barrens.

Echinodorus tenellus (little bur-head)

Emergent, to 4 in., creeping, colonial. Flowers white, small, July–sept.; fruit Aug.–Oct. **Habitat requirements:** Mud or wet sand (OBL). **Uses:** Secondary or minor species for increasing diversity in wetland restoration and mitigation.

Elodea canadensis (*Anacharis c.*) (waterweed)

Rooted or drifting aquatic, to 3 ft. long, aggressively colonial, usually in dense beds, growth rate rapid, potentially invasive. Flowers white, tiny, blooming infrequent, April–Nov. **Habitat requirements:** Water depth 1–6 ft., pH 6.5–10. Tolerant of brackish water to 10 ppt salt (OBL). **Notes:** Provides cover for small fish and aquatic invertebrates that help control mosquito populations in artificial ponds (*Elodea nuttallii* is also a native aquatic, very similar to *E. canadensis*). **Uses:** Cover for fish and invertebrates in ponds, quiet water. Nutrient uptake.

Epigaea repens (trailing arbutus)

To 4 in., evergreen, colonial, very slow growing. Flowers white, fragrant, April–May; fruit whitish capsules, July. Wildlife value low. Host for some butterfly species. **Habitat requirements:** Wooded slopes and banks of oak woods or pine barrens, sandy, dry low-nutrient acid soil, pH 4.5–6 (UPL). Tolerant of shade, salt, drought. Intolerant of soil compaction, flooding, disturbance. Will not tolerate trampling or competition from weedy plants. May be difficult to establish. **Uses:** Minor species, only in restoration of undisturbed areas in pine or oak woods on small banks or slopes where leaf litter does not accumulate.

Epilobium angustifolium (*Chamerion angustifolium*) (fireweed)

To 8 ft. Flowers magenta, showy, June–Sept.; fruit June–Sept. **Habitat requirements:** Moist, rich soil, open soil, burned woodlands (FAC). **Uses:** Secondary or minor species for increased diversity and aesthetics in restoration of forest understories, burned-over areas with moist soil, disturbed wetland edges.

Epilobium coloratum (willow herb)

To 3 ft., prolific, weedy. Flowers pinkish white, July–Sept.; fruit Aug.–Oct. **Habitat requirements:** Wet soil, disturbed areas, marshes, pond edges (OBL). Soil pH 4.5–7.5. **Uses:** Secondary or minor species for erosion control and increased diversity in wetland restoration and mitigation.

Epilobium leptophyllum (narrow-leaved willow herb)

To 3 ft., colonial. Flowers white, July–Sept. **Habitat requirements:** Wet meadows (OBL). Soil pH 4.0–6.5. **Uses:** Secondary or minor species for increasing diversity in wetland restoration and mitigation.

Epilobium strictum (northern willow herb)

To 2 ft., colonial. Flowers pink, July–Sept. **Habitat requirements:** Bogs, swamps, wet woods (OBL). Tolerant of shade. **Uses:** Secondary or minor species for increasing diversity and aesthetics in wetland restoration and mitigation. Possibly also soil-holding capacity.

Equisetum arvense (field horsetail)

To 2 ft. colonial (aggressive). No flowers, spores on tan stems, March–May. **Habitat requirements:** Moist to wet open areas, roadsides, ditches, disturbed sterile soil, railroad embankments (FAC). Soil pH 4–7. **Notes:** Aggressive, but good for soil holding. May be possible to propagate from spores as well as rhizome cuttings. Common in NYC and region. **Uses:** Secondary species for erosion control and diversity on slopes, disturbed edges, moist to wet open areas, old road beds, highway margins.

Equisetum fluviatile (water horsetail)

To over 40 in., colonial. Fertile (spores) May–Aug. No flowers. **Habitat requirements:** Shallow water, muddy shores, neutral soils (OBL). Soil pH 4.5–6.0. **Notes:** Should be possible to propagate from spores as well as rhizome cuttings. **Uses:** Secondary or minor species for increased diversity and soil-holding capacity in wetland restoration and mitigation. Marshes, pond and lake shores.

Equisetum hyemale (rough scouring rush)

To about 4 ft., evergreen, densely colonial, unbranched, rough. Fertile May–Aug. No flowers. **Habitat requirements:** Open or partly shaded areas in moist to wet sandy soil, shady stream margins (FACW). Tolerant of partial shade. **Notes:** May be difficult to find. Should be possible to propagate from spores as well as rhizome cuttings. Occasional in NYC. **Uses:** Secondary or minor species for increased diversity and soil-holding capacity in wetland restoration and mitigation. May be useful along stream banks for soil holding in light shade.

Erechtites hieraciifolia (fireweed, pilewort)

Annual, to 8 ft. (rarely), usually under 3 ft. Flowers green, seed head with bright white plumes, Aug.–Oct. **Habitat requirements:** Weed of roadsides, disturbed woodlands, edges (FACU). Tolerant of partial shade. **Uses:** Secondary species for addition to erosion control seed mix on open soil in new restoration.

Erigeron annuus (annual fleabane)

Annual, to 5 ft. Flowers white and yellow, June–Oct. Host for some butterfly species. **Habitat requirements:** Weedy, open, disturbed areas, fill (FACU). **Notes:** Grows easily from seed. Common in our region. **Uses:** Secondary species for addition to erosion control seed mix on open soil in new restoration. Increased diversity and aesthetics in vegetation of fill, open areas, roadside wildflowers.

Erigeron philadelphicus (daisy fleabane)

To 30 in. Flowers pinkish white, May–Aug. Host for some butterfly species. **Habitat requirements:** Weedy; open woods, meadows, edges, in rich, moist soil (FACU). Soil pH 4.8–7.8. Tolerant of partial shade. **Notes:** Reproduces very well from seed. Common in our region. **Uses:** Secondary or minor species for increased diversity and aesthetics in vegetation of fill, open areas, roadside wildflowers.

Erigeron pulchellus (robin's plantain)

To 20 in. Flowers violet to whitish, May–June. **Habitat requirements:** Rich, open woods, meadows, stream banks (FACU). Tolerant of partial shade. **Uses:** Secondary or minor species for increased diversity and aesthetics in restoration of open woodlands, meadows, roadside wildflowers.

Erigeron strigosus (rough fleabane)

Annual to 28 in. Flowers white, June–Aug. **Habitat requirements:** Dry, open soil, disturbed habitats, roadsides (FACU+). Soil pH 4.8–7.2. **Uses:** Secondary species for addition to erosion control seed mix on open soil in new restorations.

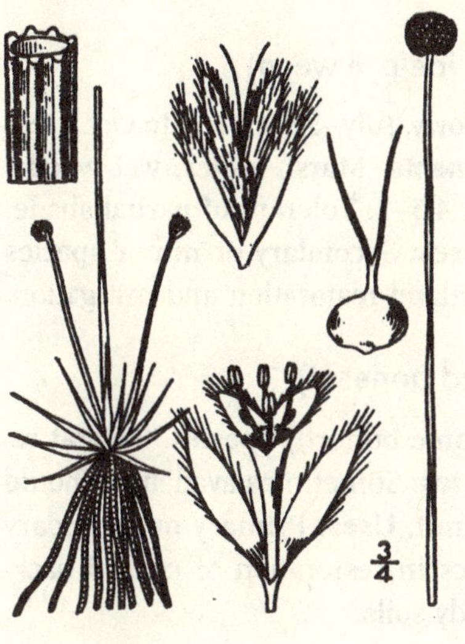

Eriocaulon aquaticum

Eriocaulon aquaticum (pipewort, white buttons)

To 8 in. Flowers white, July–Sept.; fruit to Oct. **Habitat requirements:** Shallow water, muddy shores (OBL). **Uses:** Secondary or minor species for increasing diversity and in wetland restoration and mitigation.

**Erythronium americanum* (trout lily)

Spring ephemeral, to 8 in., colonial from bulb offshoots, spreads slowly, leaves blue-green mottled with brown. Flowers yellow, showy, April–May; fruit late May. **Habitat requirements:** Usually found in rich, moist to wet soil of stream floodplains and moist understories of lowland forests (UPL). Found in soil pH 5–6. **Notes:** Often found mixed with colonies of *Claytonia virginica*. **Uses:** Primary or secondary species for increased diversity and aesthetics in restoration of floodplain forest understories, moist upland woods.

Eupatorium album (white boneset)

To 3 ft. Flowers white, July–Sept. Host for some butterfly species. **Habitat requirements:** Dry open sites, sandy acid soil, thin woodlands, pine barrens (UPL). Tolerant of partial shade. Long Island northern limit. **Uses:** Primary or secondary species for increased diversity and aesthetics in restoration of open woodlands in sandy soil, especially oak woods. Back-dune and outwash plain, coastal grassland restoration.

Eupatorium aromaticum (*Ageratina aromatica*) (smaller white snake root)

Rare (NYS S1, E); to 5 ft. Flowers white, Aug.–Sept. Host for some butterfly species. **Habitat requirements:** Dry, open woods, sandy soil, pine barrens (UPL). Tolerant of partial shade. NYC, northern limit. Plant in coordination with conservation organization restoration specialist. Use only local seed sources. **Uses:** Minor element in restoration of dry woodlands on sandy soil.

Eupatorium dubium (three-nerved joe-pye weed)

To 3 ft. Flowers purple, Aug.–Sept.; fruit to Oct. Host for some butterfly species. **Habitat requirements:** Open, moist, sandy, gravelly acid soil, wet woods, edges (FACW). Tolerant of partial shade. **Notes:** Available. **Uses:** Secondary or minor species for increasing diversity and aesthetics in wetland restoration and mitigation.

Eupatorium fistulosum (hollow-stemmed joe-pye weed)

To 6 ft., stem purple. Flowers purple-pink, showy, July–Sept.; fruit to Oct. Host for some butterfly species. **Habitat requirements:** Marsh edges, wet woods, roadside ditches, not fussy (FACW). Soil pH 4.5–7. Tolerant of partial shade. **Notes:** Common in our region. Available. **Uses:** Secondary or minor species for increasing diversity and aesthetics in wetland restoration and mitigation.

**Eupatorium hyssopifolium* (hyssop-leaved boneset)

To 3 ft. Flowers white, July–Oct. Host for some butterfly species. **Habitat requirements:** Dry, open, sandy soil (UPL). **Notes:** Sometimes available. Should be propagated more often. NYC northern limit. **Uses:** Primary or secondary species for increased diversity and aesthetics in restoration of coastal back-dune scrublands and grasslands, on dry, sandy soils.

Eupatorium maculatum (spotted joe-pye weed)

To 6 ft. Flowers purple, July–Sept.; fruit to Oct. Host for some butterfly species. **Habitat requirements:** Moist to wet open or partly shaded sites, often on calcareous soil (FACW). Should tolerate concrete debris. **Notes:** Fairly common. Available. **Uses:** Secondary or minor species for increasing diversity in wetland restoration and mitigation.

******Eupatorium perfoliatum* (boneset)

To 4 ft., hairy. Flowers white, Aug.–Sept.; fruit to Oct. Host for some butterfly species. **Habitat requirements:** Wet soil of marshes, low meadows, open wet woods, edges (FACW+). Tolerant of partial shade. **Notes:** Usually easy to obtain. Available. Use regional stock. **Uses:** Primary or secondary species for increasing diversity in wetland restoration and mitigation.

Eupatorium pilosum (ragged Eupatorium)

To 4 ft. Flowers white, Aug.–Sept.; fruit to Oct. Host for some butterfly species. **Habitat requirements:** Open bogs or part shade, acid, wet, sandy soil (FACW). **Uses:** Secondary or minor species for increasing diversity in acid bog restoration.

Eupatorium purpureum

Eupatorium purpureum (purple joe-pye weed)

To 10 ft. Flowers pink-purple, July–Oct. Host for some butterfly species. **Habitat requirements:** Rich, moist to dry, open woods, calcareous soils (UPL). Tolerant of shade. Should tolerate concrete debris. **Uses:** Secondary or minor species for increased diversity and aesthetics in restoration of moist to dry disturbed woodlands, especially on concrete rubble or somewhat alkaline fill soils.

Eupatorium rotundifolium (round-leaved joe-pye weed)

Rare (NYS S1, E; northern limit); to 5 ft. Flowers white, July–Oct. Host for some butterfly species. **Habitat requirements:** Open woods, dry to moist soil (FAC−). Tolerant of shade. **Notes:** Plant in coordination with conservation organization restoration specialist. Use local stock. **Uses:** Minor element in restoration of dry to moist open woodlands or meadows.

******Eupatorium rugosum* (*Ageratina altissima*) (white snakeroot)

To 5 ft. Plant poisonous. Flowers bright white, July–Oct. Host for some butterfly species. **Habitat requirements:** Disturbed woods, often on alkaline soils, not fussy (UPL). Widely tolerant of soils, shade, moisture regimes.

Notes: Very common in NYC woodlands. Often found with white wood aster and jumpseed. **Uses:** Primary or secondary species for erosion control, stabilization of dry, shady slopes in restoration of disturbed forest understories.

Eupatorium sessilifolium (upland boneset)

To 6 ft., colonial. Flowers white, July–Sept.; fruit Oct. Host for some butterfly species. **Habitat requirements:** Dry woods, meadows, on rich, often calcareous soils (UPL). Tolerant of partial shade. Should tolerate concrete debris. (Also supposedly tolerant of acid, sandy soils). **Uses:** Secondary or minor species for increased diversity and aesthetics in restoration of moist to dry meadows, disturbed sites.

Euphorbia corollata (flowering spurge)

Euphorbia corollata

To 40 in. Flowers (bracts) white, June–Oct. **Habitat requirements:** Dry, open woods, fields, meadows (UPL). Tolerant of partial shade. **Note:** *Euphorbia cyparissias* (Cypress spurge) is an invasive Eurasian plant. **Uses:** Secondary or minor species for increased diversity and aesthetics in restoration of moist to dry meadows, open woodlands, edges.

Euphorbia maculata (*Chamaesyce maculata*) (spotted spurge, milk purslane)

Annual, stems prostrate, forming mats to 16 in. wide, leaves with red spot. Flowers inconspicuous, June–Sept.; fruit July–Oct. **Habitat requirements:** An attractive sidewalk and path weed, open, dry, disturbed habitats (FACU−). **Uses:** Minor species for addition to seed mix for initial erosion control on open soil in new restoration.

Euphorbia polygonifolia (seaside spurge)

Annual, prostrate, forming mats to 10 in. wide. Flowers inconspicuous; blooms and fruits July–Oct. **Habitat requirements:** Coastal. Beach sand above high-tide line, dune swales (FACU). **Uses:** Minor species for holding sand, increased diversity in beach dune restoration.

**Euthamia graminifolia* (grass-leaved goldenrod)

To 3 ft., colonial. Flowers yellow, July–Oct. Host for some butterfly species. **Habitat requirements:** Open areas, moist to dry soil (FAC). Common in NYC. Appears widely tolerant of soil conditions. **Notes:** Common in our region. Available. **Uses:** Primary or secondary species for erosion control, vegetation cover, for fill, open soil, meadows, roadside banks.

**Euthamia tenuifolia* (slender-leaved goldenrod)

To 2 ft., colonial. Flowers yellow, Aug.–Oct. Host for some butterfly species. **Habitat requirements:** Open, sandy soil, sandy fill, back dunes, coastal scrub, weedy, disturbed areas (FACU). Appears widely tolerant of soil conditions. **Notes:** Common in NYC. Available. **Uses:** Primary or secondary species for erosion control, vegetation cover, for dry fill, open soil, meadows, roadside banks.

Floerkea proserpinacoides (false mermaid)

Annual, to 1 ft. Flowers small, white, April–May. **Habitat requirements:** Moist, rich, dense woods, calcareous soil, floodplain forests (FAC). Tolerant of shade. **Uses:** Minor species for increased diversity and aesthetics in restoration of moist woodlands.

Fragaria vesca (woodland strawberry)

About 6 in., colonial. Flowers white, May–June; fruit fleshy, red, edible, June–July. **Habitat requirements:** Rich, moist, soil, rocky woods (UPL). Tolerant of light shade. **Uses:** Minor species for increased diversity and aesthetics in restoration of open woodlands.

Fragaria virginiana (wild strawberry)

About 6 in., colonial. Flowers white, April–June; fruit fleshy, red, edible, May–June. **Habitat requirements:** Open fields, woods, edges (FACU). Tolerant of light shade. **Uses:** Minor species for increased diversity and aesthetics in restoration of edges, open woods.

Galium aparine (cleavers)

To about 5 ft. long, annual, stems weak, reclining, bristly. Flowers small, white, April–June; fruit May–July. **Habitat requirements:** Rich woods, thickets, meadows (FACU). Soil pH 5.4–7.2. Tolerant of shade. **Uses:** Minor species for addition to seed mix for initial erosion control in new woodland restoration.

Galium asprellum (rough bedstraw)

To 6.5 ft. long, stems sprawling. Flowers white, small (uncommon), July–Sept.; fruit Sept.–Oct. **Habitat requirements:** Wet woods, thickets (OBL). Tolerant of partial shade. **Uses:** Secondary or minor species for increasing diversity in restoration of wooded wetlands.

Galium asprellum

Galium circaezans (forest bedstraw)

To 2 ft. Flowers greenish, May–July; fruit July–Sept. **Habitat requirements:** Rich, dry woods, thickets, sandy soil (UPL). Tolerant of shade. **Uses:** Minor species for increased diversity and aesthetics in restoration of open woodlands.

Galium lanceolatum (wild licorice)

To 28 in. Flowers yellowish becoming purplish, May–July; fruit Aug.–Sept. **Habitat requirements:** Dry, rocky woods, thickets (UPL). Tolerant of shade. **Uses:** Minor species for increased diversity and aesthetics in restoration of open woodlands.

Galium obtusum (blunt-leaf bedstraw)

To 32 in., colonial, stems matted. Flowers white, May–July. **Habitat requirements:** Wet thickets, shores and meadows (FACW+). Soil pH 5.0–7.0. **Uses:** Minor species for increasing diversity and aesthetics in moist or wet meadows, open wet woods. Possible soil-holding ability.

Galium pilosum (bedstraw, cleavers)

To 40 in., stems tufted. Flowers greenish to purplish, June–Aug.; fruit Aug.–Oct. **Habitat requirements:** Dry, sandy woods, dunes, bog edges (UPL). Tolerant of shade. **Uses:** Minor species for increased diversity and aesthetics in restoration of upland woods.

Galium trifidum (small bedstraw)

To 2 ft. long, stems weak, scrambling on other plants. Flowers whitish, June–Aug.; fruit to Sept. **Habitat requirements:** Swamps, wet shores (FACW+). Soil pH 4.6–8.0. **Uses:** Minor species for increasing diversity in wetland restoration and mitigation.

Galium triflorum (sweet-scented bedstraw)

To 32 in. Flowers greenish white, June–Aug.; fruit to Sept. **Habitat requirements:** Dry woods, thickets (FACU). Tolerant of shade. **Uses:** Minor species for increased diversity in restoration of woodlands.

Gaultheria hispidula (creeping snowberry)

4–6 in. long, evergreen, prostrate, creeping. Flowers white, April–May; fruit to Aug, fleshy, white, edible. Host for some butterfly species. **Habitat requirements:** Wet, mossy woods, decayed wood, Atlantic white cedar bog edges, in acid soil (FACW). Soil pH 4.0–6.5. Tolerant of shade. **Notes:** Principally a northern and mountain plant. Has been found on Staten Island (historical). **Uses:** Minor species for increasing diversity and aesthetics in moist to wet oak forest restoration, possibly around acid bog margins.

Gaultheria procumbens (wintergreen)

To 8 in., evergreen, colonial, slow growing. Plant aromatic. Flowers white, June–Aug., fruit fleshy, red, Sept.–Oct., persisting into winter. Wildlife value low. **Habitat requirements:** Open woods, dry, acid, rocky or sandy low-nutrient soil of oak woods or pine barrens, pH 4–6.5 (FACU). Needs at least partial shade. Tolerant of soil compaction. Moderately tolerant of drought. Intolerant of flooding or competition from weedy plants. **Uses:** Minor species, only use for restoration of undisturbed areas in pine or oak barrens on small banks, slopes or rocky ledges where deep leaf litter does not accumulate.

Gentiana andrewsii (fringe-tip closed gentian)

To 3 ft. Flowers blue, showy, Aug.–Sept.; fruit Sept.–Oct. **Habitat requirements:** Open, wet woods and swamps (FACW). Calcareous soils. Soil pH 5.8–7.2. Tolerant of partial shade. Probably not tolerant of competition with aggressive species. **Notes:** Available. **Uses:** Minor species for increasing diversity and aesthetics in moist or wet meadows, open wet woods.

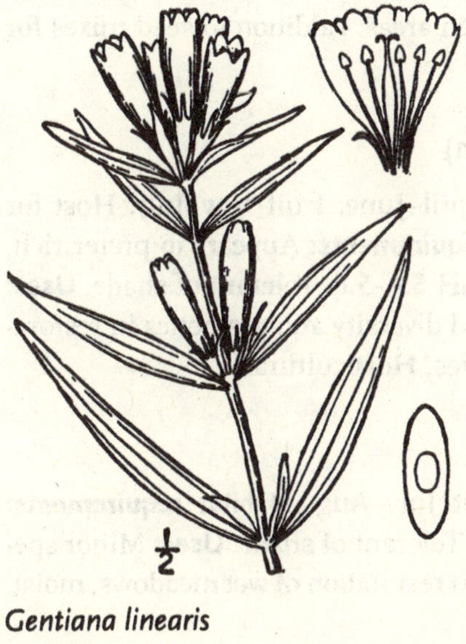

Gentiana linearis

Gentiana clausa (closed gentian)

To 3 ft. Flowers blue-purple, Sept.–Oct. **Habitat requirements:** Rich soil of wet meadows, open swamp forests (FACW). Soil pH 5.8–7.2. Tolerant of partial shade. **Notes:** Available. **Uses:** Minor species for increasing diversity and aesthetics in moist or wet meadows, open swamp forests, stream banks, pond margins.

Gentiana linearis (narrow-leaf gentian)

To 18 in. Flowers blue, showy, July–Sept. **Habitat requirements:** Open, wet woods, meadows (OBL). Tolerant of partial shade. **Uses:** Minor species for increasing diversity and aesthetics in moist or wet meadows, open wet woods, pond margins.

Gentiana saponaria (soapwort gentian)

Rare (NYS S1, E); to 2 ft. Flowers blue, showy, Sept.–Oct. **Habitat requirements:** Moist woods, bogs, wet acid, sandy soil (FACW). Tolerant of partial shade. **Notes:** Plant in coordination with a conservation organization restoration specialist. Use local stock. **Uses:** Minor species for increasing diversity and aesthetics in moist or wet meadows, open wet woods, pond margins.

Gentianopsis crinita (*Gentiana c.*) (fringed gentian)

To 32 in. Flowers violet, Sept.–Oct. **Habitat requirements:** Wet meadows, stream banks (OBL). **Uses:** Minor species for increasing diversity and aesthetics in moist or wet meadows, open wet woods, pond margins, stream banks.

Geranium bicknellii (Bicknell's crane's-bill)

Annual or biennial to 2 ft. Flowers pale purple, July–Sept. **Habitat requirements:** Open woods (UPL). Tolerant of partial shade. **Uses:** Minor species for increased diversity and aesthetics in restoration of open woodlands. Addition to woodland seed mixes for initial erosion control.

Geranium carolinianum (Carolina crane's-bill)

Annual, to 20 in. Flowers pale pink, May–Aug.; fruit June–Sept. **Habitat requirements:** Dry, barren, sandy soil, fields, open woods (UPL). Tolerant of partial shade. **Uses:** Minor species for increased diversity and aesthetics in restoration of open, dry, rocky woods, open areas. Addition to seed mixes for dry soil.

**Geranium maculatum* (wild geranium)

To 22 in. Flowers pink-purple, showy, April–June; fruit May–July. Host for some butterfly species. Woods. **Habitat requirements:** Appears to prefer rich, moist soils (FACU). Found in forest soil pH 5.4–5.6. Tolerant of shade. **Uses:** Primary or secondary species for increased diversity and aesthetics in restoration of mixed, deciduous forest understories. Horticultural.

Geum aleppicum (yellow avens)

To 3 ft. Flowers yellow, June–July; fruit July–Aug. **Habitat requirements:** Swamps and wet woods, meadows (FAC). Tolerant of shade. **Uses:** Minor species for increased diversity and aesthetics in restoration of wet meadows, moist, open areas.

Geum canadense

Geum canadense (white avens)

To 3 ft., winter rosette evergreen. Flowers white, May–Aug.; fruit June–Oct. **Habitat requirements:** Mixed deciduous woods, floodplain forests (FACU). Soil pH 4.5–7.5. Tolerant of partial shade. Found in forest soil pH 5.6. Frequent in NYC woodlands. **Notes:** Common in our region. Available. **Uses:** Minor species for increased diversity and aesthetics in restoration of woodland understories, in moist, average soil.

Geum laciniatum (rough avens)

To 3 ft., winter rosette evergreen. Flowers white, June–July; fruit July–Aug. **Habitat requirements:** Damp thickets, moist to wet open woodlands (FAC+). Soil pH 5.0–7.0. Tolerant of partial shade. **Uses:** Secondary species for increasing diversity and aesthetics in restoration of moist to wet meadows, successional habitats, open woodlands.

Gnaphalium obtusifolium (*Pseudognaphalium o.*) (sweet everlasting)

Annual, to 3 ft., plant fragrant. Flowers white, blooms and fruits Aug.–Oct. Host for some butterfly species. **Habitat requirements:** Dry, low-nutrient, sandy soil (UPL). Probably a poor competitor with more aggressive vegetation in moist or high-nutrient soil. **Uses:** Addition to seed mix for erosion control on dry, open soil of newly restored sites. Minor species for increased diversity and aesthetics in restoration of dry meadows or grasslands on, sandy soil.

Gratiola aurea (golden pert)

To 12 in., stems creeping, colonial. Flowers yellow, July–Aug.; fruit Sept. **Habitat requirements:** Sandy or gravelly swamps, pond shores, in acid soil, along coastal plain (OBL). **Uses:** Minor species for increasing diversity in restoration or mitigation of open swamps, pond and lake shores.

Gratiola neglecta (hedge-hyssop)

Annual, to 1 ft. Flowers white and yellow, May–July; fruit to Oct. **Habitat requirements:** Wet woods or open habitats (OBL). Tolerant of partial shade. **Uses:** Minor species for increasing diversity and aesthetics in restoration/mitigation of swamp forests or open marshes, shores. Addition to initial erosion control seed mixes for wet sites.

Hackelia virginiana (tickseed, beggar-lice)

Biennial, to 40 in., stems stout. Flowers white to pale blue, July–Aug.; fruit Aug.–Oct. **Habitat requirements:** Calcareous, rocky, or gravelly upland woods (FACU). Tolerant of shade. Should tolerate concrete debris. **Uses:** Addition to seed mix for erosion control in woodland understory soil of newly restored sites. Minor species for increased diversity and aesthetics in restoration of rocky woodlands.

Hedeoma pulegioides

Hedeoma pulegioides (American pennyroyal)

Annual, to 16 in., plant aromatic. Flowers bluish, July–Oct. **Habitat requirements:** Dry, open woods (UPL). Tolerant of partial shade. **Uses:** Minor species for increased diversity and aesthetics in restoration of dry woodland understories. Addition to woodland seed mixes.

Hedyotis caerulea (*Houstonia c.*) (bluets)

To 3 in. Flowers blue, April–May; fruit June. **Habitat requirements:** Moist, open areas, edges, open woods, sandy or rocky soil (UPL). Tolerant of partial shade. Probably easily overgrown by taller vegetation. **Uses:** Minor species for increased diversity and aesthetics in restoration of low meadows.

Hedyotis longifolia (pale bluets)

To 10 in. Flowers blue, June–Aug. **Habitat requirements:** Dry, gravelly, open areas (UPL). **Uses:** Minor species for increased diversity and aesthetics in restoration of low meadows.

Helenium autumnale (common sneezeweed)

To 6 ft. Flowers yellow, blooms and fruits Aug.–Nov. **Habitat requirements:** Rich moist to wet soil, open areas, thickets, freshwater tidal marshes, floodplain forests (FACW+). Soil pH 4.0–7.5. Tolerant of partial shade. **Notes:** Available. **Uses:** Minor species for increasing diversity in restoration/mitigation of open swamps, pond and lake shores.

Helianthemum bicknellii (rock rose)

To 1.5 ft. Flowers yellow, May–July; fruit July–Sept. **Habitat requirements:** Dry rocky or sandy open woods, clearings (UPL). Tolerant of partial shade. **Uses:**

Minor species for increased diversity and aesthetics in restoration of dry, open woodland understories, rocky barrens.

Helianthemum canadense (frostweed)

To 16 in. Flowers yellow, showy, May–July; fruit Aug.–Oct. **Habitat requirements:** Dry, sandy soil, wooded edges, barrens (UPL). Tolerant of partial shade. **Uses:** Minor species for increased diversity and aesthetics in restoration of dry, open woodland understories, rocky barrens.

Helianthus angustifolius (narrow-leaved sunflower)

Rare (NYS S2, T); to 6 ft. Flowers yellow, Aug.–Oct. **Habitat requirements:** Swamps, open, moist, acid soil of bogs; wetlands of pine or oak barrens (FACW). Soil pH 4.0–7.0. Tolerant of shade. **Notes:** Long Island and south. **Uses:** Minor species for increasing diversity and aesthetics in restoration/mitigation of open acid swamps, bogs. Plant in coordination with conservation organization restoration specialist.

Helianthus decapetalus (forest sunflower)

To 5 ft., colonial. Flowers yellow, showy, Aug.–Sept. **Habitat requirements:** Open woods, rich, moist soil (FACU). Tolerant of partial shade. **Uses:** Secondary or minor species for increased diversity and aesthetics in restoration of open woodlands, edges. Possibly some soil-holding capacity for erosion control on partly shady slopes, roadsides.

Helianthus divaricatus

Helianthus divaricatus (woodland sunflower)

To 5 ft., colonial. Flowers yellow, July–Sept. Host for some butterfly species. **Habitat requirements:** Dry, thin woods (UPL). Tolerant of partial shade. **Uses:** Secondary or minor species for increased diversity and aesthetics in restoration of open woodlands, edges. Possibly some soil-holding capacity for erosion control on partly shady slopes, roadsides.

Helianthus giganteus (swamp sunflower)

To 9 ft., colonial. Flowers yellow; Aug.–Oct. **Habitat requirements:** Marshes, wooded swamps, rich, wet soil (FACW). Tolerant of shade. **Uses:** Secondary or minor species for increasing diversity in restoration and mitigation of open swamps, wet meadows, may have some soil-holding capacity.

Helianthus strumosus (rough-leaved sunflower)

To 6 ft., colonial. Flowers yellow, Aug.–Sept. **Habitat requirements:** Dry, open woods, clearings (UPL). Tolerant of partial shade. **Uses:** Secondary or minor species for increased diversity and aesthetics in restoration of open woodlands, edges. Possibly some soil-holding capacity for erosion control on partly shady slopes, roadsides.

Heliopsis helianthoides (oxeye)

To 5 ft. Flowers yellow, July–Sept. **Habitat requirements:** Dry, open woods, dry banks (UPL).Tolerant of partial shade. **Uses:** Secondary or minor species for increased diversity and aesthetics in restoration of open woodlands, edges.

Helonias bullata (swamp pink)

Rare (federally listed G3; NYS SX, U; NJ rare); to 3 ft. Flowers pink, spike showy, April–May; fruit June–July. **Habitat requirements:** Swamp forests, acid bogs (OBL). Not native north of south Staten Island. Tolerant of shade. **Notes:** Plant only in cooperation with recognized conservation organization advice and direction. **Uses:** Minor species for increased diversity and aesthetics in restoration of bogs and open swamp forests.

Hepatica acutiloba (sharp-lobed hepatica)

6 in., semievergreen. Flowers bluish white, April–June. **Habitat requirements:** Rich, dry woods, limestone soils (UPL). Tolerant of shade. Should tolerate concrete debris. Cannot compete with more aggressive vegetation. Found mostly north of NYC. **Uses:** Minor species for increased diversity and aesthetics in restoration of open woodlands, on slopes where deep leaf litter does not accumulate.

Hepatica americana (round-lobed hepatica)

6 in., semievergreen. Flowers blue-lavender, March–April; fruit May–June. **Habitat requirements:** Rich, dry, acidic, rocky woods (UPL). Tolerant of shade. Cannot compete with taller, more aggressive vegetation. **Uses:** Minor species for increased diversity and aesthetics in restoration of open woodlands, on slopes where deep leaf litter does not accumulate.

Heracleum lanatum (cow parsnip)

To 10 ft. Flowers white, June–July; fruit to Aug. Host for some butterfly species. **Habitat requirements:** Moist, rich soil, salt marsh edges (FACU–). Soil pH 5.4–7.3. **Uses:** Secondary species for increased diversity and aesthetics in restoration of moist meadows, open areas in good soil.

Heuchera americana (alum root)

To 3 ft., semievergreen. Flowers purplish, May–June; fruit June–July. **Habitat requirements:** Rich, rocky, woods (UPL), limestone soils. Tolerant of shade. Should tolerate concrete debris. **Uses:** Secondary species for increased diversity and aesthetics in restoration of mixed woodland understories.

**Hibiscus moscheutos* (rose mallow)

To 6 ft., growth rate slow. Flowers pink to red and white, showy, July–Aug.; fruit Sept.–Oct. Wildlife value low. Host for some butterfly species. Attractive to hummingbirds. **Habitat requirements:** Open marshes, pond edges, fresh and brackish tidal marshes (OBL). Soil pH 4.0–7.5. Tolerant of partial shade; tolerant of brackish water to 15 ppt salt, inundation to 3 in. for up to 75% growing season. **Notes:** Common in freshwater and brackish marshes in our region. Available. **Uses:** Primary or secondary species for restoration or mitigation of open marshes, pond and lake edges, brackish marshes. Water gardens.

Hieracium gronovii (beaked hawkweed)

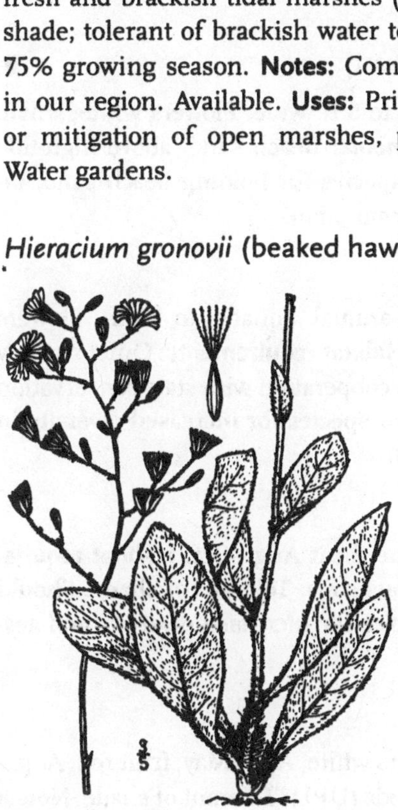

Hieracium gronovii

To 3 ft. Flowers yellow, July–Sept. **Habitat requirements:** Open woods, often in sandy soil (UPL). Tolerant of shade. **Uses:** Minor species for increased diversity and aesthetics in restoration of open woodlands, successional areas.

Hieracium kalmii (*H. canadense*) (Canada hawkweed)

To 5 ft. Flowers yellow, showy, July–Oct. **Habitat requirements:** Thickets, edges; open, rocky woods; sandy soil (UPL). Tolerant of partial shade. North of NYC. **Uses:** Minor species for increased diversity and aesthetics in restoration of open sandy or rocky woodlands, oak barrens.

Hieracium paniculatum (panicled hawkweed)

To 4 ft. Flowers yellow, July–Aug.; fruit to Oct. **Habitat requirements:** Dry, thin woods (UPL). Tolerant of shade. **Uses:** Minor species for increased diversity and aesthetics in restoration of woodlands.

Hieracium scabrum (rough hawkweed)

To 5 ft. Flowers yellow, June–Oct. **Habitat requirements:** Dry, open woods, clearings, in sandy soil (UPL). Tolerant of partial shade. **Uses:** Minor species for increased diversity and aesthetics in restoration of open woodlands, sandy soil of oak barrens.

Hieracium venosum (rattlesnake weed)

To 3 ft., leafy rosette very low, leaves with purple veins. Foliage very attractive. Flowers yellow, May–July. **Habitat requirements:** Open, rocky, acid woods, on slopes where leaf litter does not accumulate (UPL). Tolerant of shade. **Uses:** Minor species for increased diversity and aesthetics in restoration of mixed woodlands in rocky or sandy soil.

Honckenya peploides (sea-beach sandwort)

To 20 in., forming deeply rooted colonies to 6 ft. wide. Flowers white, small, May–June; fruit to Aug. **Habitat requirements:** Beach sand, above high-tide line (FACU). **Uses:** Secondary or minor species for holding beach sand, increased diversity, and aesthetics in dune restoration.

Hottonia inflata (featherfoil)

Rare (NYS S1S2, T), submerged, winter annual, aquatic, to 20 in. Flowers white, small, May–June; fruit June–Aug. **Habitat requirements:** Quiet shallow water, saturated soil (OBL). **Notes:** Plant in cooperation with state conservation organizations. Use local stock. **Uses:** Minor species for increased diversity in wetland restoration in appropriate habitats.

Hybanthus concolor (green violet)

To 3 ft. Flowers greenish white, May–June; fruit Aug.–Oct. **Habitat requirements:** Rich, moist woods (UPL), calcareous soils. Tolerant of shade. Should tolerate concrete debris. **Uses:** Minor species for increased diversity and aesthetics in restoration of mixed woodlands.

Hydrastis canadensis (golden-seal)

Rare (NYS S2, T); to 20 in., colonial. Flowers white, Apr.–May; fruit red, Aug.–Sept. **Habitat requirements:** Rich, deep woods (UPL). Tolerant of shade. **Notes:** Plant in coordination with conservation organization restoration specialist. Use only local stock. **Uses:** Minor species for increased diversity and aesthetics in restoration of mixed woodlands.

Hydrocotyle americana (marsh pennywort)

2–5 in., colonial, low, creeping. Flowers white small, June–Sept.; fruit July–Oct. Host for some butterfly species. **Habitat requirements:** Moist to wet soil, wet woods, meadows (OBL). Tolerant of shade. **Uses:** Minor element for increasing diversity of wetland restoration and mitigation. Possible soil-holding attributes.

Hydrophyllum canadense (broad-leaved waterleaf)

To 20 in., colonial. Flowers purplish or white, May–June; fruit July–Aug. **Habitat requirements:** Rich, moist woods, streamsides (FACU). Tolerant of shade. **Uses:** Secondary or minor species for increased diversity and aesthetics in restoration of moist forest understories. Possibly useful as one element for slope stabilization in disturbed woodlands.

Hydrophyllum virginianum

Hydrophyllum virginianum (Virginia waterleaf)

12–30 in., colonial. Flowers lavender to white, May–June; fruit July–Aug. **Habitat requirements:** Moist to wet, open woods, floodplain forests (FAC). Tolerant of shade. **Uses:** Secondary or minor species for increased diversity and aesthetics restoration of moist to wet forest understories. Possibly useful as one element for slope stabilization in disturbed woodlands.

Hypericum ellipticum

Hypericum canadense (Canada St.-John's-wort)

Annual, or perennial by short stolons, to 2 ft. Flowers yellow, July–Sept.; fruit capsules purplish or red, Sept.–Oct. **Habitat requirements:** Wet meadows, shores, bogs, sandy soil (FACW). **Uses:** Minor element for increasing diversity and aesthetics of wetland restoration and mitigation.

Hypericum ellipticum (pale St.-John's-wort)

To 5 in., colonial creeping. Flowers yellow, July–Aug.; fruit Sept.–Oct.

Habitat requirements: Wet shores, open marshes (OBL). **Uses:** Minor element for increasing diversity and aesthetics of wetland restoration and mitigation. Possible soil-holding attributes.

Hypericum gentianoides (orange-grass, pineweed)

Annual, to 20 in. Flowers yellow, tiny, July–Sept.; fruit Sept.–Oct. **Habitat requirements:** Open barrens, dry, sterile, open rocky or sandy soil (UPL). Soil pH 4.8–7.0. **Uses:** Minor species for increased diversity and aesthetics in restoration of pine barrens, open or rocky sandy habitats.

Hypericum majus (large Canada St.-John's-wort)

To 28 in., perennial by short, leafy stolons. Flowers yellow, July–Sept., fruit capsules maroon, Sept.–Oct. **Habitat requirements:** Wet meadows, shores, calcareous soils, pond shores (FACW). Might tolerate concrete debris. **Uses:** Minor element for increasing diversity and aesthetics of wetland restoration and mitigation.

Hypericum mutilum (dwarf St.-John's-wort)

Annual or perennial, to 32 in. Flowers yellow, July–Sept. **Habitat requirements:** Wet soil, marshes (FACW). Soil pH 4.8–7.2. **Uses:** Minor element for increasing diversity of wetland restoration and mitigation.

Hypericum punctatum (St.-John's-wort)

To 3 ft. Flowers yellow, July–Sept.; fruit Sept.–Oct. **Habitat requirements:** Moist soil, open areas, thin woods (FAC−). Soil pH 4.7–6.5. Tolerant of partial shade. **Note:** *Hypericum perforatum* is a European weed often used medicinally. **Uses:** Secondary or minor species for increased diversity and aesthetics in restoration of meadows.

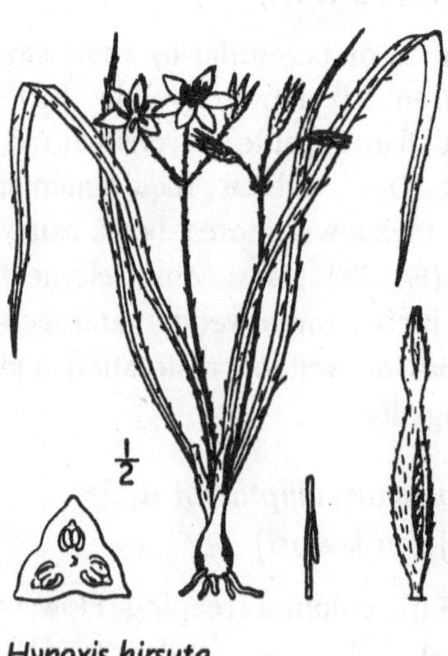

Hypoxis hirsuta

Hypoxis hirsuta (yellow star grass)

To 2 ft., usually less than 1 ft. Flowers yellow, showy, April–July; fruit Aug.–Oct. **Habitat requirements:** Moist to dry, sandy soil, open woods, edges (FAC). Soil pH 5.2–7.3. Tolerant of partial shade. **Uses:** Secondary or minor species for increased diversity and aesthetics in restoration of woodlands in habitats where deep leaf litter does not collect.

Impatiens capensis (*I. biflora*) (jewelweed, touch-me-not)

Annual, to 5 ft., often in large stands. Flowers orange, July–Aug.; fruit to Oct. Attractive to hummingbirds. **Habitat requirements:** Open to part shady swamp forests, wet gaps, edges, freshwater tidal marshes (FACW). Found in soil pH 5.6–7.4. Tolerant of partial shade. **Uses:** Secondary species for increasing diversity of wetland restoration and mitigation. Some soil-holding attributes. Might be useful in seed mixes of annuals on open soil of new restoration/mitigation.

Impatiens pallida (pale touch-me-not)

Annual, to 5 ft. Flowers yellow, June–Sept. Attractive to hummingbirds. **Habitat requirements:** Found in limestone regions, wet soil (FACW). Soil pH 6.8–7.4. More shade tolerant than *I. capensis*, less common. **Uses:** Minor species for increasing diversity of wetland restoration and mitigation. Some soil-holding attributes. Might be useful in seed mixes of annuals on open soil of new restoration/mitigation.

Iris prismatica (slender blueflag)

Rare (G4G5, NYS S2, T); to 28 in., colonial. Flowers blue, showy, June–July; fruit July–Aug. Attractive to hummingbirds. **Habitat requirements:** Marshes, pond shores, open swamp forests, wet meadows, apparently tolerant of brackish water (OBL). Tolerant of partial shade. Appears more shade tolerant than *I. versicolor*. **Notes:** Use only local seed stock. Plant in coordination with conservation organization restoration specialist. **Uses:** Secondary or minor species for increasing diversity and aesthetics of wetland restoration and mitigation. Erosion control along stream banks.

**Iris versicolor* (blueflag)

To 32 in., growth rate slow. Flowers blue, showy, June–July; fruit July–Aug. Wildlife value moderate. Attractive to hummingbirds. **Habitat requirements:** Pond shores, swamp forest gaps, marshes, freshwater and brackish tidal marshes near mean high water (OBL). Prefers acid soil. Persists, but will not flower, in shade. Tolerates moderately brackish water of tidal marshes, flooding, or saturated soil entire growing season. Available. **Uses:** Primary species for erosion control along stream banks and pond shores, increased diversity and aesthetics of wetland restoration and mitigation. Good for planting into water gardens. **Bioengineering:** Organic fiber mats, blankets, and logs.

Justicia americana (water willow)

NJ rare; to 3 ft., colonial. Flowers pale violet, July–Sept. Host for some butterfly species. **Habitat requirements:** Mud, shallow water, or lake and pond shores, river banks (OBL). Soil pH 5.4–7.6. May be hard to find. Growers should be encouraged to try this one. **Uses:** Secondary species for increasing diversity and aesthetics of wetland restoration and mitigation. Erosion control along stream banks and pond shores.

Krigia biflora (orange dandelion)

To 2.5 ft. Flowers orange, May–June. **Habitat requirements:** Open, rich woods. Fields (FACU). Tolerant of partial shade. **Uses:** Secondary or minor species for increased diversity and aesthetics in restoration of moist, open forest understories.

Krigia virginica (dwarf dandelion)

To 16 in. Flowers yellow, May–July; fruit persists until Aug. **Habitat requirements:** Dry, sterile, open soil (UPL). **Uses:** Secondary or minor species for increased diversity and aesthetics in restoration of dry, open habitats.

Kosteletzkya virginica

Kosteletzkya virginica (seashore mallow)

Rare (NYS SX, U; Global G5T3T4); to 4 ft. Flowers pink, showy, blooms and fruits, July–Sept. Grows slowly. Wildlife value low. **Habitat requirements:** Coastal. High salt marsh, mean high water to spring tide (OBL). Long Island northern limit. Tolerant of brackish water to 10 ppt salt. Intolerant of shade. **Notes:** Plant only in coordination with a conservation organization restoration specialist. Use local stock. **Uses:** Secondary or minor species for increased diversity and aesthetics in salt-marsh restoration and mitigation.

Lactuca biennis (tall blue lettuce)

Annual or biennial, to 6.5 ft. Flowers pale blue to white; blooms and fruits, Aug.–Sept. **Habitat requirements:** Rich, moist woods, thickets, open habitats, often near rivers (FACU). Tolerant of partial shade. **Uses:** Minor species for addition to annual seed mix for erosion control on open soil of new restoration. Increased diversity and aesthetics in restoration of successional habitats.

Lactuca canadensis (tall lettuce)

Annual or biennial, to 8 ft. Flowers yellow; blooms and fruits, June–Sept. **Habitat requirements:** Open woods, edges, fields (FACU−). Tolerant of shade. Frequent in NYC open woodlands. **Uses:** Minor species for addition to annual seed mix for erosion control on open soil of new restoration. Increased diversity and aesthetics in restoration of open woodlands, meadows.

Laportea canadensis (wood-nettle)

To 40 in., colonial from rhizomes, armed with stinging hairs. Flowers green, July–Aug.; fruit Aug.–Sept. **Habitat requirements:** Rich, moist woods, shady floodplains (FACW). Tolerant of shade. **Uses:** Secondary species for erosion control in floodplains, away from human usage.

Lathyrus maritimus (*Lathyrus japonicus*) (beach pea)

To 3 ft. long, colonial, reclining. Flowers pink-purple, showy, May–July. **Habitat requirements:** Coastal. Beaches above high high-tide line, primary dunes (FACU). **Notes:** Potentially a nitrogen fixer, may improve soil nutrients. **Uses:** Secondary or minor species for holding sand, increased diversity and aesthetics in back-dune restoration.

Lathyrus ochroleucus (wild pea)

To 30 in., colonial. Flowers whitish, May–July. **Habitat requirements:** Dry woods, rocky banks (UPL). Tolerant of shade. Potentially a nitrogen fixer; may improve soil nutrients. **Uses:** Secondary or minor species for increased diversity in restoration of dry upland forests. Addition to erosion control plantings on slopes, roadside banks. Should tolerate rocky or sandy sterile soils.

Lechea intermedia (large-pod pinweed)

6 in. to 2 ft., leafy basal shoots overwintering. Flowers tiny, reddish, blooms and fruits July–Oct. **Habitat requirements:** Dry, sterile, often sandy soil, beaches, back dunes (UPL). **Uses:** Secondary or minor species for increased diversity in restoration of dry, open areas, sandy soils.

Lechea maritima (beach pinweed)

To 16 in., basal shoots overwintering. Flowers tiny, reddish brown, blooms and fruits Aug.–Nov. **Habitat requirements:** Coastal. Beaches, above high high-tide line, primary and back dunes (UPL). **Uses:** Minor species for holding sand, increased diversity, and aesthetics in beach and back-dune restoration.

Lechea minor (thyme-leaf pinweed)

To 20 in., basal shoots overwintering. Flowers tiny, reddish, July–Aug.; fruit Aug.–Oct. **Habitat requirements:** Dry, open woods, open areas, sandy soils (UPL). **Uses:** Secondary or minor species for increased diversity in restoration of dry open areas, sandy soils.

Lechea mucronata (*L. villosa*) (hairy pinweed)

To 32 in., basal shoots overwintering. Flowers tiny, reddish, June–Aug.; fruit July–Nov. **Habitat requirements:** Dry, open woods, fields; sandy or gravelly

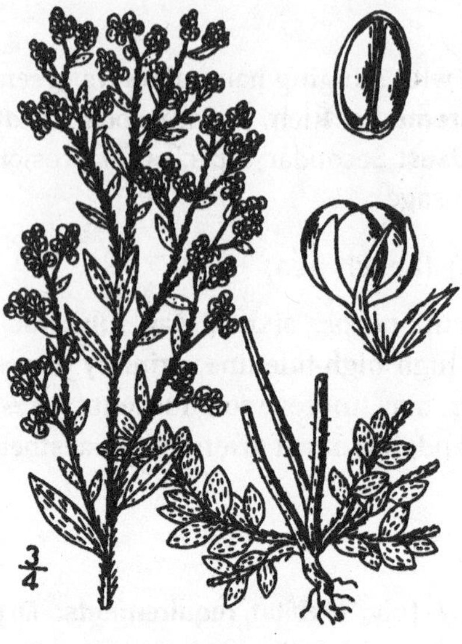

Lechea mucronata

soil (UPL). Tolerant of partial shade. **Uses:** Secondary or minor species for increased diversity in restoration of dry, open habitats, sandy soils.

Lemna minor (duckweed)

Colonial (aggressive); tiny floating aquatic plants, to 1/4 in. wide, often covering pond surfaces. Wildlife value high. **Habitat requirements:** Standing water pH 4.1–7.1, freshwater tidal areas (OBL). Intolerant of salinity over 0.5 ppt. Tolerant of partial shade. **Uses:** Minor species as food for many aquatic birds and mammals, cover for fish, shades water surface, preventing high temperatures in hot weather.

Lepidium virginicum (poor-man's pepper)

Annual or biennial, to 20 in. Flowers white, April–Nov.; fruit July–Nov. **Habitat requirements:** Open soil, roadsides, disturbed habitats (FACU−). **Uses:** Secondary or minor species as an addition to seed mix for initial erosion control on open soil of newly restored slopes, meadows, roadsides.

Lespedeza angustifolia (narrow-leaf bush clover)

To 3 ft. Flowers whitish, Aug.–Sept.; fruit Aug.–Nov. Host for some butterfly species. **Habitat requirements:** Sand barrens of the coastal plain or pinelands in acid soils (FAC). Potentially a nitrogen fixer; may improve soil nutrients. **Uses:** Secondary or minor species for increased diversity in restoration of oak or pine barrens. Sandy sterile soils. Butterfly gardens.

**Lespedeza capitata* (round-headed bush clover)

To 4 ft. Flowers whitish, Aug.–Sept.; fruit Sept.–Oct. Host for some butterfly species. **Habitat requirements:** Open fields, thin woods, tolerates sterile soil (FACU−). Potentially a nitrogen fixer; may improve soil nutrients. Tolerant of partial shade. **Notes:** Common in our region. Available. **Uses:** Primary species for restoration of sand-barren grasslands or successional communities with little bluestem, broom sedge, Indian grass, bayberry, eastern red cedar. Sandy back-dune and coastal-plain soils. Butterfly gardens.

Lespedeza hirta (hairy bush clover)

To 4 ft. Flowers white, Aug.–Sept.; fruit Sept.–Oct. Host for some butterfly species. **Habitat requirements:** Dry, open, rocky or sandy soil, open woods, fields

Lespedeza hirta

(UPL). Soil pH 5.7–8.2. Potentially a nitrogen fixer; may improve soil nutrients. Tolerant of partial shade. **Uses:** Secondary species for restoration of sand barren grasslands or successional, communities with little bluestem, broom sedge, Indian grass, bayberry, eastern red cedar, etc. Sandy back dunes and coastal plain. Butterfly gardens.

Lespedeza intermedia (wandlike bush clover)

To 30 in. Flowers purple, Aug.–Sept.; fruit Aug.–Oct. Host for some butterfly species. **Habitat requirements:** Dry, open woods, fields, roadsides (UPL). Potentially a nitrogen fixer; may improve soil nutrients. Tolerant of partial shade. **Uses:** Secondary species for increased diversity and aesthetics in restoration of oak woodlands, successional scrub on sandy soils. Butterfly gardens.

Lespedeza procumbens (trailing bush clover)

To 3 ft. long, ground cover. Flowers pink-purple, Aug.–Sept.; fruit Sept.–Oct. Host for some butterfly species. **Habitat requirements:** Open, rocky woods, fields (UPL). Potentially a nitrogen fixer; may improve soil nutrients. Tolerant of partial shade. **Uses:** Secondary species for increased diversity and aesthetics in restoration of oak woodlands on rocky or sandy soils, successional scrub on sandy soils. Butterfly gardens.

Lespedeza repens (creeping bush clover)

Stems to 3 ft. long, ground cover. Flowers pink-purple, July–Sept.; fruit Sept.–Oct. Host for some butterfly species. **Habitat requirements:** Sandy or rocky open woods (UPL). Potentially a nitrogen fixer; may improve soil nutrients. Tolerant of partial shade. **Uses:** Secondary species for increased diversity and aesthetics in restoration of mixed oak woodlands, meadows or grasslands on dry, rocky, or sandy soils. Butterfly gardens.

Lespedeza stuevei (tall bush clover)

Rare (NYS S2, T); to 3 ft. Flowers purple, Aug.–Sept.; fruit Aug.–Oct. Host for some butterfly species. **Habitat requirements:** Barrens and open, dry woods (UPL). Potentially a nitrogen fixer; may improve soil nutrients. Tolerant of partial shade. **Uses:** Secondary species for increased diversity and aesthetics in restoration of mixed oak woodlands, meadows, or grasslands on dry, rocky, or sandy soils. Butterfly gardens. Plant in coordination with conservation organization restoration specialist.

Lespedeza violacea (violet bush clover)

Rare (NYS S2, R); to 30 in. Flowers purple, July–Sept.; fruit Oct.–Nov. Host for some butterfly species. **Habitat requirements:** Dry, open woods (UPL). Potentially a nitrogen fixer; may improve soil nutrients. Tolerant of partial shade. **Uses:** Secondary species for increased diversity and aesthetics in restoration of open woodlands on dry, rocky, or sandy soils. Butterfly gardens. Plant in coordination with conservation organization restoration specialist.

Lespedeza virginica (slender bush clover)

To 3 ft. Flowers purple, Aug.–Sept.; fruit Sept.–Oct. Host for some butterfly species. **Habitat requirements:** Dry, open woods, fields (UPL). Potentially a nitrogen fixer; may improve soil nutrients. Tolerant of partial shade. **Uses:** Secondary species for increased diversity and aesthetics in restoration of open woodlands, on dry, rocky, or sandy soils. Butterfly gardens.

Liatris scariosa var. *novae-angliae* (*Liatris borealis*) (northern blazing star)

Rare (NYS S2, T); to 2.5 ft. Flowers purple, showy, Aug., Sept. **Habitat requirements:** Dry, open woods, gaps (UPL). Tolerant of partial shade. **Uses:** Secondary species for increased diversity and aesthetics in restoration of open woodlands, on dry, rocky, or sandy soils.

Lilium philadelphicum

Lilium canadense (Canada lily)

To 4 ft. Flowers yellow, showy, July (mostly); fruit to Aug. Attractive to hummingbirds. **Habitat requirements:** Moist to wet open meadows, shores (FAC+). **Notes:** Bulbs may be eaten by voles and muskrats. **Uses:** Secondary species for increasing diversity and aesthetics of wetland restoration and mitigation. Horticultural.

Lilium philadelphicum (wood lily)

To 32 in. Flowers red-orange, showy, June–July; fruit to Aug. **Habitat requirements:** Dry to moist open woods, gaps, meadows, shores (FACU+). Tolerant of partial shade. **Uses:** Secondary species for increased diversity and aesthetics in restoration of open woodlands, successional habitats, meadows. Horticultural.

Lilium superbum (Turk's cap lily)

To 6 ft. Flowers orange, showy, July–Aug.; fruit Aug.–Sept. Attractive to hummingbirds. **Habitat requirements:** Swamp forests or wet meadows (FACW+). Found in soil pH 4.4–4.8. Tolerant of bright, high shade. Often available. **Notes:** Bulbs may be eaten by voles and muskrats in open areas. Bulbs in woodlands not as vulnerable. **Uses:** Secondary species for increasing diversity and aesthetics of wetland restoration and mitigation. Horticultural.

Limonium carolinianum (sea lavender)

To 12 in. Flowers blue-lavender; blooms and fruits July–Oct. **Habitat requirements:** Coastal. Lower edge of high salt marsh, high tide line along marshy beaches, wet dune swales (OBL). **Uses:** Secondary or minor species for increased diversity and aesthetics in salt-marsh restoration and mitigation.

Limosella subulata (Atlantic mudwort)

Rare (NYS S3, R); annual, to 6 in. Flowers white to pinkish, July–Sept. **Habitat requirements:** Fresh to brackish muddy or sandy tidal river shores along coast (OBL). **Uses:** Minor species for increasing diversity in wetland restoration. Addition to initial erosion control seed mixes.

Linaria canadensis (*Nuttallanthus c.*) (blue toadflax)

Annual, to 24 in. Flowers blue, April–May; fruit June–Sept. **Habitat requirements:** Open, sterile, sandy soil (UPL). **Uses:** Secondary species for increased diversity and aesthetics in restoration of open sand barren and coastal grassland habitats. Addition to erosion control seed mixes for new restoration.

Lindernia dubia (false pimpernel)

Annual, to 8 in. Flowers bluish white, June–Oct. **Habitat requirements:** Open, wet soil, shores, wet roadsides (OBL). A small, sturdy, attractive weed. Tolerant of disturbance. **Uses:** Minor species to increase diversity and aesthetics in wetland restoration and mitigation. Addition to initial erosion control seed mixes for wet soil.

Linum medium var. *texanum* (southern yellow flax)

Rare (NYS S2, T); to 2 ft., plant waxy blue-green. Flowers yellow, June–Aug.; fruit July–Sept. **Habitat requirements:** Dry, sterile soil, fields, beaches, salt-marsh edges (FACU). **Notes:** Plant in coordination with a conservation organization restoration specialist. Use local stock. **Uses:** Secondary species for increased diversity and aesthetics in restoration of dry, open woodlands, coastal grasslands.

Linum striatum (stiff yellow flax)

To 3 ft. Flowers yellow, June–Aug.; fruit July–Sept. **Habitat requirements:** Wet woods, bogs, marshes, damp sand (FACW). Soil pH 5–8. Tolerant of partial shade. **Uses:** Minor species for increasing diversity and aesthetics of wetland restoration and mitigation.

Linum virginianum (wild yellow flax)

To 2 ft. Flowers yellow, June–Aug.; fruit July–Sept. **Habitat requirements:** Open woods, dry, sandy soil (FACU). Tolerant of partial shade. **Uses:** Secondary species for increased diversity and aesthetics in restoration of dry, open woodlands.

Lobelia cardinalis (cardinal flower)

To 4 ft., growth rate slow. Flowers red, showy, July–Aug.; fruit to Sept. Wildlife value moderate. Host for some butterfly species. Attractive to hummingbirds. **Habitat requirements:** Open or shady wet soil, stream banks, freshwater tidal and nontidal marshes, pond edges (FACW+). Tolerant of partial shade, flooding or saturated soil up to 100% of growing season. Intolerant of salt. **Notes:** Available. Reproduces well from seed if pollination and open soil are adequate. **Uses:** Secondary species for increasing diversity and aesthetics of wetland restoration and mitigation. Horticultural.

Lobelia inflata (Indian-tobacco)

Annual, to 40 in. *Plant poisonous.* Winter rosette evergreen. Flowers pale violet to whitish, June–Oct. **Habitat requirements:** Open woodlands, edges, sometimes a garden weed (FACU). Tolerant of partial shade. **Uses:** Secondary species for increased diversity and aesthetics in restoration of open woodlands, gaps, edges. Addition to seed mix for initial erosion control of new restoration.

Lobelia kalmii (brook lobelia)

To 18 in. Flowers blue to white, July–Sept. **Habitat requirements:** Marshes, shores (OBL). Prefers calcareous (somewhat alkaline) soils, should tolerate concrete debris. **Uses:** Secondary species for increasing diversity and aesthetics of wetland restoration and mitigation, especially where concrete fill is a problem.

Lobelia nuttallii (Nuttall's lobelia)

To 18 in. Flowers blue and white, July–Sept.; fruit to Oct. **Habitat requirements:** Wet sand of coastal plain, woods, bogs (FACW). Long Island and south. Tolerant of partial shade. **Uses:** Minor element species for increasing diversity and aesthetics of wetland restoration and mitigation in open sandy soil.

Lobelia siphilitica (great lobelia)

To 4 ft. Flowers blue, showy, Aug.–Sept.; fruit to Oct. **Habitat requirements:** Rich soil of open swamps, wet, open woods, wet meadows (FACW+). **Notes:** Spreads from seed if pollination and open soil adequate, but individual plants not persistent. Apparently not reproducing as freely as *L. cardinalis*. Available. **Uses:** Secondary species for increasing diversity and aesthetics of wetland restoration and mitigation.

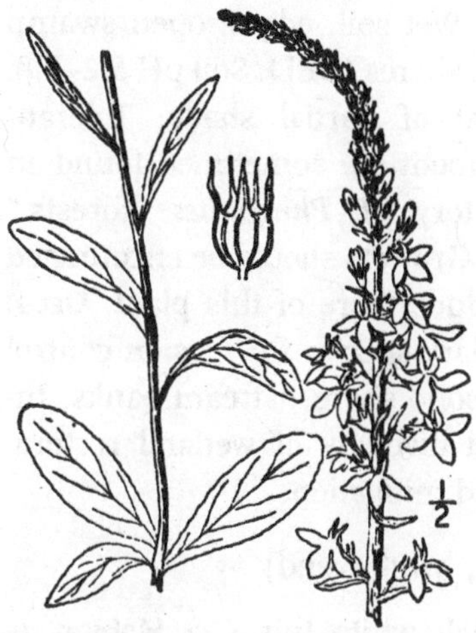

Lobelia spicata

Lobelia spicata (spiked lobelia)

To 3 ft. Flowers blue or white, June–Aug. **Habitat requirements:** Rich, open woods, meadows, sandy soils, often weedy (FAC−). Tolerant of bright, partial shade. **Uses:** Secondary species for increased diversity and aesthetics in restoration of meadows on rich, moist soil. Vegetation of high-nutrient fill soils in open habitats.

Ludwigia alternifolia (seedbox)

To 3 ft. Flowers yellow, June–Aug.; fruit Aug.–Oct. **Habitat requirements:** Open marshes, shores, wet edges (FACW+). **Uses:** Minor element species for increasing diversity of wetland restoration and mitigation.

Ludwigia palustris (water purslane)

Creeping, colonial, forming mats or emergent; foliage often reddish. Flowers green, inconspicuous, June–Sept.; fruit July–Oct. **Habitat requirements:** Wet soil, or in shallow water (OBL). **Uses:** Secondary or minor species for addition to erosion control mix along pond shores, stream banks, freshwater mudflats of seasonal ponds.

Ludwigia sphaerocarpa (globe-fruit seedbox)

To 40 in., colonial. Flowers inconspicuous, July–Sept.; fruit Aug.–Nov. **Habitat requirements:** Marshes, pond margins, bogs (OBL). **Uses:** Secondary or minor species for increased erosion control in wetland restoration, mitigation, along pond shores, in swamps.

Lupinus perennis (wild blue lupine)

To 2 ft. Flowers blue, showy, May–June; fruit June–July; Host for some butterfly species. **Habitat requirements:** Dry, open woods, gaps, sandy or rocky soils (UPL). Numerous other species are sold as horticultural plants. Potentially a nitrogen fixer; may improve soil nutrients. Tolerant of partial shade. **Uses:** Secondary species for increased diversity and aesthetics in restoration of dry, open woodlands, gaps.

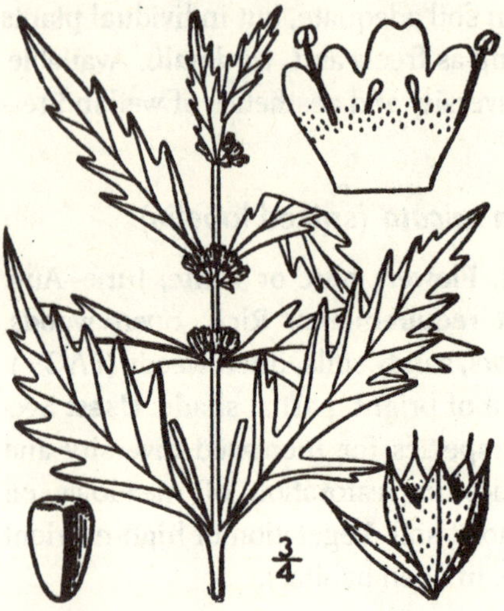

Lycopus americanus

Lycopus americanus (water horehound, bugleweed)

To 2 ft., colonial. Flowers white, small, July–Aug.; fruit to Oct. **Habitat requirements:** Wet soil, edges, open swamp forests, shores (OBL). Soil pH 5.2–7.8. Tolerant of partial shade. Tolerant of competition, sometimes found in understory of *Phragmites* "forests." **Notes:** Growers should be encouraged to produce more of this plant. **Uses:** Secondary species for erosion control along pond shores, stream banks. Increased diversity of wetland restoration and mitigation.

Lycopus rubellus (stalked water horehound, bugleweed)

Rare (NYS S1, E); to 4 ft., colonial. Flowers small, white, July–Oct. **Habitat requirements:** Wet woods, thickets (OBL). Soil pH 5.2–7.2. Tolerant of partial shade. **Uses:** Minor species for increasing diversity of wetland restoration, swamp forests, and mitigation. Use only local seed stock. Plant in coordination with conservation organization restoration specialist.

Lycopus uniflorus (northern bugleweed)

To 2 ft., colonial. Flowers white, small, June–Sept. **Habitat requirements:** Wet soil, shores (OBL). **Uses:** Secondary or minor species for increasing diversity of wetland restoration and mitigation. Erosion control along pond shores, stream banks.

Lycopus virginicus (Virginia bugleweed)

To 2 ft., colonial; leaves often dark purple. Flowers white, small, Aug.–Sept.; fruit to Oct. **Habitat requirements:** Rich, wet soil, bogs, woods (OBL). Soil pH 5.0–6.3. Tolerant of partial shade. **Uses:** Secondary species for increasing diversity of wetland restoration and mitigation. Erosion control along pond shores, stream banks.

Lysimachia ciliata (fringed loosestrife)

To 3 ft., colonial. Flowers yellow, showy, June–July; fruit to Sept. **Habitat requirements:** Swamp forests, floodplains, rich, wet soil (FACW). Tolerant of

3/5

Lysimachia ciliata

shade. **Notes:** A very attractive plant, should be propagated and used. Occasional in our region. **Uses:** Secondary species for increasing diversity and aesthetics of wetland restoration and mitigation. Pond shores, stream banks, swamp forests. Possibly useful for erosion control. Horticultural.

Lysimachia quadrifolia (whorled loosestrife)

To 3 ft. Flowers yellow, June–Aug.; fruit Aug.–Oct. **Habitat requirements:** Open woods, gaps, edges (FACU−). Tolerant of partial shade. Found in forest soil pH 4.8–5.0. **Notes:** Common in our region. **Uses:** Secondary species for increased diversity and aesthetics in restoration of open woodlands, gaps, edges.

Lysimachia terrestris (swamp candles, yellow loosestrife)

To 32 in., colonial. Flowers yellow, showy, June–July; fruit Aug.–Oct. **Habitat requirements:** Open swamps, wet woods, shores (OBL). Tolerant of partial shade. **Notes:** Should be propagated and used. **Uses:** Secondary species for increasing diversity and aesthetics of wetland restoration and mitigation. Pond shores, marshes. Possibly a useful element for erosion control.

Lysimachia thyrsiflora (tufted loosestrife)

To 2 ft., colonial. Flowers yellow, May–July. **Habitat requirements:** Cold northern swamps, acid bogs (OBL). NYC southern limit. **Uses:** Minor element for increasing diversity and aesthetics of wetland restoration and mitigation. Possibly a useful element for erosion control in appropriate habitats.

Lythrum alatum (winged loosestrife)

To 4 ft. Flowers purple, July–Aug.; fruit Sept.–Oct. **Habitat requirements:** Open swamps, marshes, wet soil (FACW+). **Notes:** *Warning! Lythrum salicaria* (purple loosestrife) is a notoriously invasive wetland plant from Eurasia. Still sold as a garden plant. **Uses:** Secondary species for increasing diversity and aesthetics of wetland restoration and mitigation. Possibly horticultural.

Maianthemum canadense (Canada mayflower)

To 8 in., leaves to about 4 in., colonial, starting very slowly. Flowers white, May–June; fruit fleshy, speckled, becoming red, June–Aug. (often persisting

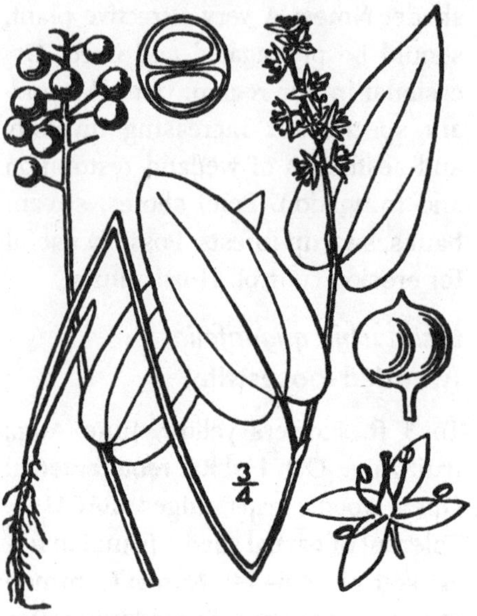

Maianthemum canadense

until Nov.). **Habitat requirements:** Moist, beech, oak, or conifer woods (FAC). Found in soil with pH 4.4–5.4, tolerates acid soils down to pH 3.8. Very shade tolerant. **Notes:** A frequent summer ground cover in NYC forest understories. Difficult to establish, but should be used more often in forest restoration. **Uses:** Secondary species for increased diversity and aesthetics in restoration of moist forest understories with Solomon's seal, false Solomon's seal, sessile-leaved bellwort, and wild sarsaparilla.

Medeola virginiana (Indian cucumber-root)

To 28 in. Flowers greenish yellow, May–June; fruit July. **Habitat requirements:** Rich, moist woods (UPL). Tolerant of shade. **Uses:** Secondary species for increased diversity and aesthetics in restoration of dry to moist forest understories in rich soil.

Melanthium virginicum (bunch flower)

Rare (NYS SH, E); to 4 ft. Flowers greenish, June–July; fruit Aug.–Sept. Poisonous. **Habitat requirements:** Swamp forests, wet meadows (FACW+). Tolerant of partial shade. NYC apparently the northern limit. **Notes:** Plant with cooperation of state conservation organizations. Use local stock. **Uses:** Minor element for increasing diversity and aesthetics of wetland restoration in appropriate habitats.

Mentha arvensis var. *canadensis* (wild mint)

To 30 in., plant fragrant. Flowers lilac, July–Aug.; fruit to Sept. **Habitat requirements:** Shores, wet meadows, open swamp forests (FACW). Soil pH 5–7. Tolerant of partial shade. **Notes:** *Warning! Mentha arvensis* var. *arvensis* is European. Be sure to obtain the native variety, sometimes categorized as *M. canadensis*. **Uses:** Minor element for increasing diversity, wetland restoration and mitigation.

Menyanthes trifoliata (buckbean)

Emergent, to 1 ft., colonial. Flowers white, May–June; fruit Aug.–Sept. **Habitat requirements:** Quiet, shallow water, bogs, marshes (OBL). Needs acid soil, pH 4.8–6.5. **Notes:** Unusual, interesting appearance. **Uses:** Minor element for increasing diversity and aesthetics of bog restoration. Possibly useful for erosion control in appropriate habitats.

Mertensia virginica (Virginia bluebells)

Spring ephemeral, to 28 in., disappears by July. Flowers blue, showy, April–May. **Habitat requirements:** Moist to wet forests, floodplains, rich, moist, well-drained soil (FACW). Soil pH 4.5–8.0. Found in Central NJ but not in NYC. Mostly south and west of our region. **Uses:** Secondary species for aesthetic enhancement and diversity of moist to wet woodlands, floodplain forests. Horticultural.

Mimulus alatus (winged monkey flower)

Rare (NYS S3, R); to 3 ft. Flowers pink-purple, showy, July–Aug.; fruit to Sept. **Habitat requirements:** Swamp forests, shady stream banks, wet meadows (OBL). Soil pH 6.2–7.8. Tolerant of partial shade. **Notes:** Plant with cooperation of conservation organizations. Use local stock. **Uses:** Minor element for increased diversity and aesthetics in wetland restoration.

Mimulus ringens (monkey flower)

To 3 ft. Flowers pink-purple, showy, July–Aug.; fruit Aug.–Sept. **Habitat requirements:** Swamp forests, gaps, wet meadows (OBL). Tolerant of partial shade. **Notes:** Individual plants not persistent but reproduces easily from seed. **Uses:** Secondary species for aesthetic enhancement and diversity of moist to wet woodland and wet meadow restoration.

Mitchella repens (partridge berry)

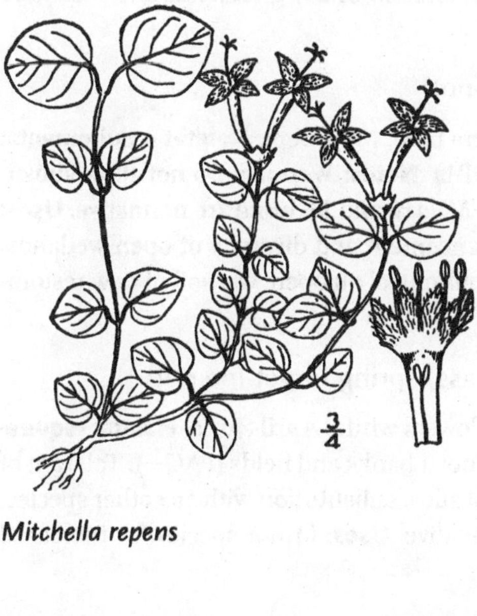

Mitchella repens

To 8 in., usually prostrate, evergreen, colonial, stems creeping. Flowers white, June–July; fruit fleshy, red, Aug.–Oct., persistent. Eaten by birds and small mammals. **Habitat requirements:** Rich, moist to dry woods (FACU). Tolerant of shade. Uncommon in NYC, usually indicative of mature, undisturbed, forest habitats. Tolerates acid soils. Found in soil pH 5.0. **Uses:** Secondary species for increased diversity and aesthetics in restoration of moist forest understories.

Mitella diphylla (mitrewort)

To 16 in., colonial. Flowers white, April–May; fruit May–June. **Habitat requirements:** Rich, moist woods (FACU). Tolerant of shade. **Uses:** Secondary species for increased diversity and aesthetics in restoration of moist forest understories.

Monarda didyma (Oswego tea, bee balm)

To 4 ft., colonial, plant fragrant. Flowers red, showy, July–Aug.; fruit Sept.–Oct. Host for some butterfly species. Attractive to hummingbirds. **Habitat requirements:** Open, moist woods, meadows (FAC+). Tolerant of partial shade. Not very persistent, apparently outcompeted easily. **Uses:** Secondary species for aesthetic enhancement and diversity of moist to wet open woodland and wet meadow restoration. Horticultural, butterfly, and hummingbird gardens.

Monarda fistulosa (wild bergamot)

To 4 ft., plant fragrant, colonial. Flowers lilac or pink, July–Sept.; fruit Aug.–Oct. Host for some butterfly species. Attractive to hummingbirds. **Habitat requirements:** Upland, open woods (UPL). Soil pH 6–8. Tolerant of partial shade. **Uses:** Secondary species for increased diversity and aesthetics in restoration of dry, open woods, meadows, successional habitats, woodland edges. Butterfly gardens.

Monarda punctata (horsemint)

To 3 ft., plant fragrant. Flowers yellowish with purple spots, July–Oct., fruit Sept.–Oct. Host for some butterfly species. Attractive to hummingbirds. **Habitat requirements:** Dry, open, sandy soil (UPL). **Uses:** Secondary species for increased diversity and aesthetics in restoration of dry grasslands and meadows of coastal plain.

Myosotis laxa (smaller forget-me-not)

Annual to perennial; to 16 in. Flowers blue, May–Sept. **Habitat requirements:** Moist to wet soil or shallow water (OBL). **Notes:** *Warning!* Do not allow substitution with any other species; all but *M. laxa* and *M. verna* are nonnative. **Uses:** Secondary species for aesthetic enhancement and diversity of open wetlands. Addition to seed mix for initial erosion control on open, wet soil of new restoration and mitigation.

Myosotis verna (early scorpion-grass, spring forget-me-not)

Annual or winter annual, to 16 in. Flowers white, April–June. **Habitat requirements:** Rocky, open, upland woods, moist banks and fields (FAC−). Tolerant of partial shade. **Notes:** *Warning!* Do not allow substitution with any other species; all but *M. laxa* and *M. verna* are nonnative. **Uses:** Minor species for increased diversity as an addition to initial erosion control seed mix on open soil of new restoration.

Myriophyllum humile (low-water milfoil)

Aquatic, submerged form to 40 in. long; terrestrial form rooted in mud, stems to 3 in. (may be aggressive in nutrient-rich water). Flowers inconspicuous, June–Oct.; fruit June–Nov. **Habitat requirements:** Ponds, muddy shores (OBL). Seeds and plants eaten by some water fowl. **Notes:** *Warning!* European water milfoil, *M. spicatum,* is a very aggressive, invasive plant. **Uses:** Minor species as cover for fish and invertebrates in ponds, quiet water. Nutrient uptake.

Najas flexilis (northern water nymph)

Annual, submerged, rooted aquatic to 20 in. Flowers inconspicuous, July–Oct. **Habitat requirements:** Shallow fresh to brackish water of lakes and rivers (OBL). Water/soil pH 6.5–7.5. **Uses:** Cover for fish and invertebrates in ponds, quiet water. Possibly also for nutrient uptake.

**Nuphar advena* (*N. lutea*) (southern pond lily, spatterdock)

Colonial rooted, submerged aquatic, leaves to 16 in. wide, floating or emerging above water surface; growth rate slow. Flowers yellow, June–Aug.; fruit to Sept. Wildlife value high. Food for some aquatic birds and some mammals, cover for fish, habitat for invertebrates; shades water surface, preventing high temperatures in hot weather. **Habitat requirements:** Sluggish streams, freshwater tidal and nontidal marshes, ponds in water depth 1–6 ft (OBL). Tolerant of slightly brackish water, partial shade, acidic water down to pH 5. Available. **Uses:** Primary species for increased diversity and aesthetics in restoration of shallow ponds and lake edges. Wetland mitigation and habitat improvement for fish and aquatic invertebrates.

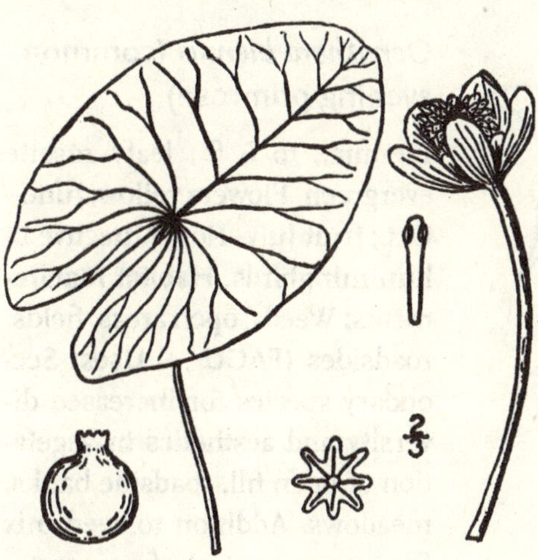

Nuphar microphylla

Nuphar microphylla (small yellow pond lily, yellow cowlily, dwarf spatterdock)

Colonial rooted aquatic, leaves to 4 in. wide, floating. Flowers yellow, June–Sept. **Habitat requirements:** Ponds, 1–6 ft. deep, lake edges (OBL). **Uses:** Primary or secondary species for increased diversity and aesthetics in restoration of shallow ponds and lake edges. Wetland mitigation and habitat improvement for fish and invertebrates.

Nuphar variegata (yellow pond lily, spatterdock)

Colonial rooted aquatic, leaves to 6 in. wide, floating. Flowers yellow, June–Sept. **Habitat requirements:** Ponds 1–6 ft. deep, lake edges (OBL). **Uses:** Primary or secondary species for increased diversity and aesthetics in restoration of shallow ponds and lake edges. Wetland mitigation and habitat improvement for fish and invertebrates.

**Nymphaea odorata* (water lily)

Colonial rooted, aquatic, leaves to 10 in. wide, floating. Flowers white, showy, fragrant, July–Aug.; fruit to Sept. Wildlife value moderate. Food for some aquatic birds and some mammals, cover for fish, habitat for invertebrates; shades water surface preventing high temperatures in hot weather. **Habitat requirements:** Ponds in water depth 1–6 ft., freshwater tidal areas (OBL). Intolerant of salinity over 0.5 ppt. **Notes:** Occasional in our region. Available. **Uses:** Primary species for increased diversity and aesthetics in restoration of shallow ponds and lake edges. Wetland mitigation and habitat improvement for fish and invertebrates. Water gardens, decorative.

Nymphoides cordata (little floating heart)

Colonial floating aquatic, leaves to 2 in. wide. Flowers white, small, July–Aug. Provides cover and shade for fish and invertebrates. **Habitat requirements:** Quiet water (OBL). **Notes:** *Warning! N. peltata* is an invasive exotic species with larger yellow flowers. **Uses:** Secondary species for increased diversity and aesthetics in restoration of shallow ponds and lake edges. Wetland mitigation and habitat improvement.

Oenothera biennis

Oenothera biennis (common evening primrose)

Biennial, to 6 ft., leafy rosette evergreen. Flowers yellow, June–Oct.; fruit July–Nov. Attractive to hummingbirds. **Habitat requirements:** Weedy, open areas, fields, roadsides (FACU−). **Uses:** Secondary species for increased diversity and aesthetics in vegetation of open fill, roadside banks, meadows. Addition to seed mix for erosion control of new restoration, roadside banks.

Oenothera fruticosa (sundrops)

To 3 ft. Flowers yellow, showy, June–Aug.; fruit July–Sept. Attractive to hummingbirds. **Habitat requirements:** Meadows, fields, disturbed sites, thin woods, marsh edges (FAC). Soil pH 4.5–7.0. Tolerant of bright, partial shade. **Uses:** Secondary species for increased diversity and aesthetics in vegetation of moist roadside banks, meadows, brackish marsh edges. Horticultural.

Oenothera parviflora (northern evening primrose)

Biennial, to 6 ft. Flowers yellow, July–Sept. Attractive to hummingbirds. **Habitat requirements:** Fields, disturbed habitats, rocky, calcareous soils, open woods (FACU−). Tolerant of bright, partial shade. Should tolerate concrete debris. **Uses:** Secondary species for increased diversity and aesthetics in vegetation of open concrete fill, roadside banks, meadows.

Oenothera perennis (small sundrops)

To 2 ft. Flowers yellow, showy, May–July; fruit June–Aug. Attractive to hummingbirds. **Habitat requirements:** Meadows, fields, open woods (FAC−). Tolerant of partial shade. **Uses:** Secondary species for increased diversity and aesthetics in vegetation of moist roadside banks, meadows, wetland edges.

Onosmodium virginianum (false gromwell)

To 2 ft., bristly. Flowers yellow or orange, June–July; fruit July–Aug. **Habitat requirements:** Sandy soil of barrens, upland oak woods (UPL). Tolerant of partial shade. **Uses:** Secondary species for increased diversity and aesthetics in restoration of open or oak barren habitats.

Opuntia humifusa (prickly pear cactus)

About 1 ft., evergreen, colonial, prickly. Flowers yellow, showy, June–July; fruit fleshy, reddish, edible, Oct.–Nov. **Habitat requirements:** Coastal back dunes, sometimes on cliffs or rocks in full sun (UPL). **Uses:** Secondary or minor species for holding sand, increased diversity, and aesthetics in back-dune restoration.

Orontium aquaticum (golden club)

Rare (NYS S2, T); emergent, to 30 in., colonial. Flowers yellow, April–June; fruit July–Aug. **Habitat requirements:** Shallow water along sandy or muddy shores, acid bogs, Atlantic white cedar swamps (OBL). Tolerant of partial shade. **Uses:** Secondary species for aesthetic enhancement and diversity of swamp or pond shore restoration. Plant in coordination with conservation organizations.

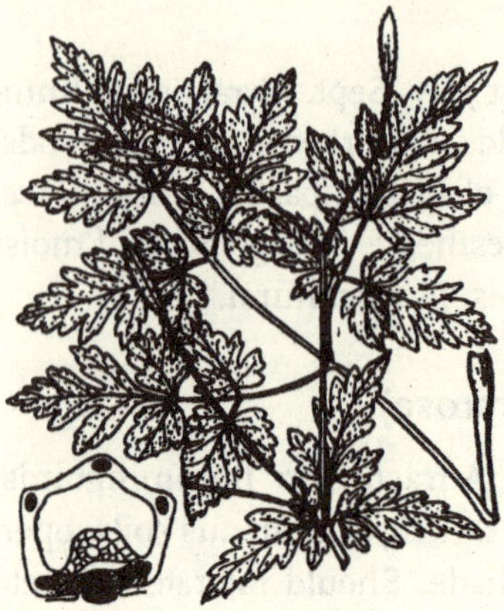

Osmorhiza claytonii

Osmorhiza claytonii (hairy sweet cicely)

To 2 ft. Flowers white, May–June; fruit June–Aug. Host for some butterfly species. **Habitat requirements:** Rich, moist woods (FACU). Tolerant of shade. **Uses:** Secondary species for increased diversity and aesthetics in restoration of moist, mixed deciduous woodlands. Butterfly gardens.

Osmorhiza longistylis (anise root)

To 3 ft., plant anise scented. Flowers white, May–June; fruit July–Aug. Host for some butterfly species. **Habitat requirements:** Rich, moist woods, floodplain forests (FACU−). Tolerant of shade. **Uses:** Secondary species for increased diversity and aesthetics in restoration of moist, mixed deciduous woodland understories. Butterfly gardens.

Oxalis stricta (*O. dillenii*) (common yellow wood sorrel)

To 20 in., colonial. Flowers yellow, May–Nov.; fruit June–Nov. **Habitat requirements:** Weed of roadsides, disturbed woodlands, and fields (UPL). Tolerant of partial shade. **Uses:** Secondary or minor species for increased diversity and aesthetics in restoration of open areas; some soil-holding capacity.

Oxalis violacea (violet wood sorrel)

To 16 in. Flowers rose-violet, showy, May–June; fruit Aug.–Oct. **Habitat requirements:** Woods, shady banks, well-drained soil of floodplain forest (UPL). Tolerant of shade. **Uses:** Secondary species for increased diversity and aesthetics in restoration of woodland understories, on small banks and slopes where leaf litter does not collect deeply.

Oxypolis rigidior (cowbane)

Rare (NYS SH, E); to 6 ft., plant poisonous. Flowers white, Aug.–Sept.; fruit Sept.–Oct. Host for some butterfly species. Should attract black swallowtail butterflies and others. **Habitat requirements:** Marshes, bogs, wet woods (OBL). A coastal plain and pine barrens plant. Tolerant of partial shade. **Uses:** Minor element for increased diversity in wetland restoration. Butterfly gardens. Plant in cooperation with conservation organizations.

Panax quinquefolius (American ginseng)

To 2 ft. Flowers white, June–July; fruit fleshy, red, Aug.–Sept. **Habitat requirements:** Rich, cool, moist woods, in deep shade (UPL).Tolerant of shade. **Uses:**

Secondary species for increased diversity and aesthetics in restoration of mixed deciduous forest understories.

Panax trifolius (dwarf ginseng)

Spring ephemeral to 8 in. Flowers white, April–May, fruit fleshy, yellow, May–June. **Habitat requirements:** Rich woods (UPL). **Uses:** Secondary species for increased diversity and aesthetics in restoration of mixed deciduous forest understories, edges of swamp forests.

Parietaria pensylvanica (pellitory)

Annual, to 16 in. Flowers greenish, blooms and fruits June–Sept. **Habitat requirements:** Dry woods, rocky or gravelly shade, circumneutral soil (FACU). Tolerant of shade. **Uses:** Minor species, possibly as addition to annual seed mixes for initial erosion control in shady sites.

Parnassia glauca (grass of Parnassus)

To 16 in., leaves waxy gray-green. Flowers white, July–Sept.; fruit to Oct. **Habitat requirements:** Cold, calcareous bogs, swamps (OBL). Should tolerate concrete debris. **Uses:** Minor element for increased diversity and aesthetics of wetland restoration.

Paronychia canadensis (smooth forked nailwort)

Annual to 16 in., stems very slender. Flowers white, July–Oct. **Habitat requirements:** Open dry woods, sandy, rocky open areas (UPL). Tolerant of partial shade. **Uses:** Minor species, possibly as addition to annual seed mixes.

Paronychia fastigiata (hairy forked nailwort)

Annual to 16 in. Flowers white, July–Oct. **Habitat requirements:** Open dry woods, sandy, rocky open areas (UPL). Tolerant of partial shade. **Uses:** Minor species, possibly as addition to annual seed mixes.

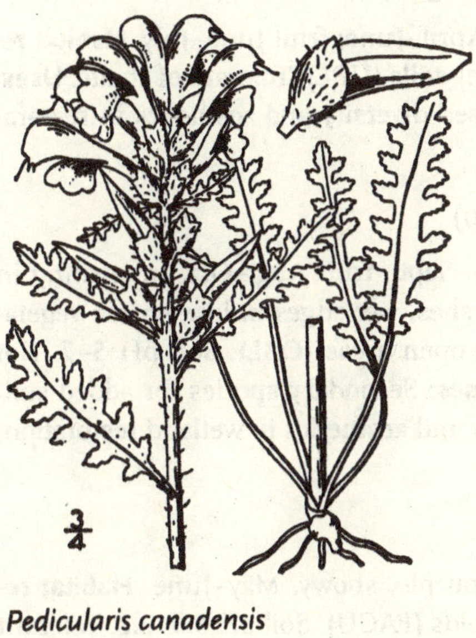

Pedicularis canadensis

Pedicularis canadensis (wood betony)

To 16 in. Flowers yellow, April–May; fruit June–July. **Habitat requirements:** Open, dry to moist woods, gaps, meadows (FACU). Soil pH 4–7. Tolerant of partial shade. **Uses:**

Secondary or minor species for increased diversity and aesthetics in restoration of forest understories.

Pedicularis lanceolata (swamp lousewort)

To 30 in. Flowers pale yellow, Aug.–Sept.; fruit Sept.–Oct. **Habitat requirements:** Swamps, open wet woods (FACW). Often on calcareous soil, should tolerate concrete debris. Tolerant of partial shade. **Uses:** Minor element for increased diversity and aesthetics in wetland restoration and mitigation.

**Peltandra virginica* (arrow arum)

Emergent, to 30 in., colonial, growth rate slow. Flowers green-white, June–July; fruit Aug. Wildlife value moderate. Cover for invertebrates, small fish. Not eaten by muskrats or geese. **Habitat requirements:** Fresh to slightly brackish tidal and nontidal marshes, pond edges (OBL). Soil pH 5.0–9.5. Tolerant of partial shade, concrete debris, tolerates slightly brackish water to 2 ppt salt; inundation to 1 ft. or saturated soil to 100% of growing season. **Notes:** Provides shade for shallow water of pond and lake edges. Available. **Uses:** Primary species for erosion control, vegetation, diversity, and aesthetics in restoration of pond and lake margins. Wetland mitigation.

Penstemon hirsutus (white beard-tongue)

To 32 in. Flowers white and purplish, May–June; fruit July–Aug. **Habitat requirements:** Dry sandy or rocky fields, open woods (UPL). Tolerant of partial shade. **Uses:** Secondary or minor species for increased diversity and aesthetics in restoration of dry woodlands or meadows on sandy or rocky soils.

Penstemon pallidus (eastern beard-tongue)

To 28 in. Flowers white and purplish, April–June; fruit June–July. **Habitat requirements:** Woods, gaps, sandy or loamy soils (UPL). Tolerant of shade. **Uses:** Secondary or minor species for increased diversity and aesthetics in restoration of dry woodlands or meadows.

Penthorum sedoides (ditch stonecrop)

To 2 ft., colonial. Flowers whitish, July–Sept.; fruit Aug.–Oct. Interesting in appearance. **Habitat requirements:** Marshes, wet edges in low, sparse vegetation. Often found in rather disturbed, open areas (OBL). Soil pH 5–7. Not a good competitor in tall vegetation. **Uses:** Secondary species for added soil-holding capacity and increased diversity and aesthetics in wetland restoration, pond edges.

Phlox divaricata (blue phlox)

To 20 in., colonial. Flowers pale blue-purple, showy, May–June. **Habitat requirements:** Moist, rich, open woods, fields (FACU). Soil pH 5.5–7.2. Tolerant of partial shade. **Notes:** Technically native to western and northern NYS, northern NJ, southwestern CT. **Uses:** Secondary or minor species for increased diversity and aesthetics in restoration of open woodlands or meadows. Gardens.

Phlox maculata (wild sweet william)

Rare (NYS S1, E); to 32 in. Flowers red-purple, June–July. **Habitat requirements:** Wet meadows, open floodplains (FACW). **Uses:** Secondary species for added soil-holding capacity and increased diversity and aesthetics in wetland restoration. Plant in cooperation with conservation organizations.

Phlox subulata (mountain phlox)

To 8 in., ground cover. Flowers purple, pink, showy, May–July. **Habitat requirements:** Gravelly, sandy soil, rocky ledges (UPL). Soil pH 5–8. Will be quickly overgrown by taller vegetation in rich soil. **Uses:** Secondary or minor species for increased diversity and aesthetics in restoration of rock outcrops, gravelly meadows. Rock gardens.

Phryma leptostachya

Phryma leptostachya (lopseed)

To 40 in. Flowers purple to white, July–Aug.; fruit Aug.–Sept. **Habitat requirements:** Moist, rich woods (UPL). Tolerant of shade. **Uses:** Secondary or minor species for increased diversity and aesthetics in restoration of woodlands.

Physalis heterophylla (clammy ground cherry)

To 3 ft., colonial. Flowers yellow with dark center, June–Sept.; fruit fleshy, yellow, Aug.–Oct. **Habitat requirements:** Rich, dry, open woods, gaps (UPL). Tolerant of partial shade. **Uses:** Secondary or minor species for increased diversity and aesthetics in restoration of dry, open woodlands or meadows.

Physalis longifolia (long-leaf ground cherry)

To 32 in., colonial. Flowers yellow, July–Sept.; fruit Aug.–Oct. **Habitat requirements:** Dry open fields, rich soil (UPL). **Uses:** Secondary or minor species for increased diversity and aesthetics in restoration of dry meadows.

Physalis pubescens (downy ground-cherry)

Annual, to 1 ft. Flowers yellow with dark center, July–Sept.; fruit yellow, fleshy, July–Oct. **Habitat requirements:** Moist open woods, disturbed soil, back dunes

(FACU−). Tolerant of partial shade. **Uses:** Secondary or minor species for increased diversity and aesthetics in restoration of open woodlands, back dunes, vegetation of sandy fill. Addition to initial erosion control seed mixes for open sites.

Physalis virginiana (Virginia ground-cherry)

Rare (NYS SH, E); to 2 ft., colonial. Flowers yellow, center dark, June–Aug.; fruit fleshy, yellow. **Habitat requirements:** Open rocky woods, gaps (UPL). Tolerant of partial shade. **Uses:** Secondary or minor species for increased diversity and aesthetics in restoration of dry, open woodlands or meadows. Plant in coordination with a conservation organization.

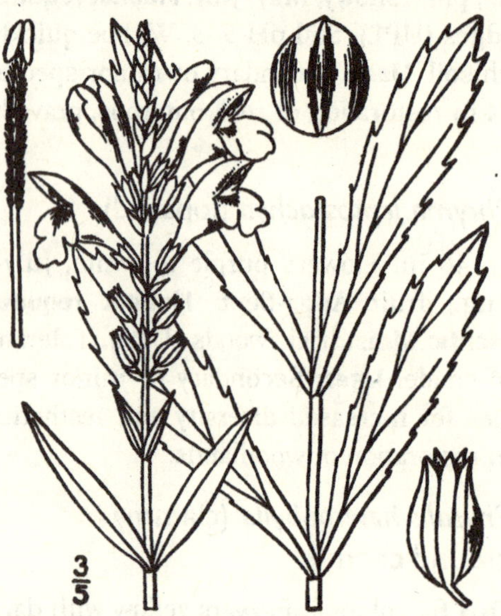

Physostegia virginiana

Physostegia virginiana (obedient plant)

To 5 ft., colonial. Flowers pale pink, showy, July–Aug. **Habitat requirements:** River banks, moist soil (FAC+). **Notes:** Apparently uncommon in our region. **Uses:** Secondary species for added soil-holding capacity and increased diversity and aesthetics in wetland restoration. Horticultural.

Phytolacca americana (pokeweed)

To 9 ft. (usually about 4 ft.), weedy, coarse plant. Flowers white, small, June–Oct.; fruit fleshy, purple, Aug.–Nov. Fruit very attractive to birds, especially valuable to fall migrants. **Habitat requirements:** Fields, woodland gaps, edges (FACU+). Soil pH 4.7–8.0. **Notes:** Common in our region. **Uses:** Secondary or minor species for wildlife value. Let the birds plant this one.

Pilea fontana (springs clearweed)

Annual, to 20 in. Flowers greenish, July–Oct. **Habitat requirements:** Swamps, wet shores (FACW+). **Uses:** Minor species, possibly as addition to annual seed mixes for initial erosion control in wetland restoration and mitigation.

Pilea pumila (clearweed)

Annual, to 20 in. Flowers greenish, July–Oct.; fruit Sept.–Oct. **Habitat requirements:** Moist to wet shade (FACW). **Uses:** Minor species, possibly as addition to annual seed mixes for initial erosion control in shady wetland restoration.

Plantago cordata (heartleaf plantain)

Rare (G4, NYS S3, T); to 12 in. Flowers greenish, May–July. **Habitat requirements:** Stream and swap forests (OBL). Lower Hudson River estuary. **Notes:** Apparently not found in NJ. Plant in coordination with conservation groups. **Uses:** Minor component for diversity and aesthetics in wetland mitigation and restoration in appropriate areas.

Plantago maritima (*Plantago oliganthos*) (seaside plantain)

Rare (S2S3, T); to 8 in. Flowers greenish, July–Sept. **Habitat requirements:** Coastal. High salt marsh, beaches, brackish shores (FACW). **Uses:** Minor species for increased diversity and aesthetics in salt marsh restoration and mitigation. Plant in coordination with conservation groups.

[*Plantago rugelii* (American plantain)

To 15 in., weedy. Flowers greenish, July–Oct. **Habitat requirements:** Moist soil of roadsides, vacant lots (FACU). **Notes:** Almost identical to the more common European *P. major*, very difficult to distinguish and not recommended.]

Plantago virginica (pale-seed plantain)

Spring ephemeral, to 8 in. Flowers pale greenish, April–June. **Habitat requirements:** Dry, open, sandy soil (UPL). **Uses:** Secondary or minor species for increased diversity and aesthetics in restoration of dry, open sites.

Pluchea odorata (*Pluchea purpurascens*) (salt marsh fleabane)

Annual, to 2 ft., plant aromatic. Flowers pink-purple, showy, blooms and fruits July–Sept. **Habitat requirements:** Coastal. High salt marshes, open brackish shores (FACW). **Uses:** Secondary or minor species for increased diversity and aesthetics in salt-marsh restoration and mitigation.

Podophyllum peltatum (mayapple)

To 20 in., colonial, spreading slowly at first. Flowers white, showy, May–June; fruit fleshy, yellow, Aug.–Sept. Fruit eaten by turtles, possibly by mammals. **Habitat requirements:** Moist woods, edges (FACU). Tolerant of shade. Tolerates soil acidity down to pH 3.9. **Uses:** Secondary species for increased diversity and aesthetics in restoration of moist forest understories.

Polygonatum biflorum (smooth Solomon's seal)

To 4 ft. Flowers greenish white, May–June; fruit fleshy, blue, July–Aug. **Habitat requirements:** Mixed woods, moist to dry sandy or rocky soils (FACU). Frequent in our woodlands. Tolerates soil pH 3.9–7.6. Tolerant of shade.

Polygonatum biflorum

Notes: Usually an indicator of high-quality, mature forest. Occasionally a remnant in disturbed forests. **Uses:** Secondary species for increased diversity and aesthetics in restoration of moist forest understories with Canada mayflower, false Solomon's seal, bellwort, and wild sarsaparilla.

Polygonatum pubescens (hairy Solomon's seal)

To 3 ft. Flowers greenish white, May–June; fruit fleshy, blue, July–Aug. **Habitat requirements:** Rich, moist to dry woods, rocky soil (UPL). Tolerates soil acidity down to pH 3.9. Found in moist forest soil pH 5–7.6. Tolerant of shade. **Notes:** Frequent in our woodlands. Usually an indicator of high quality mature forest. **Uses:** Secondary species for increased diversity and aesthetics in restoration of moist forest understories with Canada mayflower, false Solomon's seal, bellwort, and wild sarsaparilla.

Polygonella articulata (jointweed)

Annual, to 20 in. Flowers small, white to pink; blooms and fruits Sept.–Oct. **Habitat requirements:** Dry, acid, sandy soil of coastal plain, back dunes (UPL). **Notes:** Occasional in our region. **Uses:** Secondary species for increased diversity and aesthetics in restoration of coastal dune communities. Addition to annual seed mix for open dry soil in newly restored sites.

Polygonum amphibium (water smartweed)

Floating to emergent, to 3 ft., colonial. Flowers pink to red, July–Sept. Seeds eaten by waterfowl. **Habitat requirements:** Saturated soil, or water to 3 ft. deep (OBL). Soil pH 4–7. **Uses:** Minor component for diversity and aesthetics in wetland mitigation and restoration. Cover for fish, food for waterfowl.

Polygonum arifolium (halberd-leaved tearthumb)

Annual to 6 ft. long, reclining on other plants, stems prickly. Flowers pink, Aug.–Sept.; fruit to Oct. **Habitat requirements:** Open freshwater tidal and nontidal marshes, swamps, wet meadows (OBL). **Uses:** Secondary species for

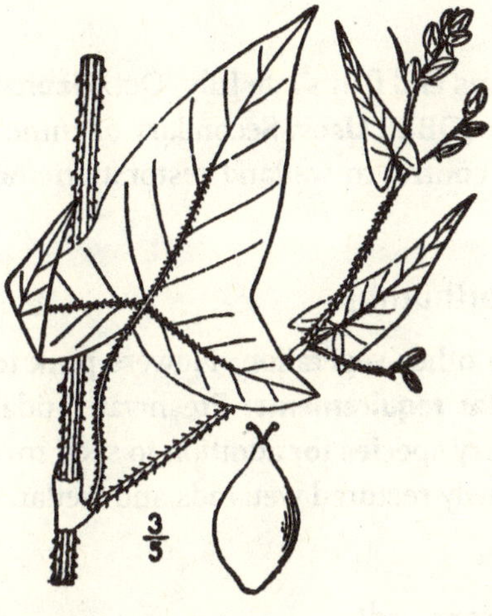

Polygonum arifolium

addition to seed mix for initial erosion control on open soil of newly restored wetlands and wetland mitigation

Polygonum hydropiperoides (mild water-pepper)

To 6 ft., reclining, colonial. Flowers pink (white); blooms and fruits July–Oct. Wildlife value moderate. **Habitat requirements:** Freshwater tidal and nontidal marshes, wet soil (OBL). Soil pH 4.5–8.0. Tolerant of partial shade; flooding or saturated soil to 100% of growing season. Intolerant of salt and drought. **Notes:** Occasional in our region. **Uses:** Minor species for diversity and aesthetics in restoration of marsh and swamp habitats. Wetland mitigation.

Polygonum pensylvanicum (Pennsylvania smartweed)

Annual, to 6 ft., reseeds well. Flowers pink, June–Oct.; fruit Aug.–Nov. Wildlife value high (seeds). **Habitat requirements:** Rich, moist to wet soil, marshes, wet meadows (FACW). Soil pH 4.0–8.5. Should tolerate concrete debris. Intolerant of shade, salt. **Notes:** Frequent in our region. **Uses:** Minor species for diversity and aesthetics in restoration of open swamps or wet meadows. Wetland mitigation. Additions to wetland erosion control seed mixes.

Polygonum punctatum (dotted smartweed)

To 3 ft. Flowers greenish white, July–Oct.; fruit Sept.–Oct. Wildlife value moderate. Seeds eaten by birds and small mammals. **Habitat requirements:** Freshwater tidal and nontidal marshes, pond edges, wet ditches (OBL). Prefers slightly alkaline soils, pH 6.0–8.7. Tolerant of flooding or saturated soils to 100% of growing season. Should tolerate concrete debris. Intolerant of shade, salt. **Notes:** Occasional in our region. **Uses:** Minor species for diversity in restoration of open swamps or wet meadows. Wetland mitigation.

Polygonum ramosissimum (bushy knotweed)

Annual, to 40 in. Flowers green; blooms and fruits Aug.–Oct. **Habitat requirements:** Moist to wet soil, open areas (FAC). Apparently tolerant of saline habitats. **Uses:** Secondary species for addition to annual seed mix for open dry soil in newly restored sites. Probably useful for roadside mixes.

Polygonum robustius (stout smartweed)

To over 40 in., colonial. Flowers white; blooms and fruits late July–Oct. **Habitat requirements:** Wet, open soil, shallow water (OBL). **Uses:** Secondary or minor species for increased diversity and erosion control in wetland restoration and mitigation.

Polygonum sagittatum (arrow-leaved tearthumb)

Annual to 6 ft., stems slender reclining on other vegetation. Flowers pink to green; blooms and fruits Aug.–Nov. **Habitat requirements:** Freshwater tidal and nontidal marshes (OBL). **Uses:** Secondary species for addition to seed mix for initial erosion control on open soil of newly restored wetlands and wetland mitigation.

**Polygonum virginianum* (*Tovara v.*) (jumpseed)

To 6 ft, colonial. Flowers greenish white, July–Oct.; fruit Aug.–Nov. **Habitat requirements:** Woods, floodplain forests (FAC). Tolerant of shade. Widely tolerant of soil types and moisture regimes. **Notes:** Common in disturbed woodlands. A sturdy, urban forest plant. **Uses:** Primary species for erosion control, and soil cover in degraded forest understories. Plant along with white wood aster, Virginia creeper, heart-leaved aster, white snake root, and Pennsylvania sedge. Can be planted through jute mat.

**Pontederia cordata* (pickerelweed)

Emergent, to 3 ft., colonial, growth rate moderate. Flowers blue, spike showy, July–Sept. Wildlife value high, cover for fish, invertebrates, shading water to prevent high temperatures. Plants eaten by muskrats and geese. **Habitat requirements:** Shallow water, to 1 ft. but tolerates brief tidal submersion, pond edges, freshwater to slightly brackish tidal marshes (OBL). Circumneutral to alkaline soil, soil pH 6–8. Tolerant of partial shade, brackish water to 3 ppt salt, flooding or saturated soil to 100% of growing season. Should tolerate alkaline fill and concrete debris. **Notes:** Occasional in our region, often planted in wetland mitigations. Available. **Uses:** Primary species for erosion control, diversity, and aesthetics in restoration of pond and lake edges, marshes. Wetland mitigation.

Potamogeton amplifolius (big-leaf pondweed)

Colonial, submerged, rooted aquatic with some floating leaves. Flowers greenish spikes, June–July; fruit July–Oct. Wildlife value high. Provides shade and shelter for fish and invertebrates, seeds and plants eaten by many waterfowl, also by muskrats. **Habitat requirements:** Ponds, lakes, and streams in water not more than 6 ft. deep (OBL). **Notes:** *Warning!* The European species, *P. crispus*, with wavy leaf margins, is very invasive. *Do not use.* **Uses:** Secondary species for habitat improvement of ponds, lake shallows. Wetland mitigation with open water habitat.

Potamogeton diversifolius (common snailseed-pondweed)

Rare (NYS S1, E); colonial, submerged, rooted aquatic with some floating leaves, stems to 4 ft long. Flowers greenish spikes, June–July; fruit July–Oct. Wildlife value high. Provides shade and shelter for fish and invertebrates; seeds and plants eaten by many waterfowl, also by muskrats. **Habitat requirements:** Shallow ponds, lake edges, and streams in water not more than 4 ft. deep (OBL). **Uses:** Secondary species for habitat improvement of shallow ponds. Wetland mitigation with open water habitat. Plant in cooperation with conservation organizations.

Potamogeton foliosus

Potamogeton foliosus (leafy pondweed)

Colonial, submerged, rooted aquatic with some floating leaves. Flowers greenish spikes, July–Sept.; fruit July–Sept. Wildlife value high. Provides shade and shelter for fish and invertebrates; seeds and plants eaten by many waterfowl, also by muskrats. **Habitat requirements:** Shallow ponds, in water not more than 2 ft. deep (OBL). **Uses:** Secondary species for habitat improvement of shallow ponds. Wetland mitigation with open water habitat.

Potamogeton gramineus (variable pondweed)

Colonial, submerged, rooted aquatic with some floating leaves. Flowers greenish spikes (rarely blooms), June; fruit July–Sept. Wildlife value high. Provides shade and shelter for fish and invertebrates; seeds and plants eaten by many waterfowl, also by muskrats. **Habitat requirements:** Ponds, lakes, and streams in water not more than 3 ft. deep (OBL). **Uses:** Secondary species for habitat improvement of shallow ponds. Wetland mitigation with open water habitat.

Potamogeton natans (floating pondweed)

Colonial, submerged, rooted aquatic with some floating leaves to 5 ft. long. Flowers greenish spikes; blooms and fruits July–Aug. Wildlife value high. Provides shade and shelter for fish and invertebrates; seeds and plants eaten by many waterfowl, also by muskrats. **Habitat requirements:** Ponds, lakes, and streams in water not more than 4 ft. deep (OBL). Uses: Secondary species for habitat improvement of shallow ponds. Wetland mitigation with open water habitat.

**Potamogeton pectinatus* (sago pondweed)

Colonial, submerged, rooted aquatic, to 2 ft. long. Water depth less than 2 ft. depending on turbidity. Flowers pinkish; blooms and fruits May–July. Wildlife value very high. Eaten by many waterfowl, muskrats; shelter for fish and invertebrates; provides shade during hot weather. **Habitat requirements:** Prefers alkaline, high-nutrient water, pH 7–10 (OBL). Tolerates brackish tidal water (2–10 ppt salt) and strong currents. Intolerant of wave action. **Notes:** *Warning!* May be aggressive. Available. **Uses:** Primary species for improvement of eutrophic ponds and brackish water.

Potamogeton perfoliatus (redhead grass)

Colonial, submerged, rooted aquatic, stems short. Growth rate rapid. Flowers June–July; fruit July–Sept. Wildlife value high. Eaten by waterfowl; shelter for fish and invertebrates; provides shade during hot weather. **Habitat requirements:** Fresh and brackish tidal areas, ponds, streams, water depth 1–3 ft., depending on turbidity, freshwater to brackish tidal zones, below mean low water (OBL). Prefers alkaline water. Tolerates brackish water to 5 ppt salt. **Uses:** Potential improvement of eutrophic ponds and brackish water.

Potamogeton pulcher (spotted pondweed)

Rare (NYS S2, T); submerged, rooted aquatic, colonial from rhizomes, stems to 5 ft. Growth rate rapid. Flowers May–July; fruit June–July. Wildlife value high. **Habitat requirements:** Prefers shallow acid water and muddy shores, water depth to 5 ft., depending on turbidity (OBL). **Uses:** Potential improvement of small ponds. Eaten by waterfowl; shelter for fish and invertebrates; provides shade during hot weather.

Potamogeton pusillus (slender pondweed)

Colonial, submerged, rooted aquatic, stems to 5 ft. Growth rate rapid. Flowers May–June; fruit June–Sept. Wildlife value high. Eaten by waterfowl; shelter for fish and invertebrates; provides shade during hot weather. **Habitat requirements:** Water depth to 5 ft., depending on turbidity (OBL). Tolerates acid to alkaline water. **Uses:** Secondary species for habitat improvement of ponds, lake edges. Wetland mitigation with open water habitat.

Potamogeton spirillus (northern snailseed-pondweed)

Colonial, submerged, rooted aquatic with some floating leaves, stems to 5 ft long. Flowers greenish spikes, June–Aug.; fruit July–Oct. Wildlife value high. Provides shade and shelter for fish and invertebrates; seeds and plants eaten by many waterfowl, also by muskrats. **Habitat requirements:** Shallow ponds, lake edges, and streams in water not more than 5 ft. deep (OBL). **Uses:** Secondary species for habitat improvement of shallow ponds. Wetland mitigation with open water habitat.

***Potentilla anserina* (*Argentina anserina*) (silverweed)**

To 1 ft., colonial, open ground cover. Flowers yellow, June–Aug., leaves silvery-hairy. **Habitat requirements:** Open, moist to wet gravelly or sandy soil, shores (OBL). Soil pH 7–8. **Uses:** Minor species for increased diversity and aesthetics in restoration of open shores, wet sandy soil. Some soil-holding capacity possible.

Potentilla arguta

***Potentilla arguta* (tall Potentilla)**

To 3 ft. Flowers white, May–June; fruit July–Aug. **Habitat requirements:** Dry, rocky, open woods, fields (UPL). Soil pH 6–8. Tolerant of partial shade. **Uses:** Secondary or minor species for increased diversity and aesthetics in restoration of dry woodlands, fields, edges.

***Potentilla canadensis* (running cinquefoil)**

To about 1.5 ft. or prostrate, colonial ground cover. Flowers yellow, April–June. **Habitat requirements:** Dry to moist soil in woods and fields (UPL). **Uses:** Secondary species for addition to erosion control plantings and soil cover in degraded, open woodlands, roadsides and meadows. **Notes:** Very similar to *P. simplex*.

***Potentilla simplex* (old-field cinquefoil)**

Semievergreen, to 1 ft., colonial ground cover. Flowers yellow, April–June; fruit to July. **Habitat requirements:** Open woods, edges, low meadows, roadsides, mowed areas (FACU−). Tolerant of partial shade. **Uses:** Secondary species for addition to erosion control plantings and soil cover in degraded, open woodlands, roadsides, and low meadows.

***Prenanthes alba* (rattlesnake root)**

To 5 ft., leaves with whitish bloom. Flowers white, Sept.–Oct. **Habitat requirements:** Rich dry to moist woods (FACU). Tolerant of shade. **Uses:** Secondary or minor species for increased diversity and aesthetics in restoration of moist, mixed deciduous forest understories.

Prenanthes altissima (tall rattlesnake root)

To 6 ft., basal leaves variable, interesting. Flowers whitish, Aug.–Oct. **Habitat requirements:** Moist, rich woods (FACU). Tolerant of shade. **Uses:** Secondary or minor species for increased diversity and aesthetics in restoration of moist, mixed deciduous forest understories.

Prenanthes serpentaria (lion's foot)

To 5 ft., basal leaves variable, interesting. Flowers yellowish, Aug.–Oct. **Habitat requirements:** Dry woods, sandy soil (UPL). Tolerant of shade. **Uses:** Secondary or minor species for increased diversity and aesthetics in restoration of oak barren woodlands, mixed woodlands on dry, sandy soils.

Prenanthes trifoliolata (gall-of-the-earth)

Prenanthes trifoliolata

To 7 ft., basal leaves variable, interesting. Flowers whitish, Aug.–Oct. **Habitat requirements:** Dry to moist woods, gaps, edges, in sandy soil (UPL). Found in forest soil pH 5.0–5.2. Tolerant of partial shade. **Notes:** Occasional in our region. **Uses:** Secondary or minor species for increased diversity and aesthetics in restoration of dry woodlands on sandy soils.

Proserpinaca palustris (mermaid-weed)

Colonial submerged to emergent, rooted aquatic. Flowers small, purplish, June–Sept.; fruit July–Oct. **Habitat requirements:** Shallow water, swamps, marshes, shores (OBL). **Uses:** Secondary species for habitat improvement of shallow ponds, marshes. Wetland mitigation.

Ptilimnium capillaceum (mock bishop's weed)

To 3 ft.. Flowers white, July–Sept.; fruit Aug.–Oct. Host for some butterfly species. **Habitat requirements:** Marshes (OBL). Tolerant of brackish water. **Uses:** Minor species for increased diversity in restoration of open wetlands, brackish marshes.

Pycnanthemum clinopodioides (basil mountain mint)

To 3 ft., plant fragrant. Flowers purple to white, July–Sept. **Habitat requirements:** Open, rocky woods, slopes (UPL). Tolerant of partial shade. **Uses:** Secondary or minor species for increased diversity and aesthetics in restoration of dry, open woodlands, coastal grasslands and dry meadows.

Pycnanthemum incanum (hoary mountain mint)

To 40 in. Flowers white and purple, July–Sept.; fruit Sept.–Oct. **Habitat requirements:** Dry, open, rocky, or sandy woods (UPL). Tolerant of partial shade. **Uses:** Secondary or minor species for increased diversity and aesthetics in restoration of dry, open woodlands.

Pycnanthemum muticum (blunt mountain mint)

Rare (NYS S2S3, T); to 3 ft., plant fragrant. Flowers purple to white, July–Sept.; fruit Sept.–Oct. **Habitat requirements:** Moist to wet meadows or open woods (FACW). Tolerant of partial shade. **Notes:** Plant in coordination with a conservation organization. Use local stock. **Uses:** Secondary or minor species for increased diversity and aesthetics in restoration of wet meadows or woods.

Pycnanthemum tenuifolium (slender mountain mint)

To 32 in. Flowers white, purple dotted, June–Aug.; fruit Sept.–Oct. **Habitat requirements:** Dry to moist open meadows, open woods (FACW). Tolerant of partial shade. **Uses:** Secondary or minor species for increased diversity and aesthetics in restoration of moist meadows or open woods.

Pycnanthemum torrei (Torrey's mountain mint)

Rare (NYS S1, E); to 4 ft., plant fragrant. Flowers white, July–Sept.; fruit Sept.–Oct. **Habitat requirements:** Open woods, fields, dry soil (UPL). Tolerant of partial shade. **Notes:** Plant in coordination with a conservation organization. Use local stock. **Uses:** Secondary or minor species for increased diversity and aesthetics in restoration of dry, open woodlands, meadows, grasslands.

2/3

Pycnanthemum virginianum

Pycnanthemum virginianum (Virginia mountain mint)

To 3 ft., plant fragrant. Flowers white, July–Sept.; fruit Sept.–Oct. **Habitat requirements:** Open woods, fields (UPL). Tolerant of partial shade. **Uses:** Secondary or minor species for increased diversity and aesthetics in restoration of dry open woodlands, meadows, grasslands.

Ranunculus abortivus (small-flowered crow-foot)

To 20 in. Flowers yellow, small, April–June; fruit June–Sept. **Habitat requirements:** Wet woods, shores (FACW). Soil pH 5.0–7.5. Tolerant of partial shade.

Uses: Minor species for increased diversity in restoration of wet woodlands, open areas.

Ranunculus ambigens (spearwort)

To 3 ft., colonial, reclining. Flowers yellow, June–July; fruit July–Aug. **Habitat requirements:** Marshes, pond shores, in heavy soil (OBL). **Uses:** Minor species for increased diversity and aesthetics in restoration of open wetlands. May also have erosion control capacity.

Ranunculus fascicularis

Ranunculus fascicularis (early buttercup)

To 10 in. Flowers yellow, showy, April–May. **Habitat requirements:** Open woods, ledges, on thin, often calcareous, soil (FACU). Should tolerate concrete debris. Tolerant of partial shade. **Notes:** Probably a poor competitor in better soils. **Uses:** Secondary or minor species for increased diversity and aesthetics in restoration of dry, open woodlands, rocky areas.

Ranunculus flabellaris (yellow water buttercup)

Emergent, rooted aquatic. Flowers yellow, May–June; fruit July–Aug. Provides shelter for fish and invertebrates, provides shade during hot weather. **Habitat requirements:** Quiet water, ponds, muddy shores (OBL). **Uses:** Secondary species for habitat improvement of shallow ponds. Wetland mitigation with open water habitat.

Ranunculus hispidus (hispid buttercup)

To 3 ft. Flowers yellow, showy, April–May; fruit May–June. **Habitat requirements:** Rich, dry to moist woods (FAC). Soil pH 4.5–8.0. Tolerant of partial shade. **Uses:** Secondary or minor species for increased diversity and aesthetics in restoration of mixed forest understories.

Ranunculus pensylvanicus (bristly buttercup)

Annual or perennial to 28 in. Flowers pale yellow, July–Aug.; fruit July–Sept. **Habitat requirements:** Wet meadows, ditches, marshes (OBL). Soil pH 5.0–7.5. **Uses:** Secondary or minor species for increased diversity in wetland restoration and mitigation. Addition to erosion control seed mixes for new mitigation.

Ranunculus recurvatus (hooked crowfoot)

To 2 ft. Flowers yellow, May–June; fruit to late June. **Habitat requirements:** Moist, rich woods, stream banks (FAC+). Tolerant of shade. **Uses:** Minor species for increased diversity and aesthetics in restoration of wooded wetlands, woodland streams.

Ranunculus trichophyllus (*R. aquatilis*) (white water crowfoot)

Submerged, rooted aquatic. Flowers white, floating, June–July; fruit July–Aug. **Habitat requirements:** Ponds, slow streams (OBL). Apparently tolerates brackish water. **Uses:** Secondary species for habitat improvement, increased diversity, and aesthetics of shallow ponds. Wetland mitigation with open water habitat.

Rhexia virginica (meadow beauty)

To 3 ft. Flowers rose-lavender, showy, July–Sept.; fruit Aug.–Oct. **Habitat requirements:** Wet open meadows, sandy, acid soil (OBL). **Uses:** Minor species for increased diversity and aesthetics in restoration of open wetlands.

Rubus hispidus (swamp dewberry)

To 5 ft., evergreen, colonial, open ground cover, scarcely woody, trailing. Flowers white, June–July; fruit fleshy, black, Aug.–Sept. Wildlife value moderate. **Habitat requirements:** Swamp forests, moist woods, Atlantic white cedar swamps (FACW). Soil, pH 4.5–7.0. Tolerant of shade. Vigorous grower in full sun. **Notes:** Frequent in our woodlands. **Uses:** Secondary species for evergreen ground cover in swamp forest understories, moist woodlands. Some soil-holding capacity for moist, shady habitats. Possibly useful as a horticultural ground cover for moist sites.

Rubus pubescens (dwarf raspberry)

Flowering stems to 16 in., colonial, herbaceous trailer, unarmed. Flowers white, May–July; fruit red fleshy, edible, June–Aug. **Habitat requirements:** Moist woods, bogs, thickets, rocky shores (FACW). Tolerant of partial shade. **Uses:** Secondary species for ground cover in swamp forest understories, moist woodlands. Some soil holding capacity for moist, shady habitats.

Rudbeckia laciniata (cut-leaf coneflower)

10 ft. Flowers yellow, July–Sept.; fruit Aug.–Oct. **Habitat requirements:** Moist to wet soil (FACW). Soil pH 4.5–7.0. Tolerant of partial shade. **Uses:** Minor species for increased diversity in wetland restoration and mitigation.

Rudbeckia triloba (thin-leaved coneflower)

To 5 ft. Flowers yellow, showy, July–Sept.; fruit Sept.–Oct. **Habitat requirements:** Moist open woods, fields (FACU). Tolerant of partial shade. **Uses:**

Secondary or minor species for increased diversity and aesthetics in restoration of open woodlands, meadows.

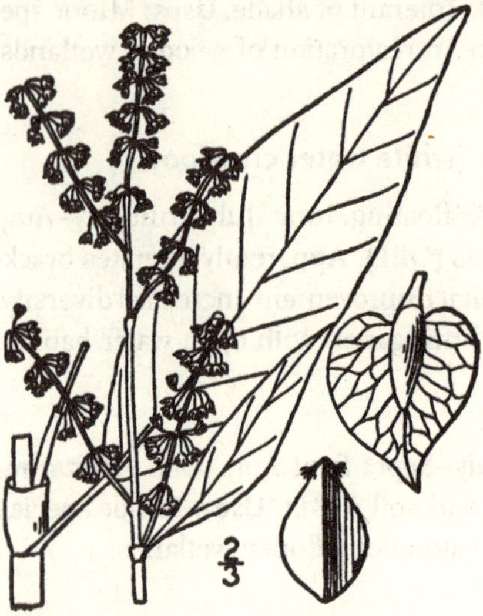

Rumex altissimus

Rumex altissimus **(pale dock)**

To 40 in., leaves pale. Flowers green, April–Aug.; fruit May–Aug. Seeds eaten by many birds. **Habitat requirements:** Moist to wet soil (FACW−). **Uses:** Secondary or minor species for increased diversity in wetland restoration and mitigation.

Rumex orbiculatus **(great water dock)**

To 8 ft., stems stout. Flowers green, June–Sept. **Habitat requirements:** Marshes, shallow water (OBL). **Uses:** Minor species for increased diversity in wetland restoration and mitigation.

Rumex verticillatus **(swamp dock)**

Emergent, to 3 ft., colonial, growth rate slow. Flowers green, becoming brown, June–Sept. Wildlife value high, seeds eaten by birds. **Habitat requirements:** Pond and lake edges, freshwater tidal and nontidal marshes (OBL). Tolerant of partial shade; tolerant of flooding to 0.5 ft. or saturated soil to 100% of growing season. Intolerant of salt. **Uses:** Minor species for increased diversity in wetland restoration and mitigation. An addition to erosion control of pond edges, marshes, shallow water.

Ruppia maritima **(widgeon grass, ditch grass)**

To 2.5 ft. long, rooted, colonial, submerged tidal aquatic. Blooms and fruits July–Oct. Growth rate rapid. Wildlife value high. **Habitat requirements:** Coastal. Sandy substrates, calm, brackish to salt water, 5–20 ppt salt (OBL). Soil pH 5.4–8.5. Water depth 1–6 ft. below mean low water. **Uses:** Potential improvement of eutrophic, brackish water in degraded salt marshes. Eaten by waterfowl, muskrats, shelter for fish and invertebrates, provides shade during hot weather.

Sabatia angularis **(rose pink)**

Rare (NYS S1, E); biennial to 30 in., from a basal rosette. Flowers pink, showy, July–Aug.; fruit Sept.–Oct. **Habitat requirements:** Open meadows, rich, moist, sandy soil (UPL). Probably does not compete well in dense vegetation. Sow seed. **Notes:** Plant in coordination with a conservation organization restoration specialist. Use local stock. **Uses:** Secondary or minor species for increased diversity and aesthetics in restoration of open meadows, successional areas.

Sabatia dodecandra (perennial sea-pink)

To 2 ft. Flowers pink and yellow, showy; blooms and fruits July–Sept. **Habitat requirements:** Coastal. Brackish to salt water of high salt marshes (OBL). **Uses:** Secondary or minor species for increased diversity and aesthetics in salt marsh restoration and mitigation.

Sabatia stellaris (annual sea-pink)

Annual, to 2 ft. Flowers pink, showy; blooms and fruits July–Oct. **Habitat requirements:** Coastal. High salt marsh (FACW+). **Uses:** Secondary or minor species for increased diversity and aesthetics in salt marsh restoration and mitigation.

Sagittaria calycina (spongy arrowhead)

Annual, emergent to submerged, to about 2 ft. Flowers white to purple; blooms and fruits June–Oct. **Habitat requirements:** Coastal. Brackish marshes, estuaries, ponds (OBL). Prefers circumneutral to alkaline water; should tolerate concrete debris. **Uses:** Minor species for increased diversity and aesthetics in restoration and mitigation of open pond edges.

Sagittaria engelmanniana (acid water arrowhead)

Emergent, to 30 in. Flowers white, July–Sept.; fruits Sept.–Oct. **Habitat requirements:** Acid bogs and ponds (OBL). **Uses:** Secondary species for increased diversity and aesthetics in restoration and mitigation of acid bogs. Wetlands of pine and oak barrens.

Sagittaria graminea

Sagittaria graminea (grass-leaved arrowhead)

Emergent to submerged, plant to 2 ft., colonial. Flowers white to pink, June–Aug. Wildlife value moderate. **Habitat requirements:** Swamps, shallow water, mud, freshwater to brackish tidal marshes (OBL). Soil pH 7. Tolerant of brackish water, flooding to 1 ft. for 100% growing season. **Uses:** Secondary or minor species for increased erosion control, diversity, and aesthetics in restoration of pond edges, brackish or freshwater marshes. Wetland mitigation.

**Sagittaria latifolia* (duck potato)

Emergent, to 3 ft., colonial. Flowers white, showy, July–Aug.; fruit Aug.–Sept. Wildlife value high.

Plants and tubers eaten by muskrats and ducks, tubers edible. **Habitat requirements:** Shallow water, saturated soil, pond and lake shores, freshwater tidal marshes (OBL). Soil pH 4.7–8.6. Tolerant of partial shade, tolerant of flooding to 2 ft. for 100% of growing season. Intolerant of salt. **Notes:** Available. **Uses:** Primary species for erosion control, diversity, and aesthetics in restoration of pond edges, marshes. Wetland mitigation.

Sagittaria subulata (Hudson arrowhead)

To 14 in., floating or emergent. Flowers white; blooms and fruits July–Sept. **Habitat requirements:** Coastal to somewhat inland on mudflats. Saline to freshwater tidal marshes (OBL). **Uses:** Secondary or minor species for increased diversity in restoration of high salt marsh habitats.

Salicornia europaea (*Salicornia maritima*) (glasswort, sapphire)

Annual, to 16 in., plant succulent, often turning bright red in autumn. Flowers inconspicuous, bloom July–Oct.; fruit Oct.–Nov. **Habitat requirements:** Coastal; high salt marsh, on open soil (OBL). **Uses:** Minor species for increased diversity in salt marsh restoration.

Salicornia virginica (perennial glasswort)

To 1 ft., colonial, growth rate rapid, forming mats, plants often turn red in autumn. Flowers green, inconspicuous; blooms and fruits Aug.–Oct. Wildlife value low. **Habitat requirements:** Coastal. High salt marsh, high tide to spring tide (high high tide, OBL). Soil pH 6.6–8.5. Tolerant of brackish to ocean water, to 60 ppt salt. Substrate, peat, or soil pH 8. Intolerant of shade. **Uses:** Secondary or minor species for increased diversity in restoration of high salt marsh habitats.

Samolus floribundus (water pimpernel)

To 12 in. Flowers white, June–Oct. **Habitat requirements:** Marshes, muddy ditches (OBL). Tolerant of brackish water. **Uses:** Secondary or minor species for increased diversity in restoration of pond edges, brackish or freshwater marshes. Wetland mitigation.

Sanguinaria canadensis (bloodroot)

Spring ephemeral, to 10 in., colonial, spreads very slowly. Flowers white, showy, March–April; fruit May–June. **Habitat requirements:** Rich, moist to dry woods, often on rocky soil (UPL). **Uses:** Secondary or minor species for increased diversity and aesthetics in restoration of forest understories.

Sanguisorba canadensis

Sanguisorba canadensis (American burnet)

To 5 ft., colonial. Flowers white, June–Oct.; fruit Sept.–Oct. **Habitat requirements:** Wet meadows, acid bogs (FACW+). **Uses:** Secondary or minor species for increased diversity and aesthetics in wetland restoration and mitigation.

Sanicula canadensis (short-styled snakeroot)

To 4 ft. Flowers greenish, May–June; fruit July–Sept. Host for some butterfly species. **Habitat requirements:** Dry, open, woods (UPL). Tolerant of partial shade. **Uses:** Secondary or minor species for increased diversity and aesthetics in restoration of dry, open, woodlands. Butterfly gardens.

Sanicula gregaria (clustered snakeroot)

To 4 ft. Flowers greenish yellow, May–June; fruit Aug.–Sept. Host for some butterfly species. **Habitat requirements:** Rich, moist, rocky woods, thickets (FACU). Tolerant of shade. **Uses:** Secondary or minor species for increased diversity and aesthetics in restoration of rich, moist woodlands, successional shrub lands. Butterfly gardens.

Sanicula marilandica (Maryland sanicle)

To 4 ft. Flowers whitish, May–June; fruit Aug.–Sept. Host for some butterfly species. **Habitat requirements:** Rich, open woods, thickets, shores (UPL). Tolerant of shade. **Uses:** Secondary or minor species for increased diversity and aesthetics in restoration of open woodlands, successional shrub lands. Butterfly gardens.

**Saururus cernuus* (lizard's tail)

To 3 ft., colonial, growth rate rapid. Flowers white, June–Aug.; fruit Aug.–Sept. Wildlife value low. Eaten by muskrats. **Habitat requirements:** Swamp forests, shallow water, freshwater tidal and nontidal marshes, pond edges, wet soil (OBL). Tolerant of open shade. Tolerant of flooding to 100% of growing season. Intolerant of salt. **Notes:** Occasional in our region. Available. **Uses:** Primary to secondary species for erosion control, diversity, and aesthetics in restoration of open swamp forests, pond edges, marshes. Wetland mitigation. Best for use in sites not heavily infested by muskrat.

Saxifraga pensylvanica (swamp saxifrage)

To 4 ft. Flowers greenish white, May; fruit June–July. **Habitat requirements:** Wet meadows, bogs (OBL). **Uses:** Secondary or minor species for increased diversity in wetland restoration and mitigation.

Saxifraga virginiensis (early saxifrage)

To 4 in. Flowers white, April–May; fruit May–June. **Habitat requirements:** Open, rocky woods, ledges, gravelly slopes (FAC). Tolerant of partial shade. **Uses:** Secondary or minor species for increased diversity and aesthetics in restoration of wet to dry rocky ledges, gravelly slopes, rocky woods. Rock gardens.

Scrophularia lanceolata (American figwort)

To 6.5 ft. Flowers reddish brown, May–July. **Habitat requirements:** Open woods, edges, thickets (FACU+). Tolerant of partial shade. **Uses:** Secondary or minor species for increased diversity and aesthetics in restoration of open woodlands, edges, successional shrub lands.

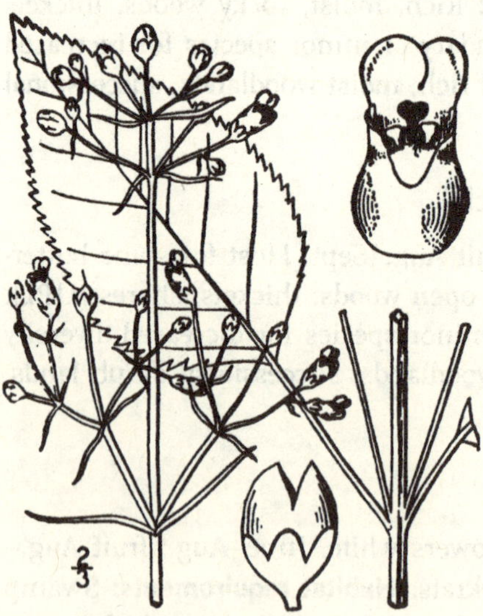

Scrophularia marilandica

Scrophularia marilandica (eastern figwort)

To 10 ft. Flowers reddish brown, July–Sept.; fruit Aug.–Oct. **Habitat requirements:** Rich, open woods, thickets (FACU−). Tolerant of partial shade. **Uses:** Secondary or minor species for increased diversity and aesthetics in restoration of open woodlands, edges.

Scutellaria elliptica (hairy skullcap)

To 8 in. Flowers blue; blooms and fruits June–July. **Habitat requirements:** Dry woods, thickets, meadows (UPL). Tolerant of partial shade. **Uses:** Secondary or minor species for increased diversity and aesthetics in restoration of dry woodlands, successional shrub lands.

Scutellaria galericulata (marsh scullcap)

Colonial, to 32 in. Flowers blue, showy, June–Sept. **Habitat requirements:** Wet soil, rocky or sandy shores (OBL). **Uses:** Secondary or minor species for increased diversity and aesthetics in wetland restoration and mitigation. Additional species for erosion control along pond edges, stream banks, open wet sandy soil.

Scutellaria integrifolia (hyssop skullcap)

To 25 in. Flowers blue, showy, June–July; fruit July–Aug. **Habitat requirements:** Moist fields, open woods (FACW). Tolerant of partial shade. **Uses:** Secondary or minor species for increased diversity and aesthetics in wetland restoration and mitigation.

Scutellaria lateriflora

Scutellaria lateriflora (mad-dog skullcap)

To 30 in., colonial. Flowers blue, small, July–Sept. **Habitat requirements:** Moist bottomlands, swampy woods (FACW+). Understory of *Phragmites* "forests." Tolerant of partial shade. **Uses:** Secondary or minor species for increased diversity in wetland restoration and mitigation in open or partly shaded habitats. Additional species for erosion control along pond edges, stream banks, wet soil.

Senecio aureus (*Packera aurea*) (golden ragwort)

To 3 ft., colonial. Tolerant of shade. Flowers yellow, showy, May–July. **Habitat requirements:** Moist woods, marshes (FACW). Soil pH 4.5–8.5. Often found in calcareous soil. Should tolerate concrete debris. **Uses:** Secondary or minor species for increased diversity and aesthetics in wetland restoration and mitigation. Additional species for erosion control along pond edges, open swamp forests, wet soil.

Senecio obovatus (*Packera obovata*) (round-leaved ragwort)

To 28 in. Flowers yellow, April–June. **Habitat requirements:** Calcareous rocks and slopes, rich woodland banks (FACU). Tolerant of partial shade. Should tolerate concrete debris. Probably not a good competitor in dense vegetation. **Uses:** Secondary or minor species for increased diversity and aesthetics in restoration of rocky woodlands and open slopes. Vegetation of woodland soil with concrete rubble.

Senecio pauperculus (*Packera paupercula*) (balsam groundsel)

To 20 in. Flowers yellow, May–June. **Habitat requirements:** Moist, calcareous meadows, stream banks, wet rocks (FAC). Should tolerate concrete debris. Probably not a good competitor in dense vegetation. **Uses:** Secondary or minor species for increased diversity and aesthetics in restoration of moist to wet rocky meadows and open rocky slopes. Vegetation of moist soil with concrete rubble.

Senna hebecarpa (*Cassia h.*) (northern wild senna)

To 5 ft. Flowers yellow, July–Sept.; fruit Sept.–Oct. **Habitat requirements:** Moist, open woods, stream banks, floodplain forests, roadsides (FAC). Tolerant of partial shade. Potentially a nitrogen fixer; may improve soil nutrients. **Uses:** Secondary or minor species for increased diversity and aesthetics in restoration of moist, open woods, roadsides, stream banks.

Silene antirrhina (sleepy catch-fly)

Annual, to 32 in. Flowers white to pink, May–July; fruit to Sept. **Habitat requirements:** Dry, open woods, roadside edges, sandy soil (UPL). Tolerant of partial shade. **Uses:** Minor species for addition to annual seed mixes for dry uplands.

Silene caroliniana (wild pink)

Rare (NYS S3, V); to 8 in. Flowers pink, showy, April–June. **Habitat requirements:** Open, rocky woods. Often growing on soil pockets in large, partly shady rock outcrops (UPL). Found in humus soil pH 5.0. Tolerant of partial shade. **Uses:** Secondary or minor species for increased diversity and aesthetics in restoration of rocky woodlands and outcrops. Rock gardens.

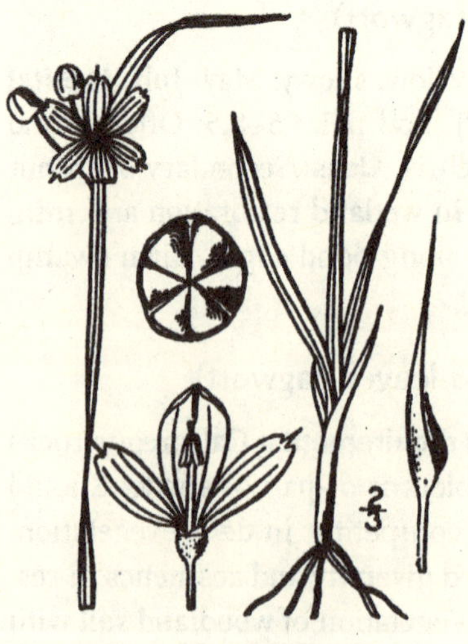

Sisyrinchium angustifolium

Silene stellata (starry campion)

To 4 ft. Flowers white, showy, July–Aug. **Habitat requirements:** Open woods (UPL). Tolerant of partial shade. **Uses:** Secondary or minor species for increased diversity and aesthetics in restoration of open woodlands.

Sisyrinchium angustifolium (stout blue-eyed grass)

To 20 in. Flowers blue, June–July; fruit July–Aug. **Habitat requirements:** Moist, open soil, open woods, fields (FACW). Soil pH 5–7. **Uses:** Minor species for increased diversity and aesthetics in wetland restoration and mitigation.

Sisyrinchium atlanticum (eastern blue-eyed grass)

To 20 in. Flowers blue, May–June; fruit June–July. **Habitat requirements:** Moist, open soil, salt marsh edges (FACW). **Uses:** Minor species for increased diversity and aesthetics in wetland restoration and mitigation.

Sisyrinchium montanum (common blue-eyed grass)

To 20 in. Flowers blue, May–July. **Habitat requirements:** Moist to wet sandy open areas, shores (FAC). Cannot compete with tall vegetation. **Uses:** Secondary or minor species for increased diversity and aesthetics in restoration of open moist sandy soil, pond shores.

Sisyrinchium mucronatum (slender blue-eyed grass)

To 20 in. Flowers blue, May–June; fruit June–July. **Habitat requirements:** Moist, sandy soil, open woods, meadows (FAC+). **Uses:** Minor species for increased diversity and aesthetics in wetland restoration and mitigation.

Sium suave (water parsnip)

To 6 ft. Flowers white, July–Sept.; fruit Sept.–Oct. Host for some butterfly species. **Habitat requirements:** Open, wet meadows, freshwater to slightly brackish tidal marshes (OBL). Tolerates flooding to 0.5 ft. or saturated soil for up to 100% of growing season; tolerant of dry-down, slightly brackish water. **Uses:** Minor element for increased diversity of wetland restoration and mitigation.

**Smilacina racemosa* (*Maianthemum racemosum*) (false Solomon's seal)

To 32 in., colonial, spreads very slowly. Flowers white, May–June; fruit fleshy, speckled, becoming red Sept.–Oct. Dispersed by birds and possibly small mammals. **Habitat requirements:** Mixed deciduous woods (FACU−). Frequent in NYC woodlands. Tolerant of shade. An indicator of good to high-quality natural forest. Apparently more tolerant of disturbance than *Polygonatum.* Tolerates acid to alkaline soils pH 3.8–7.7. **Uses:** Primary to secondary species for increased diversity and aesthetics in restoration of moist forest understories with Canada mayflower, Solomon's seal, bellwort, and wild sarsaparilla.

Smilacina stellata (*Maianthemum stellatum*) (star-flowered Solomon's seal)

To 2 ft., colonial. Flowers white, May–July; fruit fleshy, becoming red, June–Sept. **Habitat requirements:** Moist, sandy, gravelly open woods, floodplains, margins of seasonal or temporary streams and flooded areas, moist swales in back-dune holly forests (FACW). Tolerant of partial shade. **Uses:** Secondary or minor species for increased diversity and aesthetics in restoration and mitigation of wetlands in sandy soil, coastal woodlands.

Solidago bicolor (silver-rod)

To 3 ft. Flowers white, Aug.–Oct. Host for some butterfly species. **Habitat requirements:** Dry, open, often oak woods on sterile, rocky soils (UPL). Tolerant of partial shade. Probably not a good competitor in dense vegetation. **Uses:** Secondary or minor species for increased diversity and aesthetics in restoration of open, dry woodlands. Butterfly gardens.

**Solidago caesia* (blue-stemmed goldenrod)

To 3 ft. Flowers yellow, showy, Aug.–Oct. Host for some butterfly species. **Habitat requirements:** Rich, open, moist fairly dry, deciduous woods (FACU). Soil pH 5.5–7.0. Tolerates acid soil down to pH 4.0. Tolerant of shade. **Notes:** Frequent in woodland understories of our region. **Uses:** Primary to secondary species for increased diversity and aesthetics in restoration of moist forest understories, with white wood aster, Pennsylvania sedge, heart-leaved aster. Can also be planted with false Solomon's seal, Solomon's seal, etc. Butterfly gardens.

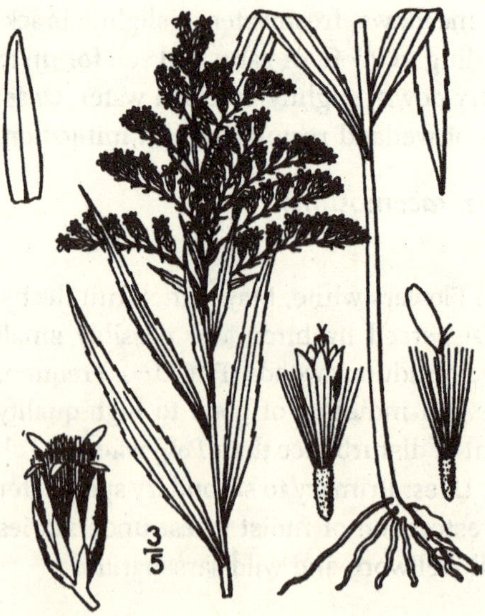
Solidago canadensis

**Solidago canadensis* (Canada goldenrod)

To 6 ft., colonial, aggressive. Flowers yellow, showy, Aug.–Oct. Host for some butterfly species. **Habitat requirements:** Open areas, old fields (FACU). Soil pH 4.8–7.5. Competes fairly well with mugwort. Very tolerant of soil types and moisture regimes, does well in fill, tolerates part shade of edges. Forms dense stands. **Notes:** Very common in our region. Typical of "old field" vegetation. **Uses:** Primary to secondary species for erosion control on open slopes, degraded open areas, meadows with concrete or other fill soils, roadsides. Plant along with common milkweed (*Asclepias syriaca*), Indian hemp (*Apocynum cannabinum*), *Aster pilosus*, etc. to help prevent invasion by mugwort in nutrient-rich, open fill soils.

Solidago elliottii (*S. latissimifolia*) (coastal swamp goldenrod)

Rare (NYS S1, U); to 10 ft., colonial from creeping rhizomes. Flowers yellow, Aug.–Oct. **Habitat requirements:** Fresh or brackish marshes (OBL). Tolerates brackish water. **Notes:** Plant in cooperation with a conservation organization restoration specialist. Use only local stock. **Uses:** Secondary or minor species for increased diversity and aesthetics of wetland restoration and mitigation. Increased erosion control.

Solidago flexicaulis (zigzag goldenrod)

To 4 ft. Flowers yellow, showy, Aug.–Oct. Host for some butterfly species. **Habitat requirements:** Rich, cool woods, thickets (FACU). Soil pH 5.3–7.0. Tolerant of partial shade. **Uses:** Secondary or minor species for increased diversity and aesthetics in restoration of moist forest understories in good soils. Shady butterfly gardens.

Solidago gigantea (late goldenrod)

To 6 ft., colonial. Flowers yellow, Aug.–Oct. **Habitat requirements:** Open, moist to wet meadows, fields, marshes (FACW). Soil pH 4–8. **Notes:** Frequent in our region. Good soil-holding capacity. **Uses:** Secondary species for erosion control of lake and pond shores, moist to wet soil. Wetland mitigation.

Solidago juncea (early goldenrod)

To 4 ft. Flowers yellow, showy, blooms mostly July–Aug. Host for some butterfly species. **Habitat requirements:** Dry to moist fields, roadsides (UPL). Tolerates partial shade. **Notes:** Common in our region. **Uses:** Secondary species for increased diversity and aesthetics in vegetation of open slopes, degraded open areas, roadsides, meadows with concrete or other fill soils, roadsides. Plant along with Canada goldenrod, common milkweed (*Asclepias syriaca*), Indian hemp (*Apocynum cannabinum*), *Aster pilosus*, etc. to help prevent invasion by mugwort in nutrient-rich, open fill soils.

**Solidago nemoralis* (gray goldenrod)

To 3 ft. Flowers yellow, showy; blooms mostly Aug.–Sept. Host for some butterfly species. **Habitat requirements:** Open, dry, sandy soil, fill, fields, thin woods, edges (UPL). Soil pH 6.5–7.5. Most likely tolerates more acid soils. Probably not a good competitor in moist, high-nutrient soils. **Uses:** Primary to secondary species for restoration of coastal grasslands and meadows on dry, sandy, sterile soils. Use with *Aster ericoides*, *Aster laevis*, little bluestem, Indian grass, etc.

Solidago odora (sweet goldenrod)

To 5 ft., plant licorice scented, colonial. Flowers yellow, showy, July–Oct. Host for some butterfly species. **Habitat requirements:** Dry, sandy soil of open oak woods, fields, edges (UPL). Tolerant of shade. Found in soil pH 5.0. **Uses:** Secondary species for increased diversity and aesthetics in restoration of thin meadows, open woodlands on dry, sandy, sterile soils.

Solidago patula (rough-leaved goldenrod)

To 6 ft. Flowers yellow, Aug.–Oct. **Habitat requirements:** Marshes, often on calcareous soil (OBL). Should tolerate concrete debris. **Uses:** Secondary or minor species for increased diversity and aesthetics of wetland restoration and mitigation. Vegetation of wet fill with concrete debris.

Solidago puberula (dusty goldenrod)

To 6.5 ft. Stems finely hairy-sticky, often purplish. Flowers yellow, Aug.–Oct. Host for some butterfly species. **Habitat requirements:** Moist to dry soils of oak or pine barrens habitats, rocky or sandy, acid soils (FACU−). **Uses:** Secondary species for increased diversity and aesthetics in restoration of open pine or oak barrens on dry, sandy, or rocky sterile soils.

**Solidago rugosa* (rough-leaved goldenrod)

To 4 ft., colonial, aggressive. Flowers yellow, showy, Aug.–Nov. **Habitat requirements:** Moist to somewhat dry, open areas (FAC). Tolerant of varying soil types, does well in fill, tolerates part shade of edges. Tolerates acid soil pH 3.8–7.5. Forms dense stands. **Notes:** Common in our region. **Uses:** Primary to secondary species for erosion control on moist open slopes, degraded open areas, meadows with concrete or other fill soils, roadsides. Plant along with common milkweed (*Asclepias syriaca*), Indian hemp (*Apocynum cannabinum*), lined aster (*Aster lanceolata*), Canada goldenrod, etc. to help prevent invasion by mugwort in nutrient-rich, moist fill soils.

**Solidago sempervirens* (seaside goldenrod)

To 5 ft. Flowers yellow, showy; blooms and fruits Sept.–Nov. **Habitat requirements:** Coastal. Low dunes, brackish wet areas, salt marsh edges (FACW). Soil pH 5.5–7.5. Intolerant of shade. **Uses:** Primary, secondary, or minor species for increased diversity in restoration of high salt marsh habitats, back-dune swales, and low foredunes (secondary to *Ammophila*).

Solidago speciosa (showy goldenrod)

To 5 ft. Flowers yellow, showy, Aug.–Oct. Host for some butterfly species. **Habitat requirements:** Meadows, woodland edges, dry, rocky fields (UPL). Tolerant of partial shade. Less common and less aggressive than *S. juncea*. **Uses:**

Secondary species for increased diversity and aesthetics in vegetation of open slopes, meadows, roadsides. Plant along with Canada goldenrod, common milkweed (*Asclepias syriaca*), Indian hemp (*Apocynum cannabinum*), *Aster pilosus*, etc. to help prevent invasion by mugwort in nutrient-rich, open fill soils. Butterfly gardens.

Solidago squarrosa (squarrose goldenrod)

To 5 ft. Flowers yellow, Aug.–Oct. **Habitat requirements:** Rich, dry, rocky, open woods (UPL). Tolerant of partial shade. **Uses:** Secondary species for increased diversity and aesthetics in restoration of open woodlands on dry, rocky soils.

Solidago uliginosa (swamp goldenrod)

To 5 ft. Flowers yellow, Aug.–Oct. **Habitat requirements:** Swamps, bogs, acid soil (OBL). **Uses:** Secondary or minor species for increased diversity and aesthetics of wetland restoration and mitigation in pine or oak barrens, in acid soil.

Solidago ulmifolia (elm-leaved goldenrod)

To 4 ft. Flowers yellow, Aug.–Oct. Host for some butterfly species. **Habitat requirements:** Open, rocky woods (UPL). Tolerant of partial shade. **Uses:** Secondary species for increased diversity and aesthetics in restoration of open woodlands on dry, rocky soils.

Sparganium americanum (American bur-reed)

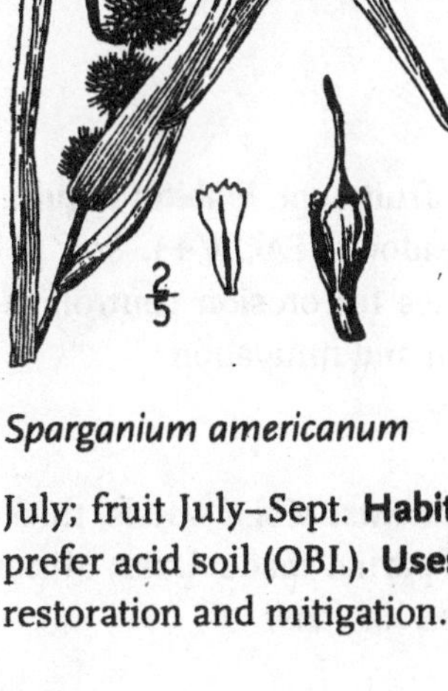

Sparganium americanum

Emergent, to 3 ft., colonial, growth rate rapid. Flowers green, burlike, June–July; fruit July–Sept. Wildlife value moderate. Rhizomes eaten by muskrats. **Habitat requirements:** Shallow water, pond and lake shores, streams (OBL). Soil pH 4.9–7.3. Tolerant of partial shade. Tolerant of flooding to 0.5 ft. or saturated soil to 100% of growing season. Intolerant of salt. Available. **Uses:** Secondary species for erosion control and increased diversity of lake and pond shores. Wetland mitigation.

Sparganium androcladum (branching bur-reed)

Emergent, to 3 ft. Flowers green, burlike, June–July; fruit July–Sept. **Habitat requirements:** Shallow water, pond shores, may prefer acid soil (OBL). **Uses:** Minor element for increased diversity in wetland restoration and mitigation.

Sparganium eurycarpum (giant bur-reed)

Colonial emergent, to 4 ft., growth rate rapid. Flowers green, burlike, June–July; fruit July–Sept. Wildlife value moderate. Seeds eaten by some waterfowl. Rhizomes eaten by Canada geese and muskrats. **Habitat requirements:** Shallow water, pond and lake shores (OBL). Soil pH 5.0–8.5. Should tolerate concrete debris. Tolerant of partial shade, flooding to 1 ft. or saturated soil up to 100% of growing season. Intolerant of salt. Available. **Uses:** Secondary species for erosion control and increased diversity, lake and pond shores. Wetland mitigation.

Spergularia canadensis (northern sand-spurrey)

Rare (NYS SX, U); annual, to 10 in., plant reclining or prostrate. Flowers white to pink, blooms and fruits July–Sept. **Habitat requirements:** Coastal. Tidal areas in mud or sand (OBL). NYS and New England. Apparently not found in NJ. **Uses:** Minor species for increased diversity in salt marsh restoration. Plant in coordination with a conservation organization restoration specialist.

Spirodela polyrhiza (big duckweed)

Colonial free-floating aquatic, body to 1/3 in. wide. Rarely flowers. Wildlife value high. Eaten by waterfowl; shades water surface, shelter for fish and invertebrates. **Habitat requirements:** Permanently inundated freshwater habitats (OBL). Salinity less than 0.5 ppt. Tolerates partial shade. **Uses:** Secondary species for increased diversity and potential improvement of eutrophic ponds.

Stachys hyssopifolia (hyssop hedge-nettle)

Rare (NYS S1S2, T); to 20 in., colonial. Flowers pale purple, June–Aug.; fruit Aug.–Oct. **Habitat requirements:** Moist sand or peat near coast, acid bogs (FACW+). **Uses:** Secondary species for erosion control, increased diversity and aesthetics, lake and pond shores, especially in coastal areas. Wetland mitigation. Plant in coordination with conservation organization restoration specialist.

Stachys tenuifolia (common hedge-nettle)

To 3 ft., colonial. Flowers rose-purple, June–Aug.; fruit Sept. **Habitat requirements:** Moist shade, rich swamp forests, wet meadows (FACW+). Soil pH 5.7–7.4. Tolerant of shade. **Uses:** Secondary species for erosion control, increased diversity and aesthetics, wetland restoration and mitigation.

Stellaria longifolia (long-leaved stitchwort)

To 20 in. Flowers white, May–July. **Habitat requirements:** Moist woods, thickets, and shores (UPL). Soil pH 4.0–6.5. Tolerant of partial shade. **Uses:** Minor species for increased diversity in restoration of open habitats.

Stylosanthes biflora (pencil flower)

To 20 in. Flowers orange-yellow, June–Sept.; fruit Aug.–Oct. Host for some butterfly species. **Habitat requirements:** Dry, open woods, barrens, fields, on sandy or rocky soil (UPL). Potentially a nitrogen fixer; may improve soil nutrients. Tolerant of partial shade. **Uses:** Secondary species for increased diversity and aesthetics in restoration of open woodlands and back-dune grasslands on dry soil.

Symplocarpus foetidus (skunk cabbage)

Spring ephemeral; to 2 ft., colonial, spreading slowly; leaves die back in midsummer. Floral bract (spathe) purple-green, Feb.–March; fruit fleshy, blackish green, Aug.–Sept. Wildlife value low. **Habitat requirements:** Swamp forests, freshwater tidal and nontidal marshes, shady seeps, stream banks (OBL). Tolerant of partial shade. Tolerant of saturated soil to 100% growing season. Intolerant of salt. Found in soil pH 5.0–6.2. **Uses:** Secondary species for increased diversity and aesthetics in restoration of swamp forests herb layer. Wetland mitigation.

Taenidia integerrima (yellow pimpernel)

To 3 ft. Flowers yellow, May–June; fruit June–July. Host for some butterfly species. **Habitat requirements:** Dry, rocky slopes, open woods on gravelly soils (UPL). Tolerant of partial shade. **Uses:** Secondary species for increased diversity and aesthetics in restoration of open woodlands on dry, rocky soil. Butterfly gardens.

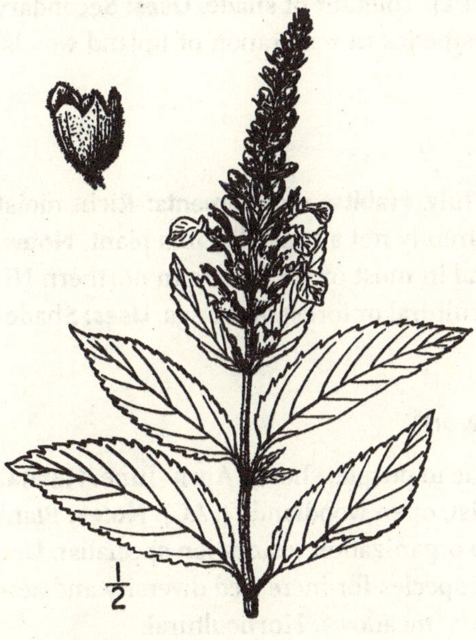

Teucrium canadense

Tephrosia virginiana (goat's rue)

To 28 in. Flowers pale yellow and pink, June–July; fruit Aug.–Oct. Host for some butterfly species. **Habitat requirements:** Sandy or rocky soil of back-dune grasslands, open pine or oak barrens (UPL). Potentially a nitrogen fixer; may improve soil nutrients. Tolerant of partial shade. **Uses:** Secondary species for increased diversity and aesthetics in restoration of open woodlands or barrens on dry, sandy soil.

Teucrium canadense (American germander)

To 3 ft., colonial. Flowers pink-purple, June–Aug.; fruit Sept.–Oct.

Habitat requirements: Marshes, open swamp forests (FACW−). Soil pH 4.5–8.0. Tolerant of partial shade. **Uses:** Secondary species for erosion control, increased diversity and aesthetics in wetland restoration and mitigation.

Thalictrum dioicum (early meadow rue)

Spring ephemeral, to 28 in. Flowers greenish yellow, April–May; fruit May. **Habitat requirements:** Moist woods (FAC). **Uses:** Secondary species for increased diversity and aesthetics in restoration of moist forest understories, swamp forest edges.

Thalictrum pubescens (*T. polygamum*) (tall meadow rue)

To 9 ft. Flowers white, June–Aug.; fruit Aug.–Oct. **Habitat requirements:** Open marshes, wet edges (FACW+). **Uses:** Secondary species for increased diversity and aesthetics in wetland restoration and mitigation.

Thalictrum revolutum (waxy meadow rue)

To 6.5 ft., plant with skunklike odor. Flowers white to purplish, May–July; fruit July–Oct. **Habitat requirements:** Dry, open rocky woods, barrens, riverbanks (UPL). Tolerant of partial shade. **Uses:** Secondary species for increased diversity and aesthetics in restoration of open, upland woods.

Thaspium trifoliatum (meadow parsnip)

To 3 ft. Flowers purple, May–July; fruit Aug.–Oct. Host for some butterfly species. **Habitat requirements:** Woods (UPL). Tolerant of shade. **Uses:** Secondary species for increased diversity and aesthetics in restoration of upland woods. Butterfly gardens.

Tiarella cordifolia (foamflower)

To 1 ft. Flowers white, May; fruit to July. **Habitat requirements:** Rich, moist woods (FAC). Tolerant of shade. Apparently not a coastal plains plant. **Notes:** Mostly north of NYC region. Historical in most of NYS. Rare in northern NJ. Does not appear to reproduce in horticultural or forest plantings. **Uses:** Shade-tolerant garden plant.

Tradescantia ohiensis (Ohio spiderwort)

Rare (NYS S1, R); to 40 in. Flowers blue to purple, showy, April–June. **Habitat requirements:** Meadows, thickets, moist, open woodlands (FAC). **Notes:** Plant only in coordination with conservation organization restoration specialist. Use local stock. **Uses:** Secondary or minor species for increased diversity and aesthetics in restoration of open woodlands, meadows. Horticultural.

Triadenum virginicum (marsh St.-John's-wort)

To 2 ft., colonial. Flowers coppery pink, showy, July–Sept.; fruit Sept.–Oct.; fruit capsules red. **Habitat requirements:** Pond edges, open wet sandy soil, bogs, cedar swamps (OBL). Acid soil. **Uses:** Secondary species for increased diversity and aesthetics, erosion control, in wetland restoration and mitigation.

Trichostema dichotomum (blue curls)

Annual, to 28 in. Flowers blue, Aug.–Oct. **Habitat requirements:** Dry meadows, open woods, edges, rocky or sandy soils (UPL). Tolerant of partial shade. **Uses:** Secondary or minor species for increased diversity and aesthetics in restoration of dry grasslands or coastal meadows.

Trichostema setaceum (narrow-leaf blue curls)

Rare (NYS SH, E); annual to 28 in. Flowers blue, Aug.–Sept. **Habitat requirements:** Dry meadows, edges (UPL). **Notes:** Plant in coordination with conservation organization restoration specialist. Use local stock. **Uses:** Secondary or minor species for increased diversity and aesthetics in restoration of dry grasslands or coastal meadows.

Trientalis borealis (starflower)

To 8 in. Flowers white, May–June. **Habitat requirements:** Rich moist woods, swamp forest edges (FAC). Tolerant of shade. **Uses:** Secondary or minor species for increased diversity and aesthetics in restoration of moist to seasonally wet forest understories.

Triglochin maritima (seaside arrow grass)

To 32 in.; blooms and fruits May–Aug. **Habitat requirements:** Saline, brackish, or freshwater marshes (OBL). **Uses:** Minor species for increasing diversity in salt marsh restoration.

Trillium cernuum (nodding trillium)

To 16 in., colonial, grows slowly. Flowers white, showy, May–June; fruit red. **Habitat requirements:** Moist to wet, rich, acid forest understories (FACW). Tolerant of bright shade. Intolerant of disturbance. **Uses:** Secondary species for increased diversity and aesthetics in restoration of swamp forest understories in protected habitats.

Trillium erectum (purple trillium)

To 16 in., colonial. Flowers maroon, showy, April–June; fruit red, to mid-July. **Habitat requirements:** Rich, moist woods (FACU−). Tolerant of shade. Probably very intolerant of disturbance, competition from aggressive species, or invasives. **Uses:** Secondary species for increased diversity and aesthetics in restoration of moist forest understories. Plant in protected sites.

Triodanis perfoliata (*Specularia p.*) (round-leaved Triodanis)

Annual, to 3 ft. Flowers purple, May–Aug. **Habitat requirements:** Open, sterile soil (FAC). **Uses:** Minor species for soil stabilization mix in sandy, dry soil.

Triosteum angustifolium

Triosteum angustifolium (horse gentian)

To 32 in. Flowers dark red, April–June; fruit fleshy, orange, July–Sept. **Habitat requirements:** Moist to dry woods, thickets (UPL). Tolerant of partial shade. **Uses:** Secondary or minor species for increased diversity and aesthetics in restoration of open woodlands, edges.

Triosteum perfoliatum (feverwort)

To 4 ft. Flowers purple, May–June; fruit fleshy, orange, Aug.–Oct. **Habitat requirements:** Rocky woods, thickets (UPL). Tolerant of partial shade. **Uses:** Secondary or minor species for increased diversity and aesthetics in restoration of open woodlands, edges.

Trollius laxus (globe flower)

Rare (Global G4T3Q, NYS S3, T); to 1.5 ft. Flowers yellow, April–May; fruit June–Aug. **Habitat requirements:** Rich soil, marshes, wet meadows, woods, often on calcareous soils (OBL). Tolerant of shade. **Uses:** Secondary species for increased diversity and aesthetics in restoration of protected open wetland habitats. Plant only in cooperation with conservation organization restoration specialist. Plant only local stock.

**Typha latifolia* (cattail)

Emergent, to 9 ft., can be aggressively colonial. Flowers brown, June–July; fruit July–Aug. Wildlife value moderate. Rhizomes eaten by muskrats; used for nesting by red-winged blackbirds. **Habitat requirements:** Shallow water, freshwater tidal and nontidal marshes, pond margins, saturated soil (OBL). Soil pH 5.5–7.5. Tolerant of flooding to 1 ft. or saturated soil for 100% of growing season. Intolerant of salt, shade, alkaline soil. *Typha latifolia* competes well with *Phragmites* if nutrient content of water or soil is not excessive.

Notes: Available. More tolerant of moving water than *Phragmites.* However, Typha may slow water flow and encourage invasion by *Phragmites. Warning! Typha angustifolia* is now known to be nonnative. Do not use this aggressive plant. **Uses:** Primary species for erosion control, bank stabilization in freshwater wetlands, restoration of pond margins, marshes, and wetland mitigation, especially where aggressive soil holding is required.

Utricularia geminiscapa (mixed bladderwort)

Submerged, free floating, aquatic, stems elongate. Flowers yellow, July–Sept. Shelter for small fish and invertebrates, provides shade during hot weather. **Habitat requirements:** Quiet, nutrient-poor water, slow streams, ponds (OBL). **Uses:** Secondary species for increased diversity, aesthetics, and potential improvement of ponds.

Utricularia gibba (creeping bladderwort)

Submerged aquatic, stems creeping, to 4 in. long, forming mats along bottom. Flowers yellow, June–Sept. **Habitat requirements:** Shallow, clean water, bogs (OBL). **Uses:** Minor species for increased diversity in shallow ponds.

Utricularia purpurea (purple bladderwort) (NJ rare)

Submerged, free-floating aquatic, to 3 ft. Flowers red-purple, July–Sept. Shelter for small fish and invertebrates, provides shade during hot weather. **Habitat requirements:** Quiet, shallow, nutrient-poor acid water along coastal plain, ponds, sluggish streams (OBL). **Uses:** Secondary species for increased diversity, aesthetics, and potential improvement of ponds.

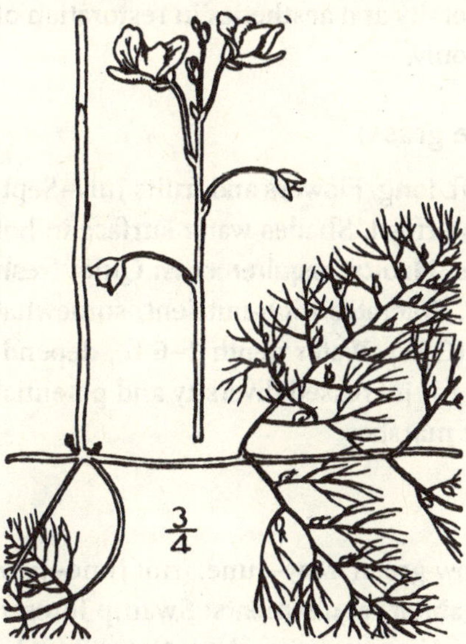

Utricularia vulgaris

Utricularia radiata (floating bladderwort)

2–8 in. above water surface, free-floating submerged aquatic, stems elongate. Flowers yellow, May–Sept. Shelter for small fish and invertebrates, provides shade during hot weather. **Habitat requirements:** Ponds (OBL). **Uses:** Secondary species for increased diversity, aesthetics, and potential improvement of ponds.

Utricularia vulgaris (common bladderwort)

To 6 ft. long, free-floating aquatic. Flowers yellow, showy, June–Sept. Shelter for small fish; provides shade during hot weather. **Habitat requirements:** Deep or shallow, quiet water, slow streams, ponds (OBL). **Uses:** Secondary species for increased diversity, aesthetics, and potential improvement of ponds.

Uvularia perfoliata (bellwort)

To 1 ft., colonial. Flowers yellow, May–June; fruit July–Aug. **Habitat requirements:** Moist woods, acid soil (FACU). Tolerant of shade. **Uses:** Secondary species for increased diversity and aesthetics in restoration of moist forest understories.

Uvularia sessilifolia (sessile-leaved bellwort)

To 1 ft., colonial. Flowers greenish yellow, April–June; fruit June–Sept. **Habitat requirements:** Moist woods (FACU−). Tolerant of shade. Found in soil pH 4.8–5.6. Frequent in high-quality woodlands of NYC. **Uses:** Secondary species for increased diversity and aesthetics in restoration of moist forest understories with Canada mayflower, Solomon's seal, false Solomon's seal, and wild sarsaparilla.

Vaccinium macrocarpon (cranberry)

To 1 ft., evergreen, prostrate, growth rate slow. Flowers white, June–July; fruit fleshy, red, edible (sour), Sept.–Nov., persistent. Wildlife value low. Host for some butterfly species. **Habitat requirements:** Acid bogs, soil pH 4–6 (OBL). Tolerant of flooding, soil compaction. Moderately tolerant of shade. Intolerant of drought, salt. Cannot compete with weedy species in high-nutrient soils. **Uses:** Secondary species for increased diversity and aesthetics in restoration of acid bogs of pine or oak barrens habitats only.

Vallisneria americana (wild celery, tape grass)

Colonial, submerged, rooted aquatic, to 7 ft. long. Flowers and fruits July–Sept. Dioecious (plant both sexes). Eaten by waterfowl. Shades water surface in hot weather; shelter for fish and invertebrates. **Habitat requirements:** Quiet fresh to slightly brackish water, soil pH 6–7.3. Tolerates high-nutrient, somewhat turbid, brackish tidal water to 5 ppt salt (OBL). Water depth 1–6 ft., depending on turbidity. **Uses:** Secondary species for increased diversity and potential improvement of eutrophic ponds and salt marshes.

Veratrum viride (false hellebore)

To 6 ft. Plant very poisonous. Flowers yellow-green, May–June; fruit June–July. Roots probably not eaten by muskrats. **Habitat requirements:** Swamp forests, stream banks (FACW+). Tolerant of shade. Very attractive plant. **Notes:** May be difficult to obtain but should be grown for wetland restorations. **Uses:** Second-

Veratrum viride

ary or minor species for increased diversity and aesthetics in restoration of woodland stream banks, swamp forest edges.

Verbena hastata (blue vervain)

To 4 ft. Flowers blue, July–Sept. Host for some butterfly species. Attractive to hummingbirds. **Habitat requirements:** Open, wet meadows, marshes, ditches (FACW+). Usually available. **Uses:** Secondary species for increased diversity and aesthetics in restoration of pond edges, open swamp, and marshes, wetland mitigation. Butterfly and hummingbird gardens.

Verbena simplex (narrow-leaved vervain)

To 2 ft. Flowers purple, June–Aug. **Habitat requirements:** Dry, open woods, roadsides, rocky or sandy habitats in nonacid (circumneutral) soil (UPL). Tolerant of partial shade. **Uses:** Secondary or minor species for increased diversity and aesthetics in restoration of open, dry woodlands.

Verbena urticifolia (white vervain)

Annual or short-lived perennial to 5 ft. Flowers white, June–Oct. **Habitat requirements:** Roadsides, moist fill, meadows, open woods (FACU). Tolerant of partial shade. Appears to tolerate concrete debris. **Uses:** Secondary or minor species for increased diversity and aesthetics in restoration of open areas, meadows, vegetation of moist roadsides, and fill soils with concrete.

Vernonia noveboracensis (New York ironweed)

To 10 ft. Flowers purple, July–Sept. Host for some butterfly species. **Habitat requirements:** Marshes, wet meadows (FACW+). Soil pH 4.5–8.0. Usually available. **Uses:** Secondary species for increased diversity and aesthetics in restoration of pond edges, open swamp, and marshes, wetland mitigation. Butterfly gardens.

Veronica americana (American brooklime)

To 3 ft., colonial. Flowers blue, June–Aug. **Habitat requirements:** Marshes, stream banks (OBL). Soil pH 5.7–7.5. **Uses:** Secondary or minor species for increased diversity and aesthetics in restoration of wetlands, stream banks, addition to erosion control plantings.

Veronica scutellata (marsh speedwell)

To 16 in., colonial. Flowers blue, May–Aug. **Habitat requirements:** Marshes, pond and lake shores (OBL). **Uses:** Secondary or minor species for increased diversity and aesthetics in restoration of wetlands, addition to erosion control plantings.

Veronicastrum virginicum (Culver's root)

To 6.5 ft. Flowers white to purplish, clusters showy, June–Sept. **Habitat requirements:** Rich, moist to dry woods, gaps, dry meadows (FACU). **Uses:** Minor species to increase diversity and aesthetics of open woodlands, gaps, edges.

Viola blanda (*V. incognita*) (sweet white violet)

About 6 in. Flowers white, May–June. Host for some butterfly species. **Habitat requirements:** Moist shady slopes, in deep humus, deciduous woods, but tolerates acid soil under evergreens (FACW). Northern parts of our region. **Uses:** Secondary or minor species for increased diversity and aesthetics in restoration of wooded wetlands in appropriate habitats.

Viola canadensis (tall white violet)

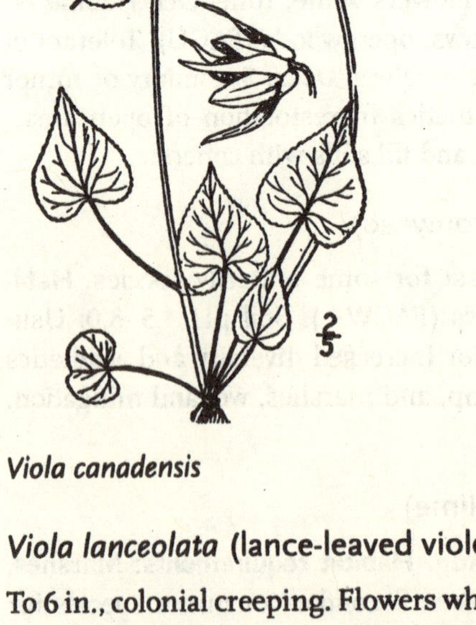

Viola canadensis

To 1 ft., colonial. Flowers white, April–July. Host for some butterfly species. **Habitat requirements:** Rocky woods (UPL). Tolerant of dappled shade. **Uses:** Secondary or minor species for increased diversity and aesthetics in restoration of forest understories.

Viola conspersa (American dog violet)

To 8 in. Flowers light blue-violet, April–May; fruit June–July. Host for some butterfly species. **Habitat requirements:** Moist woods, meadows (FACW). Tolerant of partial shade. **Uses:** Secondary or minor species for increased diversity and aesthetics in restoration of wooded wetlands. Butterfly gardens.

Viola lanceolata (lance-leaved violet)

To 6 in., colonial creeping. Flowers white with purple-brown veins, April–June; fruit Sept.–Oct. Host for some butterfly species. **Habitat requirements:** Wet, open areas, sunny marshes, stream banks (OBL). **Uses:** Secondary or minor species for increased diversity and aesthetics in restoration of open wetlands, stream banks, marshes. Butterfly gardens.

Viola macloskeyi (*V. pallens*) (wild white violet)

To 3 in., colonial. Flowers white, April–May; fruit June. **Habitat requirements:** Along streams and springs (OBL). Soil pH 6.0–7.3. **Uses:** Minor species for increased diversity and aesthetics in restoration of stream banks.

Viola palmata (*V. brittoniana*) (early blue violet)

About 6 in. Flowers violet, April–May; fruit June–July. Host for some butterfly species. **Habitat requirements:** Rich, open woods, gaps, calcareous soil (FAC). Tolerant of partial shade. **Uses:** Secondary or minor species for increased diversity and aesthetics in restoration of open forest understories.

Viola pedata (birdfoot violet)

About 6 in. Flowers purple, showy, April–May. Host for some butterfly species. **Habitat requirements:** Dry, sunny openings, fields (UPL). **Uses:** Secondary or minor species for increased diversity and aesthetics in restoration of open woodlands. Butterfly gardens.

Viola primulifolia (primrose-leaved violet)

Rare (NYS S2, T); about 6 in., colonial, creeping. Flowers white, marked with purple, April–June; fruit Aug.–Oct. Host for some butterfly species. **Habitat requirements:** Moist, open meadows, open swamp forests, sandy soil (FAC+). Listed as a hybrid, *Viola* × *primulifolia* L. (pro sp.) [*lanceolata* × *macloskeyi*] by the www.usda.plants Web site. **Uses:** Secondary or minor species for increased diversity and aesthetics in restoration of wooded wetlands in appropriate habitats.

Viola pubescens (yellow forest violet)

To 18 in. Flowers yellow, showy, April–May; fruit July–Aug. Host for some butterfly species. **Habitat requirements:** Rich woods (FACU). Tolerant of shade. Found in floodplain forest, soil pH 6–7. **Uses:** Secondary or minor species for increased diversity and aesthetics in restoration of forest understories.

Viola rostrata (long-spurred violet)

To 10 in. Flowers violet, April–May. Host for some butterfly species. **Habitat requirements:** Deep humus, moist woods (FACU). Tolerant of shade. **Uses:** Secondary or minor species for increased diversity and aesthetics in restoration of forest understories.

Viola rotundifolia (round-leaved violet)

To 4 in. Flowers yellow, April–May; fruit June–Aug. Host for some butterfly species. **Habitat requirements:** Rich, moist conifer or deciduous woods

(FAC+). Tolerant of shade. **Uses:** Secondary or minor species for increased diversity and aesthetics in restoration of wooded wetlands. Butterfly gardens.

Viola sagittata (*V. fimbriatula*) (arrow-leaved violet)

About 4 in. Flowers violet, April–May; fruit June–Aug. Host for some butterfly species. **Habitat requirements:** Open woods, gaps, meadows (FACW). Tolerant of partial shade. **Uses:** Secondary or minor species for increased diversity and aesthetics in restoration of open wooded wetlands, wet meadows. Butterfly gardens.

Viola sororia (common violet)

Spring ephemeral, about 6 in. Flowers violet, showy, April–May; fruit June–July. Host for some butterfly species. **Habitat requirements:** Open woods, shady lawns (FAC−). Tolerant of shade. Weedy, and tolerant of disturbance. Soil pH 6.0–7.8. **Uses:** Secondary or minor species for shady edges. Disturbed areas.

Viola striata (cream violet)

To 1 ft. Flowers cream color, April–June. Host for some butterfly species. **Habitat requirements:** Sunny ditches, stream banks, often weedy (FACW). Often in calcareous soil. Should tolerate concrete debris. **Uses:** Secondary or minor species for increased diversity and aesthetics in restoration of open wetlands.

Xanthium strumarium (cocklebur)

Annual to 4 ft. (rarely). Flowers green, fruit burlike, Oct.–Nov. **Habitat requirements:** Beaches or open, weedy areas (FAC). Fill soils. **Uses:** Addition to annual seed mix for initial soil stabilization on beaches or open areas (FAC).

Xyris difformis (yellow-eyed grass)

To 30 in. Flowers yellow, June–Sept.; fruit Aug.–Oct. **Habitat requirements:** Wet areas, sandy soil, coastal areas (OBL). **Uses:** Secondary or minor species for increased diversity and aesthetics in restoration of open coastal wetlands in sandy soil.

Xyris torta (slender yellow-eyed grass)

To 34 in. Flowers yellow, July–Aug.; fruit Aug.–Oct. **Habitat requirements:** Wet, acid soil of pine barrens (OBL). **Uses:** Secondary or minor species for increased diversity and aesthetics in restoration of pine barren bogs or swamps.

Zizia aurea (golden alexanders)

To 32 in. Flowers yellow, showy, April–June; fruit Aug.–Oct. Host for some butterfly species. **Habitat requirements:** Rich, moist meadows, wet, open woods, rich soil (FAC). Tolerant of shade. **Uses:** Secondary or minor species for increased diversity and aesthetics in restoration of wet forest understories, low, wet meadows.

Zostera marina (eelgrass)

To 3 ft. long, colonial, rooted, submerged, tidal aquatic, growth rate moderate, grows slowly during winter. Blooms and fruits May–July. Wildlife value high. Eaten by waterfowl. **Habitat requirements:** Coastal. Water depth 2–6 ft. depending on turbidity, below mean low water (OBL). Salinity 20–35 ppt, brackish to ocean water. Traps sediment. Roots associated with nitrogen-fixing bacteria. **Uses:** Secondary species for salt marsh and bay restoration. Improvement of habitat for fish and invertebrates.

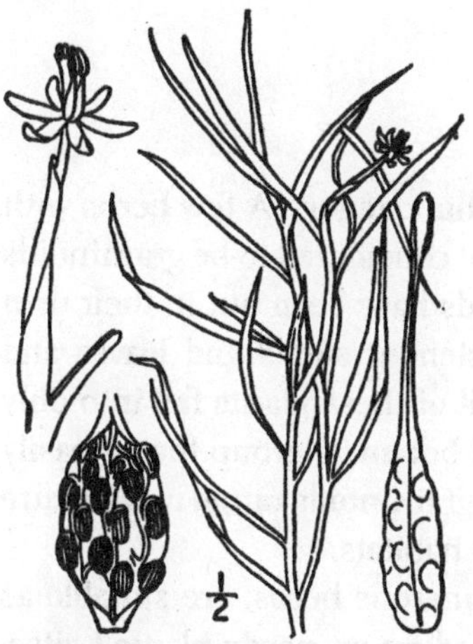

Zosterella dubia

Zosterella dubia (water star grass)

Floating aquatic. Flowers yellow, bloom and fruit mostly in June. Shelter for small fish; provides shade during hot weather. **Habitat requirements:** Quiet water, mud (OBL). **Uses:** Minor species for increased diversity, aesthetics and potential improvement of ponds.

Chapter 5

Graminoids

Grasses, sedges, and rushes are all included in this category. A few herbs with grasslike leaves (Iris, blue-eyed grass, etc.) are not considered to be graminoids and are included in the herb chapter. Graminoids have been put in their own chapter as they stand out as a group, having slender stems and leaves and mostly inconspicuous flowers and fruit. Also, all of these plants fall into only three plant families and tend to make a natural botanical group that is easily recognizable. Only a few are shade tolerant, but graminoids range in moisture tolerance from emergent aquatics to dry upland habitats.

A number of annual grasses, along with numerous herbs, are suitable as substitutes for annual rye as erosion-control seeding on newly planted sites. It is important to restore annual herbs and grasses as well as perennials since their habitats are becoming scarce.

GRAMINOID SPECIES

Agrostis hyemalis (*A. scabra*) (tickle grass, winter bent grass)

To 3 ft., tufted. Blooms and fruits June–Sept. **Habitat requirements:** Open, dry to moist sterile soil, thin woods (FAC). Soil pH 5.0–7.5. Tolerant of partial shade (FAC). Soil pH 6–8. **Notes:** *Agrostis scabra* (rough bent grass) is listed as a separate species by USDA. **Uses:** Secondary or minor species for restoration of coastal grasslands, open oak barrens, or sparse woodlands.

Agrostis perennans (*A. altissima*) (autumn bent grass)

To 3 ft., tufted. Blooms and fruits Aug.–Oct. **Habitat requirements:** Open woods, thickets (FACU). Soil pH 5.5–7.5. Tolerant of partial shade. **Uses:** Secondary species for erosion control and increased diversity in restoration of open woodlands, grasslands, or meadows.

Alopecurus aequalis (short-awn foxtail)

Annual or short-lived perennial, to 20 in., stems solitary or in small tufts. Blooms and fruits June–Sept. **Habitat requirements:** Mud or shallow water

(OBL). Soil pH 5.5–8.0. **Uses:** Minor species for increased diversity or initial erosion control in wetland restoration and mitigation.

Alopecurus aequalis

Ammophila breviligulata (beach grass)

To 3 ft., dune grass, colonial. Blooms and fruits July–Sept. **Habitat requirements:** Beach foredunes (FACU−). Soil pH 5.5–7.9. Needs a moving substrate, i.e., dune sand. **Uses:** Primary species for restoration and stabilization of beach dunes.

Andropogon gerardii (big bluestem)

To 9 ft., tufted, sometimes colonial. Blooms and fruits June–Sept. Host plant for some butterflies. **Habitat requirements:** Open areas (FAC). Soil pH 6.5–7.5. **Notes:** Available. **Uses:** Minor species for restoration of coastal grassland habitats, meadows.

**Andropogon virginicus* (broom sedge)

To 5 ft., tufted, growth rate slow. Blooms and fruits Aug.–Oct. Inhibits nitrogen-fixing plants (*Myrica*). Wildlife value moderate. Host plant for some butterflies. Persistent; winter plants dark yellow. **Habitat requirements:** Open, sterile soil, sand, acid soil, grasslands, scrub, open woods (FACU). Soil pH 4.9–7.0. Tolerant of drought. Intolerant of shade, flooding, salt. **Notes:** Available. Common in our region. **Uses:** Primary species for restoration of grasslands and dry, open habitats, especially with other warm-season grasses and eastern red cedar.

Andropogon virginicus var. *abbreviatus* (*Andropogon glomeratus*) (bunch broom sedge)

To 4 ft., stems tufted; growth rate slow. Blooms Aug.–Nov. Yellow-orange stalks persistent in winter. Wildlife value moderate. Host plant for some butterflies. **Habitat requirements:** Open, moist to wet soil, swamps and pond edges, low ground (FACW+). Tolerates saturated soil to 25% of growing season. Tolerant of drought. Intolerant of shade, salt. **Uses:** Secondary species for increased diversity and aesthetics in restoration of wetlands and transition zones.

Aristida dichotoma (churchmouse three-awn)

Annual to 16 in., stems usually tufted. Blooms and fruits Aug.–Oct. **Habitat requirements:** Dry, sterile soil (UPL). **Notes:** Occasional in our region.

Aristida dichotoma

Uses: Secondary species with seed mix for initial erosion control on open soil in new restoration of upland sites.

Aristida longespica (slimspike three-awn)

Annual to 20 in., stems loosely tufted. Blooms and fruits Aug.–Oct. **Habitat requirements:** Moist to dry soil, tolerates sterile sandy soil (UPL). **Notes:** USDA spelling: *A. longispica* **Uses:** Secondary species with seed mix for initial erosion control on open soil in new restoration of upland sites.

Aristida purpurascens (arrowfeather)

To 3 ft., stems tufted. Blooms and fruits Aug.–Oct. **Habitat requirements:** Dry, sandy or rocky soil. Sometimes on limestone (UPL). Should tolerate concrete. **Uses:** Secondary species for restoration of dry grasslands or meadows on open, sterile, sandy soil, concrete debris.

Aristida tuberculosa (three-awn)

Annual, to 32 in. Blooms and fruits Aug.–Oct. **Habitat requirements:** Open, dry, sandy soil, coastal dunes (UPL). **Uses:** Secondary species with seed mix for initial erosion control on open soil in restoration of upland sites. Restoration of back-dune grasslands.

Brachyelytrum erectum (long-awned wood grass)

To 40 in., stems tufted. Blooms and fruits June–Aug. **Habitat requirements:** Dry to moist woods (UPL). Tolerant of light shade. **Uses:** Secondary species for increased diversity in restoration of woodlands.

Bromus ciliatus (fringed brome)

To 4 ft., stems few together. Blooms and fruits May–June; fruit July–Sept. **Habitat requirements:** Moist woods, bogs, wet areas (FACW). Soil pH 5.5–7.5. Tolerant of part shade. **Uses:** Secondary species for increased diversity and aesthetics in restoration or mitigation of forested wetlands.

Bromus latiglumis (*B. altissimus*) (Canada brome)

40 in., stems solitary or loosely clustered. Blooms July–Aug.; fruit Aug.–Sept. **Habitat requirements:** Rich, moist woods, floodplain forests (FACW). Tolerant

of shade. **Notes:** Available. **Uses:** Secondary species for increased diversity in wetland restoration of forested wetlands.

Bromus pubescens (*B. purgans*) (hairy woodland brome)

To 5 ft., stems solitary or loosely clustered. Blooms and fruits June–Sept. **Habitat requirements:** Moist open woods (FACU). Tolerant of light shade. **Uses:** Secondary species for increased diversity in restoration of woodlands.

Bulbostylis capillaris (sand rush)

Annual to 12 in., stems tufted. Blooms and fruits Aug.–Oct. **Habitat requirements:** Dry rocky or sandy soil (FACU). **Uses:** Secondary species for addition to initial erosion control seed mix in restoration of dry, sandy grasslands, backdunes habitats.

Calamagrostis canadensis (bluejoint)

To 5 ft., aggressively colonial, growth rate moderate to fast. Blooms and fruits June–Aug. Inflorescence often purplish. Wildlife value moderate. Attractive to muskrats; host plant for some butterflies. **Habitat requirements:** Wet meadows, open swamps, floodplains, freshwater tidal areas (FACW+). Soil pH 4.5–8.0. Tolerates flooding. Intolerant of shade, salt. **Notes:** Available. *Warning!* May overwhelm other vegetation. Use only for degraded sites requiring rapid erosion control where aesthetics are not an issue. **Uses:** Secondary species for wetland restoration or mitigation, erosion control.

Calamagrostis cinnoides

Calamagrostis cinnoides (reed grass)

To 4 ft., colonial. Fruit Aug.–Oct. Host plant for some butterflies. **Habitat requirements:** Swamps, open, wet forests (OBL). Soil pH 4–7. **Uses:** Secondary species for wetland restoration and mitigation.

Carex abscondita (thicket sedge)

Evergreen; rare (G4G5, NYS S2, T); to 10 in., stems tufted, rosettes of wide leaves, spreads slowly. Blooms and fruits May–July. Host plant for some butterflies. **Habitat requirements:** Moist woods (FAC). Soil pH 4.8–6.8. Tolerant of shade. **Notes:** Occasional in our region. Plant in coordination with conservation organization restoration specialist. Use only local seed. Very attractive plant, good substitute for lily-turf type plants. **Uses:** Secondary species for increased diversity and aesthetics in restoration of woodlands.

Carex albicans (white-tinge sedge)

Semievergreen; to 18 in., stems densely tufted. Blooms and fruits April–June. Host plant for some butterflies. **Habitat requirements:** Dry oak woods; sandy, acid soil (UPL). Tolerant of open, summer shade. **Uses:** Secondary species for increased diversity and aesthetics in restoration of dry woodlands.

Carex albursina (white bear sedge)

To 2 ft., stems tufted. Blooms and fruits April–June. Host plant for some butterflies. **Habitat requirements:** Rich woods (FACU). Tolerant of shade. Should tolerate concrete debris. **Uses:** Secondary species for increased diversity and aesthetics in restoration of woodlands.

Carex amphibola (narrow-leaf sedge)

To 3 ft., stems tufted. Blooms and fruits May–July. Host plant for some butterflies. **Habitat requirements:** Moist woods (FAC). Soil pH 5.9–7.0. Tolerant of shade. **Uses:** Secondary species for increased diversity and aesthetics in restoration of woodlands.

Carex appalachica (Appalachian sedge)

To 32 in., stems tufted, slender. Blooms and fruits June–July. Host plant for some butterflies. **Habitat requirements:** Moist, open forest understories (UPL). Tolerant of part shade. (*C. appalachica, C. radiata* and *C. rosea* often referred to as "*C. rosea* complex," as they are very similar.) **Uses:** Minor species for increased diversity and aesthetics in restoration of open woodland understories.

Carex aquatilis (water sedge)

To 3 ft., aggressively colonial. Blooms and fruits June–Aug. Plant waxy, blue-green. Host plant for some butterflies. **Habitat requirements:** Shallow water, wet soil (OBL), tolerates brackish water. Soil pH 4.0–7.5. Available. **Uses:** Secondary or minor species for wetland restoration and mitigation, including brackish areas.

Carex atlantica (prickly bog sedge)

To 32 in., stems tufted. Blooms and fruits June–Aug. Host plant for some butterflies. **Habitat requirements:** Open swamps (FACW+). Soil pH 4.5–6. **Uses:** Secondary species for increased diversity in wetland restoration and mitigation.

Carex bebbii (Bebb's sedge)

To 32 in., stems tufted. Blooms and fruits June–Aug. Host plant for some butterflies. **Habitat requirements:** Wet meadows, shores (OBL). Soil pH 4.6–7.0. **Notes:** Available. **Uses:** Secondary or minor species for increased diversity and aesthetics in wetland restoration and mitigation.

Carex blanda

Carex blanda (woodland sedge)

Semievergreen, to 2 ft., but usually reclining; stems tufted, plant often waxy blue-green. Blooms and fruits April–June. **Habitat requirements:** Host plant for some butterflies. Moist woods, shady, disturbed sites (FAC). Soil pH 4.4–7.0. Considered weedy, but is attractive. Not fussy. Tolerant of shade. **Uses:** Secondary species for increased diversity and aesthetics in restoration of woodlands.

Carex bromoides (brome-like sedge)

To 32 in., stems tufted. Blooms and fruits May–July. Host plant for some butterflies. **Habitat requirements:** Rich, low woods, bogs, swamps (FACW). Tolerant of part shade. **Uses:** Secondary or minor species for increased diversity and aesthetics in wetland restoration and mitigation.

Carex bullata (button sedge)

To 3 ft., colonial. Blooms and fruits June–Oct. Host plant for some butterflies. **Habitat requirements:** Acid bogs of coastal plain (OBL). **Uses:** Secondary or minor species for increased diversity and aesthetics in restoration of acid bogs.

Carex canescens (hoary sedge)

To 2 ft., stems tufted. Blooms and fruits May–July. Plants waxy gray-green. Host plant for some butterflies. **Habitat requirements:** Swamps, pond edges (OBL). Soil pH 5.1–7.2. **Uses:** Secondary or minor species for increased diversity and aesthetics in wetland restoration and mitigation.

Carex cephalophora (oval-leaf sedge)

To 2 ft., leaves usually much shorter. Blooms and fruits May–July. Host plant for some butterflies. **Habitat requirements:** Dry woods, gaps, openings (FACU). Soil pH 4.8–7.0. Tolerant of partial shade. **Uses:** Minor species for increased diversity and aesthetics in restoration of open woodland understories.

Carex comosa (bearded sedge)

To 3 ft., stems tufted, growth rate slow. Blooms and fruits June–Sept. Wildlife value high. Host plant for some butterflies. **Habitat requirements:** Marshes, wet meadows, pond edges (OBL). Soil pH 4.6–7.5. Tolerant of flooding, partial shade. Intolerant of salt. Available. **Uses:** Secondary species for increased diversity and aesthetics in wetland restoration and mitigation.

*Carex crinita (fringed sedge)

To 4 ft., stems densely tufted. Blooms and fruits May–Aug. Aesthetically appealing. Host plant for some butterflies. **Habitat requirements:** Open swamp forests, marshes (OBL). Soil pH 4.0–7.5. Tolerant of partial shade. Frequent in NYC wooded and open freshwater wetlands. Available. **Uses:** Primary or secondary species for restoration of open wooded wetlands. Wetland mitigation.

Carex cristatella (crested sedge)

To 3 ft., stems tufted. Blooms and fruits June–Aug. **Habitat requirements:** Marshes, shores, wet meadows (FACW). Soil pH 4.9–6.8. Available. **Uses:** Minor species for increased diversity in wetland restoration and mitigation in open areas, marshes, pond shores.

Carex debilis

Carex debilis (white-edge sedge)

To 3 ft. (usually about 1 ft.), stems tufted. Blooms and fruits May–June. Host plant for some butterflies. **Habitat requirements:** Swamp forest edges, moist woods (FAC). Soil pH 4.6–6.6. Tolerant of shade. **Uses:** Minor species for increased diversity and aesthetics in restoration of open moist woodland understories, swamp forest, or wetland edges.

Carex digitalis (slender woodland sedge)

To 20 in., stems densely tufted. Blooms and fruits May–July. Host plant for some butterflies. **Habitat requirements:** Dry woods (UPL). Tolerant of shade. **Uses:** Minor species for increased diversity and aesthetics in restoration of open woodland understories.

Carex eburnea (bristle-leaf sedge)

To 12 in., stems slender, tufted, and colonial from underground stems (rhizomes). Blooms and fruits June–Aug. Host plant for some butterflies. **Habitat requirements:** Calcareous ledges, gravels (FACU). Should tolerate concrete debris. **Uses:** Secondary or minor species for erosion control, increased diversity, and aesthetics in restoration of concrete debris soils, fill.

Carex echinata (star sedge)

To 20 in., stems densely tufted. Blooms and fruits July–Sept. **Habitat requirements:** Swamps, bogs (FACW). Soil pH 5.6–7.2. **Uses:** Minor species for increased diversity in wetland restoration and mitigation.

Carex flaccosperma var. *glaucodea* (thin-fruit sedge)

Evergreen, rare (NYS S1, E), to 2 ft. (smaller), stems tufted, plant waxy gray-green. Blooms and fruits May–June. Host plant for some butterflies. **Habitat requirements:** Swamp forests, wet fields (FAC). Soil pH 4.6–7.1. Tolerant of shade. **Notes:** Plant in coordination with conservation organization restoration specialist. Use only local seed. **Uses:** Minor species for increased diversity and aesthetics in restoration of open woodland, understories.

Carex foenea (*Carex aenea*) (dry spike sedge)

To 40 in., stems densely tufted. Blooms and fruits May–July. Host plant for some butterflies. **Habitat requirements:** Dry open soil (UPL). **Uses:** Minor species for increased diversity and aesthetics in restoration of dry, open grasslands, meadows.

Carex folliculata (northern long sedge)

To 3 ft., stems densely tufted. Blooms and fruits June–Aug. Host plant for some butterflies. **Habitat requirements:** Wet or swampy woods (FACW), Atlantic white cedar bogs, acid soil. Tolerant of shade. **Uses:** Primary or secondary species for increased diversity and aesthetics in restoration of bogs, wooded wetlands. Wetland mitigation in acid soil.

Carex gracilescens (slender loose-flower sedge)

To 32 in., stems tufted. Blooms and fruits May–June. Host plant for some butterflies. **Habitat requirements:** Dry sandy or rocky woods (UPL), often on calcium-rich soils. Tolerant of shade. Should tolerate concrete debris. **Uses:** Minor species for increased diversity and aesthetics in restoration of dry, open woods, disturbed woodland with concrete debris or fill.

Carex granularis (limestone meadow sedge)

Evergreen, to 32 in., stems tufted, leaves wide, overwintering leaves often waxy pale green. Blooms and fruits May–June. Host plant for some butterflies. **Habitat requirements:** Rich, moist to wet woods, meadows (FACW+), on calcareous soils, pH 6.0–7.2. Should tolerate concrete debris. **Uses:** Minor species for increased diversity and aesthetics in wetland restoration and mitigation in calcium-rich soils.

Carex hystericina (porcupine sedge)

To 3 ft., colonial, growth rate moderate. Blooms and fruits June–Aug. Wildlife value high. Host plant for some butterflies. **Habitat requirements:** Open wetlands, swamps, pond edges (OBL), usually on calcareous soils. Tolerant of flooding. Should tolerate concrete debris. Intolerant of salt, shade. Available. **Uses:** Secondary or minor species for increased diversity in wetland restoration and mitigation in open areas, marshes, pond margins.

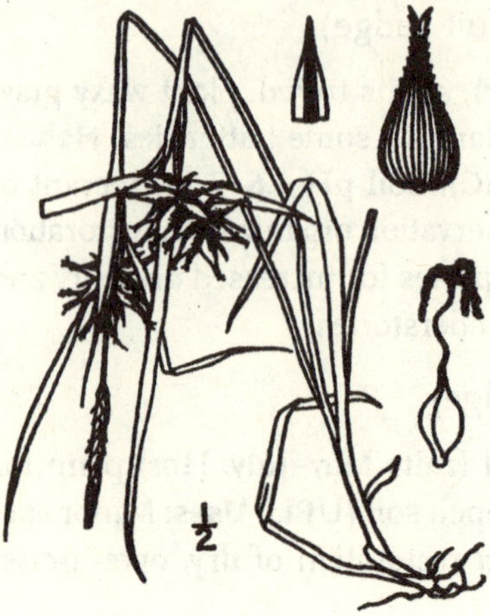

Carex intumescens

Carex intumescens (bladder sedge)

To 32 in., stems sparsely tufted. Blooms and fruits May–Aug. Host plant for some butterflies. **Habitat requirements:** Open swamp forests, wet meadows, floodplain forests (FACW+). Soil pH 4.8–6.9. Tolerant of shade. **Notes:** Available. **Uses:** Secondary species for increased diversity and aesthetics in restoration of open wooded wetlands. Wetland mitigation.

Carex lacustris (lake-bank sedge)

To 4 ft., colonial, growth rate rapid. Blooms and fruits May–Aug. Wildlife value high. **Habitat requirements:** Wet soil of open swamps, marshes, pond edges (OBL). Tolerant of flooding. Intolerant of salt, shade. Soil pH 5.6–6.8. **Notes:** Available. **Uses:** Secondary or minor species for increased diversity and aesthetics in wetland restoration and mitigation in open areas.

Carex laxiflora (loose-flowered sedge)

To 28 in., stems tufted, plant waxy blue-green. Blooms and fruits May–June. Host plant for some butterflies. **Habitat requirements:** Rich woods (FACU). Tolerant of partial shade. **Uses:** Minor species for increased diversity and aesthetics in restoration of moist to dry forest understories.

Carex longii (greenish white sedge)

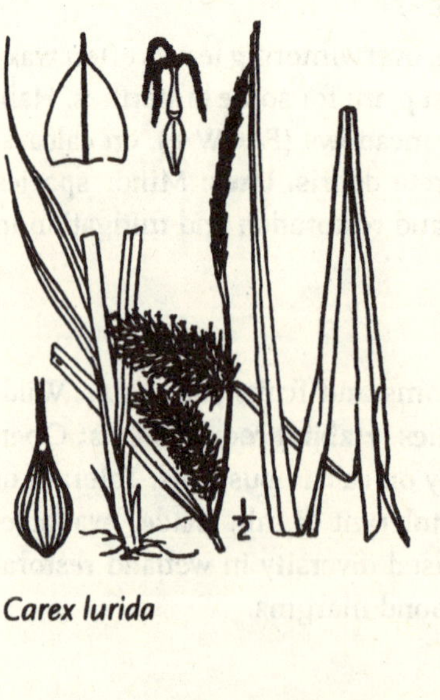

Carex lurida

To 4 ft., stems densely tufted. Blooms and fruits May–Sept. Host plant for some butterflies. **Habitat requirements:** Wet soil of swamps and bogs (OBL), usually near the coast. Needs acid soil. **Uses:** Secondary or minor species for increased diversity and aesthetics in wetland restoration and mitigation.

**Carex lurida* (shallow sedge)

To 3 ft., stems tufted. Blooms and fruits June–Oct. Host plant for some butterflies. **Habitat requirements:** Wet, open soil of marshes, wet meadows (OBL). Soil pH 4.9–6.8. Intolerant of shade. Common in our region. **Notes:**

Available. **Uses:** Primary or secondary species for restoration of open freshwater wetlands and wetland mitigation. Marshes, pond and lake edges.

Carex muehlenbergii (Muhlenberg's sedge)

To 3 ft. (leaves much shorter), stems tufted, plant pale green. Blooms and fruits June–July. Host plant for some butterflies. **Habitat requirements:** Dry, open woods, sandy soil (UPL). Tolerant of partial shade. **Uses:** Minor species for increased diversity and aesthetics in restoration of grasslands, barrens, or open woodlands.

Carex nigromarginata (black edge sedge)

To 8 in. Rare (NYS S1S2, E), colonial, mat forming. Blooms and fruits April–June. Host plant for some butterflies. **Habitat requirements:** Dry woods (UPL). Acid soils. **Uses:** Minor species for increased diversity and aesthetics in restoration of open woodland understories. Plant in coordination with conservation organization restoration specialist. Use only local seed.

Carex normalis (larger straw sedge)

To 32 in., stems tufted. Blooms and fruits June–Aug. Host plant for some butterflies. **Habitat requirements:** Rich woods, meadows (FACU). Soil pH 4.7–6.7. Tolerant of partial shade. **Uses:** Minor species for increased diversity and aesthetics in restoration of understories in moist to dry, open woodlands.

Carex pallescens (pale sedge)

To 20 in., stems tufted. Blooms and fruits May–Aug. Host plant for some butterflies. **Habitat requirements:** Moist woods, meadows (UPL). Tolerant of partial shade. **Uses:** Minor species for increased diversity and aesthetics in restoration of woodland understories and meadows.

Carex pellita (*C. lanuginosa*) (wooly sedge)

To 3 ft. (usually less), aggressively colonial. Blooms and fruits May–Aug. Wildlife value high. Host plant for some butterflies. **Habitat requirements:** Wet meadows, pond edges, shallow water (OBL). Tolerant of flooding. Intolerant of salt, shade. **Uses:** Secondary or minor species for increased erosion control, and diversity in wetland restoration and mitigation in open areas.

Carex pensylvanica (Pennsylvania sedge)

Semievergreen; to 20 in. (leaves smaller); stems tufted, spreading, colonial, forming patchy ground cover. Blooms and fruits April–July. Host plant for some butterflies. **Habitat requirements:** Typically in dry oak or pine woods (UPL), found in soil pH 5.0. Needs acid soil. Tolerant of bright, high shade. **Notes:** Available. Common in our region. **Uses:** Primary species for restoration of forest understories, eroded slopes, holding soil in disturbed understories.

Carex platyphylla (broad-leaf sedge)

Semievergreen; to 16 in., stems tufted; basal leaves wide, waxy pale green. Blooms and fruits May–June. Host plant for some butterflies. **Habitat requirements:** Rich, mixed deciduous woods (UPL). Tolerant of shade. **Uses:** Minor species for increased diversity and aesthetics in restoration of woodland understories.

Carex projecta (necklace sedge)

To 3 ft., stems tufted. Blooms and fruits June–Aug. Host plant for some butterflies. **Habitat requirements:** Marshes, wet meadows (FACW). Soil pH 4.8–7.0. **Uses:** Minor species for increased diversity and aesthetics in wetland restoration and mitigation in open areas.

Carex radiata (eastern star sedge)

To 32 in., stems tufted, very slender. Blooms and fruits June–July. Host plant for some butterflies. **Habitat requirements:** Moist, open forest understories, wetland edges (UPL). Tolerant of shade. **Notes:** Fairly common in NYC. **Uses:** Secondary or minor species for increased diversity and aesthetics in restoration of moist, woodland understories, edges of wooded wetlands.

Carex retrorsa (retrorse sedge)

To 3 ft., colonial, growth rate slow. Blooms and fruits July–Oct. Wildlife value high. Wet meadows, swamp, and floodplain forests, vernal ponds (FACW+). Tolerant of shade, flooding. Intolerant of salt. **Uses:** Secondary or minor species for increased erosion control and diversity in wetland restoration and mitigation in open or wooded swamps, vernal pond edges.

Carex rosea (rosy sedge)

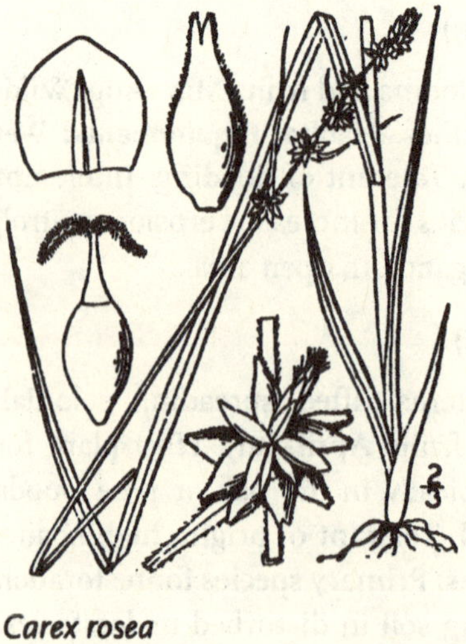

Carex rosea

To 32 in., stems tufted. Blooms and fruits June–July. Host plant for some butterflies. More robust than *C. radiata,* otherwise very similar. In drier habitats. **Habitat requirements:** Moist to dry forest understories (UPL). Tolerant of shade. **Uses:** Minor species for increased diversity and aesthetics in restoration of woodland understories.

**Carex scoparia* (pointed broom sedge)

To 3 ft., stems tufted. Blooms and fruits May–Aug. Host plant for some butterflies. **Habitat requirements:** Moist soil to temporary shallow water of marshes, open swamp forests, wet meadows (FACW). Soil pH 4.6–6.9. Tolerant of part shade. **Notes:** Common in our region. Available. **Uses:** Primary or secondary species for wetland restoration and mitigation in open or wooded swamps, open, vernal pond edges.

Carex seorsa (weak stellate sedge)

Rare (NYS S2, R); to 28 in., leaves shorter, stems densely tufted. Blooms and fruits April–June. Host plant for some butterflies. **Habitat requirements:** Wet woods, swamps of coastal areas (FACW). Tolerant of shade. **Uses:** Minor species for wetland diversity and aesthetics in restoration of swamp forests, wooded wetlands. Plant in coordination with a conservation restoration specialist.

Carex silicea (sand sedge)

To 32 in., densely tufted, stiff, waxy pale green. Blooms and fruits June–Aug. Host to some butterfly larvae. **Habitat requirements:** Moist to dry sand of coastal dunes, sand, rocky coastal shores (UPL). **Uses:** Minor species for increased diversity in restoration and stabilization of coastal sands, back dunes.

Carex squarrosa (squarrose sedge)

To 3 ft., in tussocks. Blooms and fruits June–Sept. Host plant for some butterflies. **Habitat requirements:** Calcareous wetlands and open woods (FACW). Soil pH 5.6–7.3. Should tolerate concrete debris. Tolerant of partial shade. **Uses:** Minor species for wetland diversity and aesthetics in restoration of swamp forests, wooded wetlands with concrete debris or alkaline fill.

Carex stipata (awl-fruited sedge)

To 3 ft., stems tufted, growth rate slow, eventually colonial. Blooms and fruits May–Aug. Wildlife value high. **Habitat requirements:** Wet meadows, swamps (OBL). Soil pH 4.9–7.9. Should tolerate concrete debris. Tolerant of some partial shade, drought, brief flooding (to 25% of the growing season). Intolerant of salt. **Notes:** Occasional in our region. Available. **Uses:** Secondary species for increased diversity and aesthetics in wetland restoration and mitigation, open marshes, pond shores.

**Carex stricta* (tussock sedge)

To 3 ft., emergent, densely tufted, forming permanent, low tussocks, growth rate moderate, eventually colonial. Blooms and fruits May–Aug. Wildlife value high. Host plant for some butterflies. **Habitat requirements:** Shallow, calm, undisturbed swamps, freshwater tidal areas, margins of woodland ponds (OBL), often with red maple. Soil pH 3.5–7.0, in low-nutrient water. Tolerant of partial shade. Intolerant of salt. **Notes:** Frequent in our region. Available.

Uses: Primary species for restoration and mitigation of woodland pond margins, shrub swamps, open swamp forests.

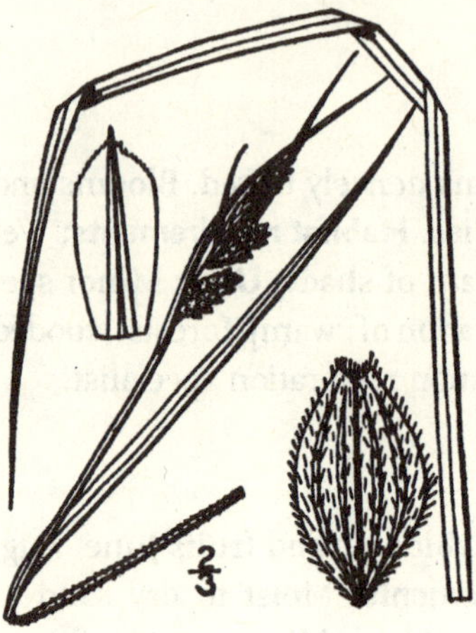

Carex swanii

Carex swanii (Swan's sedge)

To 3 ft. (leaves much shorter), stems tufted, plant gray-green. Blooms and fruits June–July. Host plant for some butterflies. **Habitat requirements:** Moist woods (UPL). Tolerates disturbed habitats. Tolerant of shade. **Notes:** Fairly common in our region. **Uses:** Minor species for increased diversity and aesthetics in restoration of woodland understories.

Carex tenera (slender sedge)

To 3 ft., stems very slender, densely tufted. Blooms and fruits June–Aug. Host plant for some butterflies. **Habitat requirements:** Moist to wet open woodlands, meadows (FAC). Tolerant of partial shade. **Uses:** Minor species for increased diversity and aesthetics in restoration of moist woodland understories, wetland edges.

Carex tribuloides (blunt broom sedge)

To 40 in., stems tufted. Blooms and fruits June–Sept. Host plant for some butterflies. **Habitat requirements:** Wet woods, meadows (FACW+). Soil pH 4.8–7.0. Tolerant of partial shade. **Notes:** Available. **Uses:** Secondary to minor species for increased diversity in wetland restoration and mitigation in swamp forests and open marshes, wet meadows.

Carex typhina (cattail sedge)

Rare (NYS S2, R); to 3 ft., stems tufted. Blooms and fruits June–Sept. Leaves wide, gray-green, similar to *C. squarrosa* but more stout. Host plant for some butterflies. **Habitat requirements:** Moist to wet woods, marshes (FACW+), soils, pH 5.7–7.0. Tolerant of shade. **Uses:** Minor species for wetland diversity and aesthetics in restoration of swamp forests, wooded wetlands, open marshes.

Carex umbellata (umbel-like sedge)

To 8 in., stems densely tufted, mat forming, flowers among leaves. Blooms and fruits April–July. Host plant for some butterflies. **Habitat requirements:** Dry to moist soil, part shade to full sun (UPL). **Uses:** Minor species for increased diversity and aesthetics in restoration of woodland understories, open areas.

Carex vestita (velvet sedge)

To 32 in., extensively colonial by underground stems (rhizomes). Blooms and fruits May–Aug. Host plant for some butterflies. **Habitat requirements:** Dry, sandy woods (UPL). Tolerant of partial shade. **Uses:** Minor species for increased diversity and aesthetics in restoration of woodland understories. Potentially a useful erosion control plant for dry forest slopes. Needs to be found and propagated.

Carex virescens (ribbed sedge)

To 40 in., stems densely tufted, plant pale green. Blooms and fruits May–July. Host plant for some butterflies. **Habitat requirements:** Dry woods, thickets (UPL). Tolerant of partial shade. **Uses:** Minor species for increased diversity and aesthetics in restoration of dry woodland understories.

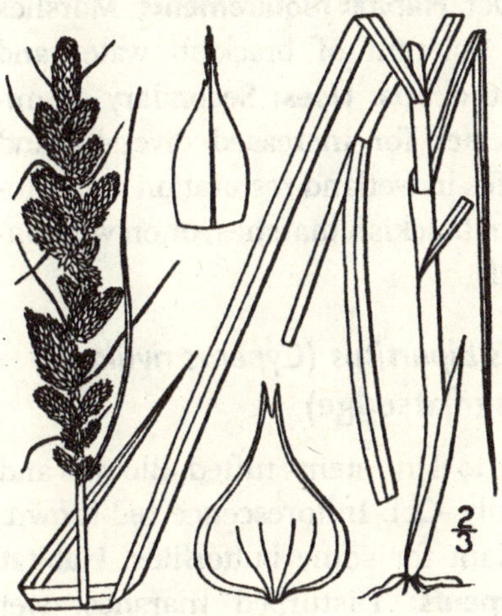
2/3

Carex vulpinoidea

**Carex vulpinoidea* (fox sedge)

To 3 ft., tufted, growth rate slow. Blooms and fruits June–Aug. Wildlife value high. Host plant for some butterflies. **Habitat requirements:** Moist to wet meadows, marshes (OBL). Soil pH 6.8–8.9. Should tolerate concrete debris. Tolerant of partial shade, flooding or saturated soil up to 75% of growing season. Intolerant of salt. **Notes:** Common in our region. Available. **Uses:** Primary or secondary species for open freshwater wetland restoration and mitigation.

Cenchrus longispinus (common sandbur)

Annual, to 32 in., stems tufted. Blooms and fruits July–Oct. Inflorescence spiny. **Habitat requirements:** Dry sandy or disturbed soil (UPL). **Notes:** Weedy. Common in dry waste sites. **Uses:** Secondary or minor species for initial erosion control seeding in dry, open restoration sites.

Cenchrus tribuloides (dune sandbur)

Annual, to 40 in., spiny. **Habitat requirements:** Coastal sand dunes (UPL). **Uses:** Secondary or minor species for initial stabilization of coastal sands, back dunes in newly restored habitats.

Cinna arundinacea (stout woodreed)

To 5 ft., stems few together. Blooms and fruits Aug.–Oct. **Habitat requirements:** Moist woods, swamp forests (FACW+). Soil pH 4.0–8.5. Should tolerate concrete debris. Tolerant of shade. Tolerant of disturbed conditions. **Notes:** Frequent in our woodlands. Available. **Uses:** Secondary species for increased diversity in wetland restoration and mitigation in swamp forests, and margins of woodland vernal ponds.

Cinna latifolia (drooping woodreed)

To 5 ft. Blooms and fruits July–Oct. **Habitat requirements:** Moist woods (FACW). Soil pH 4.7–7.0. Tolerant of shade. **Uses:** Secondary or minor species for increased diversity and aesthetics in wetland restoration of swamp forests.

Cladium mariscoides

Cladium mariscoides (twig rush)

To 3 ft., colonial. Blooms and fruits Aug.–Oct. **Habitat requirements:** Marshes (OBL). Tolerant of brackish water and concrete debris. **Uses:** Secondary or minor species for increased diversity and aesthetics in wetland restoration and mitigation in brackish marshes, or on wet concrete fill.

Cyperus bipartitus (*Cyperus rivularis*) (shining flatsedge)

Annual, to 8 in., stems tufted. Blooms and fruits July–Oct. Inflorescence red-brown. Host plant for some butterflies. **Habitat requirements:** Disturbed marshes, wet roadsides, ditches (FACW+). Soil pH 4.5–6.5. Occasional in NYC. **Uses:** Secondary or minor species for increased diversity and aesthetics in wetland restoration and mitigation. Sow seed. Potentially useful for initial seeding on open soil for erosion control.

Cyperus dentatus (toothed flatsedge)

To 18 in. Blooms and fruits July–Oct. Wildlife value high. Host plant for some butterflies. **Habitat requirements:** Wet, sandy soil (FACW+). **Uses:** Secondary or minor species for increased diversity and aesthetics in wetland restoration and mitigation.

Cyperus diandrus (umbrella flatsedge)

Annual, to 8 in. Blooms and fruits June–Oct.; Wildlife value high. Host plant for some butterflies. **Habitat requirements:** Wet to moist soil, shores (FACW). **Uses:** Secondary or minor species for increased diversity and aesthetics in wetland restoration and mitigation.

Cyperus echinatus (*C. ovularis*) (globe flatsedge)

Rare (NYS S1, E); to 3 ft. (usually much shorter), stems solitary or in small tufts. Blooms and fruits July–Sept. **Habitat requirements:** Sandy soil or fill, open woods, oak barren edges (UPL). **Notes:** Use seed of plants only from metro region stock. Plant in coordination with conservation organization restoration specialist. **Uses:** Minor species for increased diversity and aesthetics in restoration of sand barrens, coastal grasslands, open dry woodlands.

Cyperus erythrorhizos (red-rooted flatsedge)

Rare (NYS S3, R); annual, to 28 in., stems tufted. Blooms and fruits Aug.–Oct. Wildlife value high. Host plant for some butterflies. **Habitat requirements:** Stream banks, wet soil (FACW+). Soil pH 5.0–6.5. **Notes:** Plant in coordination with conservation organization restoration specialist. Use local seed stock. **Uses:** Secondary or minor species for increased diversity and aesthetics in wetland restoration and mitigation.

[*Cyperus esculentus* (nutsedge)

Plants in our region are most likely to be European genotypes. *Do not use.*]

Cyperus flavescens (yellow flatsedge)

Rare (NYS S1 U); annual, to 16 in., stems solitary or tufted. Blooms and fruits July–Oct. Wildlife value high. Host plant for some butterflies. **Habitat requirements:** Wet, sandy soil (OBL). Soil pH 5–7. **Notes:** Plant in coordination with conservation organization restoration specialist. Use local seed stock. **Uses:** Secondary or minor species for increased diversity and aesthetics in wetland restoration and mitigation. Sow seed. Potentially useful for initial seeding on open soil for erosion control.

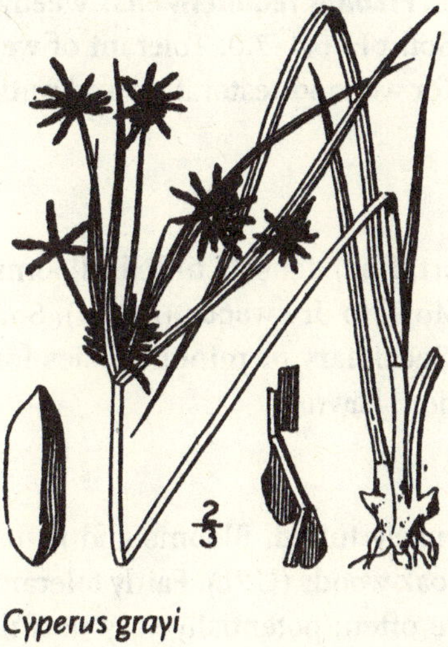

Cyperus grayi

Cyperus grayi (Gray's umbrella sedge)

To 16 in. Blooms and fruits July–Oct. **Habitat requirements:** Back dunes, dry sandy fill (UPL). **Notes:** Occasional along our back dunes. **Uses:** Minor species for increased diversity and aesthetics in restoration of back dunes, sandy fill.

Cyperus lupulinus (slender flatsedge, hop sedge)

To 18 in., colonial. Blooms and fruits Aug.–Oct. **Habitat requirements:** Dry rocky or sandy soil (UPL). **Uses:** Minor species for increased diversity and aesthetics in restoration of dry rocky or sandy soil. Potential for soil-holding uses. Use seed of plants only from metro region stock.

Cyperus odoratus (rusty flatsedge)

Rare (NYS S3, U); annual to 32 in., stems stout. Blooms and fruits Aug.–Oct. Wildlife value high. Host plant for some butterflies. **Habitat requirements:** Moist to wet soil (FACW). Soil pH 5.0–7.2. Apparently tolerant of brackish water. **Notes:** Plant in coordination with conservation restoration specialist. Use local stock. **Uses:** Secondary or minor species for wetland restoration and mitigation. Possibly in brackish marshes, saline soil of roadsides. Potentially useful for initial seeding on open soil for erosion control.

Cyperus polystachyos (many-spike flatsedge)

Annual, to 2 ft., stems tufted. Blooms and fruits Aug.–Oct. Wildlife value high. Host plant for some butterflies. **Habitat requirements:** Damp sandy or wet soil of coastal areas (FACW+). Soil pH 4.5–6.5. **Uses:** Secondary or minor species for wetland restoration and mitigation. Potentially useful for initial seeding on open soil for erosion control.

Cyperus schweinitzii (Schweinitz's flatsedge)

Rare (NYS S3, R); to 3 ft., colonial. Blooms and fruits July–Sept. **Habitat requirements:** Dry to moist sandy soil (FACU). **Notes:** Use seed of plants only from local stock. Plant in coordination with conservation organization restoration specialist. **Uses:** Minor species for increased diversity and aesthetics in restoration of dry rocky or sandy soil. Potential for soil-holding uses.

Cyperus strigosus (false nutsedge)

To 2 ft., stems solitary or few together. Blooms and fruits Aug.–Oct. Wildlife value high. Host plant for some butterflies. **Habitat requirements:** Weedy, open, wet areas, ditches, roadsides (FACW). Soil pH 6.4–7.0. Tolerant of wet fill soils, part shade. **Uses:** Secondary species for wetland restoration and mitigation, especially in weedy disturbed areas.

Danthonia compressa (flattened oatgrass)

To 8 in., flowering stems to 32 in., leaves short, fine, densely tufted. Blooms and fruits June–Aug. **Habitat requirements:** Moist to dry woods (FACU). Soil pH 4.8–7.0. Tolerant of partial shade. **Uses:** Secondary or minor species for diversity, erosion control in woodland restoration. Lawns.

Danthonia spicata (poverty oatgrass)

Inflorescence to 2 ft., leaves to 5 in., wiry, densely tufted. Blooms and fruits May–Sept. **Habitat requirements:** Rocky, open oak woods (UPL). Fairly tolerant of disturbance. **Notes:** Should be grown more often; potentially very useful.

Danthonia spicata

Uses: Primary or secondary species for erosion control and increased diversity in woodland restoration. Lawns.

Deschampsia cespitosa (tufted hairgrass)

To 3.5 ft., stems densely tufted. Blooms and fruits June–Aug. Leaves wiry, short, flowers purplish. Host plant for some butterflies. **Habitat requirements:** Wet soil, shores, cool banks (FACW). Soil pH 4.8–7.2. **Notes:** Available. **Uses:** Secondary or minor species for increased diversity and aesthetics in wetland restoration and mitigation.

Deschampsia flexuosa (common hairgrass)

To 3 ft., leaves much shorter, stems wiry, tufted. Blooms and fruits June–Aug. **Habitat requirements:** Open, rocky oak woods (UPL). Soil pH 4.8–6.8. Shade tolerant and slow growing. **Uses:** Secondary species for erosion control and increased diversity in woodland restoration.

Digitaria filiformis (slender crabgrass)

Annual, to 3 ft., tufted. Blooms and fruits Aug.–Oct. **Habitat requirements:** Dry, open, sandy soil (UPL). **Uses:** Secondary or minor species for initial erosion control seeding on newly restored dry, open sites. Substitute for annual rye.

**Distichlis spicata* (salt-grass)

To 16 in., colonial, growth rate moderate, plant usually reclining, gray-green, turning tan in autumn, persistent through winter. Blooms and fruits Aug.–Oct. Wildlife value moderate. **Habitat requirements:** High salt marsh (FACW+), mean high water to mean high high water. Often codominant with, but sometimes slightly upland of, *Spartina patens*. Tolerant of saltwater to 50 ppt, soil pH 4–10.5; tolerates spring tide flooding. Intolerant of shade. **Uses:** Primary or secondary species for restoration of high salt marsh.

**Dulichium arundinaceum* (three-way sedge)

To 3 ft., colonial. Blooms and fruits July–Oct. Leaves in three ranks. Wildlife value moderate. Host plant for some butterflies. **Habitat requirements:** Open freshwater marshes and tidal areas, pond edges (OBL). Soil pH 4.7–7.5. Tolerant of partial shade, permanently saturated soil or flooding to 1 ft. Intolerant of salt. **Notes:** Available. **Uses:** Secondary species for increased diversity and aesthetics in wetland restoration and mitigation.

Echinochloa muricata (barnyard grass)

Annual, to 40 in. Blooms and fruits July–Sept. Inflorescence usually dark purple. Wildlife value high. **Habitat requirements:** Damp or muddy soil, open, disturbed wet sites, roadsides (FACW+). **Notes:** Frequent in our region. **Uses:** Primary or secondary species for initial erosion control in newly restored areas with moist to wet soil. Substitute for annual rye in moist to wet soil. Sow seed.

Echinochloa walteri (coast cockspur grass)

Annual to 6.5 ft. Blooms and fruits Aug.–Sept. Wildlife value high. **Habitat requirements:** Marshes, wet soil, coastal, probably tolerates brackish water (FACW+). Soil pH 3.8–9.4. Should tolerate concrete debris. **Uses:** Secondary species for initial erosion control in newly restored areas with moist to wet soil. Substitute for annual rye. Sow seed.

Eleocharis acicularis (least spikerush)

To 5 in., tufted, also colonial. Blooms and fruits July–Oct. Wildlife value moderate. Host plant for some butterflies. **Habitat requirements:** In mud, along shores (OBL). Soil pH 4.5–7.0. **Uses:** Secondary species for increased diversity and aesthetics in wetland restoration and mitigation.

Eleocharis melanocarpa (black-fruited spikerush)

To 2 ft., stems densely tufted. Blooms and fruits July-Oct. Wildlife value moderate. Host plant for some butterflies. **Habitat requirements:** Wet sandy shores, pine barrens (FACW+). Needs acid soil. **Uses:** Secondary species for increased diversity and aesthetics in wetland restoration and mitigation in sandy soil, pine barrens, wetlands.

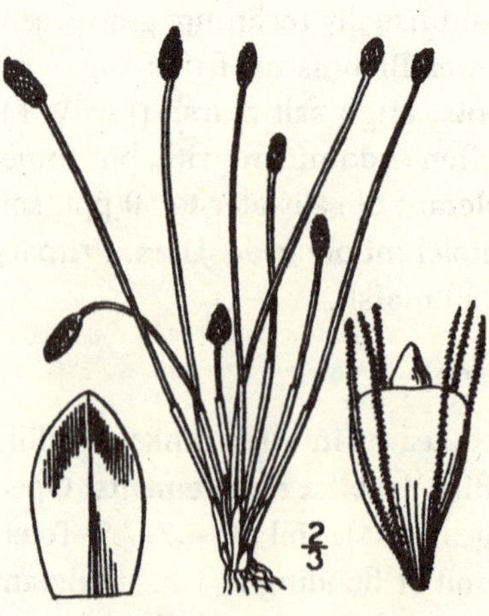

Eleocharis ovata

**Eleocharis ovata* (*E. obtusa*) (blunt spikerush)

Annual, to 2.5 ft., stems tufted. Blooms and fruits June–Aug. Wildlife value moderate. Host plant for some butterflies. **Habitat requirements:** Wet, open soil (OBL). Soil pH 4.6–6.8. Appears very tolerant of fill soils and disturbance. **Notes:** Common in our region. Often available. **Uses:** Primary or secondary species for additional erosion control, increased diversity in wetland restoration and mitigation. Probably useful as a fast-growing plant for quick erosion control.

**Eleocharis palustris* (creeping spikerush)

To 3 ft., colonial, growth rate moderate. Blooms and fruits June–Sept. Wildlife value high. Host plant for some butterflies. **Habitat requirements:** Wet soil, pond margins, marshes, freshwater tidal areas (OBL). Soil pH 4–8. Tolerant of alkaline soil, concrete debris, partial shade, flooding or saturated soil 100% of growing season. **Notes:** Available. **Uses:** Primary or secondary species for increased erosion control in wetland restoration and mitigation. Should be useful for wet, alkaline fill and demolition debris. Brackish marshes.

Eleocharis quadrangulata (square-stem spikerush)

Rare (G4, NYS S1, E); to 3 ft., stems tufted, also colonial. Blooms and fruits June–Oct. Wildlife value high. Host plant for some butterflies. **Habitat requirements:** Shallow water along the coastal plain, often tidal (OBL). Soil pH 5.8–7.2. **Uses:** Secondary species for increased diversity and aesthetics in wetland restoration and mitigation. Plant in coordination with conservation organization restoration specialist.

Eleocharis rostellata (beaked spikerush)

To 40 in., colonial, plant in tussocks, stems reclining, rooting at tips. Blooms and fruits June–Aug. Wildlife value moderate. Host plant for some butterflies. **Habitat requirements:** Saline or calcareous marshes, coastal (OBL). Soil pH 6–8. Should tolerate concrete debris. **Uses:** Secondary species for increased erosion control in wetland restoration and mitigation. Should be useful in brackish salt marsh restoration and for wet, alkaline fill and demolition debris.

Eleocharis tenuis (slender spikerush)

To 3 ft., colonial, stems in small tufts. Blooms and fruits May–June. Wildlife value moderate. Host plant for some butterflies. **Habitat requirements:** Wet, open soil (FACW). Soil pH 6.2–7.0. **Uses:** Primary or secondary species for increased erosion control in wetland restoration and mitigation.

Eleocharis tuberculosa (long-tubercle spikerush)

Annual, rare (NYS S2, T); to 32 in., stems tufted. Blooms and fruits June–Sept. Wildlife value moderate. Host plant for some butterflies. **Habitat requirements:** Wet, sandy soil, coastal (OBL). Probably prefers acid soils. **Uses:** Secondary or minor species for increased diversity and aesthetics in wetland restoration and mitigation. Plant in coordination with conservation organization restoration specialist.

Elymus canadensis (Canada wild rye)

To 5 ft., stems in small tufts, often waxy blue-green. Blooms and fruits July–Oct. **Habitat requirements:** Dry to moist rocky, sandy soil (FACU+). Soil pH 5.0–7.9. **Notes:** Available. **Uses:** Secondary species for erosion control and increased diversity in restoration of open areas, meadow mixes.

Elymus hystrix (*Hystrix patula*) (bottlebrush grass)

To 5 ft., stems in small tufts. Blooms and fruits June–Aug. **Habitat requirements:** Open woods (UPL). Tolerant of partial shade. **Notes:** Available. **Uses:** Secondary species for erosion control and increased diversity in restoration of woodlands.

Elymus riparius (streambank wild rye)

To 3 ft., stems tufted. Blooms and fruits July–Sept. **Habitat requirements:** Moist woods, stream banks (FACW). Soil pH 4.5–7.2. Tolerant of partial shade. **Notes:** Available. **Uses:** Secondary species for increased diversity and aesthetics in wetland restoration and mitigation of wooded streams and vernal pond edges.

Elymus trachycaulus (*Agropyron t.*) (slender wheat grass)

To 3 ft., stems tufted. Blooms and fruits July–Aug. **Habitat requirements:** Open areas, variable (FACU). Soil pH 5.6–9.0. Should tolerate concrete debris. **Uses:** Secondary species for erosion control and increased diversity in restoration of open areas, meadow mixes, roadsides.

Elymus villosus (hairy wild rye)

40 in., stems tufted. Blooms and fruits June–Aug. **Habitat requirements:** Dry woods (FACU−). Tolerant of partial shade. **Notes:** Available. **Uses:** Secondary species for erosion control and increased diversity in restoration of woodlands.

Elymus virginicus

Elymus virginicus (Virginia wild rye)

To 4 ft., stems tufted. Blooms and fruits June–Aug. **Habitat requirements:** Open, moist woods (FACW). Soil pH 5.0–7.4. Tolerant of partial shade. **Notes:** Available. **Uses:** Secondary species for increased diversity and aesthetics in wetland restoration and mitigation of wooded vernal pond edges and swamp forests.

Eragrostis capillaris (lace-grass)

To 28 in., stems tufted, often lemon scented. Blooms and fruits July–Oct. **Habitat requirements:** Dry sandy or rocky soil, open woods (UPL). Tolerant of partial shade. **Uses:**

Secondary species for erosion control and increased diversity in restoration of dry, open woodlands, edges, grasslands, meadows, roadsides.

Eragrostis hypnoides

Eragrostis hypnoides (teal lovegrass)

Annual, to 6 in.; plant creeping, rooting at nodes, forming mats. Blooms and fruits July–Oct. **Habitat requirements:** Gravelly, sandy shores, mudflats (OBL). Soil pH 4.5–8.5. Should tolerate concrete debris. **Uses:** Secondary species for addition to erosion control seed mix on open soil in new wetland restoration and mitigation. Sow seed.

Eragrostis pectinacea (Carolina lovegrass)

Annual, to 2 ft. Blooms and fruits July–Oct. **Habitat requirements:** Weedy on open, moist soil (FAC). **Uses:** Primary or secondary species for initial erosion control seeding on newly restored open sites. Good substitute for annual rye.

Eragrostis spectabilis (purple lovegrass)

To 2 ft., stems usually in low tufts, forming colonies. Blooms and fruits Aug.–Sept. Inflorescence purple, showy, fall. **Habitat requirements:** Tolerates dry, sandy soil or fill; occasional high mowing (UPL). Soil pH 4.0–7.5. **Uses:** Secondary species for erosion control and increased diversity in restoration of open areas, dry grasslands, roadsides.

Eriophorum gracile (slender cotton grass)

To 8 in., colonial. Blooms and fruits April–July. Inflorescence whitish, cottony. Host plant for some butterflies. **Habitat requirements:** Bogs, marshes, shores, wet peat (OBL). Acid soil pH 4.0–6.5. **Uses:** Secondary or minor species for increased diversity and aesthetics in wetland restoration and mitigation of open wetlands.

Eriophorum virginicum (tawny cotton grass)

To 3 ft., colonial. Blooms and fruits Aug.–Oct. Inflorescence brownish cottony. Host plant for some butterflies. **Habitat requirements:** Marshes, bogs, peaty meadows (OBL). Acid soil, pH 3.8–6.5. **Notes:** Available. **Uses:** Secondary or minor species for increased diversity and aesthetics in wetland restoration and mitigation of open wetlands.

Eriophorum viridicarinatum (dark-scale cotton grass)

To 2 ft., colonial. Blooms and fruits June–Aug. Inflorescence buff-cottony. Host plant for some butterflies. **Habitat requirements:** Marshes, bogs, wet meadows (OBL). **Uses:** Secondary or minor species for increased diversity and aesthetics in wetland restoration and mitigation of open wetlands.

Festuca subverticillata (*F. obtusa*) (nodding fescue)

To 4 ft., stems tufted. Blooms and fruits May–Aug. **Habitat requirements:** Moist woods, thickets (FACU). Soil pH 5.5–7.2. Tolerant of shade. **Uses:** Secondary species for erosion control and increased diversity in restoration of moist woodlands, edges.

Fimbristylis autumnalis (slender fimbry)

Annual, to 8 in., stems tufted. Blooms and fruits Aug.–Oct. **Habitat requirements:** Moist to wet soil (FACW). Tolerates disturbance. **Uses:** Secondary species for increased erosion control on open soil in new wetland restoration and mitigation. Sow seed.

Fimbristylis castanea (marsh fimbry)

To 4 ft., stems densely tufted. Blooms and fruits July–Oct. Host plant for some butterflies. **Habitat requirements:** Open wetlands, brackish marshes (OBL). Tolerates brackish water. **Uses:** Secondary or minor species for increased diversity and aesthetics in wetland restoration and mitigation of open, brackish wetlands.

Glyceria acutiflora (creeping mannagrass)

To 40 in., stems often reclining, rooting at lower nodes. Blooms and fruits May–July. **Habitat requirements:** Muddy soil, pond margins, shallow water (OBL). **Uses:** Secondary species for increased erosion control, diversity, and aesthetics in wetland restoration and mitigation.

Glyceria canadensis (rattlesnake mannagrass)

To 3 ft., stems solitary or few together, colonial, growth rate moderate. Blooms and fruits June–Aug. Wildlife value moderate. Eaten by muskrat and deer. **Habitat requirements:** Marshes, open, wet woods (OBL). Soil pH 5.0–8.5. Tolerant of flooding to 50% of growing season. Tolerant of light, partial shade. Intolerant of salt, competition (plant in dense stands). **Notes:** Available. **Uses:** Secondary species for increased erosion control, diversity, and aesthetics in wetland restoration and mitigation.

Glyceria grandis (American mannagrass)

To 5 ft., colonial, stems tufted; growth rate rapid. Blooms and fruits June–Aug. Wildlife value moderate. Eaten by deer and muskrat. **Habitat requirements:** Wet meadows, stream banks, marshes (OBL). Intolerant of flooding beyond late spring; intolerant of shade or competition (plant in monocultures). Available. **Uses:** Secondary species for increased erosion control, diversity, and aesthetics in wetland restoration and mitigation.

Glyceria melicaria (melic mannagrass)

To 40 in., stems solitary from a creeping base, colonial. Blooms and fruits June–Aug. **Habitat requirements:** Swamps, wet woods (OBL). Soil pH 4.5–8.0. Tolerant of shade. **Notes:** Available. **Uses:** Secondary species for increased erosion control, diversity, and aesthetics of restoration in swamps, marshes, forested wetlands.

Glyceria obtusa (coastal mannagrass)

To 3 ft., colonial. Blooms and fruits July–Sept. Inflorescence dense. **Habitat requirements:** Swamps, wet woods (OBL). Soil pH 4–7. Tolerant of shade. **Uses:** Secondary species for increased erosion control, diversity, and aesthetics of restoration in forested wetlands.

Glyceria septentrionalis (eastern mannagrass)

To 5 ft., colonial, growth rate rapid. Blooms and fruits May–July. Wildlife value moderate. Eaten by deer and muskrat. **Habitat requirements:** Wet soil, marshes, pond edges (OBL). Intolerant of flooding beyond late spring, intolerant of shade and competition (plant in monocultures). **Notes:** Available. **Uses:** Secondary species for increased erosion control, diversity, and aesthetics in wetland restoration and mitigation.

Glyceria striata

**Glyceria striata* (fowl mannagrass)

To 4 ft., stems tufted, colonial, growth rate slow to moderate. Blooms and fruits June–Sept. Wildlife value moderate. **Habitat requirements:** Swamp forests, shrub swamps (OBL). Soil pH 4–8. Tolerates partial shade. Tolerant of flooding or saturated soil to 25% of growing season. Intolerant of salt. **Notes:** Available. Frequent in our region. **Uses:** Primary or secondary species for wooded wetland restoration and mitigation, shrub swamps.

Hierochloe odorata (vanilla grass)

To 2 ft., sparsely colonial. Blooms and fruits April–July. Inflorescence sometimes reddish. Host for some butterfly species larvae. **Habitat requirements:** Wet soil of upper salt marsh edges (FACW). Soil pH 5.7–7.4. **Uses:** Secondary or minor species for salt marsh restoration, mitigation. Addition to erosion control plantings.

Hordeum jubatum (foxtail barley, squirrel-tail grass)

To 28 in., stems tufted. Blooms and fruits July–Aug. **Habitat requirements:** Roadside weed on moist soil (FAC). **Notes:** Available. **Uses:** Secondary species for erosion control and increased diversity in restoration of open areas, meadows, roadside seed mixes.

Juncus acuminatus (taper-tip rush)

To 32 in., stems tufted. Blooms and fruits June–Aug. Host plant for some butterflies. **Habitat requirements:** Wet meadows (OBL). Soil pH 4.4–7.2. Occasional in NYC. **Uses:** Secondary species for increased diversity and aesthetics in wetland restoration and mitigation.

Juncus arcticus var. *littoralis* (*J. balticus*) (wire rush, Baltic rush)

To 32 in., stems single along underground stem (rhizome), colonial. Blooms and fruits July–Sept. Host plant for some butterflies. **Habitat requirements:** Alkaline and brackish water, open shores (OBL). Tolerates concrete debris. **Uses:** minor species for increased diversity and aesthetics in wetland restoration and mitigation, brackish marshes, wet soil with concrete debris. Possibly useful for additional erosion control.

Juncus articulatus (jointed rush)

To 2 ft., stems single along underground stem (rhizome), plant colonial. Blooms and fruits July–Aug. Host plant for some butterflies. **Habitat requirements:** Wet meadows, bogs, shores (OBL). Soil pH 4.8–7.5. **Uses:** Minor species for increased diversity and aesthetics in wetland restoration and mitigation.

Juncus bufonius (toad rush)

Annual to 12 in. Blooms and fruits June–Nov. **Habitat requirements:** Salt marshes and moist, wet, open ground (FACW). Soil pH 4.6–7.6. **Uses:** Secondary species for addition to initial erosion control annuals on new wetland restoration, pond shores, wet edges.

Juncus canadensis (Canada rush)

To 3 ft., stems tufted. Blooms and fruits July–Oct. Host plant for some butterflies. **Habitat requirements:** Swamps, marshes, wet shores (OBL). Soil

Juncus canadensis

pH 4.5–5.9. **Notes:** Available. **Uses:** Secondary species for wetland restoration and mitigation.

**Juncus effusus* (soft rush)

Semievergreen; to 3 ft., densely tufted, spreading, growth rate slow. Blooms and fruits July–Sept. Wildlife value high. Host plant for some butterflies. **Habitat requirements:** Wet meadows, freshwater tidal and nontidal marshes, ditches, pond edges (FACW+). Soil pH 5.5–7.0. Tolerant of partial shade, flooding (to 100% of growing season). Intolerant of salt. Usually a tough, reliable plant with wide tolerances for soil type, pH, and moisture regime. Resistant to goose depredations once established. **Notes:** Common in our region. Available. **Uses:** Primary species for wetland restoration and mitigation.

**Juncus gerardii* (black grass)

To 16 in., stems tufted, colonial. Blooms and fruits June–Sept., inflorescence becoming dark. **Habitat requirements:** High salt marsh, generally just upland of or with *Spartina patens* and *Distichlis spicata* (FACW+). **Notes:** Usually available. **Uses:** Primary or secondary species for salt marsh restoration, mitigation.

Juncus greenei (Greene's rush)

To 32 in., stems tufted. Blooms and fruits June–Sept. **Habitat requirements:** Moist to dry sandy or clay soil, dunes (FAC). **Uses:** Minor species for increased diversity in restoration of sandy grasslands or back dunes.

Juncus marginatus (grass-leaf rush)

To 20 in., stems tufted. Blooms and fruits June–Sept. Host plant for some butterflies. **Habitat requirements:** Wet meadows (FACW). Soil pH 5.5–6.8. **Uses:** Secondary or minor species for increased diversity in wetland restoration and mitigation.

Juncus nodosus (knotted rush)

To 16 in., colonial. Blooms and fruits July–Aug. Host plant for some butterflies. **Habitat requirements:** Bogs, marshes (OBL). Soil pH 4.0–7.5. **Uses:** Minor species for increased diversity in wetland restoration and mitigation.

Juncus scirpoides (needle-pod rush)

To 32 in., colonial. Blooms and fruits July–Oct. Host plant for some butterflies. **Habitat requirements:** Wet sandy soil (FACW). Soil pH 5.6–6.8. **Uses:** Minor species for increased diversity in wetland restoration and mitigation.

Juncus secundus (lopsided rush)

To 2 ft., stems tufted. Blooms and fruits June–Oct. **Habitat requirements:** Open, sterile soil (FACU). Soil pH 4.9–6.8. **Uses:** Minor species for increased diversity in restoration of sandy grasslands or back dunes.

Juncus tenuis

**Juncus tenuis* (path rush)

To 28 in., usually shorter, stems tufted, growth rate slow. Blooms and fruits July–Sept. Wildlife value moderate. **Habitat requirements:** Disturbed sites. Tolerant of trampling, compacted soil, fill, part shade, drought (FAC−). Soil pH 4.5–7.0. Moderately flood tolerant (to 25% of growing season). Intolerant of salt. **Notes:** Very common in our region. Available. **Uses:** Primary species for highly used areas. Path edges, play areas, lawns with high foot traffic.

Juncus torreyi (Torrey's rush)

To 3 ft., colonial, growth rate slow. Blooms and fruits July–Oct. Wildlife value moderate. Host plant for some butterflies. **Habitat requirements:** Moist to wet soil, marshes, wet meadows (FACW). Soil pH 4.5–6.5. Tolerant of high soil pH, drought, partial shade, flooding up to 25% of growing season. **Notes:** Available. **Uses:** Secondary species for wetland restoration and mitigation.

**Leersia oryzoides* (rice cut-grass)

To 5 ft., aggressively colonial, sprawling, rooting at nodes, growth rate moderate. Leaves rough, saw toothed. Blooms and fruits June–Oct. Wildlife value high. Host plant for some butterflies. **Habitat requirements:** Freshwater tidal and nontidal marshes, wet ditches, open swamp forests (OBL). Soil pH 5.1–8.8. Tolerant of partial shade, concrete debris, drought, flooding, or saturated soil to 100% of growing season. Intolerant of salt. **Notes:** Frequent in our region. Available. **Uses:** Primary species for wetland restoration and mitigation. Erosion control, stabilization of wet soils. May crowd out less aggressive plants. Best for degraded sites.

Leersia virginica (white grass)

To 5 ft. (usually about 1 ft.), colonial, sprawling, rooting at nodes. Blooms and fruits July–Oct. Host plant for some butterflies. **Habitat requirements:** Wet woods, along trails, disturbed sites (FACW). Soil pH 4.5–8.5. Tolerant of shade, concrete debris. **Notes:** Sometimes mistaken for the highly invasive alien, *Microstegium vimineum* (Japanese stilt grass), a shade-tolerant annual with stilt roots and silvery midrib. **Uses:** Secondary species for increased erosion control, slope stabilization, and diversity in restoration of moist woodlands, swamp forests.

Leptoloma cognatum (*Digitaria c.*) (fall witch-grass)

To 28 in., stems tufted. Blooms and fruits June–Oct. **Habitat requirements:** Dry, open, sandy soil (UPL). **Uses:** Minor species for increased diversity in restoration of sandy grasslands, roadsides.

Luzula acuminata (hairy wood-rush)

To 16 in., stems tufted. Blooms and fruits April–May. **Habitat requirements:** Moist to dry woods (FAC). Tolerant of bright shade. **Uses:** Minor species for increased diversity and aesthetics in restoration of moist, open woodlands.

Luzula multiflora (common wood-rush)

To 16 in., stems tufted, leaves often purplish. Blooms and fruits April–June. **Habitat requirements:** Dry to moist mixed deciduous or oak woods (FACU). Found in acid soil, pH 4.8–5.4. Tolerant of bright shade. **Uses:** Minor species for increased diversity and aesthetics in restoration of open woodlands.

Muhlenbergia frondosa (wire-stem muhly)

To 40 in., plants vigorously colonial. Blooms and fruits Aug.–Oct. **Habitat requirements:** Moist open woods, thickets, edges, sometimes weedy (FAC). Soil pH 5.9–7.9. Tolerant of shade. **Uses:** Secondary species for erosion control on open, wooded slopes, edges, roadsides, open areas. Addition to erosion control seed mix in newly restored woodland sites.

Muhlenbergia mexicana (Mexican muhly)

To 34 in., aggressively colonial. Blooms and fruits Aug.–Oct. **Habitat requirements:** Moist to wet, open areas or woods (FACW). Soil pH 5.5–7.5. Tolerant of partial shade. **Uses:** Secondary species for increased erosion control and diversity in restoration of open swamp forests or open wetlands, wetland mitigation.

Muhlenbergia schreberi (nimblewill)

To 2 ft., usually about 8 in., stems tufted, later sprawling, rooting at nodes, colonial, sometimes aggressive. Blooms and fruits July–Nov. **Habitat requirements:**

Muhlenbergia schreberi

Weedy sites in woods, part shade, or open areas; tolerates fill soil and concrete debris (FAC). Soil pH 4.5–7.5. Tolerates mowing well. Good lawn grass. Common in NYC and region. **Notes:** Should be propagated as seed or plugs for erosion control. **Uses:** Primary or secondary species for erosion control on wooded slopes, roadsides, open areas. Addition to erosion control seed mix in newly restored woodland sites.

Muhlenbergia sobolifera (creeping muhly)

To 34 in., vigorously colonial. Blooms and fruits July–Oct. **Habitat requirements:** Dry woods, rocky habitats, often on calcareous soils (UPL). Should tolerate concrete debris. Tolerant of shade. **Notes:** Needs to be commercially propagated. **Uses:** Primary or secondary species for erosion control on dry wooded or rocky slopes, roadsides, fill soils, open areas. Addition to erosion control seed mix in newly restored woodlands.

Muhlenbergia sylvatica (forest muhly)

To 30 in., colonial. Blooms and fruits July–Oct. **Habitat requirements:** Moist woods, thickets, stream banks (FAC+). Soil pH 5.9–7.5. Tolerant of shade. **Uses:** Secondary species for erosion control on wooded slopes, edges, roadsides, open areas. Addition to erosion control seed mix in newly restored woodland sites.

Muhlenbergia tenuiflora (slender-flowered muhly)

To 40 in., vigorously colonial. Blooms and fruits July–Sept. **Habitat requirements:** Upland rocky or gravelly woods, shaded slopes, cliffs (UPL). Tolerant of shade. **Notes:** Potentially very useful. Needs propagation. **Uses:** Secondary species for erosion control on dry, wooded slopes, edges, shady roadsides. Addition to erosion-control seed mix in newly restored woodland sites.

Panicum amarum (bitter panic grass)

To 6 ft., colonial, waxy blue-green. Blooms and fruits Aug.–Nov. **Habitat requirements:** Beach foredunes (FACU−). Soil pH 5.0–7.6. **Notes:** *Warning!* Use local stock. Some commercial breeds are very aggressive. **Uses:** Restoration and stabilization of coastal dunes with *Ammophila*.

Panicum boscii (Bosc's panic grass)

To 28 in., winter rosette evergreen. Blooms and fruits July–Oct. Wildlife value high. **Habitat requirements:** Rich dry woods (UPL). Tolerant of shade. **Uses:**

Panicum boscii

Secondary or minor species for increased diversity and aesthetics in restoration of open woodlands, partly shady roadside banks.

Panicum capillare (witch-grass)

Annual to 28 in. Blooms and fruits Aug.–Oct. Wildlife value high. Inflorescence often purple. **Habitat requirements:** Weedy, in gardens, open soil (FAC−). **Notes:** Should be propagated for seed. Potential substitute for annual rye. **Uses:** Primary or secondary species for initial erosion control in new restoration with open soil. Initial slope stabilization. Roadside banks, annual grass seed mixes.

**Panicum clandestinum* (*Dichanthelium clandestinum*) (deer-tongue grass)

To 5 ft., stems tufted, aggressively colonial. Blooms and fruits July–Nov. Leaves wide. Wildlife value high. Host plant for some butterflies. **Habitat requirements:** Moist fields, open woods (FAC+). Soil pH 4.0–7.5. **Notes:** Common in our region. Available. **Uses:** Primary species for erosion control, stabilization of moist soils on roadside banks wetland margins, moist open woodlands, and meadow restoration. Wetland mitigation.

Panicum columbianum (*Dichanthelium sabulorum* var. *thinium*) (Columbia panic grass)

To 34 in., winter rosette evergreen, stems tufted, plant blue-green to purplish, hairy. Blooms and fruits June–Nov. Wildlife value high. **Habitat requirements:** Sandy soil, open areas, thin woods (UPL). Tolerant of partial shade. **Uses:** Secondary or minor species for increased diversity and aesthetics in restoration of open woodlands, meadows, partly shady roadside banks.

Panicum commonsianum (*Dichanthelium ovale*) (rosette grass)

To 2 ft., winter rosette evergreen, stems tufted, plant gray-green, sometimes purplish. Blooms and fruits May–Nov. Wildlife value high. **Habitat requirements:** Open, dry, sandy soil (UPL). **Uses:** Secondary or minor species for increased diversity and aesthetics in restoration of open dry soil, grassland restoration.

Panicum commutatum (*Dichanthelium c.*) (variable panic grass)

To 32 in., winter rosette evergreen, stems tufted, plant waxy gray-green to purplish. Blooms and fruits May–Nov. Wildlife value high. **Habitat requirements:** Open sandy or rocky soil, thin woods (FACU+). Soil pH 4.0–6.5. Tolerant of partial shade. **Uses:** Secondary or minor species for increased diversity and aesthetics in restoration of open woodlands, sandy meadows, partly shady roadside banks.

Panicum depauperatum (*Dichanthelium d.*) (poverty panic grass)

To 16 in., winter rosette evergreen, stems densely tufted, slender, hairy. Blooms and fruits May–Oct. Wildlife value high. **Habitat requirements:** Dry open areas, thin woods (UPL). Tolerant of partial shade. **Uses:** Secondary or minor species for increased diversity and aesthetics in restoration of open woodlands, sandy meadows, partly shady roadside banks.

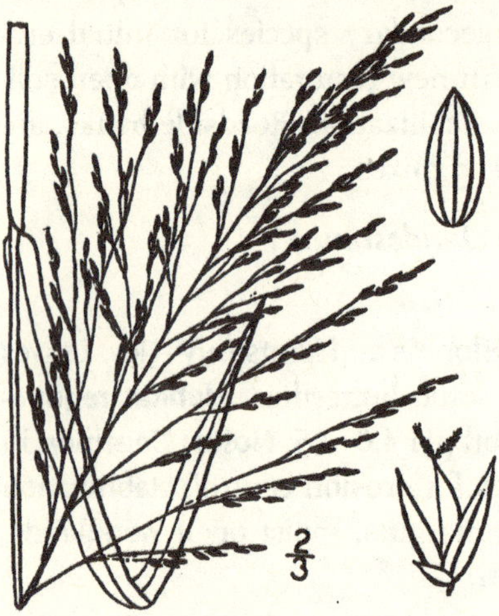

Panicum dichotomiflorum

Panicum dichotomiflorum (fall panic grass)

Annual, to 40 in., stems tufted, weedy, often aggressive. Blooms and fruits July–Oct. Wildlife value high. Stems often reddish. **Habitat requirements:** Open damp sand, pond edges, moist to wet street curbs and roadsides (FACW−). Soil pH 4.8–7.0. Appears tolerant of urban conditions. **Notes:** Very common. Available. **Uses:** Secondary species with seed mix for initial erosion control on open soil in wetland restoration and mitigation. Possible substitute for annual rye.

Panicum dichotomum (*Dichanthelium d.*) (cypress witch-grass)

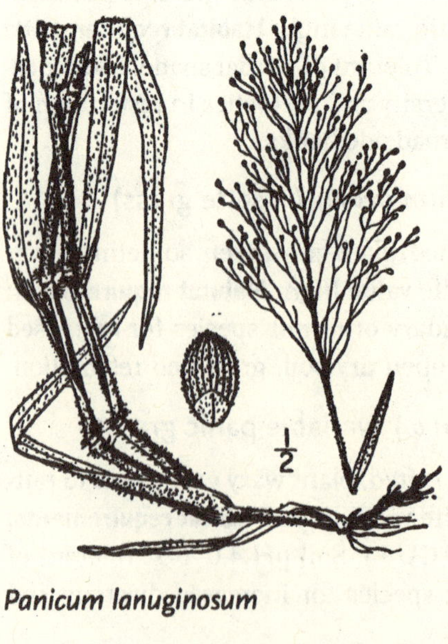

Panicum lanuginosum

To 28 in., winter rosette evergreen, stems tufted, slender, often purplish. A delicate, attractive plant. Blooms and fruits May–Nov. **Habitat requirements:** Thin woods, open disturbed habitats (FAC). Tolerant of partial shade. **Uses:** Secondary or minor species for increased diversity and aesthetics in restoration of open woodlands, meadows, partly shady roadside banks.

Panicum lanuginosum (*Dichanthelium acuminatum* var. *fasciculatum*) (downy panic grass)

To 40 in. (spring flowering stems), winter rosette evergreen, stems tufted, plants hairy, very variable. Blooms and fruits May–Nov. Wildlife value high. **Habitat requirements:** Open oak or pine woods, sandy soil, dunes, shores (UPL). Tolerant of partial shade. **Notes:** One of several very similar species including: *P. leucothrix, P. spretum, P. wrightianum, P. villosissimum,* all on sandy soils, open woods. **Uses:** Secondary or minor species for increased diversity, erosion control and aesthetics on dry, open or partly shaded sites. Barrens, back dunes, open woodlands.

Panicum latifolium (*Dichanthelium l.*) (broad-leaved panic grass)

To 40 in., winter rosette evergreen, stems tufted, usually hairy. Blooms and fruits May–Oct. Wildlife value high. **Habitat requirements:** Dry, open woods, thickets (UPL). Soil pH 4.0–6.5. Tolerant of partial shade. **Uses:** Secondary or minor species for increased diversity, erosion control and aesthetics in restoration of dry, partly shaded sites. Open woodlands, roadside banks.

Panicum oligosanthes (*Dichanthelium o.*) (few-flowered panic grass)

To 28 in., winter rosette evergreen, stems loosely tufted. Blooms and fruits June–Nov. Wildlife value high. **Habitat requirements:** Dry open woods, gaps, sandy soil (UPL). Tolerant of partial shade. **Uses:** Secondary or minor species for increased diversity, erosion control, and aesthetics in restoration of dry, partly shaded sites. Open woodlands, roadside banks.

Panicum philadelphicum (Philadelphia panic grass)

Annual to 32 in., stems slender. Blooms and fruits June–Oct. Wildlife value high. **Habitat requirements:** Dry rocky or sandy soil or thin woods (UPL). Tolerant of partial shade. **Uses:** Secondary species for addition to erosion control seed mixes for open soil of new restoration in dry, open, or partly shaded sites. Seed mix for roadside banks.

Panicum rigidulum (*Panicum agrostoides*) (red-top panic grass)

To 4 ft., stems tufted. Blooms and fruits July–Oct. Often purplish, stout. Wildlife value high. Host plant for some butterflies. **Habitat requirements:** Marshes, wet meadows (FACW+). Soil pH 5.0–7.5. **Uses:** Secondary species for increased diversity, erosion control on open soil in wetland restoration and mitigation.

Panicum scoparium (*Dichanthelium s.*) (velvet panic grass)

To 5 ft., stems solitary or few together. Blooms and fruits June–Nov. Plants hairy. Wildlife value high. **Habitat requirements:** Marshes, wet meadows (FACW). Soil pH 4.5–7.5. **Uses:** Secondary or minor species for increased diversity, erosion control on open soil in wetland restoration and mitigation.

Panicum sphaerocarpon (*Dichanthelium s.*) (round-seed panic grass)

To 20 in., winter rosette evergreen, stems tufted, pale green, reclining. Blooms and fruits May–Nov. Wildlife value high. **Habitat requirements:** Dry to moist woods (FACU). Tolerant of shade. **Uses:** Secondary or minor species for increased diversity, erosion control and aesthetics in restoration of moist to dry, forest understories, shaded roadside banks.

Panicum verrucosum (warty panic grass)

Annual, to 3 ft., stems solitary or tufted. Blooms and fruits Aug.–Oct. Wildlife value high. **Habitat requirements:** Moist to wet woods, shores, along coastal plain (FACW). Tolerant of partial shade. **Uses:** Secondary species with seed mix for initial erosion control on shady soil in wetland restoration and mitigation. Woodlands, roadside banks.

**Panicum virgatum* (switchgrass)

To 6 ft., tufted, growth rate slow. Blooms and fruits July–Sept. Wildlife value high. **Habitat requirements:** Back dunes, dry to wet meadows, successional shrub lands, grasslands, upper edges of salt marsh with *Baccharis,* at or above mean high high water (FAC). Soil pH 4.5–7.5. Tolerates sterile, acid, sandy soil, low nutrient fill, drought, partial shade, flooding or saturated soil up to 25% of growing season, brackish water to 10 ppt salt. Widely tolerant of soil moisture variations. Often associated with broom sedge, little bluestem and Indian grasses, eastern red cedar. Does not compete well with mugwort or other aggressive weeds in high-nutrient soils. **Notes:** Common in our region. Available. Try to get local stock. *Warning!* There is apparently an overly aggressive selection being grown for commercial use. **Uses:** Primary species for establishment of meadows, shrub lands, and dry grasslands on sandy soil. Restoration of back-dune habitats. Upper edges of open wetlands. Wetland mitigation.

Paspalum setaceum

Paspalum setaceum (thin paspalum)

To 24 in., tufted, often reclining, leaves hairy, mostly basal. Blooms and fruits June–Oct. **Habitat requirements:** Moist to dry sandy soil, open sites, or thin woodlands (FACU+). Tolerates light shade. **Uses:** Minor species for increased diversity in restoration of open woodlands, gaps, edges, roadsides.

Phalaris arundinacea (reed canary grass)

To 5 ft., aggressively colonial, growth rate fast, may be invasive. Blooms and fruits June–Aug. Wildlife value moderate. Host plant for some butterflies. **Habitat requirements:** Freshwater tidal and nontidal marshes, shores, moist areas (FACW+). Soil pH 4.9–8.2. Tolerant of concrete debris, drought, flooding, or saturated soil to 100% of growing season. Intolerant of shade, salt. **Notes:** Available. Warning: Invasive in western NYS and other areas. **Uses:** Secondary species for erosion control, soil stabilization, in wet habitats where rapid, permanent cover is desired. Use only in degraded sites subject to disturbance.

Phragmites australis (common reed, phragmites)

To 15 ft. (in high-nutrient soils), colonial from deep rhizome system. Blooms and fruits Aug.–Oct. **Habitat requirements:** Moist upland to standing water (FACW). Tolerant of brackish tidal water (to 20 ppt; inundation to 2 ft. for 100% growing season; soil pH 3.7–10—data from nonnatives). Prefers high-nutrient soils. Not tolerant of saltwater or dry, sterile soil. **Notes:** *Warning!* Nonnative genotypes *very invasive.* New genetic information indicates the common form of *Phragmites* in the northeastern U.S. is not native. However, a few remnant populations of native *Phragmites* remain in some sites in Delaware, Massachusetts, and southern New Jersey. **Uses:** Erosion control and uptake of high-nutrient levels. Use native genotypes.

Piptochaetium avenaceum (*Stipa a.*) (black oatgrass)

To 40 in., tufted. Blooms and fruits April–June. **Habitat requirements:** Dry, open woods (UPL). Tolerant of partial shade. **Uses:** Minor species for increased diversity in restoration of open woodland understories, edges, gaps.

Poa alsodes (speargrass, grove bluegrass)

To 3 ft., stems tufted. Blooms and fruits May–June. Host plant for some butterflies. **Habitat requirements:** Moist woods (FACW−). Tolerant of shade. **Notes:** One of only a few native species of *Poa.* **Uses:** Secondary species for increased diversity in restoration of moist to wet forest understories.

Poa cuspidata (early bluegrass)

To 2 ft., colonial, also loosely tufted. Blooms and fruits March–June. **Habitat requirements:** Rocky, moist woods (UPL). Tolerant of shade. **Uses:** Minor species for increased diversity in restoration of woodlands.

Poa palustris (fowl meadow grass)

To 5 ft., stems tufted. Blooms and fruits June–Aug. Host plant for some butterflies. **Habitat requirements:** Wet meadows (FACW+). Soil pH 4.9–7.5. **Notes:** Available. **Uses:** Secondary species for increased diversity in restoration of moist to wet meadows, marshes. Wetland mitigation.

Poa sylvestris (woodland bluegrass)

To 32 in. Blooms and fruits April–June. **Habitat requirements:** Rich, moist woods (FACW). Soil pH 5.9–7.0. Tolerant of shade. **Uses:** Secondary species for increased diversity in restoration of moist forest understories.

Puccinellia fasciculata (salt-marsh alkali grass)

To 24 in. Blooms and fruits May–July. **Habitat requirements:** Wet soil of high salt marsh borders (OBL). **Uses:** Secondary species for salt marsh restoration, mitigation. Use seed or stock from NYC metro region sources only.

Puccinellia pallida (*Torreyochloa p.*) (pale false mannagrass)

To 40 in., stems reclining or creeping from base. Blooms and fruits May–Aug. **Habitat requirements:** Swamps, shallow water (OBL). **Uses:** Secondary or minor species for increased diversity in restoration of swamps, marshes. Wetland mitigation.

Rhynchospora alba (white beak rush)

To 28 in., stems tufted. Blooms and fruits July–Sept. Host plant for some butterflies. **Habitat requirements:** Sphagnum bogs (OBL), sandy or acid peaty soil. **Uses:** Secondary or minor species for increased diversity in restoration of bogs, swamps.

Rhynchospora capitellata (brownish beak rush)

To 32 in., stems tufted. Blooms and fruits July–Oct. Host plant for some butterflies. **Habitat requirements:** Bogs, wet sand (OBL). Needs acid soil. **Uses:** Secondary or minor species for increased diversity in restoration of bogs, swamps. Wetland mitigation.

Rhynchospora fusca (brown beak rush)

To 16 in., colonial. Blooms and fruits June–Oct. Host plant for some butterflies. **Habitat requirements:** Bogs, marshes (OBL). **Uses:** Secondary or minor species for increased diversity in restoration of bogs, marshes. Wetland mitigation.

Schizachne purpurascens (false melic)

To 3 ft., stems tufted. Blooms and fruits June–Aug. Inflorescence purplish. **Habitat requirements:** Dry rocky or sandy woods (FACU−). Tolerant of shade. **Uses:** Minor species for increased diversity in restoration of woodland understories in rocky or sandy soils.

**Schizachyrium scoparium* (*Andropogon s.*) (little bluestem)

To 4 ft., stems densely tufted, bluish purple in flower, becoming dark orange-gold over winter. Blooms and fruits Sept.–Oct. Host plant for some butterflies. **Habitat requirements:** Old fields, open areas, back dunes (FACU−). In dry, acid soils. Available. **Uses:** Primary species for restoration of grasslands and dry, open habitats, sandy soil, especially with other warm-season grasses and eastern red cedar.

**Scirpus americanus* (*S. olneyi, Schoenoplectus americanus*) (Olney three-square)

To 6 ft., colonial, growth rate rapid. Blooms and fruits June–Sept. Flowers brown. Wildlife value high. Eaten by muskrats; seeds eaten by many birds. Host plant for some butterflies. **Habitat requirements:** Brackish and freshwater tidal marshes, nontidal alkaline marshes, pond edges, moist to wet fill soils (OBL). Tolerant of brackish water to 15 ppt salt, concrete debris; flooding to 0.5ft for 100% of growing season. Moderately tolerant of some drought. Intolerant of shade. **Notes:** Available. **Uses:** Primary or secondary species for restoration of salt or freshwater marshes, pond edges. Wetland mitigation.

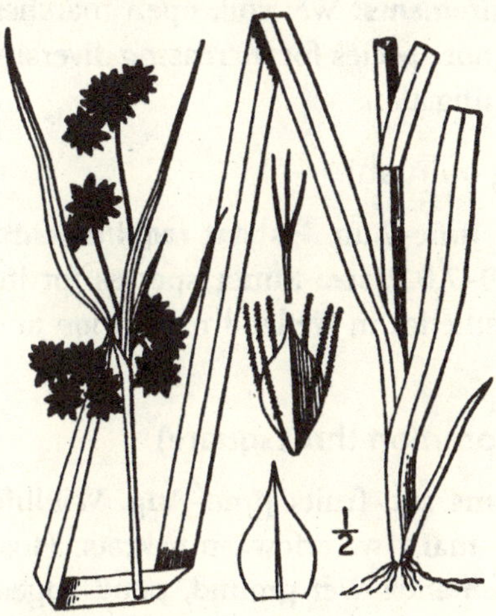

Scirpus atrovirens

**Scirpus atrovirens* (black bulrush, green bulrush)

To 4 ft., stems tufted. Blooms and fruits July–Aug. Host plant for some butterflies. **Habitat requirements:** Wet meadows, swamps, wet thickets (OBL). Soil pH 4–8. Tolerates disturbance, partial shade. **Notes:** A sturdy, robust plant. Frequent in our region. Available. **Uses:** Primary or secondary species for restoration of open or partially shaded marshes, wet, open woodlands, swamps. Wetland mitigation.

**Scirpus cyperinus* (wool grass)

To 6 ft., stems tufted, also colonial, growth rate moderate. Blooms and fruits Aug.–Oct. Flowers greenish, becoming wooly brown. Wildlife value high. Seeds and rhizomes eaten by many waterfowl, also by muskrats. Host plant for some butterflies. **Habitat requirements:** Freshwater tidal and nontidal marshes, wet fill, swamps (FACW+). Soil pH 4.8–8.0. Probably tolerates concrete debris. Tolerates flooding or saturated soil to 25% of growing season. Intolerant of shade, salt. **Notes:** Frequent in our region. Available. **Uses:** Primary to secondary species for restoration of marshes, vegetation of wet fill with concrete debris. Wetland mitigation.

Scirpus fluviatilis (river bulrush)

To 4 ft., colonial. Blooms and fruits July–Sept.; growth rate moderate. Wildlife value high, seeds or rhizomes eaten by many waterfowl and by muskrats. Host plant for some butterflies. **Habitat requirements:** Marshes, pond and lake shores (OBL). Soil pH 4.0–7.5. Probably tolerant of concrete debris. Tolerant of partial shade, flooding up to 1 ft. deep for 100% of growing season. Intolerant of salt. **Notes:** Available. **Uses:** Secondary species for restoration of freshwater wetlands, erosion control on soils with concrete fill. Wetland mitigation.

Scirpus maritimus (*Schoenoplectus maritimus*) (seaside bulrush)

Rare (NYS S1, U); to 4 ft., stems stout, colonial from rhizomes. Blooms and fruits June–Sept. Host to some butterfly larvae. **Habitat requirements:** Salt marshes (OBL). Soil pH 4–7. Tolerant of concrete debris, saltwater. **Notes:** Much like *S. robustus.* Use seed or stock from regional sources only. **Uses:** Secondary species for salt marsh restoration, mitigation.

Scirpus microcarpus (*S. rubrotinctus*) (small-fruit bulrush)

To 5 ft., colonial from underground stems (rhizomes). Stems stout, reddish. Blooms and fruits July–Aug. **Habitat requirements:** Wet soil, open marshes (OBL). Soil pH 5.4–7.4. Available. **Uses:** Minor species for increasing diversity and aesthetics in wetland restoration and mitigation.

Scirpus pendulus (*S. lineatus*) (drooping bulrush)

To 5 ft., stems tufted. Blooms and fruits June–Aug. **Habitat requirements:** Marshes, wet meadows (OBL). Soil pH 4.9–7.0. **Uses:** Minor species for increasing erosion control, diversity, and aesthetics in wetland restoration and mitigation.

**Scirpus pungens* (*Schoenoplectus p.*) (common threesquare)

To 4 ft., colonial, growth rate rapid. Blooms and fruits June–Aug. Wildlife value high. Seeds and rhizomes eaten by many waterfowl, muskrats. Host plant for some butterflies. **Habitat requirements:** Wet ground, pond edges, brackish tidal and nontidal marshes (OBL). Soil pH 3.7–7.5. Tolerant of concrete debris, fill soils. Tolerates brackish water to 15 ppt salt; tolerates drought, tolerates flooding to 0.5 ft. up to 100% of growing season. **Notes:** Frequent in our region. Available. **Uses:** Primary species for restoration of freshwater wetlands, pond edges; erosion control, vegetation of wet fill. Secondary species for brackish salt marshes. Wetland mitigation.

**Scirpus robustus* (*Schoenoplectus robustus*) (salt-marsh bulrush)

To 5 ft., colonial, growth rate moderate. Blooms and fruits July–Oct. Wildlife value high. Seeds and rhizomes eaten by many waterfowl, muskrats. **Habitat requirements:** High salt marsh, 10% intertidal and above (OBL). Soil pH 6.4–8.4. Tolerant of brackish water to 25 ppt salt. Intolerant of shade. **Notes:** Usually available. **Uses:** Primary or secondary species for salt marsh restoration, mitigation.

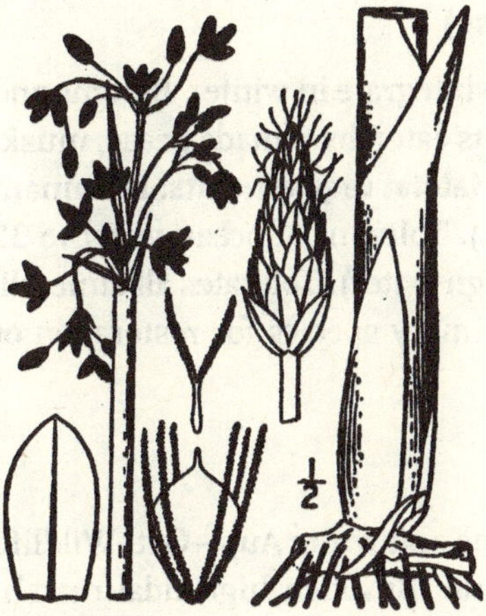

Scirpus validus

*Scirpus validus (Schoenoplectus tabernaemontani) (soft-stem bulrush)

To 7 ft., colonial, growth rate rapid. Blooms and fruits June–Sept. Wildlife value high. Seeds and rhizomes eaten by waterfowl and muskrats. Host plant for some butterflies. **Habitat requirements:** Freshwater and brackish tidal marshes, pond shores (OBL); circumneutral to alkaline soil pH 5.4–8.5. Tolerant of concrete debris. Tolerant of brackish water to 5 ppt salt, flooding to 1 ft., or saturated soil for 100% growing season. Intolerant of shade. **Notes:** Available. **Uses:** Primary or secondary species for restoration of disturbed, brackish marshes, upper 50% of intertidal zone to high high-tide line. Wetland mitigation. Erosion control of wet, alkaline fill, concrete debris.

Scirpus verecundus (*Trichophorum planifolium*) (club rush)

To 16 in., stems densely tufted, slender. Blooms and fruits May–June. **Habitat requirements:** Dry fields, open woods, often on calcareous rock ledges (UPL). **Uses:** Minor species for increased diversity and aesthetics in restoration of dry, open woodlands, gaps, edges. Open or lightly shaded areas with concrete debris.

Scleria pauciflora (few-flower nut rush)

To 20 in., colonial. Blooms and fruits June–Sept. **Habitat requirements:** Sterile, acid soil, sandy fill (FACU+). **Uses:** Minor species for increased diversity and aesthetics in restoration of dry, open, sandy soil, coastal grasslands, barrens.

Scleria triglomerata (whip nut rush)

To 3 ft., colonial. Blooms and fruits June–Sept. **Habitat requirements:** Moist to dry sandy soil (FAC). **Uses:** Minor species for increased diversity and aesthetics in restoration of sand barrens, moist sandy soil.

Setaria parviflora (*S. geniculata*) (knotroot-foxtail grass)

To 4 ft. Blooms and fruits July–Oct. **Habitat requirements:** Moist to dry open soil, salt marshes. Apparently tolerant of brackish water or slightly saline soil (FAC). **Uses:** Minor species for increased diversity and aesthetics in restoration of open habitats, grasslands, meadows, salt marsh edges.

**Spartina alterniflora* (salt-marsh cordgrass)

To 4.5 ft., colonial, growth rate rapid. Stems disintegrate in winter. Blooms and fruits July–Sept. Wildlife value moderate. Plants eaten by Canada geese, muskrats. Protect new plantings with goose fence. **Habitat requirements:** Dominant plant of low salt marsh, soil pH 4.5–8.5 (OBL). Tolerant of ocean water to 35 ppt salt, mean midtide to high water (mean high water). Tolerates alkaline fill, concrete debris. Intolerant of shade. **Uses:** Primary species for restoration of low salt marsh.

Spartina cynosuroides (big cordgrass)

To 9 ft., colonial, growth rate moderate. Blooms and fruits Aug.–Oct. Wildlife value low. Eaten by Canada geese and muskrat. Brackish high tidal marsh, mean high water to high high water (spring tide); freshwater marshes (OBL). Soil pH 5.8–7.5. Tolerant of brackish water to 10 ppt salt. Intolerant of shade. **Uses:** Secondary species for restoration of brackish high salt marsh or tidal freshwater marsh.

**Spartina patens* (salt-meadow cordgrass)

Spartina patens

To 2 ft., colonial, usually reclining, growth rate moderate; winter plants reddish tan. Blooms and fruits June–Oct. Wildlife value moderate. Eaten by Canada geese. **Habitat requirements:** Dominant plant of high salt marsh, mean high water to mean high high water (spring tide) and above (FACW+). Soil pH 4–8. Tolerant of drought; brackish to ocean water 35 ppt salt. Intolerant of shade. **Uses:** Primary species for restoration of high salt marsh.

Spartina pectinata (prairie cordgrass)

To 7 ft., colonial. Blooms and fruits July–Sept. **Habitat requirements:** Brackish to freshwater shores, marshes (OBL). Soil pH 6.0–8.5. Should tolerate concrete debris. **Notes:** Available. **Uses:** Secondary or minor species for increasing diversity in freshwater wetland restoration and mitigation.

Sphenopholis nitida (wedge-grass, wedgescale)

To 32 in., stems tufted, plant dark green. Blooms and fruits April-June. **Habitat requirements:** Dry woods or open areas (UPL). Tolerant of partial shade.

Uses: Secondary species for increased diversity in restoration of open woodland understories, meadows, grasslands.

Sphenopholis obtusata (prairie wedge-grass, prairie wedgescale)

Annual or short-lived perennial, to 4 ft. Blooms and fruits June–July. **Habitat requirements:** Wet to dry soil, lake shores, meadows, woodland edges (FAC−). Soil pH 5.0–7.5. **Uses:** Secondary species for initial erosion control on open soil of restoration. Sow seed. Possible substitute for annual rye.

Sphenopholis pensylvanica (swamp oats)

To 3 ft., stems apparently solitary or few. Blooms and fruits May–July. Host plant for some butterflies. **Habitat requirements:** Wet woods and open areas (OBL). Tolerant of partial shade. **Uses:** Secondary or minor species for increasing diversity in freshwater wetland restoration and mitigation.

**Sorghastrum nutans* (Indian grass)

To 6 ft., colonial, stems loosely tufted. Blooms and fruits Aug.–Sept., inflorescence gold-brown. **Habitat requirements:** Dry, open woods, edges, open areas, sandy low-nutrient soil (UPL). Soil pH 5.0–7.8. **Notes:** Available. **Uses:** Secondary species for increased diversity, aesthetics, erosion control in restoration of grasslands and open habitats, in dry, sandy soil, especially with other warm-season grasses. Grassland restoration.

Sporobolus asper (*S. compositus* var. *compositus*) (tall dropseed)

To 4 ft., stems tufted. Blooms and fruits Aug.–Oct. Inflorescence purplish, cylindrical. **Habitat requirements:** Dry, sandy, sterile soil, sometimes weedy (UPL). Soil pH 5.5–7.0. Tolerant of drought. **Uses:** Secondary species for increased diversity in restoration of grasslands, meadows, revegetation of roadsides.

Sporobolus neglectus (puffsheath dropseed)

Annual to 20 in. Blooms and fruits Aug.–Oct. **Habitat requirements:** Dry, sterile, often calcareous soils (FACU−). Should tolerate concrete debris. **Uses:** Secondary species for initial erosion control on open soil of restoration. Sow seed. Possible substitute for annual rye.

Sporobolus vaginiflorus (poverty grass)

Annual to 20 in. Blooms and fruits Aug.–Oct. **Habitat requirements:** Dry, sandy, sterile soil, open habitats (UPL). **Uses:** Secondary species for initial erosion control on dry, open soil of restoration. Sow seed. Possible substitute for annual rye.

**Tridens flavus* (purpletop)

To 5 ft. (inflorescence), stems tufted, colonial. Blooms and fruits Aug.–Oct. Inflorescence dark purple. Host plant for some butterflies. **Habitat**

requirements: Roadsides, fields, dry, open woods (FACU). Soil pH 4.5–6.5. Tolerant of drought and low-nutrient soils. Intolerant of shade. **Notes:** Common in our region. Available. **Uses:** Primary or secondary species for increased erosion control, diversity, and aesthetics in restoration of grasslands, meadows, revegetation of roadsides and slopes.

Triplasis purpurea (purple sand-grass)

Annual to 32 in. Blooms and fruits Aug.–Oct., inflorescence rose-purple. **Habitat requirements:** Open sand, coastal (UPL). **Uses:** Secondary to minor species for increased diversity, aesthetics, and soil stabilization on open sand of newly restored back-dune habitats, coastal grasslands.

Tripsacum dactyloides (gamma grass)

Rare (NYS S2, U); to 9 ft., colonial, sometimes also densely tufted, very robust plants, large underground stems (rhizomes). Blooms and fruits June–Sept. Host plant for some butterflies. Host to larvae of a rare moth (*Amphipoea erepta*). **Habitat requirements:** Open marshes (FACW). Soil pH 5.1–7.5. Tolerates brackish water. Occasional in Bronx and Richmond Counties. **Notes:** Available. Use stock only from NYC or NYC metro regional sources. **Uses:** Secondary species for restoration of freshwater or brackish marshes.

Vulpia octoflora (six-week fescue)

Annual to 2 ft., stems tufted. Blooms and fruits May–June; **Habitat requirements:** Dry, open, sterile soil (UPL). **Uses:** Secondary to minor species for increased diversity and soil stabilization on sand of newly restored open habitats, dry roadsides, coastal grasslands. Addition to seed mix with later flowering annual grasses; substitute for annual rye.

Zizania aquatica (wild rice)

Annual to 9 ft. Blooms and fruits June–Sept.; plants robust. Wildlife value high. Grain eaten by water fowl, plants eaten by muskrats. Host plant for some butterflies. **Habitat requirements:** Quiet waters and shores, freshwater and brackish tidal marshes (OBL). Soil pH 6.4–7.4. Tolerant of somewhat brackish water, flooding to 3 ft., or saturated soil to 100% of growing season. Intolerant of shade. **Notes:** Available. **Uses:** Minor element to enhance habitat value and diversity in restoration of marsh or shore habitats. Wetland mitigation. Enhance soil-holding annual grass seed mix for new restoration.

Chapter 6

Ferns

Ferns produce neither flowers nor fruit. They reproduce by minute, windborne spores. With a few exceptions (marsh fern and bracken, for instance), ferns do best in bright, dappled shade of moist forest floors.

Adiantum pedatum

FERN SPECIES

Adiantum pedatum (maidenhair fern)

To 3 ft., colonial, growth rate slow. Spores July–Aug. **Habitat requirements:** Rich, moist woods, stream banks (FAC−). Acid soil, pH 4.6–6.6. Tolerant of shade. **Uses:** Secondary species for increased diversity and aesthetics in restoration of moist forest understories.

Asplenium platyneuron (ebony spleenwort)

Semievergreen, to 1.5 ft. Spores June–Oct. **Habitat requirements:** Moist, open, rocky woods; rich, circumneutral soil (FACU). Does not compete well with more aggressive plants. Tolerant of part shade. **Uses:** Minor species for increased diversity and aesthetics in restoration of open woodlands, rocky banks in part shade.

Asplenium rhizophyllum (*Camptosorus r.*) (walking fern)

Evergreen, to 6 in., colonial. Spores July–Oct.; leaves rooting at tips form new plants. **Habitat requirements:** Moist, mossy, shaded, north-facing cliffs and stone walls, often on limestone (UPL). Tolerant of shade. **Uses:** Minor species for increased diversity and aesthetics in restoration of cliffs, sheltered, moist rock walls.

Asplenium trichomanes (maidenhair spleenwort)

Evergreen, to 10 in. Spores May–Oct. **Habitat requirements:** Sheltered, moist, rocky limestone areas, should tolerate concrete debris (UPL). Does not compete well with more aggressive plants. Tolerant of shade. **Uses:** Minor species for increased diversity and aesthetics in restoration of open woodlands, rocky banks, ledges in part shade.

Athyrium filix-femina (lady fern)

To 3 ft. Spores June–Sept. **Habitat requirements:** Moist woods, shady edges, not fussy (FAC). Soil pH 4.5–7. Tolerant of shade. Occasional in NYC woodlands. **Notes:** Frequent in our region. Available. **Uses:** Secondary species for increasing diversity and aesthetics in restoration of moist woodlands, swamp forest margins.

Athyrium thelypterioides (*Deparia acrostichoides*) (silvery glade fern)

To 3 ft. Spores July–Oct. **Habitat requirements:** Rich, moist woods, subacid soils (FAC). Tolerant of part shade. **Uses:** Secondary species for increasing diversity and aesthetics in restoration of moist woodlands, swamp forest margins.

Cystopteris fragilis (fragile fern)

To 8 in. Spores June–Sept. **Habitat requirements:** Moist woods, rocky slopes, cliffs, in circumneutral soil (FACU). Tolerant of shade. **Uses:** Minor species for increased diversity and aesthetics in restoration of moist, wooded ravines and rocky slopes.

Cystopteris protrusa (lowland fragile fern)

Rare (NYS S1 E); to 8 in. Spores June-Sept. Sparsely colonial from creeping stem. **Habitat requirements:** Moist, rocky, wooded slopes, shady ravines in circumneutral soil (FACU). Tolerant of shade. **Notes:** Plant in coordination with conservation organization. Use only local stock. **Uses:** Minor species for increased diversity and aesthetics in restoration of moist, rich woods, shady ravines.

Dennstaedtia punctilobula (hay-scented fern)

To 32 in., aggressively colonial. Spores June–Aug. **Habitat requirements:** Open woods, gaps, edges (UPL). Tolerates soil acidity down to pH 4.0, found in forest soil pH 4.8–5.0 Often colonizes old burn sites. Tolerant of open shade. **Notes:** *Warning!* May crowd out less aggressive plants. Available. **Uses:** Secondary species for erosion control on wooded or partly open slopes. Cover for open soil in woodlands, partly shaded roadside banks.

Dryopteris carthusiana

Dryopteris carthusiana (*D. spinulosa*) (spinulose wood fern, toothed wood fern)

Evergreen, to 2 ft. Spores May–Aug. **Habitat requirements:** Rich, moist to wet woods (FAC+), circumneutral soil, tolerant of shade. **Uses:** Secondary or minor species for increased diversity and aesthetics in restoration of wet forest understories.

Dryopteris clintoniana (Clinton's wood fern)

Evergreen, to 4 ft. Spores July–Aug. **Habitat requirements:** Rich, wet woods, swamp forests, wet to moist soil (FACW+), glaciated uplands. Tolerant of shade. **Uses:** Secondary or minor species for increased diversity and aesthetics in restoration of wet forest understories.

Dryopteris cristata (crested wood fern)

Evergreen, to 30 in. Spores July–Aug. **Habitat requirements:** Wet to moist soil (FACW+). Wet woods, swamp forests, bogs in acid soil, pH 3.5–6.5. Tolerant of shade. **Uses:** Secondary or minor species for increased diversity and aesthetics in restoration of wet forest understories.

Dryopteris goldiana (Goldie's wood fern)

Evergreen, to 4 ft. Spores May–Sept. **Habitat requirements:** Cool, rich, moist woods on calcareous to neutral soils (FAC+). Tolerant of shade. **Uses:** Secondary or minor species for increased diversity and aesthetics in restoration of moist to wet forest understories.

Dryopteris intermedia (common wood fern)

Evergreen, to 32 in. Spores June–Aug. **Habitat requirements:** Moist woods, swamp forest margins, rich soil (FACU). Tolerant of shade. **Uses:** Secondary species for increased diversity and aesthetics in restoration of moist forest understories, swamp forest margins.

Dryopteris marginalis

Dryopteris marginalis (marginal wood fern)

Evergreen, to 18 in. Spores June–Oct. **Habitat requirements:** Woods, shaded, rocky slopes (FACU−). Tolerant of shade. **Uses:** Secondary species for increased diversity and aesthetics in restoration of forest understories.

Gymnocarpium dryopteris (oak fern)

To 10 in.; spores June–Aug. **Habitat requirements:** Cool, rocky woods, acid soil (UPL). Tolerant of shade. **Uses:** Minor species for increased diversity and aesthetics in restoration of oak forest understories.

Matteuccia struthiopteris (ostrich fern)

To 5 ft. (rarely), colonial. Spores June–Sept. **Habitat requirements:** Open swamp forests, part shady stream banks, floodplain forests, calcareous soils, should tolerate concrete debris (FACW). Tolerant of shade. **Notes:** Found in the northern part of our region. Apparently not a coastal-plain plant. **Uses:** Secondary or minor species for increased diversity, aesthetics, and soil-holding capacity in restoration of moist to wet forest understories.

**Onoclea sensibilis* (sensitive fern)

To 1 ft., colonial, growth rate moderate. Spores mature Oct. Wildlife value low. **Habitat requirements:** Open swamp forests, freshwater tidal and nontidal marshes, undisturbed ditches (FACW). Rich soil, pH 4.5–7.5. Tolerant of shade, flooding, or saturated soil up to 100% of growing season. Intolerant of salt, drought. **Notes:** Common in our region. Available. **Uses:** Primary herbaceous species for swamp forest restoration. Wetland mitigation. Stabilization of wet soil in shady habitats.

**Osmunda cinnamomea* (cinnamon fern)

To 3 ft., growth rate very slow. Spores mature May–June. Wildlife value low. **Habitat requirements:** Swamp forests, shady stream banks, moist to wet forest soil (FACW). Soil pH 4.5–7.0. Tolerant of full shade (prefers partial shade), drought, flooding, or saturated soil up to 100% growing season. **Notes:** Frequent in our region. Available. **Uses:** Primary species for restoration of swamp forest habitats, woodland pond edges. Wetland mitigation in shaded sites.

Osmunda claytoniana

Osmunda claytoniana (interrupted fern)

To 3 ft. Spores May–June. **Habitat requirements:** Moist to somewhat dry open woods (FAC). Rocky or sandy acid soils, pH 4–6. Tolerant of part shade. **Notes:** Occasional in our region. **Uses:** Secondary species for increased diversity and aesthetics in forest understory restoration.

Osmunda regalis (royal fern)

To 5 ft. (rarely), growth rate very slow. Spores mature May–June. Wildlife value low. **Habitat requirements:** Stream banks, freshwater tidal marshes, swamp forests, vernal pond margins, shallow water to wet soil (OBL). Prefers acid soil, pH 4–6. Tolerant of drought, light shade, flooding, or saturated soil up to 100% of growing season. Intolerant of salt. **Notes:** Occasional in our region. Available. **Uses:** Secondary species for restoration of swamp forest habitats, woodland pond edges, stream banks. Wetland mitigation in open or partially shaded sites.

Polypodium virginianum, (*P. vulgare*) (common polypody)

Evergreen, to 1ft. (usually less). Spores June–Oct. **Habitat requirements:** Moist to dry shade, in thin, circumneutral soils on glacial erratics in rocky woods, sometimes on banks, tree bases, old logs, limestone cliffs (UPL). Tolerant of shade. **Uses:** Secondary species for increased diversity and aesthetics in restoration of moist, rocky woods, especially along stream margins. Shady rock gardens.

Polystichum acrostichoides (Christmas fern)

Evergreen, to 3 ft. Spores May–Oct. **Habitat requirements:** Rich soil of wooded slopes where deep leaf litter does not accumulate, rocky slopes (FACU−). Very tolerant of shade. **Notes:** Formerly common in our region. **Uses:** Minor species for increased diversity and aesthetics in restoration of slopes in moist, rocky woods.

Pteridium aquilinum (bracken fern)

To 4 ft. (in our area), colonial. Spores June–Sept. Dry, sterile soils (FACU), often in open, shrubby successional habitats or open woodlands in sterile, sandy soils, pH 4.5–7.0. Intolerant of full shade. **Notes:** Somewhat weedy. *Warning!*

Can be aggressive, especially in burned-over sites. **Uses:** Secondary species for additional erosion control and diversity on open slopes, roadside banks, dry meadows.

Thelypteris hexagonoptera (*Phegopteris h.*) (broad beech-fern)

To 2 ft., colonial. Spores June–Sept. **Habitat requirements:** Rich, moist woods (FAC). Tolerant of shade. **Uses:** Secondary species for increased diversity, aesthetics, and soil-holding capacity in restoration of moist woodlands.

Thelypteris noveboracensis (New York fern)

To 18 in., aggressively colonial. Spores June–Oct.; colonization rate rapid. Wildlife value low. **Habitat requirements:** Open, moist to wet woodlands (FAC). Tolerant of part shade; saturated soil for up to 75% of growing season; tolerant of drought. Tolerates acid soil down to pH 3.9. Intolerant of salt. **Uses:** Secondary species for erosion control on moist, shady slopes. Minor element for restoration of woodland understories.

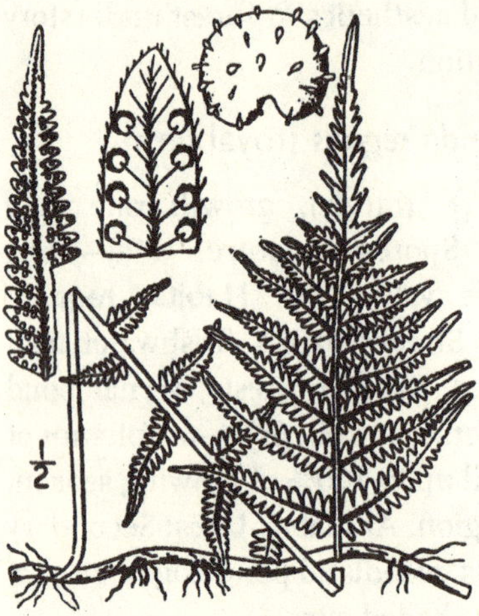

Thelypteris noveboracensis

Thelypteris palustris (marsh fern)

To 18 in., colonial, growth rate moderate. Spore production June–Oct. Wildlife value low. **Habitat requirements:** Freshwater tidal and nontidal marshes, wet meadows, rich muddy, subacid soil, stream banks (FACW+). Tolerates saturated soil for up to 100% of growing season. Moderately tolerant of shade. Intolerant of salt. **Uses:** Secondary species for increased diversity, aesthetics, and soil-holding capacity in wetland restoration and mitigation.

Thelypteris phegopteris (northern beech-fern)

To 1 ft., colonial. Spores June–Aug. **Habitat requirements:** Moist cliffs, cool woods, rocky stream banks (UPL). Tolerant of shade. **Uses:** Minor species for increased diversity and aesthetics in restoration of moist, rocky woods, especially along stream margins.

Thelypteris simulata (Massachusetts fern)

To 2 ft., colonial. Spores July–Sept. **Habitat requirements:** Swamp forests, moist to wet woods, red maple swamp forests, white cedar bogs (FACW), highly acid soil. Tolerant of shade. **Uses:** Secondary species for increased diversity, aesthetics, and soil-holding capacity in restoration of marshes, swamp forests, moist woods, or acid bog habitats.

Woodsia ilvensis (rusty woodsia)

To 6 in. Spores June–Oct. **Habitat requirements:** Dry, sunny cliffs in acid soil (UPL). **Uses:** Minor species for increased diversity and aesthetics in restoration of exposed, rocky sites.

Woodsia obtusa (blunt-lobed cliff fern)

Semievergreen, to 14 in. Spores June–Oct. **Habitat requirements:** Shady cliffs, sheltered, rocky banks, often on limestone, holes in mortar in stone walls (UPL). Tolerant of concrete. Tolerant of partial shade. **Uses:** Minor species for increased diversity and aesthetics in restoration of rocky, sheltered sites.

Woodwardia areolata (netted chain fern)

To 2 ft., colonial, growth rate slow. Spore production July–Sept. Wildlife value low. **Habitat requirements:** Swamp forests, in acid soil. Acid bogs, shrub swamps. Tolerates shade; saturated soil for 100% of growing season (FACW+). Intolerant of salt. **Notes:** Transplants well. Occasional in NYC woodlands. **Uses:** Secondary species for increased diversity, aesthetics, and soil-holding capacity in restoration of swamp forests, moist woods, or acid bog habitats.

Woodwardia virginica (Virginia chain fern)

To 4 ft. (much smaller this far north), colonial. Spores June–Sept. **Habitat requirements:** Swamp forests and mossy bogs, in acid soil (OBL). Tolerant of shade. **Notes:** Frequent in our region. **Uses:** Secondary species for increased diversity, aesthetics, and soil-holding capacity in restoration of swamp forests or acid bog habitats.

Part II

Plants for Various Habitat Types

The goals for a successful restoration project are to establish plant species that are appropriate to the region and suitable for the site. They must be able to grow and reproduce, resist invasion by exotics, and become part of a dense, diverse, thriving ecological community. In order to choose the best suite of plants for a project, the conditions of the site must be matched to the needs of the plants.

The most critical environmental factors for any plant are light, water, and soil chemistry (pH). Many habitats in the New York metropolitan area are disturbed or created by human activities. Some of these disturbed conditions include filled salt marsh, altered hydrology due to buildings and pavement, land fills, concrete or demolition debris, altered topography, stream channelization, and aggressive, exotic plants. Because plants must confront so many artificial habitats, landscape designers and restorationists must match plant materials with existing habitat characteristics. The habitats listed in this book are based on the fundamental needs of plants regardless of the ecosystems that might have covered the particular site in the past, or habitat types that "should" be there. For example, a planting site near the shore may not be suitable for back-dune plants if the soil consists of high pH, high nutrient, fill, and the surrounding vegetation is dominated by mugwort (*Artemisia vulgaris*) and tree-of-heaven (*Ailanthus altissima*). Unless it is possible to change the existing environmental conditions, one must choose plants that will thrive in the existing conditions by considering light levels, water availability, and soil pH (acidity/alkalinity).

In addition, it is necessary to project into the future and predict how a restoration project will change over time. In general, this means that open areas will slowly develop more shade and that the native vegetation will have to compete with aggressive exotic plants. If a restoration is to survive both in the present and over time, succession must be taken into account. However, plants must initially be selected for prevailing conditions. A forest restoration done on an open, southwest-facing slope dominated by mugwort should be planted with sun-loving, aggressively colonial native herbs and shrubs. Plants should be selected for both drought tolerance and slope stabilization. Aggressively colonial native herbs and shrubs such as Canada goldenrod, common milkweed, Indian hemp, and gray dogwood will fill this need. Prickly shrubs and ground covers such as blackberry, native roses, and dewberry will also help protect the site while forest trees and shrubs grow in. Sun-loving plants can be interplanted with trees and shrubs that will eventually take over. Trees can be a mixture of fast-growing pioneer species such as poplar, gray birch, wild black cherry, and sassafras, interplanted with slower-growing oaks and hickories. With few exceptions, management needs to be a part of any restoration. Provision for periodic watering, removal of invasive plants, fencing repairs, and sign replacement should be built into the specifications for any project. Overplanting is always better than underplanting because not all the plants will survive.

For more information on various aspects of ecological restoration, consult the numerous sources on the Web and in libraries.

MARITIME HABITATS: SAND DUNES

Examples of plant communities

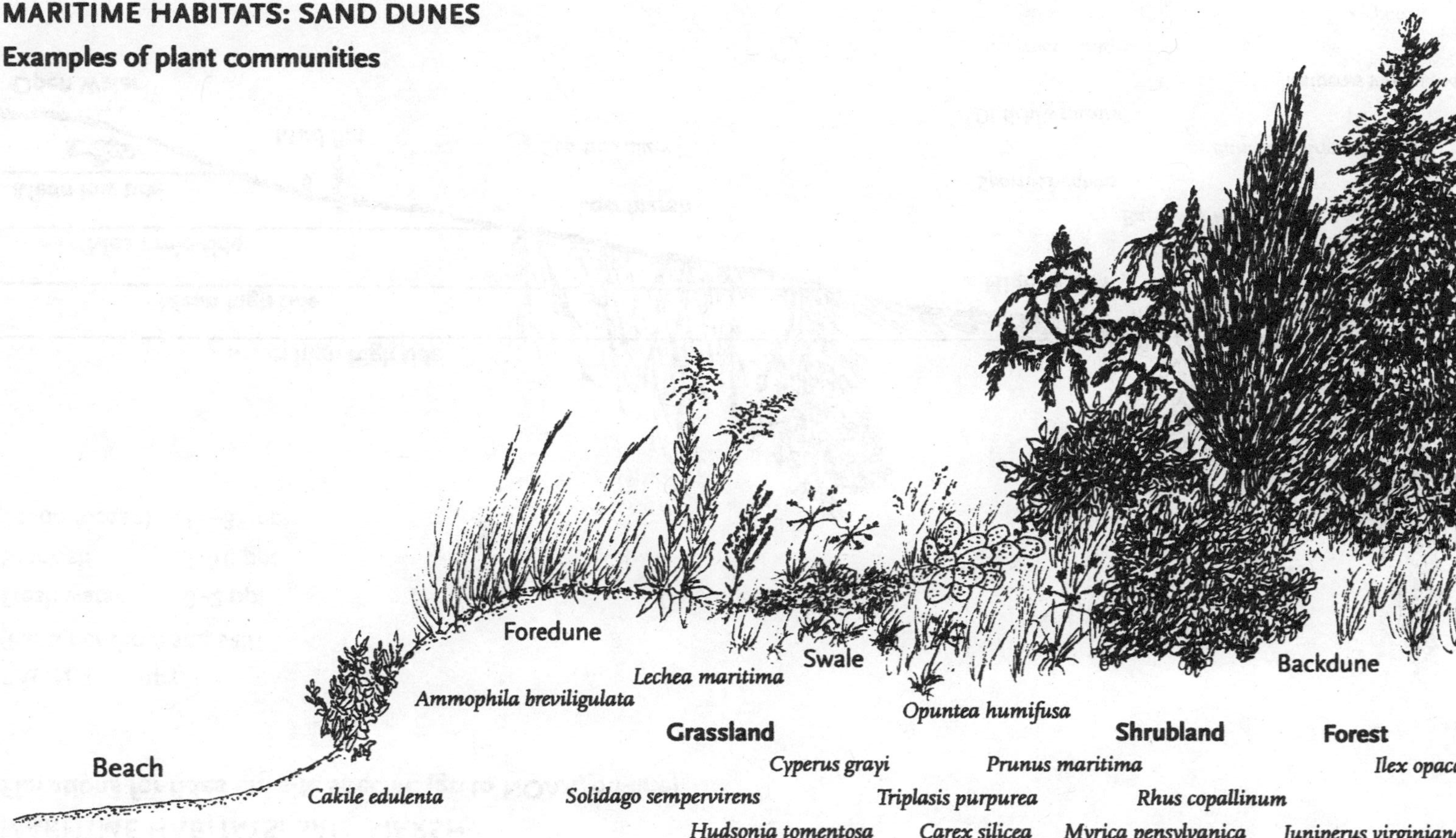

MARITIME HABITATS: SALT MARSH

Elevations for tides are site specific (go to NOAA, on-line)

SALINITY—PPT
(Parts per thousand salt)

Fresh water	0–2 ppt
Brackish	3–10 ppt
Saline (ocean)	11–35 ppt

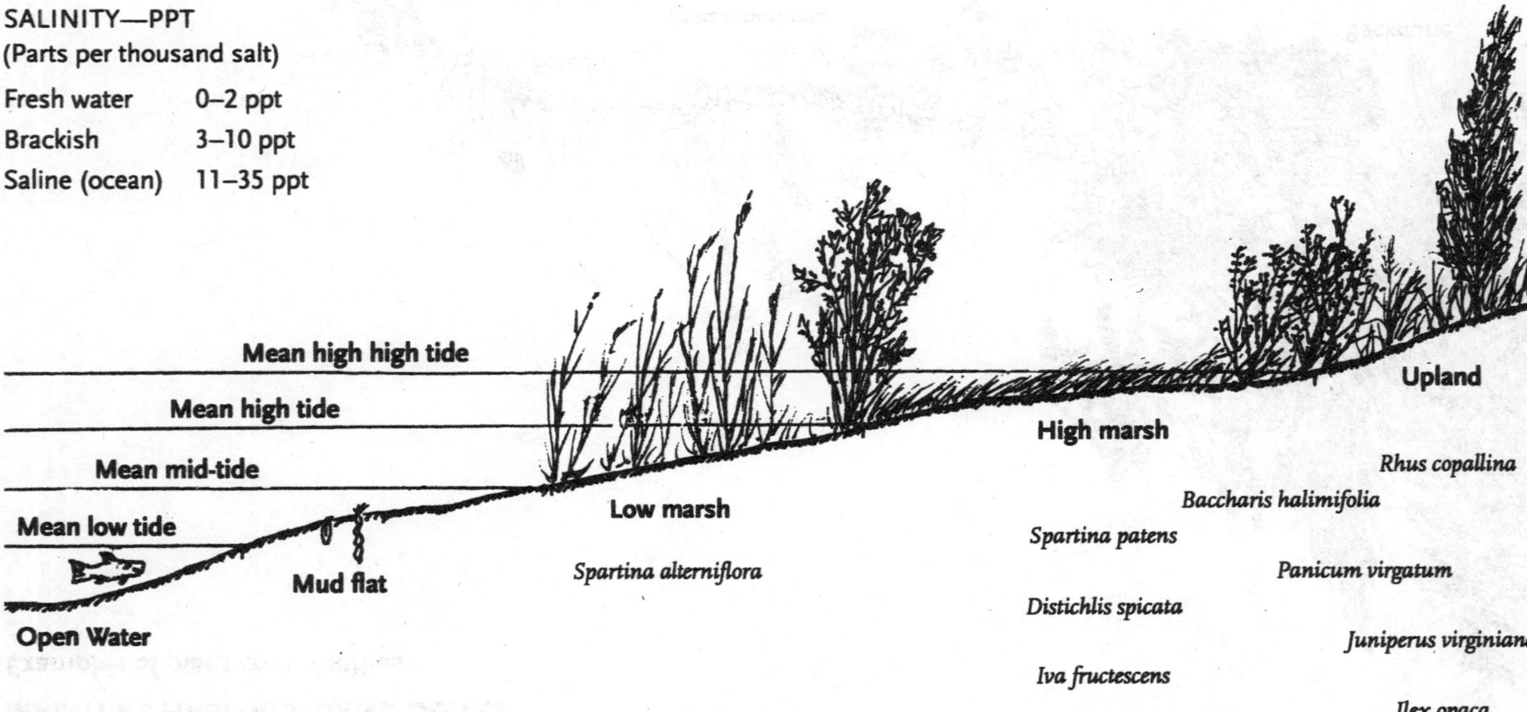

OPEN HABITATS

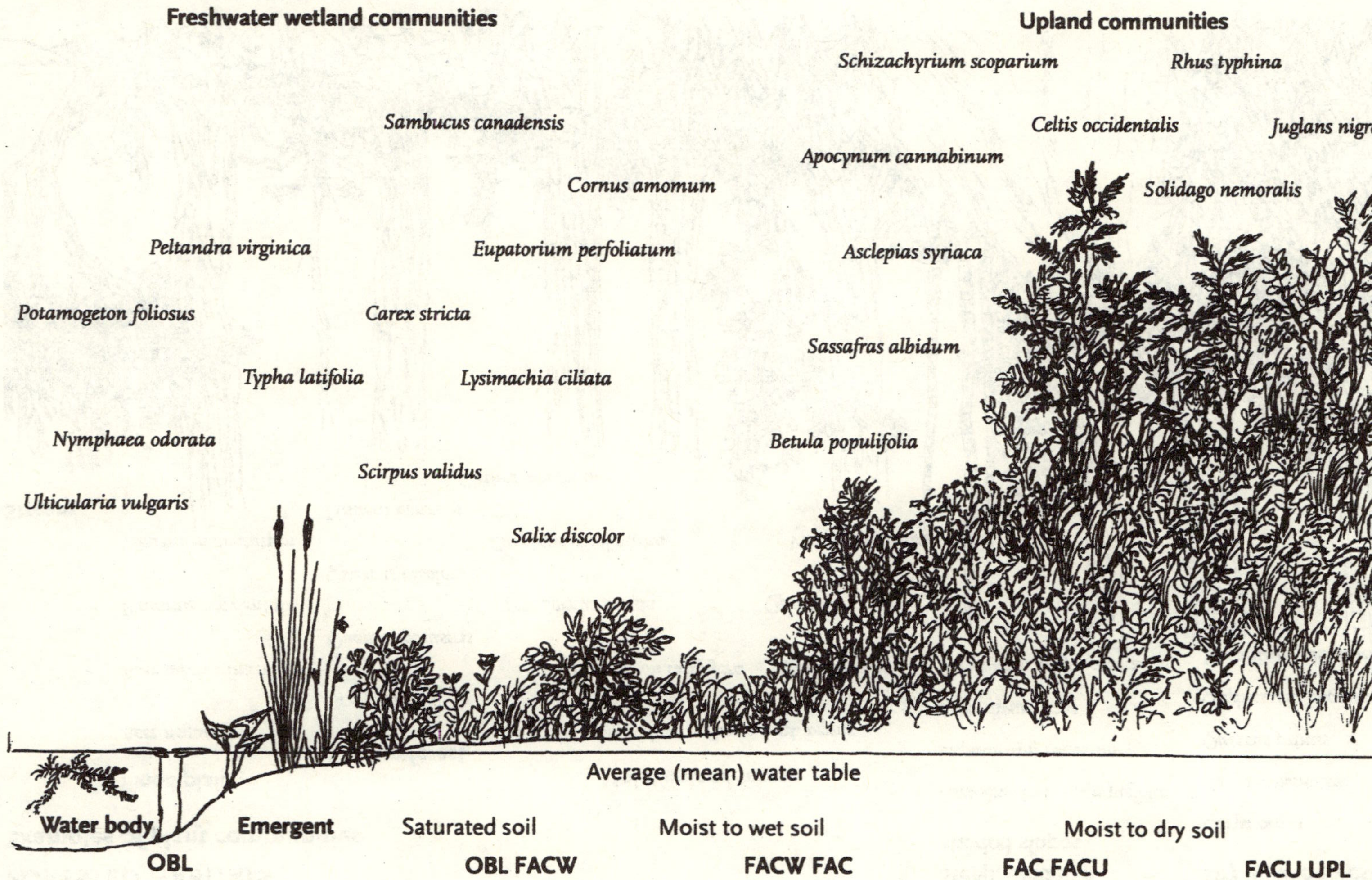

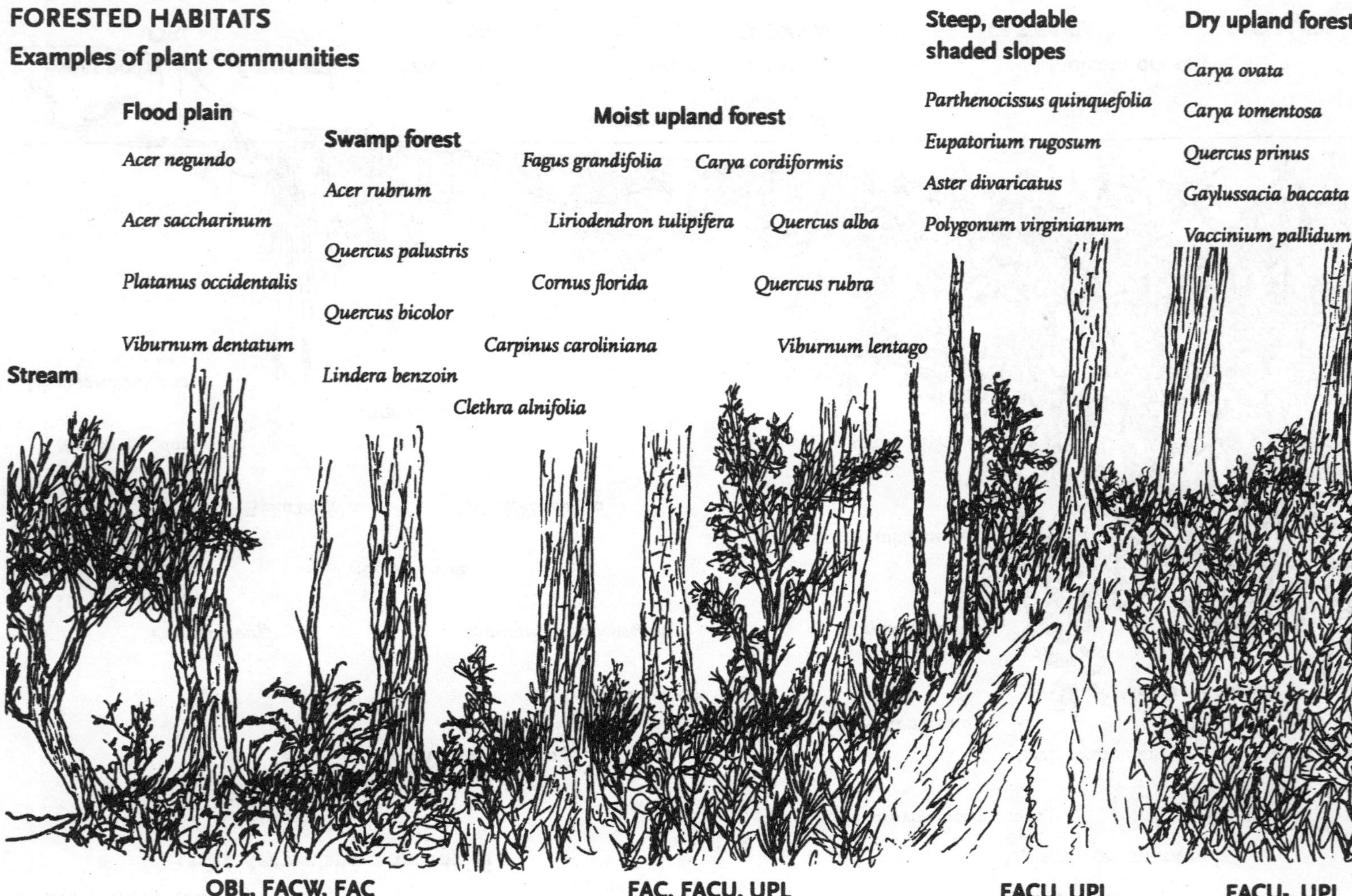
FORESTED HABITATS
Examples of plant communities
Flood plain
Acer negundo
Acer saccharinum
Platanus occidentalis
Viburnum dentatum
Swamp forest
Acer rubrum
Quercus palustris
Quercus bicolor
Lindera benzoin
Clethra alnifolia
Moist upland forest
Fagus grandifolia
Carya cordiformis
Liriodendron tulipifera
Quercus alba
Cornus florida
Quercus rubra
Carpinus caroliniana
Viburnum lentago
Steep, erodable shaded slopes
Parthenocissus quinquefolia
Eupatorium rugosum
Aster divaricatus
Polygonum virginianum
Dry upland forest
Carya ovata
Carya tomentosa
Quercus prinus
Gaylussacia baccata
Vaccinium pallidum
Stream
OBL, FACW, FAC
FAC, FACU, UPL
FACU, UPL
FACU-, UPL

Chapter 7

Plants for Open Habitats, Full Sun

SET 1. NONTIDAL, FRESHWATER OPEN WETLANDS

List 1. Freshwater Wetland Annuals (native substitutes for annual rye)

Annual Wetland Herbs

Ambrosia trifida (great ragweed) FAC; to 6 ft.
Bidens cernua (bur-marigold) OBL; to 40 in.
Bidens coronata (tick-seeded sunflower) OBL; to 4 ft.
Bidens frondosa (devil's beggar-ticks) FACW; to 4 ft.
Callitriche terrestris (*C. deflexa*) (starwort) FACW+, S; to 2 in.
Cardamine pensylvanica (Pennsylvania bitter-cress) OBL; to 2 ft.
Gratiola neglecta (hedge-hyssop) OBL; to 1 ft.
Hypericum canadense (Canada St.-John's-wort) FACW; to 2 ft.
Hypericum mutilum (dwarf St.-John's-wort) FACW; to 32 in.
Impatiens capensis (*I. biflora*) (jewelweed) FACW, H, S; to 3 ft.; soil pH 5.6–7.0
Impatiens pallida (pale touch-me-not) FACW, S; to 5 ft.
Pilea fontana (springs clearweed) FACW+; to 20 in.
Pilea pumila (clearweed) FACW, S; to 20 in.
Polygonum arifolium (halberd-leaved tearthumb) OBL; prickly, to 6 ft. long
Polygonum pensylvanicum (Pennsylvania smartweed) FACW; to 6 ft.
Polygonum sagittatum (arrow-leaved tearthumb) OBL; to 6 ft.
Ranunculus pensylvanicus (bristly buttercup) OBL; to 28 in.
Sagittaria calycina (spongy arrowhead) OBL; ca 2 ft.

Annual Wetland Graminoids

Alopecurus aequalis (short-awn foxtail) OBL; to 20 in.
Cyperus bipartitus (*C. rivularis*) (shining flatsedge) FACW+, B; to 8 in.
Cyperus flavescens (yellow flatsedge) OBL, B; to 16 in. (NYS S1 U)
Cyperus odoratus (rusty flatsedge) FACW, B; to 32 in.
Cyperus polystachyos (many-spike flatsedge) FACW+, B; to 2 ft.
Echinochloa muricata (barnyard grass) FACW+; to 40 in.

Echinochloa walteri (coast cockspur grass) FACW+; to 6.5 ft.
Eleocharis ovata (*E. obtusa*) (blunt spikerush) OBL, B; to 2.5 ft.
Eragrostis hypnoides (teal lovegrass) OBL, mat forming; to 6 in.
Fimbristylis autumnalis (slender fimbry) FACW; to 8 in.
Juncus bufonius (toad rush) FACW; to 12 in.
Panicum dichotomiflorum (fall panic grass) FACW−; to 40 in.
Panicum verrucosum (warty panic grass) FACW, S (part); to 3 ft.
Zizania aquatica (wild rice) OBL, B; to 9 ft.

List 2. Open, Freshwater Wetlands—Circumneutral Soils

(Wetland trees: See Swamp Forest list)

Shrubs for Open, Wet to Moist Soil

Alnus incana (speckled alder) FACW, B, C, N; to 35 ft.; pH 6.5–7.5; shade index 0–2; s
Alnus serrulata (smooth alder) OBL, B, C, N; to 20 ft.; pH 5.5–7.5; shade index 0–2
**Aronia arbutifolia* (red chokeberry) FACW, A, B, C, F, S (part); to 12 ft.; soil pH 5–6.5
Aronia melanocarpa (black chokeberry) FAC, A, B, C, F, S (part); to 6 ft.; soil pH 5–6.5
**Cephalanthus occidentalis* (buttonbush) OBL, C; to 12 ft.; pH 6–8.5; emergent to moist soil
**Cornus amomum* (silky dogwood) FACW, B, S (part); to 9 ft.; soil pH 6–8.5
**Ilex verticillata* (winterberry) FACW, A, D, S; to 15 ft.; soil pH 4.5–6
Rosa palustris (swamp rose) OBL, C, aggressive; to 6 ft., stems prickly
Salix bebbiana (beaked willow) FACW, B, D; to 15 ft.; soil pH 6.5–7.5; shade index 0–2
**Salix discolor* (pussy willow) FACW, B, D; to 15 ft.; soil pH 6.5–7.5; shade index 0–2
Salix lucida (shining willow) FACW, B, D; to 18 ft.; soil pH 6–7.5
Salix petiolaris (meadow willow) OBL, B, D; to 20 ft.
Salix sericea (silky willow) OBL, B, D; to 12 ft.
**Sambucus canadensis* (elderberry) FACW, C, S (part); to 12 ft.; soil pH 6–8
Spiraea alba var. *latifolia* (meadowsweet) FAC+, B, C; to 6 ft.; soil pH 6.6–7.5
Vaccinium corymbosum (highbush blueberry) FACW, A, B, F, S (part); to 9 ft.; soil pH 3.5–6.5
**Viburnum dentatum* (*V. recognitum*) (arrowwood) FAC, A, B, C, S (part); to 10 ft.; soil pH 4.4–7
Viburnum nudum (*V. cassinoides*) (possum-haw) OBL, A, B, S (part) (NYS S1, T); to 12 ft.; soil pH 5–6

Floating and Submerged Herbs

(provide shade for fish and invertebrates that help control mosquito populations in artificial ponds, uptake of excess nutrients. Water depth for rooted plants to 6 ft.)

Callitriche heterophylla (two-headed water starwort) OBL; submerged, annual; stems to 8 in. long

Callitriche palustris (vernal water starwort) OBL; submerged, annual; stems to 8 in. long

Hottonia inflata (featherfoil) OBL (NYS S1S2, T); submerged, winter annual; to 20 in.

Lemna minor (duckweed) OBL, C (aggressive); tiny floating plants

Najas flexilis (northern water nymph) OBL; submerged, annual

**Nuphar advena* (*N. lutea*) (southern pond lily) OBL, C; leaves emergent

Nuphar microphylla (small yellow pond lily, yellow cowlily, dwarf spatterdock) OBL, C; floating leaved

Nuphar variegata (yellow pond lily, spatterdock) OBL, C; floating leaved

**Nymphaea odorata* (water lily) OBL, C; floating leaved

Nymphoides cordata (floating heart) OBL, C; floating aquatic

Potamogeton amplifolius (big-leaf pondweed) OBL, C; submerged, rooted

Potamogeton diversifolius (common snailseed-pondweed) OBL, C; submerged, rooted

Potamogeton foliosus (leafy pondweed) OBL, C; submerged, rooted

Potamogeton gramineus (variable pondweed) OBL, C; submerged, rooted

Potamogeton natans (floating pondweed) OBL, C; submerged, rooted

Potamogeton pusillus (slender pondweed) OBL, C; submerged, rooted

Potamogeton spirillus (northern snailseed-pondweed) OBL, C; submerged, rooted

Proserpinaca palustris (mermaid weed) OBL, C; submerged to immersed

Ranunculus flabellaris (yellow water buttercup) OBL; immersed, rooted

Ranunculus trichophyllus (white water crowfoot) OBL; submerged, rooted

Spirodela polyrhiza (big duckweed) OBL, C; free floating

Utricularia geminiscapa (mixed bladderwort) OBL; submerged, free floating

Utricularia radiata (floating bladderwort) OBL; submerged, free floating

Utricularia vulgaris (common bladderwort) OBL; to 6 ft. long, free floating

Vallisneria americana (wild celery, tape grass) OBL, C; rooted, submerged; to 7 ft. long

Emergent Herbs for Open, Shallow Water or Saturated Soil of Pond Edges or Marshes

Acorus calamus (sweet flag) OBL, C; emergent, to 4 ft.; brackish water to 10 ppt; eaten by muskrats

**Alisma subcordatum* (southern water plantain) OBL, C; emergent, ca. 1 ft.

Alisma triviale (*A. plantago-aquatica*) (northern water plantain) OBL, C; emergent, to 3 ft.

Caltha palustris (marsh marigold) OBL, C, S (part); emergent, to 2 ft.

**Decodon verticillatus* (swamp loosestrife) OBL, C; to 4 ft.

**Hibiscus moscheutos* (rose mallow) OBL, B, H; to 6 ft.

**Iris versicolor* (blue flag) OBL, A, C, H; to 32 in.

Justicia americana (water willow) OBL, B, C; to 3 ft.

Ludwigia palustris (water purslane) OBL, C; creeping, forming mats or submerged

Orontium aquaticum (golden club) OBL, C; emergent, to 30 in.

**Peltandra virginica* (arrow arum) OBL, C, S (part); emergent, to 30 in.; soil pH 5–6.5; muskrat safe

Polygonum amphibium (water smartweed) OBL, C; floating to emergent, to 3 ft.

**Pontederia cordata* (pickerelweed) OBL, C, S (part); emergent, to 3 ft.; soil pH 6–8; eaten by muskrats

Rumex verticillatus (swamp dock) OBL, C; emergent, to 3 ft.

Sagittaria graminea (grass-leaved arrowhead) OBL, C; emergent to immersed, plant to 2 ft.; soil pH 7

**Sagittaria latifolia* (duck potato) OBL, C; emergent, to 3 ft.

**Saururus cernuus* (lizard's tail) OBL, C, S to 3 ft.

Sparganium americanum (American bur-reed) OBL, C; emergent, to 3 ft.; eaten by muskrats

Sparganium eurycarpum (giant bur-reed) OBL, C; emergent, to 4 ft.; eaten by muskrats

**Typha latifolia* (cattail) OBL, C; emergent, to 9 ft.; soil pH 5.5–7.5

Emergent Graminoids

Carex aquatilis (water sedge) OBL, B, C (aggressive); to 3 ft.

**Carex stricta* (tussock sedge) OBL, A, B, C, S (part); to 3 ft.; soil pH 6.2

Eleocharis acicularis (least spikerush) OBL, B, C; to 5 in.

**Eleocharis palustris* (creeping spikerush) OBL, B, C, K; to 3 ft.

**Juncus effusus* (soft rush) FACW+, B, E (semi-), S (part); to 3 ft.

**Scirpus americanus* (Olney three-square) OBL, B, C; to 6 in.; water to 15 ppt salt; eaten by muskrats

**Scirpus pungens* (common threesquare) OBL, B, C; to 4 ft.; soil pH 7; water to 15 ppt salt; eaten by muskrats

**Scirpus validus* (soft-stem bulrush) OBL, B, C, K; to 7 ft.; soil pH 6.5–8.5; eaten by muskrats

Zizania aquatica (wild rice) OBL, B; annual, to 9 ft.

Herbs for Open, Wet to Moist Soil

Anemone canadensis (Canadian anemone) FACW, C; to 2 ft.
Angelica atropurpurea (purple-stem angelica) OBL, B, K, S (part); to 6 ft.
**Asclepias incarnata* (swamp milkweed) OBL, B, C; to 4 ft.
Asclepias rubra (red milkweed) OBL, B (G4G5, globally rare; NYS SX, U); L.I. northern limit; to 2 ft.
**Aster lanceolatus* (*A. simplex*) (lined aster) FACW, B, C, S; to 4 ft.
Aster lateriflorus (calico aster) FACW−; to 3 ft.
**Aster novae-angliae* (New England aster) FACW−, B, C; to 6 ft.
**Aster novi-belgii* (New York aster) FACW+, B, C; to 4 ft.
Aster puniceus (bristly aster) OBL, B; to 8 ft.
Aster tradescantii (shore aster) FACW, B, C; to 2 ft.
Aster umbellatus (flat-topped aster) FACW, B, C; to 5 ft.
Bidens coronata (tick-seeded sunflower) OBL; annual, to 4 ft.
Campanula aparinoides (marsh bellflower) OBL, C; reclining on other plants; to 2 ft.
**Chelone glabra* (turtlehead) OBL, B, S; to 3 ft.
Cicuta bulbifera (water hemlock) OBL, B; to 3 ft.; plant toxic
Cicuta maculata (common water hemlock) OBL, B; to 6 ft.; plant very toxic
Cirsium muticum (swamp thistle) OBL, B, H; very spiny; to 6 ft.
Equisetum hyemale (rough scouring rush) FACW, C, E, S (part); to ca. 4 ft.
Eupatorium dubium (three-nerved joe-pye weed) FACW, A, B, S (part); to 3 ft.
Eupatorium fistulosum (hollow-stemmed joe-pye weed) FACW, B, S (part); to 6 ft.
**Eupatorium maculatum* (spotted joe-pye weed) FACW, B, K; to 6 ft.
**Eupatorium perfoliatum* (boneset) FACW+, B, S (part); to 4 ft.
Gentiana clausa (closed gentian) FACW, S (part); to 3 ft.
Gentiana linearis (narrow-leaf gentian) OBL, S (part); to 18 in.
Gentianopsis crinita (fringed gentian) OBL; to 32 in.
Helenium autumnale (common sneezeweed) FACW+; to 6 ft.
Helianthus giganteus (swamp sunflower) FACW, C; to 9 ft.
**Hibiscus moscheutos* (rose mallow) OBL, B, H; to 6 ft.
Hypericum canadense (Canada St.-John's-wort) FACW; annual or perennial by short stolons; to 2 ft.
Hypericum ellipticum (pale St.-John's-wort) OBL, C; creeping, to 5 in.
Hypericum majus (large Canada St.-John's-wort) FACW; to 28 in.
Hypericum mutilum (dwarf St.-John's-wort) FACW; Annual or perennial; to 32 in.
Hydrocotyle americana (marsh pennywort) OBL, B, C; low, creeping
Iris prismatica (slender blueflag) OBL, C, H, S (part); (NYS S2, U); to 28 in.
**Iris versicolor* (blueflag) OBL, A, C, H; to 32 in.
Justicia americana (water willow) OBL, B, C; to 3 ft.

Lilium canadense (Canada lily) FAC+, H; to 4 ft.; eaten by muskrats
Lilium superbum (Turk's cap lily) FACW+, H, S; to 6 ft.; soil pH 4.4–4.8; eaten by muskrats
**Lobelia cardinalis* (cardinal flower) FACW+, B, H, S (part); to 4 ft.
Lobelia siphilitica (great lobelia) FACW+; to 4 ft.
Ludwigia alternifolia (seedbox) FACW+; to 3 ft.
Ludwigia sphaerocarpa (globe-fruit seedbox) OBL, C; to 40 in.
Lycopus americanus (water horehound, bugleweed) OBL, C, S (part); to 2 ft.
Lycopus uniflorus (northern bugleweed) OBL, C; to 2 ft.
Lycopus virginicus (Virginia bugleweed) OBL, C; to 2 ft.
Lysimachia ciliata (fringed loosestrife) FACW, C, S; to 3 ft.
Lysimachia terrestris (swamp candles, yellow loosestrife) OBL, C; to 32 in.
Lythrum alatum (winged loosestrife) FACW+; to 4 ft.
Melanthium virginicum (bunch flower) FACW+, S (part); (NYS SX, U); to 4 ft.; toxic
Mentha arvensis var. *canadensis* (wild mint) FACW; to 30 in.
Mimulus alatus (winged monkey flower) OBL, S; (NYS S3, R); to 3 ft.
Mimulus ringens (monkey flower) OBL, S (part); to 3 ft.
Monarda didyma (Oswego tea, bee balm) FAC+, B, C, H, S (part); to 4 ft.
Oxypolis rigidior (cowbane) OBL, B; to 6 ft.
Penthorum sedoides (ditch stonecrop) OBL, C; to 2 ft.
Physostegia virginiana (obedient plant) FAC+, C; to 5 ft.
Polygonum hydropiperoides (mild water-pepper) OBL, C, S (part); reclining, to 6 ft.
Polygonum pensylvanicum (Pennsylvania smartweed) FACW; annual to 6 ft.
Polygonum robustius (stout smartweed) OBL, C; to +40 in.
Potentilla anserina (silverweed) OBL, C, G; to 1 ft.
Ptilimnium capillaceum (mock bishop's weed) OBL, B; to 3 ft.
Pycnanthemum muticum (blunt mountain mint) FACW; to 3 ft.
Ranunculus ambigens (spearwort) OBL, C; reclining, to 3 ft.
Rudbeckia laciniata (cut-leaf coneflower) FACW; to 10 ft.
Rumex altissimus (pale dock) FACW−; to 40 in.
Rumex orbiculatus (great water dock) OBL; to 8 ft.
Saxifraga pensylvanica (swamp saxifrage) OBL; to 4 ft.
Scutellaria galericulata (marsh scullcap) OBL, C; to 32 in.
Scutellaria integrifolia (hyssop skullcap) FACW, S (part); to 25 in.
Scutellaria lateriflora (mad-dog skullcap) FACW+, C, S; to 30 in.
Sisyrinchium angustifolium (stout blue-eyed grass) FACW; to 20 in.
Sisyrinchium atlanticum (eastern blue-eyed grass) FACW; to 20 in.
Sisyrinchium mucronatum (slender blue-eyed grass) FAC+; to 20 in.
Sium suave (water parsnip) OBL, B; to 6 ft.
Solidago elliotii (coastal swamp goldenrod) OBL, C; (NYS S1, U); to 10 ft.

Solidago gigantea (late goldenrod) FACW, C; to 6 ft.
Teucrium canadense (American germander) FACW−, C, S (part); to 3 ft.
Thalictrum pubescens (tall meadow rue) FACW+; to 9 ft.
Triadenum virginicum (marsh St.-John's-wort) OBL, C; to 2 ft.
Verbena hastata (blue vervain) FACW+, B, H; to 4 ft.
**Vernonia noveboracensis* (New York ironweed) FACW+, B; to 10 ft.
Veronica americana (American brooklime) OBL, C; to 3 ft.
Veronica scutellata (marsh speedwell) OBL, C; to 16 in.
Viola lanceolata (lance-leaved violet) OBL, B, C; creeping, to 6 in.

Ferns for Open, Wet to Moist Soil

**Onoclea sensibilis* (sensitive fern) FACW, C, S; to 1 ft.
Osmunda regalis (royal fern) OBL, S (part); to 5 ft.
Thelypteris palustris (marsh fern) FACW+, C; to 18 in.

Graminoids for Open, Wet to Moist Soil

Andropogon virginicus var. *abbreviatus* (*A. glomeratus*) (bunch broom-sedge) FACW+, B; to 4 ft.
Calamagrostis canadensis (bluejoint) FACW+, B, C (aggressive); to 5 ft.; potentially invasive
Carex comosa (bearded sedge) OBL, B, S (part); to 3 ft.
**Carex crinita* (fringed sedge) OBL, B, S (part); to 4 ft.
Carex cristatella (crested sedge) FACW, B; to 3 ft.
**Carex intumescens* (bladder sedge) FACW+, B, S; to 32 in.
Carex lacustris (lakebank sedge) OBL, C; to 4 ft.
**Carex lurida* (shallow sedge) OBL, B; to 3 ft.
Carex pellita (*C. lanuginosa*) (wooly sedge) OBL, B, C (aggressively); to 3 ft.
Carex projecta (necklace sedge) FACW, B; to 3 ft.
Carex retrorsa (retrorse sedge) FACW+, C, S; to 3 ft.
**Carex scoparia* (pointed broom-sedge) FACW, B, S (part); to 3 ft.
Carex stipata (awl-fruited sedge) OBL, C, B, S (partial), to 3 ft.; soil pH 4.9–7.9
Carex tribuloides (blunt broom sedge) FACW+, B, S (part); to 40 in.
**Carex vulpinoidea* (fox sedge) OBL, B, C, S (part); to 3 ft.
Cyperus strigosus (false nutsedge) FACW, B; to 2 ft.
Deschampsia cespitosa (tufted hairgrass) FACW, B; to 3.5 ft.
**Dulichium arundinaceum* (three-way sedge) OBL, B, C; to 3 ft.
**Eleocharis palustris* (creeping spikerush) OBL, B, C, K; to 3 ft.
Fimbristylis castanea (marsh fimbry) OBL, B; to 4 ft.
Glyceria acutiflora (creeping mannagrass) OBL; to 40 in.
Glyceria canadensis (rattlesnake mannagrass) OBL, C; to 3 ft.
Glyceria grandis (American mannagrass) OBL, C; to 5 ft.

Glyceria septentrionalis (eastern mannagrass) OBL, C; to 5 ft.; eaten by muskrats
Juncus acuminatus (taper-tip rush) OBL, B; to 32 in.
Juncus articulatus (jointed rush) OBL, B, C; to 2 ft.
**Juncus effusus* (soft rush) FACW+, B, E (semi-), S (part); to 3 ft.
Juncus marginatus (grass-leaf rush) FACW, B; to 20 in.
**Leersia oryzoides* (rice cut-grass) OBL, B, C (aggressive); to 5 ft.
Muhlenbergia mexicana (Mexican muhly) FACW, C (aggressive), S (part); to 34 in.
**Panicum clandestinum* (deer-tongue grass) FAC+, B, C (aggressive); to 5 ft.
Panicum rigidulum (*P. agrostoides*) (red-top panic grass) FACW+, B; to 4 ft.
Poa palustris (fowl meadow grass) FACW+, B; to 5 ft.
Puccinellia pallida (pale mannagrass) OBL; to 40 in.
**Scirpus atrovirens* (black bulrush, green bulrush) OBL, B, S (part); to 4 ft.
**Scirpus cyperinus* (wool grass) FACW+, B, C; to 6 ft.; soil pH 5–8
Scirpus fluviatilis (river bulrush) OBL, B, C; to 4 ft.; eaten by muskrats
Scirpus microcarpus (small-fruit bulrush) OBL, C; to 5 ft.
Scirpus pendulus (*S. lineatus*) (drooping bulrush) OBL; to 5 ft.
**Scirpus pungens* (common threesquare) OBL, B, C; to 4 ft.
Tripsacum dactyloides (gamma grass) FACW, B, C; (NYS S2, U); to 9 ft.

List 3. Freshwater Wetlands—Acid Soil

Shrubs for Wet to Moist, Acid Soil

(*Typical wetland shrubs of the NYC region)

Alnus serrulata (smooth alder) OBL, B, C, N; to 20 ft.; soil pH 5.5–7.5
**Aronia arbutifolia* (red chokeberry) FACW, A, B, C, F, S (part); to 12 ft.; soil pH 5–6.5
**Aronia melanocarpa* (black chokeberry) FAC, A, B, C, F, S (part); to 6 ft.; soil pH 5–6.5
**Clethra alnifolia* (sweet pepperbush) FAC, A, B, C, S; to 8 ft.; soil pH 4.5–6.5
**Eubotrys racemosa* (*Leucothoe r.*) (fetterbush) FACW, A, S; to 12 ft.; soil pH 4.4–6
Ilex laevigata (smooth winterberry) OBL, A, D; to 9 ft.; soil pH 4.5–6
**Ilex verticillata* (winterberry) FACW, A, D, S; to 15 ft.; soil pH 4.5–6
**Lindera benzoin* (spicebush) FACW, A, B, D, F, S (very); to 15 ft.; soil pH 4.5–7.7
**Lyonia ligustrina* (maleberry) FACW, A, S (part); to 12 ft.; soil pH 4–6
**Rhododendron viscosum* (swamp azalea) OBL A, C, S; to 6 ft.; soil pH 4–6
**Vaccinium corymbosum* (highbush blueberry) FACW A, B, F, S (part); to 9 ft.; soil pH 3.5–6.5
**Viburnum dentatum* (*V. recognitum*) (arrowwood) FAC, A, B, C, S (part); to 10 ft.; soil pH 4.4–7

Viburnum nudum (*V. cassinoides*) (possum-haw) OBL, A, B, S (part); (NYS S1, T); to 12 ft.; soil pH 5–6

Floating Leaved and Submerged Herbs for Acid Soil

(low pH, low-nutrient water)

Nuphar advena (*N. lutea*) (southern pond lily) OBL A, C, S (part); acidic water to pH 5
Nymphaea odorata (water lily) OBL A, C
Potamogeton pulcher (spotted pondweed) OBL, A, C, rooted, submerged
Potamogeton pusillus (slender pondweed) OBL, C
Utricularia geminiscapa (mixed bladderwort) OBL; submerged, free floating
Utricularia gibba (creeping bladderwort) OBL; submerged, to 10 in.
Utricularia purpurea (purple bladderwort) OBL; submerged, free floating, to 3 ft.

Emergent Herbs for Wet to Moist Acid Soil

Acorus calamus (sweet flag) OBL, A, C; emergent; to 4 ft., salt tolerance to 10 ppt
Calla palustris (water arum) OBL, A, C, S (part); emergent; to 12 in.
Coptis trifolia (goldthread) FACW, E, C, S; to 6 in.
Equisetum fluviatile (water horsetail) OBL, C; to + 40 in.
Eupatorium pilosum (ragged eupatorium) FACW, A, B; to 4 ft.
Gaultheria hispidula (creeping snowberry) FACW A, B, E, S; prostrate, creeping
Gratiola aurea (golden pert) OBL, A, C; to 12 in.
Helianthus angustifolius (narrow-leaved sunflower) FACW, A; (NYS S2, T); to 6 ft.
Hypericum canadense (Canada St.-John's-wort) FACW; annual, or perennial by short stolons; to 2 ft.
**Iris versicolor* (blueflag) OBL A, C, H; to 32 in.
Lysimachia thyrsiflora (tufted loosestrife) OBL, A, C; to 2 ft.
Menyanthes trifoliata (buckbean) OBL, A, C; emergent, to 1 ft.
Orontium aquaticum (golden club) OBL, A, C, S (part); emergent, to 30 in.
Rhexia virginica (meadow beauty) A, OBL; to 3 ft.
Sagittaria engelmanniana (acid water arrowhead) OBL A; emergent, to 30 in.
Sanguisorba canadensis (American burnet) FACW+, A, C; to 5 ft.
Smilacina stellata (star-flowered Solomon's seal) FACW, C, S (part); to 2 ft.
Solidago uliginosa (swamp goldenrod) OBL; to 5 ft.
Sparganium androcladum (branching bur-reed) OBL, A; emergent, to 3 ft.,
Stachys hyssopifolia (hyssop hedge-nettle) FACW+, A, C; (NYS S2S3, T); to 20 in.
Trillium cernuum (nodding trillium) FACW, A, C, S; to 16 in.
Vaccinium macrocarpon (cranberry) OBL, A, B, E, G, S (part); prostrate, to 1 ft.; soil pH 4–6

Viola blanda (*V. incognita*) (sweet white violet) FACW, B; ca 6 in.
Xyris torta (slender yellow-eyed grass) OBL A; to 34 in.

Ferns for Wet to Moist, Acid Soil

**Onoclea sensibilis* (sensitive fern) FACW, C, S; to 1 ft.; soil, pH 4.5–7.5
**Osmunda regalis* (royal fern) OBL, A, S (part); to 5 ft.; soil pH 4–6

Graminoids for Moist to Wet Acid Soil

Carex echinata (star sedge) FACW (prob.), A, B; to 20 in.
Carex folliculata (northern long sedge) FACW (prob.), A, B, S (part); to 3 ft.
Carex longii (greenish-white sedge) OBL, A, B; to 4 ft.
**Carex stricta* (tussock sedge) OBL A, B, C, S (part); to 3 ft.; soil pH 6.2
Eleocharis melanocarpa (black-fruited spikerush) FACW+, A, B; to 2 ft.
Eriophorum gracile (slender cotton grass) OBL, A, B, C; to 8 in.
Eriophorum virginicum (tawny cotton grass) OBL, A, B, C; to 3 ft.
Eriophorum viridicarinatum (dark-scale cotton grass) OBL, B, C; to 2 ft.
Juncus canadensis (Canada rush) OBL, A, B; to 3 ft.
Rhynchospora alba (white beakrush) OBL A, B; to 28 in.
**Rhynchospora capitellata* (brownish beakrush) OBL, A, B; to 32 in.
Rhynchospora fusca (brown beakrush) OBL, B, C; to 16 in.

List 4. Open, Freshwater Wetlands with Alkaline Soils (pH 7.1–8.5)

(s: salt tolerance moderate to high, or tolerates brackish water)

Shrubs for Wet to Moist Alkaline Soil

**Cephalanthus occidentalis* (buttonbush) OBL, C; to 12 ft.; soil pH 6–8.5
**Cornus amomum* (silky dogwood) FACW, B, S (part); to 9 ft.; soil pH 6–8.5
Cornus sericea (*C. stolonifera*) (red-osier dogwood) FACW, B; to 8 ft.; soil pH 6–8.5
Potentilla fruticosa (shrubby cinquefoil) FACW; to 3 ft.; soil pH 6–8.5
Ribes americanum (wild black currant) FACW, S; to 6 ft.; soil pH 6–8.5
**Sambucus canadensis* (elderberry) FACW, C, S (part); to 12 ft.; soil pH 6–8

Floating Leaved and Submerged Herbs for Alkaline Soil (high pH or high nutrient water)

Elodea canadensis (waterweed) OBL, C (aggressive); rooted or not, to 3 ft.; water to pH 6.5–10; to 10 ppt salt
Potamogeton pectinatus (sago pondweed) OBL, C, K; rooted, submerged, to 2 ft.; pH 7–10; to 10 ppt salt
Potamogeton pusillus (slender pondweed) OBL, C; rooted, submerged, to 5 ft.
Vallisneria americana (wild celery, tape grass) OBL, C; rooted, submerged, to 7 ft., long

Herbs for Wet to Moist Alkaline Soil

**Eupatorium maculatum* (spotted joe-pye weed) FACW B; to 6 ft.
Gentiana andrewsii (fringe-tip closed gentian) FACW, K, S (part); to 3 ft.
Hypericum majus (large Canada St.-John's-wort) FACW, K; to 28 in.
Lobelia kalmii (brook lobelia) OBL; to 18 in.
Parnassia glauca (grass of Parnassus) OBL; to 16 in.
Pedicularis lanceolata (swamp lousewort) FACW, S (part); to 30 in.
Polygonum punctatum (dotted smartweed) OBL; to 3 ft.
Pontederia cordata (pickerelweed) OBL, C, S (part); emergent, to 3 ft.
Sagittaria calycina (spongy arrowhead) OBL; annual emergent, ca. 2 ft.
Senecio aureus (golden ragwort) FACW, C, S; to 3 ft.
Solidago patula (rough-leaved goldenrod) OBL, B; to 6 ft.
Viola striata (cream violet) FACW, B; to 1 ft.

Graminoids for Wet to Moist Alkaline Soil

Carex atlantica (prickly bog sedge) FACW+, B; to 32 in.
Carex bebbii (Bebb's sedge) OBL, B; to 32 in.
Carex granularis (limestone meadow sedge) FACW+, B, E, K; to 32 in.
Carex hystericina (porcupine sedge) OBL, B, C, K; to 3 ft.
Carex squarrosa (squarrose sedge) FACW, B, K; to 3 ft.
Carex typhina (cattail sedge) FACW+, B, K, S; to 3 ft. (NYS S2, R)
Cladium mariscoides (twig rush) OBL, C; to 3 ft.
Eleocharis palustris (creeping spikerush) OBL, B, C; to 3 ft.
Eleocharis rostellata (beaked spikerush) OBL, B, C; to 40 in.
Juncus arcticus var. *littoralis* (*J. balticus*) (wire rush) OBL, B, C; to 32 in.
Juncus torreyi (Torrey's rush) FACW, B, C, K; to 3 ft.
**Scirpus americanus* (Olney three-square) OBL, B, C; to 6 in.
**Scirpus cyperinus* (wool grass) FACW+, B, C; to 6 ft.; soil pH 5–8
Scirpus fluviatilis (river bulrush) OBL, B, C; to 4 ft.
**Scirpus pungens* (common threesquare) OBL, B, C; to 4 ft.
Scirpus validus (soft-stem bulrush) OBL, B, C; to 7 ft.; soil pH 6.5–8.5

SET 2. TIDAL WETLAND PLANTS

Salinity levels: Freshwater, 0–2 parts per thousand salt (ppt); brackish water, 2–10 ppt salt; saline (ocean) tidal water 10–30 ppt.
High salt marsh: mean high high water (spring tides) to mean high water. Surface flooded during high high water, soil usually saturated below the surface during high tides. All plants listed for tidal wetlands are adapted to high salt marsh (except *Spartina alterniflora*).

Low salt marsh: mean high water to mid (mean) tide. Surface usually saturated during most high tides, soil drains and becomes aerated as the tide recedes (*Spartina alterniflora*).

Plants adapted to tidal wetlands, whether freshwater, brackish, or saline, tolerate periodic soil saturation but are not usually adapted to continuous anaerobic conditions such as those experienced by emergent wetland plants. In order to survive, these plants need soil that drains and becomes aerated periodically during the daily tide cycles. Heavy clay soil, which does not drain, may not permit survival of tidally adapted plants. On the East Coast we have two tidal cycles each day. The hours of high tide shift forward by about one hour each day, creating a continuously migrating set of two high and two low tides within each twenty-four-hour period. Some emergent and aquatic plants can also live in tidal wetlands.

List 5. Freshwater Tidal Wetlands

Shrubs for Freshwater Tidal Wetlands

Alnus incana (*A. rugosa*) (speckled alder) FACW, B, C, N; to 35 ft.; pH 6.5–7.5; shade index 0–2; s

**Cephalanthus occidentalis* (buttonbush) OBL, C; to 12 ft.; soil pH 6–8.5

**Cornus amomum* (silky dogwood) FACW, B, S (part); soil pH 6–8.5

Myrica pensylvanica (northern bayberry) FAC, A, C, D, N; to 6 ft.; soil pH 5–6.5

Rosa palustris (swamp rose) OBL, C, aggressive; to 6 ft.; stems prickly

**Sambucus canadensis* (elderberry) FACW, C, S (part); to 12 ft.; soil pH 6–8

**Viburnum dentatum* (*V. recognitum*) (arrowwood) FAC, A, B, C, S (part); to 10 ft.; soil pH 4.4–7

Floating and Submerged Herbs for Freshwater Tidal Wetlands

Lemna minor (duckweed) OBL, C (aggressive); tiny floating plants

**Nuphar advena* (*N. lutea*) (southern pond lily) OBL, C; leaves emergent

**Nymphaea odorata* (water lily) OBL, C; floating leaved

Emergent Herbs for Freshwater Tidal Wetlands

Acorus calamus (sweet flag) OBL, C; emergent; to 4 ft.; brackish water to 10 ppt; eaten by muskrats

**Alisma subcordatum* (southern water plantain) OBL, C; emergent; ca. 1 ft.

**Peltandra virginica* (arrow arum) OBL, C, S (part); emergent, to 30 in.; soil pH 5–6.5; muskrat safe

**Pontederia cordata* (pickerelweed) OBL, C, S (part); emergent, to 3 ft.; soil pH 6–8; eaten by muskrats

Rumex verticillatus (swamp dock) OBL, C; emergent, to 3 ft.

Sagittaria graminea (grass-leaved arrowhead) OBL, C; emergent to immersed, plant to 2 ft.; soil pH 7

**Sagittaria latifolia* (duck potato) OBL, C; emergent, to 3 ft.
**Saururus cernuus* (lizard's tail) OBL, C, S to 3 ft.
**Typha latifolia* (cattail) OBL, C; emergent, to 9 ft.; soil pH 5.5–7.5

Herbs for Moist to Wet Soil of Freshwater Tidal Wetlands

Amaranthus cannabinus (salt-marsh hemp) OBL, D; to 8 ft.
Ambrosia trifida (great ragweed) FAC; annual; to 6 ft.
**Asclepias incarnata* (swamp milkweed) OBL, B, C; to 4 ft.
Bidens cernua (bur-marigold) OBL; annual; to 40 in.
Helenium autumnale (common sneezeweed) FACW+; to 6 ft.
**Hibiscus moscheutos* (rose mallow) OBL, B, H; to 6 ft.
Impatiens capensis (*I. biflora*) (jewelweed) FACW, H, S; annual; to 3 ft.; soil pH 5.6–7.0
**Iris versicolor* (blueflag) OBL, A, H, S (part); to 32 in.
Lobelia cardinalis (cardinal flower) FACW+, B, H, S (part); to 4 ft.
Polygonum arifolium (halberd-leaved tearthumb) OBL; prickly; to 6 ft.
Polygonum hydropiperoides (mild water-pepper) OBL, C, S (part); reclining, to 6 ft.
Polygonum punctatum (dotted smartweed) OBL; to 3 ft.
Polygonum sagittatum (arrow-leaved tearthumb) OBL; annual; to 6 ft.
Sium suave (water parsnip) OBL, B; to 6 ft.
**Symplocarpus foetidus* (skunk cabbage) OBL, C; spring ephemeral; to 2 ft.; soil pH 5–6.2

Graminoids for Freshwater Tidal Wetlands

Calamagrostis canadensis (bluejoint) FACW+, B, C (aggressive); to 5 ft.; potentially invasive
**Carex stricta* (tussock sedge) OBL, A, B, C, S (part); to 3 ft.; soil pH 6.2
**Dulichium arundinaceum* (three-way sedge) OBL, B, C; to 3 ft.
**Eleocharis palustris* (creeping spikerush) OBL, B, C, K; to 3 ft.
**Juncus effusus* (soft rush) FACW+, B, E (semi-), S (part); to 3 ft.
**Leersia oryzoides* (rice cut-grass) OBL, B, C (aggressive); to 5 ft.
**Scirpus americanus* (Olney three-square) OBL, B, C; to 6 in.; water to 15 ppt salt; eaten by muskrats
**Scirpus cyperinus* (wool grass) FACW+, B, C; to 6 ft.; soil pH 5–8
**Scirpus pungens* (common threesquare) OBL, B, C; to 4 ft.; pH 7; water to 15 ppt salt; eaten by muskrats
**Scirpus validus* (soft-stem bulrush) OBL, B, C, K; to 7 ft.; soil pH 6.5–8.5; eaten by muskrats
Tripsacum dactyloides (gamma grass) FACW, B, C; (NYS S2, U); to 9 ft.
Zizania aquatica (wild rice) OBL, B; annual; to 9 ft.

List 6. Brackish Tidal wetlands (approximately 3–15 ppt salt)

Shrubs for Brackish Tidal Wetlands

Aronia arbutifolia (red chokeberry) FACW, B, C, F, S (part); to 12 ft.; soil pH 5–6.5

Baccharis halimifolia (groundsel bush) FACW, D; to 12 ft.; soil pH 7–8.5

Iva frutescens (marsh elder) FACW+; to 9 ft.; soil pH 6–7.5

Myrica pensylvanica (northern bayberry) (dioecious) FAC, A, C, D, N; to 6 ft.; soil pH 5–6.5

Floating or Submerged Herbs for Brackish Tidal Wetlands

Elodea canadensis (waterweed) OBL, C (aggressive); 10 ppt salt; water pH 6.5–10

Najas flexilis (northern water nymph) OBL

Nuphar advena (*N. lutea*) (southern pond lily) OBL; acidic water to pH 5

Potamogeton pectinatus (sago pondweed) OBL; to 10 ppt salt; water pH 7–10

Potamogeton perfoliatus (redhead grass) OBL; to 5 ppt salt

Ranunculus trichophyllus (white water crowfoot) OBL

Vallisneria americana (wild celery, tape grass) OBL; to 5 ppt salt

Emergent Herbs for Brackish Tidal Wetlands

**Pontederia cordata* (pickerelweed) OBL; to 3 ft.; to 3 ppt salt; soil pH 6–8

Herbs for Moist to Wet Soil of Brackish Tidal Wetlands

Acorus calamus (sweet flag) OBL; to 4 ft.; to 10 ppt salt

**Hibiscus moscheutos* (rose mallow) OBL; to 6 ft.; to 15 ppt salt

Iris prismatica (slender blueflag) OBL, H, S (part); (NYS S2, U); to 28 in.

**Iris versicolor* (blueflag) OBL, A, C, S (part); to 32 in.

Kosteletzkya virginica (seashore mallow) OBL; (NYS SX, U; Global G5T3T4); to 4 ft.; to 10 ppt salt

Limosella subulata (mudwort) OBL; annual; to 6 in.

Polygonum ramosissimum (bushy knotweed) FAC; annual; to 40 in.

Ptilimnium capillaceum (mock bishop's weed) OBL; to 3 ft.

Sagittaria graminea (grass-leaved arrowhead) OBL, C; to 2 ft.; soil pH 7

Samolus floribundus (water pimpernel) OBL; to 12 in.

Sium suave (water parsnip) OBL, B; to 6 ft.

Solidago elliotii (coastal swamp goldenrod) OBL, C; (NYS S1, U); to 10 ft.

Graminoids for Brackish Tidal Wetlands

Carex aquatilis (water sedge) OBL, C (aggressive); to 3 ft.

Cladium mariscoides (twig rush) OBL, C; to 3 ft.

Cyperus odoratus (rusty flatsedge) FACW, B; annual; to 32 in.
Echinochloa walteri (coast cockspur grass) FACW+; annual; to 6.5 ft.
Eleocharis palustris (creeping spikerush) OBL, B, C; to 3 ft.
Eleocharis rostellata (beaked spikerush) OBL, B, C; to 40 in.
Fimbristylis castanea (marsh fimbry) OBL, B; to 4 ft.
Juncus arcticus var. *littoralis* (*J. balticus*) (wire rush) OBL, B, C; to 32 in.
**Panicum virgatum* (switchgrass) FAC; to 6 ft.; to 10 ppt salt
**Scirpus americanus* (Olney three-square) OBL, B, C; to 6 in.; to 15 ppt salt
**Scirpus pungens* (common threesquare) OBL, B, C; to 4 ft.; to 15ppt salt
Scirpus validus (soft-stem bulrush) OBL, B, C; to 7 ft.; to 5 ppt salt; soil pH 6.5–8.5
Setaria parviflora (*S. geniculata*) (knotroot-foxtail grass) FAC; to 4 ft.
Spartina cynosuroides (big cordgrass) OBL, C; to 9 ft.;
Tripsacum dactyloides (gamma grass) FACW, B, C; to 9 ft.; (NYS S2, U)
Zizania aquatica (wild rice) OBL, B; annual; to 9 ft.

List 7. Saline Tidal Wetlands, Salt Marsh

Shrubs of Saline Tidal Wetlands

Baccharis halimifolia (groundsel bush) FACW, D; to 12 ft.; soil pH 7–8.5; upland edges of high salt marsh
Iva frutescens (marsh elder) FACW+; to 9 ft., high salt marsh

Herbs of Saline Tidal Wetlands

Aster tenuifolius (perennial salt-marsh aster) OBL; to 18 in.
Atriplex arenaria (sea-beach orach) FAC−; annual; to 20 in.
Limonium carolinianum (sea lavender) OBL; to 12 in.
Sabatia dodecandra (perennial sea-pink) OBL; to 2 ft.
Salicornia europaea (glasswort, sapphire) OBL; annual; to 16 in.
Salicornia virginica (perennial glasswort) OBL, C; to 1 ft.
Solidago sempervirens (seaside goldenrod) FACW; to 5 ft.; upper edge high salt marsh

Graminoids of Saline Tidal Wetlands

**Distichlis spicata* (salt grass) FACW+, C; to 16 in.; subdominant with *Spartina patens*
Hierochloe odorata (vanilla grass) FACW, B, C; to 2 ft.; upper edge high salt marsh
Juncus gerardii (black grass) FACW+, C; to 16 in.; subdominant; upper edge high salt marsh
Panicum virgatum (switchgrass) FAC; to 6 ft.; upper edge high salt marsh
Puccinellia fasciculata (salt-marsh alkali grass) OBL; to 24 in.

Scirpus maritimus (seaside bulrush) OBL, B, C; to 4 ft.; (NYS S1, U)
Scirpus robustus (salt-marsh bulrush) OBL, C; to 5 ft.; soil pH 4–7
**Spartina alterniflora* (salt-marsh cordgrass) OBL, C; to 4.5 ft.; low salt marsh
**Spartina patens* (salt-meadow cordgrass) FACW+, C; to 2 ft.; high salt marsh dominant
Triglochin maritima (seaside arrow grass) OBL; to 32 in.

SET 3. UPLAND PLANTS FOR OPEN SITES

List 8. Annuals for Soil Stabilization

Annual Herbs

Acalypha gracilens (three-seeded mercury) UPL; to 20 in.
Acalypha rhomboidea (*A. virginica* var. *r.*) (three-seeded mercury/copper-leaf) FACU−; to 2 ft.
Ambrosia artemisiifolia (ragweed) FACU; to 40 in.
Amphicarpaea bracteata (American hog peanut) FAC, N, S (part); twining; to 40 in. long
Arabis canadensis (sickle-pod) UPL E (winter rosette), S; to 40 in.
Arabis hirsuta var. *pycnocarpa* (hairy rock cress) FACU, E (winter rosette); to 32 in.
Arabis laevigata (smooth rock cress) UPL, E (winter rosette), S; to 40 in.
Arabis lyrata (lyre-leaved rock cress) FACU, E (winter rosette); to 16 in.
Campanula americana (tall bellflower) FAC, S (part); to 5 ft.
Cerastium nutans (nodding chickweed) FAC; to 2 ft.
Chamaecrista fasciculata (*Cassia chamaecrista*) (partridge pea) UPL, N; to 30 in.
Chamaecrista nictitans (*Cassia n.*) (dwarf partridge pea) FACU−, N; to 20 in.
Chenopodium berlandieri (pit-seed goosefoot) UPL; to 5 ft.
Chenopodium capitatum (strawberry-blite) UPL; to 2 ft.
Cirsium pumilum (pasture thistle) UPL, K; to 32 in.
Conyza canadensis (*Erigeron c.*) (horseweed) UPL; to 5 ft.
Cuphea viscosissima (blue wax-weed) FAC−; to 2 ft.
Diodia teres (buttonweed, poorjoe) UPL; prostrate, to 32 in. long
Draba reptans (Carolina whitlow-grass) UPL; to 8 in.
Erechtites hieraciifolia (fireweed, pilewort) FACU, S (part); to 8 ft.
Erigeron annuus (annual fleabane) FACU, B; to 5 ft.
Erigeron strigosus (rough fleabane) FACU+; to 28 in.
Euphorbia maculata (spotted spurge, milk purslane) FACU−; forming mats to 16 in. wide
Floerkea proserpinacoides (false mermaid) FAC; to 1 ft.
Galium aparine (cleavers) FACU, S; reclining

Geranium bicknellii (Bicknell's crane's-bill) UPL, S (part); to 2 ft.
Geranium carolinianum (Carolina crane's-bill) UPL; to 20 in.
Gnaphalium obtusifolium (sweet everlasting) UPL, B; to 3 ft.
Hackelia virginiana (tickseed, beggar-lice) FACU, S; to 40 in.
Hedeoma pulegioides (American pennyroyal) UPL, S (part); to 16 in.
Hypericum gentianoides (orange-grass, pineweed) UPL; to 20 in.
Lactuca biennis (tall blue lettuce) FACU; to 6.5 ft.
Lactuca canadensis (tall lettuce) FACU−, S; to 8 ft.
Lepidium virginicum (poor-man's pepper) FACU−; to 20 in.
Linaria canadensis (blue toadflax) UPL; to 2 ft.
Lobelia inflata (Indian-tobacco) FACU, E (winter rosette), S (part); to 40 in.
Myosotis verna (early scorpion-grass, spring forget-me-not) FAC−
Oenothera biennis (common evening primrose) FACU−, E (leafy rosette), H; to 6 ft.
Oenothera parviflora (northern evening primrose) FACU−, H; to 6 ft.
Parietaria pensylvanica (pellitory) FACU, S; to 16 in.
Paronychia canadensis (smooth forked nailwort) UPL; to 16 in.
Paronychia fastigiata (hairy forked nailwort) UPL; to 16 in.
Physalis pubescens (downy ground-cherry) FACU−; to 1 ft.
Polygonella articulata (jointweed) UPL; to 20 in.
Polygonum ramosissimum (bushy knotweed) FAC; to 40 in.
Silene antirrhina (sleepy catch-fly) UPL; to 32 in.
Trichostema dichotomum (blue curls) UPL; to 28 in.
Trichostema setaceum (narrow-leaf blue curls) UPL (NYS SH, E); to 28 in.
Triodanis perfoliata (round-leaved Triodanis) FAC; to 3 ft.,
Verbena urticifolia (white vervain) FACU; to 5 ft.

Annual, Upland Graminoids

Aristida dichotoma (churchmouse three-awn) UPL; to 16 in.
Aristida longespica (slimspike three-awn) UPL; to 20 in.
Aristida tuberculosa (three-awn) UPL; to 32 in.
Bulbostylis capillaris (sand rush) FACU; to 12 in.
Cenchrus longispinus (common sandbur) UPL; to 32 in.
Digitaria filiformis (slender crabgrass) UPL; to 3 ft.
Eragrostis pectinacea (Carolina lovegrass) FAC; to 2 ft.
Panicum capillare (witch-grass) FAC−; to 28 in.
Panicum philadelphicum (Philadelphia panic grass) UPL; to 32 in.
Sphenopholis obtusata (prairie wedge-grass) FAC−; to 4 ft.
Sporobolus neglectus (puffsheath dropseed) FACU−; to 20 in.
Sporobolus vaginiflorus (poverty grass) UPL; to 20 in.
Triplasis purpurea (purple sand-grass) UPL; to 32 in.
Vulpia octoflora (six-week fescue) UPL; to 2 ft.

List 9. Perennial Grasses for Native Turf

Danthonia compressa (flattened oatgrass) FACU, G, S; leaves to 8 in., inflorescence to 32 in.

Danthonia spicata (poverty oatgrass) UPL, S (part); leaves to 5 in., inflorescence to 2 ft.

Juncus tenuis (path rush) FAC−, S (part); usually less than 1 ft. tall

Muhlenbergia frondosa (wire-stem muhly) FAC, C (vigorously), S; leaves to 5 in., inflorescence to 3.5 ft.

Muhlenbergia schreberi (nimblewill) FAC, C (aggressive), S (part); tolerates mowing well. Less than 1 ft.

Muhlenbergia sobolifera (creeping muhly) UPL, C (vigorously), S; to 34 in. (inflorescence)

Muhlenbergia sylvatica (forest muhly) FAC+, C, S; to 30 in. (inflorescence)

Muhlenbergia tenuiflora (slender flowered muhly) UPL, C (vigorously), S; to 40 in. (inflorescence)

Tridens flavus (purpletop) FACU, B, C; to 5 ft.(inflorescence)

Buchloe dactyloides (buffalo grass) native to U.S. western short-grass prairie, very drought tolerant, hardly needs mowing. Studied extensively by Dr. James Quinn, a professor at Rutgers University, Dept. of Ecology, Evolution and Natural Resources. Paper on buffalo-grass's potential use in NJ for turf and conservation uses was in the *Journal of the Torrey Botanical Society* 125(4), 1998, pp. 319–323.

List 10. Native Woody Ornamentals (wet to dry soils)

Large Trees (to over 60 ft.)

Betula nigra (river birch) (moist soil) FACW, A; to 75 ft.; soil pH 4–6.5; shade index 2–4

Betula papyrifera (paper birch) FACU, B, F; to 80 ft.; soil pH 5–8.5; shade index 1

Chamaecyparis thyoides (Atlantic white cedar) (moist soil) OBL, A, E; to 75 ft., soil pH 3–5.5

Pinus echinata (short-leaf pine) (acid soil) UPL, A, E (NYS S1, E); to 90 ft.

Pinus resinosa (red pine) (acid soil) FACU, A, E; to 100 ft.; soil pH 4–6.5; shade, index 2.4

Pinus rigida (pitch pine) (acid soil) FACU, A, E; to 60 ft.; soil pH 3.5–6.5; shade index 0–2

Pinus strobus (white pine) (acid soil) FACU, A, E; to 110 ft.; soil pH 4–6.5; shade index 4.4

Small Trees (60 ft. and less)

Betula populifolia (gray birch) FAC, A, B, F; to 30 ft., soil pH 5–7.5; shade index 1

Carpinus caroliniana (American hornbeam) FAC, B, F, S; to 40 ft.; soil pH 4.0–7.5; shade index 8–10

Cornus florida (flowering dogwood) FACU−, B, F, S; to 40 ft.; soil pH 5.5–7; shade index 8–10

Crataegus crus-galli (cockspur hawthorn) FACU; to 30 ft.; thorns to 3-in.; soil pH 6–8.5; shade index 2–4

Ilex opaca (American holly) (dioecious) FACU+, A, D, E, S; to 40 ft.

Juniperus virginiana (eastern red cedar) (dioecious) FACU, B, D, E; to 60 ft.; soil pH 4.7–8.5; shade index 0–2

Magnolia virginiana (sweet-bay magnolia) (moist soil) FACW+, S; to 60 ft.; (NYS S1, U); soil pH 5–6

Ostrya virginiana (hophornbeam) FACU−, B, S; to 60 ft.; soil pH 4.2–8; shade index 8–10

Pinus virginiana (Virginia pine) (acid soil) UPL, A, E (NYS S1, E); to 30 ft.; pH 4.6–7.9; shade intolerant

Large Shrubs (11–30 ft.)

Amelanchier arborea (serviceberry) FAC, B, F, S (part); to 40 ft.

Amelanchier canadensis (shadbush) FAC, B, F, S (part); to 25 ft.; soil pH 5–6.5; shade index 8–10

Aronia arbutifolia (red chokeberry) (moist soil) FACW, B, C, F, S (part); to 12 ft.; soil pH 5–6.5

Aronia prunifolia (purple-fruit chokeberry) (moist soil) FACW, B, C, F, S (part); to 12 ft.; soil pH 5–6.5

Cornus alternifolia (pagoda dogwood) UPL, S; to 25 ft.; soil pH 6.5–7.5; shade index 8–10

Cornus racemosa (red-panicle dogwood, gray dogwood) FAC, C; to 15 ft.; soil pH 6–8.5

Crataegus intricata (Biltmore hawthorn) UPL, S (part); to 24 ft.; thorns 1–2 in.

Crataegus pruinosa (frosted hawthorn) UPL; to 24 ft.; very thorny; soil pH 6–8.5; shade, index 2–4

Hamamelis virginiana (witch hazel) FAC−, S; to 25 ft.; soil pH 6–6.5 (more tolerant); shade index 8–10

Ilex verticillata (winterberry) (moist soil; dioecious) FACW, A, D, S; to 15 ft.; soil pH 4.5–6

Prunus americana (hedge plum) FACU−, B, C; to 24 ft.; soil pH 6.5–7.5; shade index 2–4

Rhododendron maximum (white laurel) FAC, A, C, E, S; to 30 ft.; soil pH 4.5–6; shade index 6–8

Rhus copallina (winged sumac) (dioecious) UPL, A, C, D, F; to 25 ft.; soil pH 6–7; shade index 0–2

Rhus glabra (smooth sumac) UPL, C, D, F; to 15 ft.; soil pH 6–7; shade index 0–2

Rhus typhina (staghorn sumac) UPL, C, D, F; to 15 ft.; soil pH 6–7; shade index 0–2

Salix discolor (pussy willow) (males only; moist soil) FACW, B, D; to 15 ft.; soil pH 6.5–7.5; shade index 0–2

Sambucus canadensis (elderberry) (moist soil) FACW, C, S (part); to 12 ft.; soil pH 6–8

Staphylea trifolia (bladdernut) FAC, S (part); to 15 ft.; soil pH 6–8

Viburnum lentago (nanny berry) FAC B, C, S (part); to 30 ft.; soil pH 6–8.5; shade index 5–6

Viburnum prunifolium (black-haw) FACU, B, S (part); to 15 ft.; soil pH 5–8.5; shade index 2–4

Small Shrubs (1–10 ft.)

Amelanchier spicata (*A. stolonifera*) (dwarf serviceberry) FACU, B, C, S; to 3 ft.

Aronia melanocarpa (black chokeberry) (moist soil) FAC, B, C, F, S (part); to 6 ft., soil pH 5–6.5

Ceanothus americanus (New Jersey tea) UPL, A, B, C, S (part); to 4 ft.; soil pH 4.5–6

Clethra alnifolia (sweet pepperbush) (moist soil) FAC+, A, B, C, S; to 8 ft.; soil pH 4.5–6.5

Cornus rugosa (roundleaf dogwood) UPL, S; to 9 ft.; soil pH 6–8.5

Cornus sericea (*C. stolonifera*) (red-osier dogwood) FACW, B; to 8 ft.; soil pH 6–8.5

Crataegus uniflora (one-flower hawthorn) UPL, S (part); to 6 ft.

Diervilla lonicera (dwarf-bush honeysuckle) UPL, C, H, S; to 3 ft.; soil pH 4.8–7.0

Dirca palustris (leatherwood) FAC, S; to 6 ft.; soil pH 6–8.5

Euonymus americanus (strawberry bush) FAC, F, S; to 7 ft.; (NYS S1, T); soil pH 6–7.5

Gaylussacia baccata (black huckleberry) FACU, A, B, C, S; to 3 ft.; soil pH 4–5

Gaylussacia dumosa (dwarf huckleberry) FAC, A, B, C, S (part); to 20 in.; soil pH 4.3–6.5

Gaylussacia frondosa (tall huckleberry) FAC, A, B, C, S; to 6 ft.; soil pH 3.8–5.5

Hypericum hypericoides (St. Andrew's Cross) UPL; to 4 ft.

Hypericum prolificum (shrubby St.-John's-wort) FACU; to 3 ft.; soil pH 6–8.5; shade index very low

Ilex glabra (inkberry) (moist, acid soil; dioecious) FACW, A, E, D, S; to 6 ft.; soil pH 4.5–6

Juniperus communis (common juniper) (dioecious) UPL, A, D, E; to 6 ft.; soil pH 5–8.5

Kalmia angustifolia (sheep laurel) FAC, A, C, E, S (part); to 3 ft.; soil pH 4.5–6

Kalmia latifolia (mountain laurel) FACU, A, E, S; to 9 ft.; soil pH 4.5–6

Lonicera canadensis (fly-honeysuckle) FACU, H, S (part); to 6 ft.

Lyonia mariana (staggerbush) FAC−, A, S (part); to 6 ft.
Myrica pensylvanica (northern bayberry) (dioecious) FAC, A, C, D, N; to 6 ft.; soil, pH 5–6.5
Prunus pumila var. *depressa* (sand cherry) UPL; to 3 ft.
Physocarpus opulifolius (ninebark) FACW, C; to 10 ft.; soil pH 6–8.5
Rhododendron canadense (rhodora) FACW, A, S; (NYS S2, R); to 3 ft.
Rhododendron periclymenoides (pinkster azalea) (moist soil) FAC, A, S; to 6 ft.; soil pH 4.2–5.5
Rhododendron prinophyllum (*R. roseum*) (early azalea) (moist soil) FAC, A, S; to 9 ft.; soil pH 5–8
Ribes americanum (wild black currant) FACW, S; to 6 ft.; soil pH 6–8.5
Ribes cynosbati (dogberry) UPL, F, S; to 5 ft.; stems spiny; soil pH 6–8.5
Ribes hirtellum (smooth gooseberry) FAC, S; to 3 ft.; few spines
Ribes rotundifolium (Appalachian gooseberry) UPL, S; to 5 ft.; spiny
Rosa blanda (smooth rose) FACU, C; to 6 ft.; prickly; soil pH to over 7.5
Rosa carolina (pasture rose) UPL, C; to 3 ft.; prickly; soil pH 6–8.5
Rosa virginiana (Virginia rose) FAC, A, C; to 6 ft.; prickly
Rubus occidentalis (black raspberry) UPL, C; to 4 ft.; prickly; soil pH 4.5–6.5
Rubus odoratus (flowering raspberry) UPL, C, S (part); unarmed; to 6 ft.; soil pH 5–6
Salix humilis (upland willow) (males only) FACU, C, D; to 9 ft.; soil pH 6–7.5
Salix occidentalis (*S. tristis*) (dwarf upland willow) (males only) UPL, B, C, D; to 3 ft.
Spiraea alba var. *latifolia* (meadowsweet) FAC+, B, C; to 6 ft.; soil pH 6.6–7.5
Spiraea tomentosa (hardhack) (moist soil) FACW, B, C; to 5 ft; soil pH 5–6
Taxus canadensis (Canada yew) FAC, E, S; to 6 ft.; soil pH 5–7.5
Vaccinium angustifolium (lowbush blueberry) FACU, A, B, C, G, S (part); to 2 ft.; soil pH 4–6
Vaccinium corymbosum (highbush blueberry) FACW, A, B, F, S (part); to 9 ft.; soil pH 3.5–6.5
Vaccinium pallidum (*V. vacillans*) (early low blueberry) UPL, A, B, C, S; to 3 ft.; soil pH 4.8–5.6
Vaccinium stamineum (deerberry) (acid soil) FACU−, A, B, S; to 5 ft.; soil pH 4–6.5
Viburnum acerifolium (maple-leaved viburnum) UPL, A, B, C, F, S (very); to 7 ft.; soil pH 4.4–6
Viburnum alnifolium (*V. lantanoides*) (hobblebush) UPL, B, S; to 10 ft.; soil pH 5.5–6.5
Viburnum cassinoides (*V. nudum* var. *c.*) (withe rod) FACW, F, S; to 12 ft.; soil pH 5–6.5
Viburnum rafinesquianum (downy arrowwood) UPL, B, S; to 7 ft.; soil pH 6–8.5

List 11. Plants for Slope Stabilization in Open Sites

Plants in this list are mostly colonial, and grow or reproduce rapidly. They were chosen for their soil-holding capacity on open to lightly shaded slopes. It is assumed that there may be concrete debris present to a greater or lesser extent in many urban soils.

Oaks, pines, and plants in the heath family usually require soils with pH 6 or less. Test soil pH before planting these. *Shade tolerance:* 0 (needs full sun) to 10 (tolerates deep shade).

Trees for Open Slopes (*Generally available, tolerant of urban conditions.)

**Betula populifolia* (gray birch) FAC, A, B, F.; to 30 ft.; soil pH 5–7.5; shade index 1

**Celtis occidentalis* (common hackberry) FACU, B, K; to 70 ft.; soil pH 6.5–8.5; shade index 4–6

Diospyros virginiana (persimmon) FAC−, C; to 40 ft.; soil pH 6–6.5; shade index 2–4; (NYS S2, T)

Juglans nigra (black walnut) UPL, B, K; to 100 ft.; soil pH 4.6–8.2; shade index 4

**Populus deltoides* (eastern cottonwood) FAC, B, s; to 150 ft.; soil pH 5.5–7.5; shade index 2.2

**Populus grandidentata* (big-toothed aspen) FACU−, B, C; to 60 ft.; soil pH 5–6.3; shade index 1

Populus tremuloides (quaking aspen) UPL, B, C; to 50 ft.; soil pH 4.5–6.5; shade index <1

Prunus pensylvanica (pin cherry) FACU−, B, C; to 45 ft.; soil pH 6–7.5; shade index 0.7

**Prunus serotina* (wild black cherry) FACU, A, B, F, K; to 75 ft.; soil pH 4–8; shade index 2.4

**Sassafras albidum* (sassafras) FACU−, A, B, C, D, F; to 50 ft.; soil pH 6–7; shade index 2–4

Shrubs for Open Slopes (*Usually available, common, tough, urban-tolerant plants.)

Amelanchier spicata (A. stolonifera) (dwarf serviceberry) FACU, B, C, S; to 3 ft.

**Cornus racemosa* (red-panicle dogwood) FAC, C, K, S (part); to 15 ft.; soil pH 6–8.5

Lonicera dioica (limber honeysuckle) FACU, H, S; shrub or climber; to 9 ft.; soil pH 6–8.5

**Myrica pensylvanica* (northern bayberry) FAC, A, C, D, N; to 6 ft.; soil pH 5–6.5

Prunus americana (hedge plum) FACU−, B, C; to 24 ft.; soil pH 6.5–7.5; shade index 2–4

Quercus prinoides (dwarf oak, chinquapin) UPL, C, K; to 20 ft.; pH 5–8.5

Rhus copallina (winged sumac) UPL, A, C, D, F; to 25 ft.; soil pH 6–7; shade index 0–2
Rhus glabra (smooth sumac) UPL, C, D, F; to 15 ft.; soil pH 6–7; shade index 0–2
Rhus typhina (staghorn sumac) UPL, C, D, F; to 15 ft.; soil pH 6–7; shade index 0–2
Rosa blanda (smooth rose) FACU, C; to 6 ft.; prickly; soil pH to over 7.5
Rosa carolina (pasture rose) UPL, C, K; to 3 ft.; prickly; soil pH 6–8.5
Rubus allegheniensis (common blackberry) FACU, C; to 6 ft.; prickly; soil pH 4.5–7.5
Rubus flagellaris (dewberry) UPL, C, G; ca. 1 ft.; stems prickly; soil pH 5–7
Rubus occidentalis (black raspberry) UPL, C; to 4 ft.; prickly; soil pH 4.5–6.5
Rubus odoratus (flowering raspberry) UPL, C, S (part); to 6 ft.; unarmed; soil pH 5–6
Salix humilis (upland willow) FACU, C, D; to 9 ft.; soil pH 6–7.5
Salix occidentalis (*S. tristis*) (dwarf upland willow) UPL, B, C, D; to 3 ft.
Viburnum dentatum (*V. recognitum*) (arrowwood) FAC, B, C, S (part); to 10 ft.; soil pH 4.4–7
Viburnum lentago (nanny berry) FAC, B, C, S (part); to 30 ft., soil pH 6–8.5; shade index 5–6
Viburnum rafinesquianum (downy arrowwood) UPL, B, K, S (part); to 7 ft.; soil pH 6–8.5

Woody Vines for Open Slopes

Lonicera sempervirens (trumpet honeysuckle) FACU, C, H, S (part); to 20 ft.; soil pH 6–7.5
Menispermum canadense (moon seed) UPL, A, C, G, S (part); to 12 ft.; soil pH 5–7.5
Parthenocissus quinquefolia (Virginia creeper) FACU, A, C, F, G, S; to 35 ft.; soil pH 5–7.5
Parthenocissus vitacea (grape-woodbine) FACU, A, C, F, G, S; to 35 ft.; soil pH 5–7.5
Smilax glauca (glaucous greenbrier) FACU, C, E (semi), K, S; to 20 ft.; soil pH 6–8.5
Smilax rotundifolia (common greenbrier) FAC, A, C (vigorous), E (stems), K, S (part); to 35 ft.; soil pH 5–8.5
Toxicodendron radicans (poison ivy) FAC, A, C (vigorous), F, S; soil pH 5–6.5; all parts toxic

Herbs for Open Slopes

Apocynum cannabinum (Indian hemp) FACU, B, C; to 4 ft.; soil pH 4.5–7.0
Asclepias syriaca (common milkweed) UPL, B, C; to 6 ft.
Aster ericoides (many-flowered aster) FACU, B, C; to 3 ft.

Aster laevis (smooth aster) UPL, B; to 3 ft.
**Aster lanceolatus* (*A. simplex*) (lined aster) FACW, B, C, S; to 4 ft.
**Aster novae-angliae* (New England aster) FACW−, B, C; to 6 ft.
**Aster pilosus* (heath aster) UPL, A, B; to 5 ft.
Astragalus canadensis (milk vetch) FAC, B, C, N; to 4 ft.
**Euthamia graminifolia* (grass-leaved goldenrod) FAC, B, C; to 3 ft.
**Euthamia tenuifolia* (slender-leaved goldenrod) FACU, B, C; to 2 ft.
Helianthus strumosus (rough-leaved sunflower) UPL, C, S (part); to 6 ft.
Monarda fistulosa (wild bergamot) UPL, B, C, H; to 4 ft.
Pteridium aquilinum (bracken fern) FACU, C; to 4 ft.
**Solidago canadensis* (Canada goldenrod) FACU, B, C (aggressive); to 6 ft.
**Solidago juncea* (early goldenrod) UPL, B; to 4 ft.
**Solidago rugosa* (rough-stemmed goldenrod) FAC, C; to 4 ft., soil pH 3.8–5

Graminoids for Open Slopes

Agrostis perennans (*A. altissima*) (autumn bent grass) FACU, S (part); to 4 ft.
**Andropogon virginicus* (broom sedge) FACU, B; to 5 ft.
Elymus canadensis (Canada wild rye) FACU+; to 5 ft.
Elymus trachycaulus (*Agropyron t.*) (slender wheat grass) FACU; to 3 ft.
Festuca subverticillata (*F. obtusa*) (nodding fescue) FACU, S; to 4 ft.; tufted
**Juncus tenuis* (path rush) FAC−, S (part); to 28 in.
Muhlenbergia frondosa (wire-stem muhly) FAC, C (vigorously), S (part); to 40 in.
Muhlenbergia schreberi (nimblewill) FAC, C (aggressive), S (part); to 2 ft.
Muhlenbergia sobolifera (creeping muhly) UPL, C (vigorously), S; to 34 in.
**Panicum clandestinum* (deer-tongue grass) FAC+, B, C (aggressive); to 5 ft.
**Panicum virgatum* (switchgrass) FAC; to 6 ft.
**Schizachyrium scoparium* (*Andropogon s.*) (little bluestem) FACU−, B; to 4 ft.
Scleria pauciflora (few-flower nut rush) FACU+, C; to 20 in.
Scleria triglomerata (whip nutrush) FAC, C; to 3 ft.
Sorghastrum nutans (Indian grass) UPL, C; to 6 ft.
Sporobolus asper (tall dropseed) UPL; to 4 ft.
**Tridens flavus* (purpletop) FACU, B, C; to 5 ft.

List 12. Maritime Uplands-Coastal Sand Dune Habitats (low-nutrient, inorganic, native sand; *not* fill soils in coastal areas)

Trees for Back-Dune Woodlands

Celtis occidentalis (common hackberry) FACU, B; to 70 ft.; soil pH 6.5–8.5; shade index 4–6
Ilex opaca (American holly) FACU+, A, D, E, S; to 40 ft.; soil pH 4–5
Juniperus virginiana (eastern red cedar) FACU, A, B, D, E; to 60 ft; soil pH 4.7–8.5; shade index 0–2

Pinus rigida (pitch pine) FACU, A, E; to 60 ft.; soil pH 3.5–6.5; shade index 0–2

Prunus serotina (wild black cherry) FACU, A, B, F, K; to 75 ft.; soil pH 4–8; shade index 2.4

**Sassafras albidum* (sassafras) FACU−, A, B, C, D, F; to 50 ft.; soil pH 4.2–7; shade index 2–4

Shrubs for Dune Woodlands and Scrub Thickets

Amelanchier canadensis (shadbush) FAC, B, F, S (part); to 25 ft.; soil pH 5–6.5; shade index 8–10

Myrica pensylvanica (northern bayberry) (dioecious) FAC, A, C, D, N; to 6 ft.; soil pH 5–6.5

Prunus maritima (beach plum) UPL; to 6 ft.

Quercus ilicifolia (bear oak) UPL, A; to 15 ft.; soil pH 4–7.5

**Rhus copallina* (winged sumac) UPL, A, C, D, F; to 25 ft.; soil pH 6–7 (wider tolerance); shade index 0–2

**Rosa virginiana* (Virginia rose) FAC, A, C; to 6 ft.; prickly

Vaccinium corymbosum (highbush blueberry) FACW, A, B, F, S (part); to 9 ft.; soil pH 3.5–6.5

Vines for Dune Woodlands and Scrub Thickets

Parthenocissus quinquefolia (Virginia creeper) FACU, A, C, F, G, S; climber to 35 ft.; soil pH 5–7.5

Smilax rotundifolia (common greenbrier) FAC, A, C, E (stems), K, S (part); climber to 35 ft.; soil pH 5–8.5

Toxicodendron radicans (poison ivy) FAC, A, C (aggressive), F, S; climber to 35 ft.; soil pH 5–6.5

Herbs for Beach-Heather, Scrub, Back-Dune Swales and Grasslands

Cakile edentula (American sea rocket) FACU; annual to 32 in.; primary dune to tide line

Euphorbia polygonifolia (seaside spurge) FACU; annual, prostrate, forming mats to 10 in.

Honckenya peploides (seabeach sandwort) FACU, C; to 20 in.; mat forming.

Hudsonia tomentosa (false heather) UPL, A, E; less than 1 ft.

Lathyrus maritimus (*L. japonicus*) (beach pea) FACU−, C, N; to 3 ft.

Lechea maritima (beach pinweed) UPL, E (basal shoots); to 16 in.

Opuntia humifusa (prickly pear cactus) UPL, E, C; ca. 1 ft.; prickly

Solidago sempervirens (seaside goldenrod) FACW; to 5 ft.

Xanthium strumarium (cocklebur) FAC; annual to 4 ft. (rarely); primary dune to tide line

Graminoids for Dune Grasslands and Primary Dune Stabilization

Ammophila breviligulata (beach grass) FACU−, C; to 3 ft. (dominant)
Aristida tuberculosa (three-awn) UPL; annual to 32 in.
Carex silicea (sand sedge) UPL, B; to 32 in.
Cenchrus tribuloides (dune sandbur) UPL; annual to 40 in.; spiny
Cyperus grayi (Gray's umbrella sedge) UPL; to 16 in.
Panicum amarum (bitter panic grass) FACU−, C; to 6 ft.
Panicum virgatum (switchgrass) FAC; to 6 ft.
Schizachyrium scoparium (*Andropogon* s.) (little bluestem) FACU−, B; to 4 ft.
Triplasis purpurea (purple sand-grass) UPL; annual to 32 in.

List 13. Upland Plants for Open, Acid, Low-Nutrient Soils, Dry Sandy Fill, or Sand Barrens

This list includes plants tolerant of low-nutrient soils of pH 6 or less. Most of this information is observational, since there are no data on pH tolerance for most nonwoody plants.

Trees for Dry, Acid Soil (rocky or sandy barrens)

Betula populifolia (gray birch) FAC, A, B, F; to 30 ft.; soil pH 5–7.5; shade index 1
Ilex opaca (American holly) FACU+, A, D, E, S; to 40 ft.; soil pH 4–5
Juniperus virginiana (eastern red cedar) FACU, A, B, D, E; to 60 ft; soil pH 4.7–8.5; shade index 0–2
Pinus echinata (short-leaf pine) UPL, A, E; to 90 ft. (NYS rare)
Pinus resinosa (red pine) FACU, A, E; to 100 ft.; soil pH 4–6.5; shade index 2.4
Pinus rigida (pitch pine) FACU, A, E; to 60 ft.; soil pH 3.5–6.5; shade index 0–2
Pinus virginiana (Virginia pine) UPL, A, E; to 30 ft. (NYS rare)
Quercus alba (white oak) FACU−, A, B; to 75 ft.; soil pH 3.5–7.5
Quercus coccinea (scarlet oak) UPL, A, B, F; to 75 ft.; soil pH 4.5–6.9; shade index 2–4
Quercus marilandica (blackjack oak) UPL, A, B; to 50 ft.; soil pH 4–5.6; shade index 2–4
Quercus prinus (chestnut oak) UPL, A, B; to 70 ft.; soil pH 6–6.5 (more widely tolerant); shade index 4–6
Quercus stellata (post oak) UPL, A, B; to 60 ft.; soil pH 4.6–6.5; shade index 2–4
Quercus velutina (black oak) UPL, A, B; to 80 ft.; pH 6–6.5 (more widely tolerant); shade index 6–8

Shrubs for Dry, Acid Soil (rocky or sandy barrens, successional scrub)

Amelanchier canadensis (shadbush) FAC, B, F, S; to 25 ft.; soil pH 5–6.5; shade index 8–10
Comptonia peregrina (sweet fern) UPL, A, C, D, N; to 4 ft.; soil pH 4.5–6.5

Hudsonia ericoides (pine-barren false heather) UPL, A, E; ca. 1 ft. or less
Hypericum stans (*Ascyrum s.*) (St.-Peter's-wort) UPL; to 32 in.
Juniperus communis (common juniper) UPL, A, D, E; to 6 ft.
Kalmia angustifolia (sheep laurel) FAC A, C, E, S; to 3 ft.; soil pH 4.5–6
Myrica pensylvanica (northern bayberry) FAC, A, C, D, N; to 6 ft.; soil pH 5–6.5
Prunus maritima (beach plum) UPL; to 6 ft.
Quercus ilicifolia (bear oak) UPL, A; to 15 ft.; soil pH 4–7.5
**Rhus copallina* (winged sumac) UPL, A, C, D, F; to 25 ft.; soil pH 6–7 (wider tolerance); shade index 0–2
**Rosa virginiana* (Virginia rose) FAC, A, C; to 6 ft.; prickly
**Rubus allegheniensis* (common blackberry) FACU, C; to 6 ft.; very prickly; soil pH 4.5–7.5
Vaccinium angustifolium (lowbush blueberry) FACU, A, B, C, G, S (part); to 2 ft.; soil pH 4–6

Herbs for Dry, Acid Soil

Aletris farinosa (colic root) FAC, S (part); (NYS S2, T); to 3 ft.
Anaphalis margaritacea (pearly everlasting) UPL, B; to 3 ft.
Antennaria neglecta (field pussytoes) UPL C; to 16 in.
Apocynum cannabinum (Indian hemp) FACU, B, C; to 4 ft.
Arctostaphylos uva-ursi (bearberry) UPL, A, B, E, G; trailing to 6 in.; soil pH 4.5–6
Asclepias tuberosa (butterfly weed) UPL, B; to 2 ft.
Asclepias variegata (white milkweed) UPL, B, S; (NYS S1, T); to 3 ft.
Aster concolor (silvery aster) UPL, B, C; (NYS S1, E); to 3 ft.
Aster dumosus (bushy aster) FAC B, C; to 34 in.
Aster ericoides (many-flowered aster) FACU, B; ca. 3 ft.
Aster laevis (smooth aster) UPL B; ca. 3 ft.
Aster linariifolius (stiff aster) UPL, B; to 2 ft.
Aster patens (late purple aster) UPL, B; to 5 ft.
Aster pilosus (heath aster) UPL, A, B; to 5 ft.
Aster solidagineus (narrow-leaved white-topped aster) UPL, B; (NYS S2 U); to 2 ft.
Aster spectabilis (showy aster) UPL, A, B (NYS S2 U); to 3 ft.
Aster undulatus (clasping heart-leaved aster) UPL B, S (part); to 4 ft.
Baptisia tinctoria (wild indigo) UPL, B, N; to 3 ft.
Calystegia spithamaea (low bindweed) UPL, H; to 18 in.
Chamaecrista fasciculata (*Cassia c.*) (partridge pea) UPL, N; annual to 30 in.
Chrysopsis falcata (sickle-leaved golden aster) UPL; to 14 in.
Chrysopsis mariana (broad-leaved golden aster) UPL; to 32 in.
Eupatorium album (white boneset) UPL, B; to 3 ft.
**Eupatorium hyssopifolium* (hyssop-leaved boneset); UPL, B; to 3 ft.

Eupatorium sessilifolium (upland boneset) UPL, B, C, S; to 6 ft.
**Euthamia graminifolia* (grass-leaved goldenrod) FAC, B, C; to 3 ft.
**Euthamia tenuifolia* (slender-leaved goldenrod) FACU, B, C; to 2 ft.
Geranium carolinianum (Carolina cranesbill) UPL; annual to 20 in.
Gnaphalium obtusifolium (sweet everlasting) UPL; annual to 3 ft.
Hedyotis longifolia (pale bluets) UPL; to 10 in.
Helianthemum bicknellii (rock rose) UPL; to 1.5 ft.
Helianthemum canadense (frostweed) UPL; to 16 in.
Hieracium scabrum (rough hawkweed) UPL, S (part); to 5 ft.
Krigia virginica (dwarf dandelion) UPL; to 16 in.
Lespedeza angustifolia (narrow-leaf bush clover) FAC, B, N; to 3 ft.
Lespedeza capitata (round-headed bush clover) FACU−, B, N; to 4 ft.
Lespedeza hirta (hairy bush clover) UPL , B, N; to 4 ft.
Lespedeza stuevei (tall bush clover) UPL, S (part); B, N; (NYS, S2, R); to 3 ft.
Linaria canadensis (blue toadflax) UPL; annual to 24 in.
Linum medium (common yellow flax) FACU; (NYS S2, T); to 2 ft.
Monarda punctata (horsemint) UPL, B, H; to 3 ft.
Onosmodium virginianum (false gromwell) UPL, S (part); to 2 ft.; bristly
Pteridium aquilinum (bracken fern) FACU, C; to 4 ft.
Solidago nemoralis (gray goldenrod) UPL, B; to 3 ft.
Solidago odora (sweet goldenrod) UPL, B, S (part); to 5 ft.
Stylosanthes biflora (pencil flower) UPL, B, N, S (part); to 20 in.
Tephrosia virginiana (goat's rue) UPL, B, N, S (part); to 28 in.

Graminoids for Dry, Acid Soil

Agrostis hyemalis (*A. scabra*) (tickle grass) FAC, S (part); to 3 ft.
Andropogon gerardii (big bluestem) FAC, B, C (sometimes); to 9 ft.
Andropogon virginicus (broom sedge) FACU, B; to 5 ft.
Aristida purpurascens (arrowfeather) UPL; to 3 ft.
Cyperus echinatus (*C. ovularis*) (globe flatsedge) UPL; (NYS S1, E); to 3 ft.
Cyperus grayi (Gray's umbrella sedge) UPL; to 16 in.
Cyperus lupulinus (slender flatsedge) UPL, C; (NYS S2, U); to 18 in.
Cyperus schweinitzii (Schweinitz's flatsedge) FACU, C; (NYS S3, R); to 3 ft.
Elymus canadensis (Canada wild rye) FACU+; to 5 ft.
Eragrostis spectabilis (purple love grass) UPL; to 2 ft.
Juncus secundus (secund rush) FACU; to 2 ft.
Panicum columbianum (Columbia panic grass) UPL, E (winter rosette), S (part); to 34 in.
Panicum commutatum (variable panic grass) FACU+, E (winter rosette), S (part); to 32 in.
Panicum lanuginosum (downy panic grass) UPL, E (winter rosette), S (part); to 40 in.
Panicum virgatum (switchgrass) FAC; to 6 ft.

Paspalum setaceum (thin paspalum) FACU+, S (part); to 24 in.
Schizachyrium scoparium (*Andropogon* s.) (little bluestem) FACU−, B; to 4 ft.
Scleria pauciflora (few-flower nutrush) FACU+, C; to 20 in.
Scleria triglomerata (whip nutrush) FAC, C; to 3 ft.
Sorghastrum nutans (Indian grass) UPL, C; to 6 ft.
Sporobolus asper (tall dropseed) UPL; to 4 ft.

List 14. Upland Plants for Open Areas—Alkaline Soil, Fill

Note: Alkaline fill (above pH 7), containing concrete, old asphalt, gravel, brick, demolition debris, and similar substrates, is not a native soil type. Very little testing has been done to see what native plants can tolerate this type of material. However, one study by the forestry crew of NYC Parks Natural Resources Group (Kortebein et al. 2002) indicates a number of trees that can do well in concrete-rubble fill substrates. This list is taken from observations of plants growing in concrete rubble and listings of plants growing on calcareous soils or plants listed as at least moderately salt tolerant (s). Information on pH tolerance is included where available. For many plants, pH range tolerances may be broader than those listed.

Trees for Upland, Alkaline Soil

Betula papyrifera (paper birch) FACU, B, F; to 80 ft.; soil pH 5–8.5; shade index 1; s
Carya cordiformis (bitternut hickory) FACU+, B, F; to 90 ft.; soil pH 5.5–8.5; shade index 5.8
Celtis occidentalis (common hackberry) FACU; B; to 70 ft.; soil pH 6.5–8.5; shade index 4–6; s
Juglans nigra (black walnut) UPL, B; to 100 ft.; soil pH 4.6–8.2; shade index 4; s
Juniperus virginiana (eastern red cedar) FACU, A, B, D, E; to 60 ft; soil pH 4.7–8.5; shade index 0–2
Morus rubra (red mulberry) FACU; to 60 ft.; soil pH 6.3–8; shade index 4–6; s
Ostrya virginiana (hophornbeam) FACU−, B, s; to 60 ft.; soil pH 4.2–8; shade index 8–10
Prunus serotina (wild black cherry) FACU, A, B, F, K; to 75 ft.; soil pH 4.3–8; shade index 2.4
Quercus alba (white oak) FACU; A, B; to 75 ft.; soil pH 3.5–7.5; shade index 5.7; s
Tilia americana (American linden, basswood) FACU; to 80 ft.; soil pH 6.5–7.5; shade index 8

Shrubs for Upland, Alkaline Soil

Cornus alternifolia (pagoda dogwood) UPL, S; to 25 ft.; soil pH 6.5–7.5; shade index 8–10

Cornus racemosa (red-panicle dogwood; gray dogwood) FAC, C; to 15 ft.; soil pH 6–8.5

Cornus rugosa (round-leaf dogwood) UPL, S; to 9 ft.; soil pH 6–8.5

Corylus americana (American hazelnut) FACU– S; to 9 ft.; soil pH 6–7.5

Corylus cornuta (beaked hazelnut) FACU–, S; to 9 ft.; soil pH 6–7.5

Crataegus crus-galli (cockspur hawthorn) FACU; to 30 ft.; thorns to 3-in.; soil pH 6–8.5; shade index 2–4

Crataegus pruinosa (frosted hawthorn) UPL; to 24 ft.; very thorny; soil pH 6–8.5; shade index 2–4

Dirca palustris (leatherwood) FAC, S; to 6 ft.; soil pH 6–8.5; s

Hypericum prolificum (shrubby St.-John's-wort) FACU; to 3 ft. pH 6–8.5; s

Juniperus communis (common juniper) UPL, A, D, E; to 6 ft.; soil pH 5–8.5; s

Lonicera canadensis (fly-honeysuckle) FACU, H, S; to 6 ft.; s

Quercus prinoides (dwarf oak, chinquapin) UPL, A, B; to 9 ft.; soil pH 6–8.5; shade index 4–6

Rhus glabra (smooth sumac) UPL, C, D, F; to 15 ft.; soil pH 6–7; shade index 0–2; s

Rhus typhina (staghorn sumac) UPL, C, D, F; to 15 ft.; soil pH 6–7; shade index 0–2; s

Ribes cynosbati (dogberry) UPL, F, S; to 5 ft.; spiny; soil pH 6–8.5

Ribes hirtellum (smooth gooseberry) FAC, S; to 3 ft.; few spines

Ribes rotundifolium (Appalachian gooseberry) UPL, S; to 5 ft.; often spiny

Rosa blanda (smooth rose) FACU, C; to 6 ft., prickly; soil pH to over 7.5

Rosa carolina (pasture rose) UPL, C; to 3 ft.; prickly; soil pH 6–8.5

Rubus allegheniensis (common blackberry) FACU; C; to 6 ft.; prickly; soil pH 4.5–7.5

Rubus flagellaris (dewberry) UPL, C, G; ca. 1 ft.; stems prickly

Salix humilis (upland willow) FACU, C, D; to 9 ft.; soil pH 6–7.5

Staphylea trifolia (bladdernut) FAC, S (part); to 15 ft.; soil pH 6–8

Taxus canadensis (Canada yew) FAC , E, S; to 6 ft.; soil pH 5–7.5; s

Viburnum lentago (nanny berry) FAC B, C, S (part); to 30 ft.; soil pH 6–8.5; shade index 5–6

Viburnum prunifolium (black-haw) FACU, B, S (part); to 15 ft.; soil pH 5–8.5; shade index 2–4

Viburnum rafinesquianum (downy arrowwood) UPL, B, S; to 7 ft.; soil pH 6–8.5

Zanthoxylum americanum (prickly ash) UPL, D, S (part); to 25 ft.; stems prickly; soil pH 6–8.5; shade index 2–4

Herbs for Upland, Alkaline Soil

(*Good competitors against mugwort in open, high nutrient fill soils)

**Apocynum cannabinum* (Indian hemp) FACU, B, C; to 4 ft.; soil pH 3.5–7

Arabis hirsuta var. *pycnocarpa* (creamflower rock cress) FACU, E (winter rosette). Biennial to 32 in.

Arabis laevigata (smooth rock cress) UPL, E (winter rosette), S; biennial to 40 in.

Arabis lyrata (lyre-leaved rock cress) FACU, E (winter rosette); biennial to 16 in.

**Asclepias syriaca* (common milkweed) UPL, B, C; to 6 ft.

**Aster pilosus* (heath aster) UPL, A, B; to 5 ft.

Cirsium pumilum (pasture thistle) UPL, K; biennial to 32 in.

Eupatorium purpureum (purple joe-pye weed) UPL, B, S; to 10 ft.

Hackelia virginiana (tickseed, beggar-lice) FACU, S; biennial to 40 in.

Oenothera parviflora (northern evening primrose) FACU−, H; biennial to 6 ft.

Ranunculus fascicularis (early buttercup) FACU, S (part); to 10 in.

Senecio obovatus (round-leaved ragwort) FACU, S (part); to 28 in.

Senecio pauperculus (balsam groundsel) FAC; to 20 in.

**Solidago canadensis* (Canada goldenrod) FACU, B, C (aggressive); to 6 ft.

**Solidago juncea* (early goldenrod) UPL, B; to 4 ft.

**Solidago rugosa* (rough-leaved goldenrod) FAC, C; to 4 ft.; soil pH 3.8–5

Verbena urticifolia (white vervain) FACU; annual or perennial to 5 ft.

Graminoids for Upland, Alkaline Soils

Aristida purpurascens (arrowfeather) UPL; to 3 ft.

Carex albursina (white bear sedge) FACU, B, S; to 2 ft.

Carex eburnea (bristle-leaf sedge) FACU, B, C; to 12 in.

Muhlenbergia schreberi (nimblewill) FAC, C (aggressive), S (part); to 2 ft.

Muhlenbergia sobolifera (creeping muhly) UPL, C (vigorously), S; to 34 in.

Muhlenbergia tenuiflora (slender-flowered muhly) UPL, C (vigorously), S; to 40 in.

Scirpus verecundus (clubrush) UPL; to 16 in.

Sporobolus neglectus (puffsheath dropseed) FACU−; annual to 20 in.

Chapter 8

Plants for Forest Restorations

This list includes "aforestation" projects, which are the creation of new forest habitats on fill soils (concrete rubble, demolition debris, and landfills).

SET 4. PLANTS FOR FORESTED WETLANDS

List 15. Swamp Forests: ** Typical dominant species. * Common subdominant species

Trees for Swamp Forests

***Acer rubrum* (red maple) FAC, F, S; to 100 ft.; soil pH 4.5–7; shade index 6–8

Betula nigra (river birch) FACW, A; to 75 ft.; soil pH 4–6.5; shade index 2–4

Fraxinus nigra (black ash) FACW, F; to 75 ft.; soil pH 4.4–8.2; shade index 2–4

**Fraxinus pennsylvanica* (green ash) FACW, F; to 75 ft.; soil pH 6–8.0; shade index 2–4

***Liquidambar styraciflua* (sweetgum) FAC, F; to 100 ft.; soil pH 4.4–7; shade index 2–4

Magnolia virginiana (sweet-bay magnolia) FACW+, S; to 60 ft.; soil pH 5–6.9; (NYS S1, U)

**Nyssa sylvatica* (black tupelo) FAC, D, F, S; to 90 ft.; soil pH 5–6; shade index 2–4

Quercus bicolor (swamp white oak) FACW, B; to 70 ft.; soil pH 5–7.5; shade index 4–6

***Quercus palustris* (pin oak) FACW, A, B; to 80 ft.; soil pH 4.5–6.5; shade index 0–2

Quercus phellos (willow oak) FAC+, A, B; to 80 ft.; soil pH 4.5–6.5; (NYS S1, E) (Long Island northern limit)

Shrubs for Swamp Forest Understories

**Aronia arbutifolia* (red chokeberry) FACW, B, C, F, S (part); to 12 ft.; soil, pH 5–6.5

Aronia melanocarpa (black chokeberry) FAC, B, C, F, S (part); to 6 ft.; soil, pH 5–6.5

Aronia prunifolia (purple fruit chokeberry) FACW, B, C, F, S (part); to 12 ft.; soil, pH 5–6.5

***Clethra alnifolia* (sweet pepperbush) FAC+, A, B, C, S; to 8 ft.; soil pH 4.5–6.5

Eubotrys racemosa (*Leucothoe r.*) (fetterbush) FACW, A, S; to 12 ft.; soil pH 4.4–6

Ilex verticillata (winterberry) FACW, A, D, S (part); to 15 ft.; soil, pH 4.5–6 (probably higher)

***Lindera benzoin* (spicebush) FACW, B, D, F, S; to 15 ft.; soil pH 4.5–7.7

Lyonia ligustrina (male-berry) FACW, A, S (part); to 12 ft.; soil pH 4–6

Nemopanthus mucronatus (mountain holly) OBL, A, D, S; to 9 ft.

**Rhododendron viscosum* (swamp azalea) OBL, A, C, S (part); to 6 ft.; soil pH 4–6

Ribes americanum (wild black currant) FACW, S; to 6 ft.; soil pH 6–8.5

Ribes triste (swamp red currant) OBL, A, S; to 2.5 ft.

**Vaccinium corymbosum* (highbush blueberry)FACW, A, B, F, S (part); to 9 ft.; soil pH 3.5–6.5

Viburnum cassinoides (*V. nudum* var. *c.*) (withe rod) FACW, F, S; to 12 ft.; soil pH 5–6.5

***Viburnum dentatum* (*V. recognitum*) (arrowwood) FAC, B, C, S (part); to 10 ft.; soil pH 4.4–7

Herbs for Swamp Forest Understories

Angelica atropurpurea (purple-stem angelica) OBL, B, S (part); to 6 ft.

**Arisaema triphyllum* (jack-in-the-pulpit) FACW−, S; to 2 ft.

**Boehmeria cylindrica* (false nettle) FACW+, S; to 40 in.

**Claytonia virginica* (spring beauty) FACU, C; to 7 in.; soil pH 6; spring ephemeral

Coptis trifolia (goldthread) FACW, E, C, S; to 6 in.

**Erythronium americanum* (trout lily) UPL, C; to 8 in., soil pH 5–6; spring ephemeral

Eupatorium dubium (three-nerved joe-pye weed) FACW, A, B, S (part); to 3 ft.

**Eupatorium perfoliatum* (boneset) FACW+, B, S (part); to 4 ft.

Gentiana andrewsii (fringe-tip closed gentian) FACW, K, S (part); to 3 ft.

Geum laciniatum (rough avens) FAC+, E (winter rosette), S (part); to 3 ft.

Helenium autumnale (common sneezeweed) FACW+, S (part); to 6 ft.

Impatiens capensis (*I. biflora*) (jewelweed) FACW, H, S; annual to 3 ft.; soil pH 5.6–7.0

Iris prismatica (slender blueflag) OBL, C, H, S (part); (NYS S2, U); to 28 in.

Lilium superbum (Turk's cap lily) FACW+, H, S; to 6 ft.; soil pH 4.4–4.8
Lobelia cardinalis (cardinal flower) FACW+, B, H, S (part); to 4 ft.
Lycopus americanus (water horehound, bugleweed) OBL, C, S (part); to 2 ft.
Lysimachia ciliata (fringed loosestrife) FACW, C, S; to 3 ft.
Mimulus ringens (monkey flower) OBL, S (part); to 3 ft.
**Peltandra virginica* (arrow arum) OBL, C, S (part); emergent; to 30 in.; soil pH 5–6.5
Ranunculus recurvatus (hooked crowfoot) FAC+, S; to 2 ft.
Rubus hispidus (swamp dewberry) FACW, C, E, G, S; to 5 ft.; scarcely woody, stems trailing
**Saururus cernuus* (lizard's tail) OBL, C, S; to 3 ft.
Stachys tenuifolia (common hedge-nettle) FACW+, C, S; to 3 ft.
**Symplocarpus foetidus* (skunk cabbage) OBL, C; to 2 ft., soil pH 5–6.2; spring ephemeral
Teucrium canadense (American germander) FACW−, C, S (part); to 3 ft.
Trillium cernuum (nodding trillium) FACW, A, C, S; to 16 in.
Veratrum viride (false hellebore) FACW+, S; to 6 ft.
Viola conspersa (American dog violet) FACW, B, S (part); to 8 in.

Ferns for Swamp Forest Understories

Dryopteris cristata (crested wood fern) FACW+, E, S; to 30 in.
Matteuccia struthiopteris (ostrich fern) FACW, C, S; to 5 ft. (rarely)
**Onoclea sensibilis* (sensitive fern) FACW, C, S; to 1 ft.; soil pH 4.5–7.5
**Osmunda cinnamomea* (cinnamon fern) FACW, S; to 3 ft., soil pH 4.8–6.2
Osmunda regalis (royal fern) OBL, S (part); to 5 ft. (rarely)
Thelypteris simulata (Massachusetts fern) FACW, A, C, S; to 2 ft.
Woodwardia areolata (netted chain fern) FACW+, A, C, S; to 2 ft.

Graminoids for Swamp Forest Understories

Bromus altissimus (*B. latiglumis*) (Canada brome) FACW, S; to 3 ft.
Bromus ciliatus (fringed brome) FACW, S; to 4 ft.
Carex bromoides (brome-like sedge) FACW, B, S (part); to 32 in.
**Carex crinita* (fringed sedge) OBL, B, S (part); to 4 ft.
Carex folliculata (northern long-sedge) FACW (prob.), B, S (part); to 3 ft.
Carex intumescens (bladder sedge) FACW+, B, S; to 32 in.
Carex retrorsa (retrorse sedge) FACW+, C, S; to 3 ft.
**Carex scoparia* (pointed broom-sedge) FACW, B, S (part); to 3 ft.
Carex seorsa (weak stellate sedge) FACW, B, S, (NYS S2, R); to 28 in.
Carex stipata (awl-fruited sedge) OBL, C, B, S (partial); to 3 ft.; soil pH 4.9–7.9
**Carex stricta* (tussock sedge) OBL, A, B, C, S (part); to 3 ft.; emergent; soil pH 6.2
Carex tribuloides (blunt broom sedge) FACW+, B, S (part); to 40 in.

Carex typhina (cattail sedge) FACW+, B, K, S; to 3 ft.; tufted (NYS S2, R)
**Carex vulpinoidea* (fox sedge) OBL, B, C, S (part); to 3 ft.
Cinna arundinacea (stout woodreed) FACW+, S; to 5 ft.
Elymus riparius (stream-bank wild rye) FACW, S (part); to 3 ft.
Elymus virginicus (Virginia wild rye) FACW−, S (part); to 4 ft.
Glyceria melicaria (melic mannagrass) OBL, C, S; to 40 in.
Glyceria obtusa (coastal mannagrass) OBL, C, S; to 3 ft.
**Glyceria striata* (fowl mannagrass) OBL, C, S; to 4 ft.
**Juncus effusus* (soft rush) FACW+, B, E (semi-), S (part); to 3 ft.
Leersia virginica (white grass) FACW, B, C, S; to 5 ft. (usually 1–2 ft.)
**Scirpus atrovirens* (black bulrush, green bulrush) OBL, B, S (part); to 4 ft.

List 16. River Floodplain Forests

Subject to scouring, deep, periodic flooding, river currents, generally more open and disturbed than swamp forests or floodplain forests of small streams. However, these two habitat types are on a continuum.

Trees for Floodplain Forests

***Acer negundo* (box elder) FAC+; to 60 ft.; soil pH 5–8; shade index 1.8
**Acer rubrum* (red maple) FAC F, S; to 100 ft.; soil pH 4.5–7; shade index 6–8
***Acer saccharinum* (silver maple) FACW; to 90 ft.; soil pH 4–7; shade index 5.8
Betula nigra (river birch) FACW, A; to 75 ft.; soil pH 4–6.5; shade index 2–4
**Fraxinus pennsylvanica* (green ash) FACW, F; to 75 ft.; soil pH 6–8.0; shade index 2–4
***Liquidambar styraciflua* (sweetgum) FAC, F; to 100 ft.; soil pH 4.4–7; shade index 2–4
**Platanus occidentalis* (American sycamore) FACW; to 150 ft.; soil pH 6.5–8.5; shade index 4
***Populus deltoides* (eastern cottonwood) FAC, B; to 150 ft.; soil pH 5.5–7.5; shade index 2.2
***Quercus palustris* (pin oak) FACW, A, B; to 80 ft.; soil pH 4.5–6.5; shade index 0–2
***Salix nigra* (black willow) FACW+, B, D; to 40 ft.; soil pH 6–8; shade index 1.4

Shrubs and Vines for Floodplain Forest Understories

***Cornus amomum* (silky dogwood) FACW, B, K, S (part); to 9 ft.; soil pH 6–8.5
**Ilex verticillata* (winterberry) FACW, A, D, S; to 15 ft.; soil pH 4.5–6
**Lindera benzoin* (spicebush) FACW, B, D, F, S (dense); to 15 ft.; soil pH 4.5–7.7
***Viburnum dentatum* (*V. recognitum*) (arrowwood) FAC, B, C, S (part); to 10 ft.; soil pH 5–7

Vitis riparia (river grape) FACW, K, S; high climber to 35 ft.; woody vine; soil pH 6–8.5

Herbs for Floodplain Forest Understories

Amphicarpaea bracteata (American hog peanut) FAC, N, S (part); to 40 in.; annual twining vine
**Aster lanceolatus* (*A. simplex*) (lined aster) FACW, B, C, S; to 4 ft.
**Boehmeria cylindrica* (false nettle) FACW+, S; to 40 in.
Circaea lutetiana (*C. quadrisulcata*) (enchanter's nightshade) FACU, C, S; to 2 ft., soil pH 5.6
**Claytonia virginica* (spring beauty) FACU, C; to 7 in.; soil pH 6; spring ephemeral
**Erythronium americanum* (trout lily) UPL, C; to 8 in.; soil pH 5–6; spring ephemeral
Floerkea proserpinacoides (false mermaid) FAC, K, S; annual to 1 ft.
**Geum canadense* (white avens) FACU, E (winter rosette) S; to 3 ft.; soil pH 5.6
Helenium autumnale (common sneezeweed) FACW+, S (part); to 6 ft.
Hydrophyllum virginianum (Virginia waterleaf) FAC, C, S; to 30 in.
Lactuca biennis (tall blue lettuce) FACU, S (part); annual to 6.5 ft.
Laportea canadensis (wood nettle) FACW, C, S; to 40 in. (stinging)
Lobelia cardinalis (cardinal flower) FACW+, B, H, S; to 4 ft.
Lycopus americanus (water horehound, bugleweed) OBL, C, S (part); to 2 ft.
**Lysimachia ciliata* (fringed loosestrife) FACW, C, S; to 3 ft.
Mertensia virginica (Virginia bluebells) FACW; to 28 in.; spring ephemeral
Osmorhiza longistyis (anise root) FACU−, B, S; to 3 ft.
Oxalis violacea (violet wood sorrel) UPL, S; to 16 in.
Peltandra virginica (arrow arum) OBL, C, S (part); to 30 in.; emergent
**Polygonum virginianum* (*Tovara v.*) (jumpseed) FAC, C, S; to 6 ft.
Symplocarpus foetidus (skunk cabbage) OBL, C; to 2 ft. soil pH 5–6.2; spring ephemeral
Senna hebecarpa (*Cassia h.*) (northern wild senna) FAC, N, S (part); to 5 ft.
Trientalis borealis (starflower) FAC, S; to 8 in.

Ferns for Floodplain Forest Understories

Matteuccia struthiopteris (ostrich fern) FACW, C, S; to 5 ft. (rarely)
**Onoclea sensibilis* (sensitive fern) FACW, C, S; to 1 ft.; soil pH 4.5–7.5
**Osmunda cinnamomea* (cinnamon fern) FACW, S; to 3 ft.; soil pH 4.8–6.2

Graminoids for Floodplain Forest Understories

Bromus altissimus (*B. latiglumis*) (Canada brome) FACW, S; to 3 ft.
Carex intumescens (bladder sedge) FACW+, B, S; to 32 in.

Carex retrorsa (retrorse sedge) FACW+, C, S; to 3 ft.
Carex tribuloides (blunt broom sedge) FACW+, B, S (part); to 40 in.
Carex typhina (cattail sedge) FACW+, B, K, S; to 3 ft.; tufted (NYS S2, R)
***Cinna arundinacea* (stout woodreed) FACW+, S; to 5 ft.
Elymus riparius (stream-bank wild rye) FACW, S (part); to 3 ft.
**Glyceria striata* (fowl mannagrass) OBL, C, S; to 4 ft.
**Scirpus atrovirens* (black bulrush, green bulrush) OBL, B, S (part); to 4 ft.

List 17. Plants for Acid Bogs

Trees of Acid Bogs

Chamaecyparis thyoides (Atlantic white cedar) OBL, A, E; to 75 ft.; soil pH 3–5.5

Larix laricina (tamarack, American larch) FACW, A; to 60 ft.; soil pH 4.5–7.5; shade index 0.8

Shrubs of Acid Bog Understories

Chamaedaphne calyculata (leatherleaf) OBL, A, C, E; to 3 ft.; soil pH 4.5–6
**Clethra alnifolia* (sweet pepperbush) FAC, A, B, C, S; to 8 ft.; soil pH 4.5–6.5
**Eubotrys racemosa* (*Leucothoe r.*) (fetterbush) FACW, A, S; to 12 ft.; soil pH 4.4–6
Ilex laevigata (smooth winterberry) OBL, A, D; to 9 ft.; soil pH 4.5–6
Ilex glabra (inkberry) FACW, A, E, D, S; to 6 ft.; soil pH 4.5–6
**Ilex verticillata* (winterberry) FACW, A, D, S; to 15 ft.; soil pH 4.5–6
**Lindera benzoin* (spicebush) FACW, A, B, D, F, S (very); to 15 ft.; soil pH 4.5–6.5
**Lyonia ligustrina* (male-berry) FACW, A, S (part); to 12 ft.; soil pH 4–6
Nemopanthus mucronatus (mountain holly) OBL, A, D, S; to 9 ft.
Rhododendron canadense (rhodora) FACW, A, S; to 3 ft.; (NYS S2, R)
Rhododendron maximum (white laurel) FAC, A, C, E, S; to 30 ft.; soil pH 4.5–6
**Rhododendron viscosum* (swamp azalea) OBL A, C, S; to 6 ft.; soil pH 4–6
**Vaccinium corymbosum* (highbush blueberry) FACW A, B, F, S (part); to 9 ft.; soil pH 3.5–6.5

Herbs for Acid Bog Understories

Aster radula (rough low aster) OBL, B, C, S; to 4 ft.; (NYS SH, U)
Calla palustris (water arum) OBL, A, C, S (part); to 12 in.; emergent
Coptis trifolia (goldthread) FACW, E, C, S; to 6 in.
Epilobium strictum (northern willow herb) OBL, C, S; to 2 ft.
Eupatorium dubium (three-nerved joe-pye weed) FACW, A, B, S (part); to 3 ft.
Eupatorium pilosum (ragged eupatorium) FACW, A, B, S (part); to 4 ft.

Gaultheria hispidula (creeping snowberry) FACW, A, B, E, S; 4–6 in. long prostrate

Gentiana saponaria (soapwort gentian) FACW, A, S (part); to 2 ft.; (NYS S1, E)

Helianthus angustifolius (narrow-leaved sunflower) FACW, A, S; to 6 ft.; (NYS S2, T)

Lobelia nuttallii (Nuttall's lobelia) FACW, S (part); to 18 in.

Orontium aquaticum (golden club) OBL, A, C, S (part); to 30 in.; (NYS S2, T); emergent

Rubus hispidus (swamp dewberry) FACW, C, E, G, S; to 5 ft.; scarcely woody, trailing

Ferns for Acid Bog Understories

Dryopteris cristata (crested wood fern) FACW+, E, S; to 30 in.

Onoclea sensibilis (sensitive fern) FACW, C, S; to 1 ft.; soil, pH 4.5–7.5

**Osmunda cinnamomea* (cinnamon fern) FACW, S; to 3 ft., soil pH 4.8–6.2

Osmunda regalis (royal fern) OBL, A, S (part); to 5 ft.

Thelypteris simulata (Massachusetts fern) FACW, A, C, S; to 2 ft.

Woodwardia areolata (netted chain fern) FACW+, A, C, S; to 2 ft.

Woodwardia virginica (Virginia chain fern) OBL, A, C, S; to 4 ft.

Graminoids for Acid Bog Understories

Carex folliculata (northern long-sedge) FACW (prob.), A, B, S (part); to 3 ft.

**Carex stricta* (tussock sedge) OBL, A, B, C, S (part); to 3 ft.; soil pH 6.2

List 18. Plants for Alkaline Swamps

Trees for Alkaline Swamps

Acer saccharinum (silver maple) FACW; to 90 ft.; soil pH 4–7 (tolerates higher pH); shade index 5.8; s

Fraxinus nigra (black ash) FACW, F; to 75 ft.; soil pH 4.4–8.2; shade index 2–4; s

**Fraxinus pennsylvanica* (green ash) FACW, F; to 75 ft.; soil pH 6–8.0; shade index 2–4

***Liquidambar styraciflua* (sweetgum) FAC, F; to 100 ft.; soil pH 6–7 (tolerance is wider); shade index 2–4

**Platanus occidentalis* (American sycamore) FACW; to 150 ft.; soil pH 6.5–8.5; shade index 4

Populus deltoides (eastern cottonwood) FAC; soil pH 5.5–7.5 (grows in higher pH soils); s

Salix nigra (black willow) FACW+, B, D; to 40 ft.; soil pH 6–8; shade index 1.4

Thuja occidentalis (northern white cedar) FACW, E; to 45 ft.; soil pH 6–8.5 (calcareous bogs)

Shrubs for Alkaline Swamp Forest Understories

Cornus amomum (silky dogwood) FACW, B, S (part); soil pH 6–8.5
Physocarpus opulifolius (nine-bark) FACW, C, K, S (part); to 10 ft.; soil pH 6–8.5
Ribes americanum (wild black currant) FACW, K, S; to 6 ft.; soil pH 6–8.5
Sambucus canadensis (elderberry) FACW, C, S (part); to 12 ft.; soil pH 6–8
**Viburnum dentatum* (*V. recognitum*) (arrowwood) FAC, A, B, C, S (part); to 10 ft.; soil pH 5–7

Herbs for Alkaline Swamp Forest Understories

Angelica atropurpurea (purple-stem angelica) OBL, B, K, S (part); to 6 ft.
**Aster lanceolatus* (*A. simplex*) (lined aster) FACW, B, C, S; to 4 ft.
Cardamine douglassii (pink spring cress) FACW+, S; to 10 in.; (NYS, S3, U)
Gentiana andrewsii (fringe-tip closed gentian) FACW, K, S (part); to 3 ft.
Pedicularis lanceolata (swamp lousewort) FACW, S (part); to 30 in.
**Pontederia cordata* (pickerelweed) OBL, C, K, S (part); to 3 ft.; emergent
Senecio aureus (golden ragwort) FACW, C, K, S; to 3 ft.
Stachys tenuifolia (common hedge-nettle) FACW+, C, S; to 3 ft.

Ferns for Alkaline Swamp Forest Understories

Dryopteris carthusiana (*D. spinulosa*) (toothed wood fern) FAC+, E, S; to 2 ft.
Dryopteris goldiana (Goldie's wood fern) FAC+, E, K, S; to 4 ft.
Matteuccia struthiopteris (ostrich fern) FACW, C, K, S; to 5 ft.
**Onoclea sensibilis* (sensitive fern) FACW, C, S; to 1 ft.; soil pH 4.5–7.5

Graminoids for Alkaline Swamp Forest Understories

Carex squarrosa (squarrose sedge) FACW, B, K, S (part); to 3 ft.
Carex typhina (cattail sedge) FACW+, B, K, S; (NYS S2, R); to 3 ft.
**Juncus effusus* (soft rush) FACW+, B, E (semi-), S (part); to 3 ft.

SET 5. PLANTS FOR UPLAND FORESTS

List 19. Plants for Disturbed Forest Understories, Eroded, Shady, Dry Slopes

Amend soil with leaves or compost. Install jute or coconut fiber mat, without artificial fiber, over soil amendment. If this is not possible, use a layer of branches over soil amendment. Plant through mat or small woody debris with 2-inch plugs. Water if possible.

The most critical remedies for revegetating bare, eroded soil are to protect the site from pedestrian and vehicle traffic, and to slow rainwater runoff. Use of loose brush mats or cribbing in addition to the above-mentioned soil amendments are useful temporary measures. Heavy planting will slow and dissipate runoff permanently. Use of thorny or densely branching shrubs and vines can discourage renewed human disturbance.

Shrubs and Woody Vines for Disturbed Forest Understories

Amelanchier spicata (*A. stolonifera*) (dwarf serviceberry) FACU, B, C, S; to 3 ft.
Cornus alternifolia (pagoda dogwood) UPL, S to 25 ft.; soil pH 6.5–7.5; shade index 8–10
Cornus rugosa (round-leaf dogwood) UPL, S; to 9 ft.; soil pH 6–8.5
Corylus americana (American hazelnut) FACU−, S; to 9 ft.; soil pH 6–7.5
Corylus cornuta (beaked hazelnut) FACU−, S; to 9 ft.; soil pH 6–7.5
Crataegus intricata (Biltmore hawthorn) UPL, S (part); to 24 ft.; thorny
Diervilla lonicera (dwarf-bush honeysuckle) UPL, C, H, S; to 3 ft.
Dirca palustris (leatherwood) FAC, S; to 6 ft.; soil pH 6–8.5
Euonymus americanus (strawberry bush) FAC, F, S; to 7 ft.; soil pH 6–7.5; (NYS S1, T)
Lonicera dioica (limber honeysuckle) FACU, H, S; shrub or climber, to 9 ft.; soil pH 6–8.5
**Parthenocissus quinquefolia* (Virginia creeper) FACU, C, F, G, S; woody vine
Ribes cynosbati (dogberry) UPL, F, S; to 5 ft.; spiny
Ribes rotundifolium (Appalachian gooseberry) UPL, S; spiny, to 5 ft.
Rubus odoratus (flowering raspberry) UPL, C, S (part); stems unarmed, to 6 ft.; soil pH 5–6
Staphylea trifolia (bladdernut) FAC, S; to 15 ft.; soil pH 6–8
Taxus canadensis (Canada yew) FAC, E, S; to 6 ft.; soil pH 5–7.5
Toxicodendron radicans (poison ivy) FAC, C, F, S; woody, vining ground cover to 35 ft. Toxic.
**Viburnum dentatum* (*V. recognitum*) (arrowwood) FAC, B, C, S (part); to 10 ft.; soil pH 5–7
Viburnum lentago (nanny berry) FAC, B, C, S (part); to 30 ft.; soil pH 6–8.5; shade index 5–6
Viburnum rafinesquianum (downy arrowwood) UPL, B, S (part); to 7 ft.; soil, pH 6–8.5

Herbs for Disturbed Forest Understories

Agrimonia gryposepala (common agrimony) FACU, C, S; to 4 ft.
Agrimonia pubescens (downy agrimony) UPL, C, S; to 3 ft.
**Aster cordifolius* (heart-leaved aster) UPL, B, S; to 5 ft.
**Aster divaricatus* (white wood aster) UPL, B, C, G, S; to 3 ft.
Circaea lutetiana (enchanter's nightshade) FACU, C, S; to 2 ft.; soil pH 5.6
Collinsonia canadensis (horse balm) FAC, C, S; to 3 ft.
**Eupatorium rugosum* (white snakeroot) UPL, B, C, S; to 5 ft.
**Geum canadense* (white avens) FACU, E (winter rosette), S; to 3 ft.; soil pH 5.6

Heuchera americana (alum root) UPL, E, S; to 3 ft.
**Polygonum virginianum* (*Tovara v.*) (jumpseed) FAC, C, S; to 6 ft.
**Solidago caesia* (blue-stemmed goldenrod) FACU, B, S; to 3 ft.

Ferns for Disturbed Forest Understories

Dennstaedtia punctilobula (hay-scented fern) UPL, C (aggressive), G, S (part); to 32 in.; soil pH 4–5
Polystichum acrostichoides (Christmas fern) FACU−, E, S (very); to 3 ft.
Thelypteris noveboracensis (New York fern) FAC, C (aggressive), S (part); to 18 in.

Graminoids for Disturbed Forest Understories

Carex blanda (woodland sedge) FAC, B, E, S to 2 ft.
**Carex pensylvanica* (Pennsylvania sedge) UPL, B, C, E (part), G, S; to 20 in.; soil pH 5
Carex swanii (Swan's sedge) UPL, B, S; to 3 ft.
**Danthonia compressa* (flattened oatgrass) FACU, G, S; to 2 ft.
**Danthonia spicata* (poverty oatgrass) UPL, S (part); to 2 ft.
**Juncus tenuis* (path rush) FAC−, S (part); to 28 in.
Muhlenbergia frondosa (wire-stem muhly) FAC, C (vigorously), S; to 40 in.
Muhlenbergia schreberi (nimblewill) FAC, C (aggressive), S (part); to 2 ft.
Muhlenbergia sobolifera (creeping muhly) UPL, C (vigorously), S; to 34 in.
Muhlenbergia tenuiflora (slender flowered muhly) UPL, C (vigorously), S; to 40 in.

List 20. Plants for Moist to Moderately Dry, Upland Forests: Good quality soils, pH 5–7 (approximately). Shade index: Least shade tolerant = 1; most shade tolerant = 10

Upland Trees

Acer saccharum (sugar maple) FACU, F, S; to 100 ft.; soil pH 5.5–7.3; shade index 10
Betula lenta (black birch, sweet birch) FACU, B, F; to 70 ft.; soil pH 4–5; shade index 4–6
Betula papyrifera (paper birch) FACU, B, F; to 80 ft.; soil pH 5–8.5; shade index 1; *pioneer*
Carpinus caroliniana (ironwood) FAC, B, F, S; to 40 ft.; soil pH 4.0–7.5; *understory;* shade index 8–10
Carya cordiformis (bitternut hickory) FACU+, B, F; to 90 ft.; soil pH 5.5–8.5; shade index 5.8
Carya glabra (pignut hickory) FACU−, B, F; to 90 ft.; soil pH 6–7.5; shade index 4–6
Carya ovalis (sweet pignut hickory; false shagbark) UPL, B; to 80 ft.

Carya ovata (shagbark hickory) FACU−, B, F; to 90 ft.; soil pH 6–6.5; shade index 5.4

Carya tomentosa (mockernut hickory) UPL, B, F; to 80 ft.; soil pH 6–6.5; shade index 2–4

Celtis occidentalis (common hackberry) FACU, B; to 70 ft.; soil pH 6.5–8.5; shade index 4–6

Cornus florida (flowering dogwood) FACU−, B, F, S; to 40 ft.; soil pH 5.5–7; *understory;* shade index 8–10

Diospyros virginiana (persimmon) FAC−, C, D; to 40 ft.; soil pH 6–6.5; shade index 2–4; *pioneer*

Fagus grandifolia (American beech) FACU, S; to 90 ft.; soil pH 4.1–6.5; shade index 9.3

Fraxinus americana (white ash) FACU, D, F; to 80 ft.; soil pH 5–7.5; shade index 6–8

Juglans nigra (black walnut) UPL, B; to 100 ft.; soil pH 4.6–8.2; shade index 4; *pioneer*

Liriodendron tulipifera (tulip tree) FACU, B, F, H; to 120 ft.; soil pH 4.8–6.5; shade index 4–6

Morus rubra (red mulberry) FACU; to 60 ft.; soil pH 6.3–8; shade index 4–6

Ostrya virginiana (hophornbeam) FACU−, B, S; to 30 ft.; soil pH 4.2–8; *understory;* shade index 8–10

Populus grandidentata (big-toothed aspen) FACU−, B, C, D; to 60 ft.; soil pH 5–6.3; shade index 1; *pioneer*

Populus tremuloides (quaking aspen) UPL, B, C, D; to 50 ft.; soil pH 4.5–6.5; shade index <1; *pioneer*

**Prunus serotina* (wild black cherry) FACU, A, B, F, K; to 75 ft.; soil pH 4.3–8; shade index 2.4

Quercus alba (white oak) FACU−, A, B; to 75 ft.; soil pH 3.5–7.5; shade index 5.7

Quercus coccinea (scarlet oak) UPL, A, B, F; to 75 ft., soil pH 4.5–6.9; shade index 2–4

Quercus prinus (chestnut oak) UPL, A, B; to 70 ft.; soil pH 6–6.5; shade index 4–6

Quercus rubra (red oak) FACU−, A, B; to 90 ft.; soil pH 4.5–6.5; shade index 7.8

Quercus velutina (black oak) UPL, A, B; to 80 ft.; soil pH 6–6.5; shade index 6–8

Tilia americana (American linden, basswood) FACU; to 80 ft.; soil pH 6.5–7.5; shade index 8

Upland Forest Understory Shrubs

Amelanchier arborea (serviceberry) FAC, B, F, S (part); to 40 ft.

Amelanchier canadensis (shadbush) FAC, B, F, S (part); to 25 ft.; soil pH 5–6.5; shade index 8–10

Amelanchier spicata (*A. stolonifera*) (dwarf serviceberry) FACU, B, C, S; to 3 ft.
Cornus alternifolia (pagoda dogwood) UPL, S; to 25 ft.; soil pH 6.5–7.5; shade index 8–10
Cornus rugosa (round-leaf dogwood) UPL, S; to 9 ft.; soil pH 6–8.5
Corylus americana (American hazelnut) FACU−, S; to 9 ft.; soil pH 6–7.5
Corylus cornuta (beaked hazelnut) FACU−, S; to 9 ft.; soil pH 6–7.5
Crataegus intricata (Biltmore hawthorn) UPL, S (part); to 24 ft.; thorny
Diervilla lonicera (dwarf-bush honeysuckle) UPL, C, H, S; to 3 ft.; soil pH 6–6.5
Dirca palustris (leatherwood) FAC, S; to 6 ft.; soil pH 6–8.5
Euonymus americanus (strawberry bush) FAC, F, S; to 7 ft.; soil pH 6–7.5
Hamamelis virginiana (witch hazel) FAC−, S; to 25 ft.; soil pH 6–6.5; shade index 8–10
Lonicera canadensis (fly-honeysuckle) FACU, H, S; to 6 ft.
Ribes cynosbati (dogberry) UPL, F, S; to 5 ft.; prickly and spiny; soil pH 6–8.5
Ribes rotundifolium (Appalachian gooseberry) UPL, S; to 5 ft.; spiny
Rubus odoratus (flowering raspberry) UPL, C, S; to 6 ft.; unarmed; soil pH 5–6
Staphylea trifolia (bladdernut) FAC, S; to 15 ft.; soil pH 6–8
Taxus canadensis (Canada yew) FAC E, S; to 6 ft.; soil pH 5–7.5
Viburnum acerifolium (maple-leaved viburnum) UPL, A, B, C, F, S (very); to 7 ft.; soil pH 4.4–6
Viburnum alnifolium (*V. lantanoides*) (hobblebush) UPL, B, C, S; to 6 ft.; soil pH 5.5–6.5
Viburnum lentago (nanny berry) FAC, B, C, S (part); to 30 ft.; soil pH 6–8.5; shade index 5–6
Viburnum rafinesquianum (downy arrowwood) UPL, B, S (part); to 7 ft.; soil pH 6–8.5

Upland Forest Understory Herbs: Soil pH 5.5–7 (approximately).
* Tolerant of urban woodland soils, fairly common in NYC woodlands.
**Tough plants for disturbed woods

Actaea alba (A. pachypoda) (doll's eyes, baneberry) UPL, S; to 32 in.
Actaea rubra (A. spicata) (red baneberry) UPL, S; to 32 in.
Agrimonia gryposepala (common agrimony) FACU, C, S; to 4 ft.
Agrimonia pubescens (downy agrimony) UPL, C, S; to 3 ft.
Amphicarpaea bracteata (American hog peanut) FAC, N, S (part); to 40 in. long; annual, twining vine
Anemonella thalictroides (rue anemone) UPL, to 8 in.; spring ephemeral
Anemone quinquefolia (wood anemone) FACU, C; to 8 in.; spring ephemeral
Anemone virginiana (tall anemone) UPL, S (part); to 3 ft.
Angelica venenosa (hairy angelica) UPL, B, S; to 6 ft.
Aquilegia canadensis (wild columbine) FAC, H, S; to 8 in.

Arabis canadensis (sickle-pod) UPL, E (winter rosette), S; biennial to 40 in.
**Aralia nudicaulis* (wild sarsaparilla) FACU, C, D, S; to 15 in.
Aralia racemosa (spikenard) UPL, C, S; to 6 ft.
Aristolochia serpentaria (Virginia snakeroot) UPL, B, S; to 18 in.
Asarum canadense (wild ginger) UPL, C, G, S; ca. 8 in.
Asclepias exaltata (poke milkweed) FACU, B, S; to 5 ft.
Asclepias quadrifolia (four-leaved milkweed) UPL, B, S; to 20 in.
Asclepias variegata (white milkweed) UPL, B, S; to 3 ft.
Aster acuminatus (whorled aster) UPL, B, C, S (part); to 32 in.
**Aster cordifolius* (heart-leaved aster) UPL, B, S; to 5 ft.
***Aster divaricatus* (white wood aster) UPL, B, C, G, S; to 3 ft.
Aster infirmus (Appalachian flat-topped white aster) UPL, B, S; to 44 in.
Aster lowrieanus (smooth heart-leaved aster) UPL, B, S; to 3 ft.
Aster macrophyllus (big-leaved aster) UPL, B, C, S; to 3 ft.
Aster paternus (toothed white-topped aster) UPL, B, S; to 2 ft.
Campanula americana (tall bellflower) FAC, S (part); winter annual or biennial to 5 ft.
Cardamine concatenata (*Dentaria laciniata*) (toothwort) FACU, C, S; to 16 in.
Cardamine diphylla (*Dentaria d.*) (broad-leaved toothwort) FACU, C, S; to 16 in.
Caulophyllum thalictroides (blue cohosh) UPL, S; to 32 in.
Cimicifuga racemosa (black snakeroot) UPL, B, S; to 7 ft.
***Circaea lutetiana* (enchanter's nightshade) FACU, C, S; to 2 ft.; soil pH 5.6
Claytonia caroliniana (Carolina spring beauty) FACU; ca. 4 in.; spring ephemeral
**Claytonia virginica* (spring beauty) FACU, C; to 7 in.; soil pH 6; spring ephemeral
**Collinsonia canadensis* (horse balm) FAC, C, S; to 3 ft.
**Cryptotaenia canadensis* (Canada honewort) FAC, B, S; to 3 ft.
Cynoglossum virginianum (wild comfrey) UPL, S; to 3 ft.
Dicentra canadensis (squirrel corn) UPL; to 6 in.; spring ephemeral
Dicentra cucullaria (Dutchman's breeches) UPL; to 6 in.; spring ephemeral
**Erythronium americanum* (trout lily) UPL, C; to 8 in.; soil pH 5–6; spring ephemeral
***Eupatorium rugosum* (white snakeroot) UPL, B, C, S; to 5 ft.
***Galium aparine* (cleavers) FACU, S; to above 5 ft. long; sprawling annual
Galium circaezans (forest bedstraw) UPL, S; to 2 ft.
Galium pilosum (bedstraw, cleavers) UPL, S; to 40 in.
Galium triflorum (sweet-scented bedstraw) FACU, S; to 32 in.
**Geranium maculatum* (wild geranium) FACU, B, S; to 22 in.; soil pH 5.4–5.6
***Geum canadense* (white avens) FACU, E (winter rosette) S; to 3 ft.; soil pH 5.6
Geum laciniatum (rough avens) FAC+, E (winter rosette), S (part); to 3 ft.
Hackelia virginiana (tickseed, beggar-lice) FACU, S; biennial to 40 in.

Helianthus decapetalus (forest sunflower) FACU, C, S (part); to 5 ft.
Helianthus divaricatus (woodland sunflower) UPL, B, C, S (part); to 5 ft.
Hepatica acutiloba (sharp-lobed hepatica) UPL, E, S; to 6 in.
Hepatica americana (round-lobed hepatica) UPL, E, S; to 6 in.
Heuchera americana (alum root) UPL, E, S; to 3 ft.
Hieracium paniculatum (panicled hawkweed) UPL, S; to 4 ft.
Hybanthus concolor (green violet) UPL, S; to 3 ft.
Hydrastis canadensis (golden-seal) UPL, C, S; to 20 in.; (NYS S2, T)
Hydrophyllum canadense (broad-leaved waterleaf) FACU, C, S; to 20 in.
Hydrophyllum virginianum (Virginia waterleaf) FAC, C, S; to 30 in.
***Lactuca canadensis* (tall lettuce) FACU−, S; annual or biennial to 8 ft.
**Lysimachia quadrifolia* (whorled loosestrife) FACU−, S; to 3 ft.; soil pH 4.8–5.0
**Maianthemum canadense* (Canada mayflower) FAC−, C, G, S (very); to 8 in.; soil pH 4–5.4
Medeola virginiana (Indian cucumber root) UPL, S; to 28 in.
Mitchella repens (partridge berry) FACU, C, E, G, S; to 8 in.; soil pH 5.0
Mitella diphylla (mitrewort) FACU, C, S; to 16 in.
**Osmorhiza claytonii* (hairy sweet cicely) FACU, B, S; to 2 ft.
Osmorhiza longistyis (anise root) FACU−, B, S; to 3 ft.
Oxalis violacea (violet wood sorrel) UPL, S; to 16 in.
Panax trifolius (dwarf ginseng) UPL, to 8 in.; spring ephemeral
Pedicularis canadensis (wood betony) FACU, S; to 16 in.
Penstemon pallidus (eastern beard-tongue) UPL, S; to 28 in.
Phryma leptostachya (lopseed) UPL, S; to 40 in.
Podophyllum peltatum (mayapple) FACU, C, S; to 20 in.
**Polygonatum biflorum* (smooth Solomon's seal) FACU, S; to 4 ft.; soil pH 4.6–7.6
Polygonatum pubescens (hairy Solomon's seal) UPL, S; to 3 ft.; soil pH 5–7.6
***Polygonum virginianum* (*Tovara v.*) (jumpseed) FAC, C, S; to 6 ft.
Prenanthes alba (rattlesnake root) FACU, S; to 5 ft.
Prenanthes altissima (tall rattlesnake root) FACU, S; to 6 ft.
Ranunculus hispidus (hispid buttercup) FACU, S (part); to 10 in.
Rudbeckia triloba (thin-leaved coneflower) FACU, S (part); to 5 ft.
Sanguinaria canadensis (bloodroot) UPL, C; to 10 in.; spring ephemeral
Sanicula canadensis (short-styled snakeroot) UPL, B, S; to 4 ft.
Sanicula gregaria (clustered snakeroot) FACU, B, S; to 4 ft.
Sanicula marilandica (Maryland sanicle) UPL, B, S; to 4 ft.
Scrophularia lanceolata (American figwort) FACU+, S; to 6.5 ft.
Scrophularia marilandica (eastern figwort) FACU−, S; to 10 ft.
Scutellaria elliptica (hairy skullcap) UPL, S (part); to 8 in.
Silene stellata (starry campion) UPL, S (part); to 4 ft.

**Smilacina racemosa* (false Solomon's seal) FACU−, C, S; to 32 in.; soil pH 3.8–7.7
***Solidago caesia* (blue-stemmed goldenrod) FACU, B, S; to 3 ft.
Solidago flexicaulis (zigzag goldenrod) FACU, B, S; to 4 ft.
Thaspium trifoliatum (meadow parsnip) UPL, B, S; to 3 ft.
Trientalis borealis (starflower) FAC, S; to 8 in.
Trillium erectum (purple trillium) FACU−, C, S; to 16 in.
Triosteum angustifolium (horse gentian) UPL, S (part); to 32 in.
Triosteum perfoliatum (feverwort) UPL, S (part); to 4 ft.
Uvularia perfoliata (bellwort) FACU, C, S; to 1 ft.
**Uvularia sessilifolia* (sessile-leaved bellwort) FACU−, C, S; to 1 ft.; soil pH 4.8–5.6
Viola canadensis (tall white violet) UPL, C, S; to 1 ft.
Viola pubescens (yellow forest violet) FACU, B, S; to 18 in.
Viola rostrata (long-spurred violet) FACU, B, S; to 10 in.
***Viola sororia* (common violet) FAC−, B, S; ca 6 in.; spring ephemeral
Zizia aurea (golden alexanders) FAC, B, S; to 32 in.

Upland Forest Understory Ferns

Adiantum pedatum (maidenhair fern) FAC−, C (very slowly), S; to 3 ft.
Athyrium filix-femina (lady fern) FAC, C, S; to 3 in.
Athyrium thelypterioides (silvery glade fern) FAC, S (part); to 3 ft.
Dryopteris intermedia (common wood fern) FACU, E, S; to 32 in.
Dryopteris marginalis (marginal wood fern) FACU−, E, S; to 18 in.
Osmunda claytoniana (interrupted fern) FAC, S (part); to 3 ft.
Polystichum acrostichoides (Christmas fern) FACU−, E, S (very); to 3 ft.; slopes
Thelypteris hexagonoptera (*Phegopteris h.*) (broad beech fern) FAC, C, S; to 2 ft.

Upland Forest Understory Graminoids

Brachyelytrum erectum (long-awned wood grass) UPL, S; to 40 in.
Bromus pubescens (*B. purgans*) (hairy woodland brome) FACU, S; to 5 ft.
**Carex abscondita* (thicket sedge) FAC, B, E, S (very); to 10 in.; (NYS S1, U)
Carex albursina (white bear sedge) FACU, B, S; to 2 ft.
Carex amphibola (narrow-leaf sedge) FAC, B, S; to 3 ft.
***Carex blanda* (woodland sedge) FAC, B, E, S; to 2 ft.
Carex debilis (white-edge sedge) FAC, B, S; to 3 ft.
Carex digitalis (slender woodland sedge) UPL, B, S; to 20 in.
Carex flaccosperma var. *glaucodea* (thin-fruit sedge) FAC, B, E, S; to 2 ft.; soil pH 4.6–7.1 (NYS S1, E)
Carex gracilescens (slender looseflower sedge) UPL, B, S; to 32 in.
Carex laxiflora (broad looseflower sedge) FACU, B, S; to 28 in.
Carex normalis (larger straw sedge) FACU, B, S (part); to 32 in.

Carex pallescens (pale sedge) UPL, B, S; to 20 in.
Carex platyphylla (broad-leaf sedge) UPL, B, E (semi-), S; to 16 in.
***Carex radiata* (eastern star sedge) UPL, B, S; to 32 in.
**Carex rosea* (rosy sedge) UPL, B, S; to 32 in.
***Carex swanii* (Swan's sedge) UPL, B, S; to 3 ft.
Carex tenera (slender sedge) FAC, B, S (part); to 3 ft.
***Danthonia compressa* (flattened oatgrass) FACU, G, S; to 2 ft.
***Danthonia spicata* (poverty oatgrass) UPL, S (part); to 2 ft.
Deschampsia flexuosa (common hairgrass) UPL, S; to 3 ft.
Festuca subverticillata (*F. obtusa*) (nodding fescue) FACU, S; to 4 ft.
Luzula acuminata (hairy wood-rush) FAC, S (light); to 16 in.
**Luzula multiflora* (common wood-rush) FACU, S (light); to 16 in.; soil pH 4.8–5.4
Muhlenbergia frondosa (wire-stem muhly) FAC, C (vigorously), S; to 3 ft.
***Muhlenbergia schreberi* (nimblewill) FAC, C (aggressive), S (part); to 2 ft.
Muhlenbergia sobolifera (creeping muhly) UPL, C (vigorously), S; to 34 in.
Muhlenbergia sylvatica (forest muhly) FAC+, C, S; to 30 in.
Muhlenbergia tenuiflora (slender-flowered muhly) UPL, C (vigorously), S; to 40 in.
Panicum dichotomum (cypress witchgrass) FAC, E (winter rosette), S (part); to 28 in.
Panicum lanuginosum (downy panic grass) UPL, E (winter rosette), S (part), to 40 in.
Panicum sphaerocarpon (round-seed panic grass) FACU, E (rosette), S; to 20 in.

List 21. Forest Plants for Acid Soils: Dry, Upland Rocky Woods, or Sandy, Acid, Low-Nutrient Soils of Oak Forests and Pine Barrens

Trees for Sandy or Rocky Acid Soils

Betula lenta (black birch, sweet birch) FACU, B, F; to 70 ft.; soil pH 4–5; shade index 4–6
**Betula populifolia* (gray birch) FAC, A, B, F; to 30 ft.; soil pH 5–7.5; shade index 1
Carpinus caroliniana (American hornbeam, ironwood) FAC, B, F, S; to 40 ft.; soil pH 4.0–7.5; shade index 8–10
Fagus grandifolia (American beech) FACU, S; to 90 ft.; soil pH 4.1–6.5; shade index 9.3
Juglans nigra (black walnut) UPL, B; to 100 ft.; soil pH 4.6–8.2; shade index 4
Ostrya virginiana (hophornbeam) FACU−, B, S; to 60 ft.; soil pH 4.2–8; shade index 8–10
Picea rubens (red spruce) FACU, A, E; to 90 ft.; soil pH 4–5.5; shade intolerant
Pinus echinata (short-leaf pine) UPL, A, E; to 90 ft.; shade intolerant; (NYS, SX, U)

**Pinus rigida* (pitch pine) FACU, A, E; to 60 ft.; soil pH 3.5–6.5; shade index 0–2

Pinus strobus (white pine) FACU, A, E; to 110 ft.; soil pH 4–6.5; shade index 4.4

Pinus virginiana (Virginia pine) UPL, A, E; to 30 ft.; soil pH 4.6–7.9; shade intolerant; (NYS S1, E)

**Populus grandidentata* (big-toothed aspen) FACU−, B, C, D; to 60 ft.; soil pH 5–6.3; shade index 1

**Populus tremuloides* (quaking aspen) UPL, B, C, D; to 50 ft.; soil pH 4.5–6.5; shade index <1

**Quercus alba* (white oak) FACU−, A, B, to 75 ft.; soil pH 3.5–7.5; shade index 5.7

**Quercus coccinea* (scarlet oak) UPL, A, B, F; to 75 ft.; soil pH 4.5–6.9; shade index 2–4

Quercus marilandica (blackjack oak) UPL, A, B; to 50 ft.; soil, pH 4–5.6; shade index 2–4

Quercus prinus (*Q. montana*) (chestnut oak) UPL, A, B; to 70 ft.; soil pH 6–6.5 (tolerates lower pH); shade index 4–6

Quercus rubra (red oak) FACU−, A, B, to 90 ft.; pH 4.5–6.5; shade index 7.8

Quercus stellata (post oak) UPL, A, B; to 60 ft.; soil pH 4.6–6.5; shade index 2–4

Quercus velutina (black oak) UPL, A, B; to 80 ft.; soil pH 6–6.5 (tolerates lower pH); shade index 6–8

Shrubs for Sterile, Acid Forest Soils

Amelanchier arborea (serviceberry) FAC, B, F, S (part); to 40 ft.

Amelanchier canadensis (shadbush) FAC; B, F, S (part); to 25 ft.; soil pH 5–6.5; shade index 8–10

Amelanchier spicata (*A. stolonifera*) (dwarf serviceberry) FACU, B, C, S; to 3 ft.

Ceanothus americanus (New Jersey tea) UPL, A, B, C, S (part); to 4 ft.; soil pH 4.5–6

**Gaylussacia baccata* (black huckleberry) FACU, A, B, C, S; to 3 ft., soil pH 4–5

Gaylussacia dumosa (dwarf huckleberry) FAC, A, B, C, S (part); to 20 in.

Gaylussacia frondosa (tall huckleberry) FAC, A, B, C, S; to 6 ft.

Kalmia angustifolia (sheep laurel) FAC, A, C, E, S (part); to 3 ft.; soil pH 4.5–6

Kalmia latifolia (mountain laurel) FACU, A, E, S; to 9 ft.; soil pH 4.5–6

Lyonia mariana (staggerbush) FAC−, A, C, S (part); to 6 ft.

Rhododendron maximum (white laurel) FAC, A, C, E, S; to 30 ft.; soil pH 4.5–6; shade index 6–8

**Rhododendron periclymenoides* (pinkster azalea) FAC, A, S; to 6 ft.; soil pH 4.2–5.5

Rhododendron prinophyllum (*R. roseum*) (early azalea) FAC, A, S; to 9 ft.; soil pH 5–8

Taxus canadensis (Canada yew) FAC, E, S; to 6 ft.; soil pH 5–7.5

Vaccinium angustifolium (lowbush blueberry) FACU, A, B, C, G, S (part); to 2 ft.; soil pH 4–6

**Vaccinium pallidum* (*V. vacillans*) (early low blueberry) UPL, A, B, C, S; to 3 ft.

Vaccinium stamineum (deerberry) FACU−, A, B, S (part); to 5 ft.; soil pH 4–6.5

**Viburnum acerifolium* (maple-leaved viburnum) UPL, A, B, C, F, S (very); to 7 ft.; soil pH 4.4–6

Viburnum alnifolium (*V. lantanoides*) (hobblebush) UPL, B, S; to 10 ft.; soil pH 5.5–6.5

Herbs for Acid Forest Soil

Aralia hispida (bristly sarsaparilla) UPL, C, S; to 4 ft.

Aster concolor (silvery aster) UPL, B, C; to 3 ft.; (NYS S1, E)

Aster Desmodium ciliare (little-leaf tick-trefoil) UPL, B, N; to 40 in.; (NYS S2S3, T)

Desmodium glabellum (tall tick-clover) UPL, B, N, S; to 4 ft.; (NYS S1, T)

Desmodium laevigatum (smooth tick-trefoil) UPL, B, N, S; to 4 ft.; (NYS S1, T)

Desmodium marilandicum (Maryland tick-trefoil) UPL, B, N, S (part); to 4 ft.

Desmodium paniculatum (panicled tick-clover) UPL, B, N, S (part); to 3 ft.

Desmodium rotundifolium (round-leaf tick-trefoil) UPL, B, N, S; stems prostrate to 5 ft.

Desmodium viridiflorum (velvety tick-trefoil) UPL, B, N, S; to 6 ft.

Epigaea repens (trailing arbutus) UPL, A, B, C, E, S; to 4 in.

Eupatorium album (white boneset) UPL, A, B, S (part); to 3 ft.

Eupatorium aromaticum (smaller white snake root) UPL, B, S (part); to 5 ft.; (NYS S1, E)

Eupatorium sessilifolium (upland boneset) UPL, B, C, S; to 6 ft.

Gaultheria procumbens (wintergreen) FACU, A, C, E, G, S; to 8 in.

Geranium carolinianum (Carolina crane's-bill) UPL; annual to 20 in.

Hedeoma pulegioides (American pennyroyal) UPL, S (part); annual to 16 in.

Hieracium gronovii (beaked hawkweed) UPL, S; to 3 ft.

Hieracium kalmii (*H. canadense*) (Canada hawkweed) UPL, S (part); to 5 ft.

Hieracium scabrum (rough hawkweed) UPL, S (part); to 5 ft.

Hieracium venosum (rattlesnake weed) UPL, S; to 3 ft.

Lathyrus ochroleucus (wild pea) UPL, C, N, S; to 30 in.

Lespedeza intermedia (wandlike bush clover) UPL B, N, S (part); to 30 in.

Lespedeza procumbens (trailing bush clover) UPL, B, G, N, S; to 3 ft.

Lespedeza repens (creeping bush clover) UPL, B, G, N, S; to 3 ft.

Lespedeza stuevei (tall bush clover) UPL, B, N; to 3 ft.; (NYS, S2, R)

Lespedeza violacea (violet bush clover) UPL, B, N, S; to 30 in.; (NYS S2, R)
Lespedeza virginica (slender bush clover) UPL, B, N, S; to 3 ft.
Liatris scariosa var. *novae-angliae* (northern blazing star) UPL, S; to 2.5 ft.
Linum virginianum (wild yellow flax) FACU, S (part); to 2 ft.
Lupinus perennis (wild blue lupine) UPL, B, N, S; to 2 ft.
Lysimachia quadrifolia (whorled loosestrife) FACU−, S; to 3 ft.; soil pH 4.8–5.0
Onosmodium virginianum (false gromwell) UPL, S (part); to 2 ft.; bristly
Parietaria pensylvanica (pellitory) FACU, S; annual to 16 in.
Penstemon hirsutus (white beard-tongue) UPL, S (part); to 32 in.
Physalis heterophylla (clammy ground-cherry) UPL, C, S (part); to 3 ft.
Physalis virginiana (Virginia ground-cherry) UPL, C, S (part); to 2 ft.
Prenanthes serpentaria (lion's foot) UPL, S; to 5 ft.
Prenanthes trifoliolata (gall-of-the-earth) UPL, S (part); to 7 ft.; soil pH 5.0
Pycnanthemum clinopodioides (basil mountain mint) UPL, S (part); to 3 ft.
Pycnanthemum incanum (hoary mountain mint) UPL, S (part); to 40 in.
Sanicula canadensis (short-styled snakeroot) UPL, B, S; to 4 ft.
Saxifraga virginiensis (early saxifrage) FAC, S (part); to 4 in.
Silene antirrhina (sleepy catch-fly) UPL; annual to 32 in.
Silene caroliniana (wild pink) UPL, S (part); to 8 in.; (NYS S3, V)
Solidago bicolor (silver-rod) UPL, B, S (part); to 3 ft.
Solidago squarrosa (squarrose goldenrod) UPL, S (part); to 5 ft.
Solidago ulmifolia (elm-leaved goldenrod) UPL, B, S (part); to 4 ft.
Stylosanthes biflora (pencil flower) UPL, B, N, S (part); to 20 in.
Taenidia integerrima (yellow pimpernel) UPL, B, S (part); to 3 ft.
Tephrosia virginiana (goat's rue) UPL, B, N, S (part); to 28 in.
Thalictrum revolutum (waxy meadow-rue) UPL, S (part); to 6.5 ft.
Verbena simplex (narrow-leaved vervain) UPL, S (part); to 2 ft.

Graminoids for Acid Forest Soils

Agrostis hyemalis (*A. scabra*) (tickle grass) FAC, S (part); to 3 ft.; soil pH 5–7.5
Agrostis perennans (*A. altissima*) (autumn bent grass) FACU, S (part); to 3 ft.
Carex digitalis (slender woodland sedge) UPL, B, S; to 20 in.
Carex muehlenbergii (Muhlenberg's sedge) UPL, S (part), B; to 3 ft.
Carex pensylvanica (Pennsylvania sedge) UPL, B, C, E (part), G, S; to 20 in.; soil pH 5
Carex vestita (velvet sedge) UPL, B, C (extensively), S; to 32 in.
Carex virescens (ribbed sedge) UPL, B, S; to 40 in.
Deschampsia flexuosa (common hairgrass) UPL, S; to 3 ft.
Elymus hystrix (*Hystrix patula*) (bottlebrush grass) UPL, S (part); to 5 ft.
Eragrostis capillaris (lace-grass) UPL, S (part); to 28 in.
Luzula multiflora (common wood-rush) FACU, S (part); to 16 in.; soil pH 4.8–5.4

Panicum columbianum (Columbia panic grass) UPL, E (winter rosette), S (part); to 34 in.

Panicum depauperatum (poverty panic grass) UPL, E (winter rosette), S (part); to 16 in.

Panicum lanuginosum (downy panic grass) UPL, E (winter rosette), S (part); to 40 in.

Panicum oligosanthes (few-flowered panic grass) UPL, E (winter rosette), S (part); to 28 in.

Panicum philadelphicum (Philadelphia panic grass) UPL, S (part); annual to 32 in.

Piptochaetium avenaceum (black oatgrass) UPL, S (part); annual to 32 in.

Schizachne purpurascens (false melic) FACU−, S; to 3 ft.

Plants for List 22. Alkaline Forest Soils, Concrete Debris

Trees for Alkaline Soil

Betula papyrifera (paper birch) FACU, B, F; to 80 ft.; soil pH 5–8.5; shade index 1; s

Carya cordiformis (bitternut hickory) FACU+, B, F; to 90 ft.; soil pH 5.5–8.5; shade index 5.8

Celtis occidentalis (common hackberry) FACU; B; to 70 ft.; soil pH 6.5–8.5; shade index 4–6; s

Juglans nigra (black walnut) UPL, B; to 100 ft.; soil pH 4.6–8.2; shade index 4; s

Juniperus virginiana (eastern red cedar) FACU, A, B, D, E; to 60 ft; soil pH 4.7–8.5; shade index 0–2

Morus rubra (red mulberry) FACU; to 60 ft.; soil pH 6.3–8; shade index 4–6; s

Ostrya virginiana (hophornbeam) FACU−, B, S; to 60 ft.; soil pH 4.2–8; shade index 8–10

**Prunus serotina* (wild black cherry) FACU, A, B, F, K; to 75 ft.; soil pH 4.3–8; shade index 2.4

Tilia americana (American linden, basswood) FACU; to 80 ft.; soil pH 6.5–7.5; shade index 8

Shrubs for Forest Understories with Alkaline Soil

Amelanchier arborea (serviceberry) FAC, B, F, K, S (part); to 40 ft.

Dirca palustris (leatherwood) FAC, K, S; to 6 ft.; soil pH 6–8.5

Lonicera canadensis (fly-honeysuckle) FACU, H, S; to 6 ft.

Rhododendron prinophyllum (*R. roseum*) (early azalea) FAC, A, S; to 9 ft.; soil pH 5–8

Ribes cynosbati (dogberry) UPL, F, K, S (part); to 5 ft.; soil pH 6–8.5

Ribes rotundifolium (Appalachian gooseberry) UPL, S (part); to 5 ft.; spiny

Staphylea trifolia (bladdernut) FAC, S; to 15 ft.; soil pH 6–8

Viburnum lentago (nanny berry) FAC B, C, K, S (part); to 30 ft.; soil pH 6–8.5; shade index 5–6

Viburnum prunifolium (black-haw) FACU, B, K, S (part); small tree; to 15 ft.; soil pH 5–8.5; shade index 2–4

Viburnum rafinesquianum (downy arrowwood) UPL, B, K, S (part); to 7 ft.; soil pH 6–8.5

Zanthoxylum americanum (prickly ash) UPL, D, K, S (part); to 25 ft.; soil pH 6–8.5; shade index 2–4

Herbs for Alkaline Forest Soils (including some plants needing "rich" soil as well as those found on limestone soils)

Actaea alba (A. pachypoda) (doll's eyes, baneberry) UPL, S; to 32 in.

Actaea rubra (A. spicata) (red baneberry) UPL, S; to 32 in.

Agastache scrophulariaefolia (purple giant hyssop) UPL, S; to 4 ft.

Agrimonia pubescens (downy agrimony) UPL, C, K, S; to 3 ft.

Allium tricoccum (wild leek) FACU+, S; to 1 ft.

Anemone cylindrica (thimbleweed) UPL; to 3 ft.

Anemone quinquefolia (wood anemone) FACU, C; to 8 in.; spring ephemeral

Anemone virginiana (tall anemone) UPL, S (part); to 3 ft.

Aquilegia canadensis (wild columbine) FAC, H, S; to 18 in.

Arabis hirsuta var. *pycnocarpa* (hairy rock cress) FACU, E (winter rosette), K, S; biennial to 32 in.

Arabis laevigata (smooth rock cress) UPL, E (winter rosette), K, S; biennial to 40 in.

Arabis lyrata (lyre-leaved rock cress) FACU, E (winter rosette); biennial to 16 in.

Aralia nudicaulis (wild sarsaparilla) FACU, C, D, S; to 15 in.

Aralia racemosa (spikenard) UPL, C, S; to 6 ft.

Aristolochia serpentaria (Virginia snakeroot) UPL, B, K, S; (NYS S1, U); to 18 in.

Asarum canadense (wild ginger) UPL, C, G, K, S; ca. 8 in.

Asclepias verticillata (whorled milkweed) UPL, B, S (part); to 18 in.

Asclepias viridiflora (green milkweed) UPL, B, K, S (part); to 3 ft.; (NYS S2, R)

**Aster cordifolius* (heart-leaved aster) UPL, B, S; to 5 ft.

**Aster divaricatus* (white wood aster) UPL, B, C, G, S; to 3 ft.

Aster lowrieanus (smooth heart-leaved aster) UPL, B, S; to 3 ft.

Caulophyllum thalictroides (blue cohosh) UPL, K, S; to 32 in.

Cerastium nutans (nodding chickweed) FAC, K, S; annual to 2 ft.

Cimicifuga racemosa (black snakeroot) UPL, B, S; to 7 ft.

**Claytonia virginica* (spring beauty) FACU, C; to 7 in.; soil pH 6; spring ephemeral

Collinsonia canadensis (horse balm) FAC, C, S; to 3 ft.

Cryptotaenia canadensis (Canada honewort) FAC, B, S; to 3 ft.

Dicentra canadensis (squirrel corn) UPL; to 6 in.; spring ephemeral

Dicentra cucullaria (Dutchman's breeches) UPL; to 6 in.; spring ephemeral
Eupatorium purpureum (purple joe-pye weed) UPL, B, K, S; to 10 ft.
**Eupatorium rugosum* (white snakeroot) UPL, B, C, K, S; to 5 ft.
Eupatorium sessilifolium (upland boneset) UPL, B, C, K, S; to 6 ft.
Floerkea proserpinacoides (false mermaid) FAC, K, S; annual to 1 ft.
Fragaria vesca var. *americana* (woodland strawberry) UPL, C, G, S; ca. 6 in.
**Geranium maculatum* (wild geranium) FACU, B, S; to 22 in.; soil pH 5.4–5.6
Hackelia virginiana (tickseed, beggar-lice) FACU, K, S; biennial to 40 in.
Helianthus decapetalus (forest sunflower) FACU, C, S (part); to 5 ft.
Hepatica acutiloba (sharp-lobed hepatica) UPL, E, K, S; 6 in.
Heuchera americana (alum root) UPL, E, K, S; to 3 ft.
Hybanthus concolor (green violet) UPL, K, S; to 3 ft.
Oenothera parviflora (northern evening primrose) FACU−, H, K, S (part); biennial to 6 ft.
Ranunculus fascicularis (early buttercup) FACU, K, S (part); to 10 in.
Senecio obovatus (round-leaved ragwort) FACU, K, S (part); to 28 in.
Verbena simplex (narrow-leaved vervain) UPL, S (part); to 2 ft.
Verbena urticifolia (white vervain) FACU, S (part); annual or perennial to 5 ft.
Viola palmata (V. brittoniana) (early blue violet) FAC, B, K, S (part); ca. 6 in.

Ferns for Alkaline Forest Soils

Asplenium trichomanes (maidenhair spleenwort) UPL, E, K, S; to 10 in.
Polypodium virginianum (P. vulgare) (common polypody) UPL, C, E, S; to 1ft.

Graminoids for Alkaline Forest Soils

Carex albursina (white bear sedge) FACU, B, S; to 2 ft.
Carex gracilescens (slender looseflower sedge) UPL, B, S; to 32 in.
**Muhlenbergia schreberi* (nimblewill) FAC, C (aggressive), S (part); to 2 ft.
**Muhlenbergia sobolifera* (creeping muhly) UPL, C (vigorously), S; to 34 in.
Muhlenbergia tenuiflora (slender-flowered muhly) UPL, C (vigorously), S; to 40 in.

Glossary

Many of these definitions are a synthesis of those given in the glossaries in Gleason and Cronquist (1991), Raven et al. (1986), Harrington and Durrell (1957), and Fernald (1950).

acid: Soil or water with a pH below 7.

aforestation: The artificial establishment of forests by planting trees in an area of nonforested land.

aggressive: Plants that grow rapidly and are often colonial, producing many stems from one extensive root system. Canada goldenrod is an aggressive plant relative to butterfly weed.

alkaline: Soil or water with a pH above 7.

allelopathic: Plants that produce substances, usually in roots or fallen leaves, which inhibit the germination or growth of other plants in the vicinity. Most of these chemicals are alkaloids, terpenoids, or phenolics. *See* black walnut (*Juglans nigra*).

alternate: One leaf at each node along a stem.

anaerobic: Lacking air (oxygen). Typical condition of waterlogged soils, or compacted soils without air spaces. Aerobic refers to an organism requiring oxygen or an environment containing oxygen.

annual: Herbs (or grasses) that complete their entire life cycle within one growing season. They overwinter only as seed. Winter annuals sprout in autumn and overwinter as leafy rosettes. Ragweed is an annual.

aquatic: Plants that live in water. Some are rooted to the bottom of the water body, others simply float. Some have leaves that float on the surface of the water or emerge from the water on stalks; others are completely submerged.

barren: Habitats with dry, low-nutrient, rocky, or sandy soils. Barren habitats support specialized plant communities adapted to these inhospitable conditions. Plants adapted to barrens soils are often poor competitors on high-nutrient soils with more aggressive species. Bearberry (*Arctostaphylos uva-ursi*) is an example.

biennial: Plants that complete their life cycle in two years. They usually grow as a rosette of leaves the first growing season. The following summer they produce a flowering stalk and die after seeds mature. Evening primrose (*Oenothera biennis*) is an example.

bog: Open, quiet wetlands, poor in oxygen and nutrients that accumulate partially decayed plant remains (peat). Sphagnum bog: the ground layer is dominated by sphagnum mosses.

brackish: Water with approximately 0.6 to 17 parts per thousand salt (ppt). Freshwater has 0–0.5 ppt salt. Ocean water averages 35 ppt salt.

calcareous: Soils high in calcium, derived from limestone. Concrete is artificial limestone. These soils are generally circumneutral to alkaline. The term "rich" is often applied to calcareous soils because many nutrients (especially calcium, magnesium, phosphate, and potassium) are more available in neutral or slightly alkaline soils than in acid soils.

catkin: A (usually) dangling, spike-like inflorescence of tiny flowers, generally amid scale-like bracts, often of only one sex. Male catkins are usually larger and more conspicuous (pussy willow). Females are often smaller and more rigid (hazelnut), or not in catkins (oaks).

chlorophyll: The green pigment in plants that transfers light energy into a form used to make sugar from carbon dioxide and water. This process is photosynthesis. The waste product from photosynthesis is oxygen.

circumneutral: Around pH 7 (i.e., about pH 6.5–7.5). *See* pH.

coastal plain: Relatively flat terrain along the coast. Areas along the coast, formerly below sea level in recently past geologic eras. Outer coastal plain of our region includes Long Island and the eastern counties of New Jersey. It is usually characterized by sandy soils, often interspersed with layers of clay. Inner coastal plain in New Jersey is a strip of land running NE–SW roughly following the path of Route 1. *See* piedmont.

colonial (clonal): Plants reproducing vegetatively (asexually) by various methods: root sprouts, underground stems (rhizomes), runners, bulb offsets. They may form large stands that are essentially a single plant. All are genetically identical, e.g., lined aster, strawberries.

community: Plant species that typically are found growing together in the same habitat, e.g., dry, upland oak forest; acid bog; alkaline fill soil.

competition: The ability of one plant to shade out, crowd out, or overwhelm another plant. Plants adapted to poor soils, and marginal habitats, are often outcompeted in better habitats by more vigorous or taller plants. For instance, sweet everlasting can be outcompeted by Canada goldenrod in good-quality soil.

deciduous: Plants that lose their leaves in autumn and grow a complete new set each spring.

dioecious: Plants in which male and female flowers are on separate individual plants, e.g., *Ilex, Myrica.*

dominant: The most abundant plants in a particular plant community. In this region, swamp forests are often dominated by red maple. A codominant plant is about as equally abundant as the dominant species. Sweet gum-red maple swamp forest is an example.

dune: Ridges of sand that parallel beach or other oceanfronts. A primary dune is the sand ridge that begins slightly above high high tide level. It is highly disturbed by winds and storms and is usually dominated by dune grass (*Ammophila breviligulata*). Back-dune plant communities are those that develop behind shoreline primary dunes. They are often disturbed by storms and tend to be dominated by herbs and shrubs. Poison ivy, bayberry, and beach plum are examples. If undisturbed for some decades, forest dominated by American holly and eastern red cedar often become established (Fire Island, NY; Sandy Hook, NJ).

emergent: Plants that grow in shallow water with their leaves above the water's surface or in saturated soil that is flooded periodically, e.g., *Peltandra virginica, Carex stricta.*

freshwater: Water with salt content less than 0.5 parts per thousand (ppt). *See* brackish.

gap: In reference to forest communities, an opening in the tree canopy that allows a local increase in light reaching the forest floor. This, in turn, allows additional growth of understory herbs, shrubs, and canopy tree saplings, until the canopy gap closes as tall trees grow inwards or saplings grow upwards to fill it.

graminoid: Grasses and grasslike plants. Usually including only the grass, sedge, and rush families with very narrow, linear leaves and small, dry flowers.

herb: Plants without woody tissues that die back to the ground in winter. Usually applied to broad-leaved plants rather than grasses. Also referred to as forbs.

high high tide: Spring tide. The greatest tidal range, occurring twice a month, during the full and new moons when the sun and moon are aligned and their gravitational pulls are combined.

highlands: Mostly characterized by formerly glaciated, hilly terrain. Roughly equivalent to the northwest part of New Jersey and the rocky, glaciated parts of New York City north of Long Island, including some of Manhattan and all of the Bronx.

humus: Insoluble, partially decayed organic materials forming a blackish, soft, crumbly substance that collects as a layer between mineral soil and the surface layer of undecayed leaf litter and woody debris.

inflorescence: The part of a plant bearing flowers. Applied to plants with more than one flower.

invasive: A plant species that grows and reproduces without constraint in a plant community of which it is not a natural member. Invasive plants decrease biodiversity of a plant community by crowding out native plants.

marsh: Open, more-or-less permanently flooded wetland, dominated by emergent, herbaceous vegetation. Water may be fresh, brackish, or salt. The latter two conditions are salt marshes.

monoecious: Flowers that are unisexual but both sexes are on the same plant, e.g., *Quercus, Carya, Pinus.* (*See* dioecious).

mycorrhizas: Symbiotic association between the roots of a plant and a fungus. The fungus helps extract nutrients, especially phosphorus, from soil and, in turn, uses carbohydrates manufactured by the plant. There are several different structural types of mycorrhizas.

native plant: Plants that were growing in this region before Europeans came to North America. Our native plants are adapted to the climate and soils of the New York City region. They have evolved relationships with birds, mammals, insects, and fungi and are integrated into the ecology of this region. The native plants of this region come from seeds that spread northward after the last glaciers melted thousands of years ago.

ornamental: Plants used as horticultural specimens in gardens or developed parks, not intended to reproduce or be part of a plant natural community.

peat: Soil consisting of partially decayed organic materials, mostly plant debris that is not decomposing for lack of oxygen. Peaty soils usually form in wetlands, where there is little oxygen and few aerobic decay bacteria.

perennial: A plant that can bloom and fruit more than once. This includes all woody plants. Some perennials are short lived, others may live for 200 years (oaks). *See* annual and biennial.

pH: A measure of the acidity and alkalinity of soil or water. The lower the pH, the higher the acidity. Many native plants require acid soil with pH 4.5–6. Soils with pH above 6.5 are considered neutral, and soils with pH above 7.5 are alkaline (pH stands for the "power of hydrogen" and is the negative log of the concentration of hydrogen ions in a solution).

phytoremediation: Biological remediation of environmental problems using plants. Some plants are able to take up significant amounts of various toxic wastes from the soil.

piedmont: "Foot of the mountain." In New Jersey, the strip of land running NE–SW, between the inner coastal plain and the highlands, relatively flat to rolling terrain, both glaciated and unglaciated.

pioneer species: Plants that are the first colonizers of open, disturbed sites (*see* Succession), such as burns, blow-downs, abandoned farm fields, vacant lots, or fill soils. Most pioneer species grow quickly, reproduce abundantly, and are intolerant of shade. Most annual herbs and short-lived woody species are pioneers.

prickle: A sharp, pointed outgrowth from the bark of a plant, as, e.g., in *Rosa carolina, Ribes cynosbati.*

primary species: The dominant plant species in a habitat or for use in a restoration.

reproductive maturity: The point in the life of a plant where it has achieved sufficient size (biomass) and has access to enough resources (light, water, nutrients) to support the growth of reproductive structures (sporangia, cones, flowers). Reproduction is "costly" in terms of energy use.

rosette: A dense cluster of leaves arranged in a circle or dense spiral at the base of a plant (basal rosette), usually rather flat, as, e.g., in Indian-tobacco (*Lobelia inflata*). Many biennials produce a rosette during their first year. These leaves often die as the flowering stalk grows during the second year. Some perennials produce a winter rosette in autumn that is green all winter and dies when the plant grows flowering stems the following spring, e.g., white avens (*Geum canadense*).

salt marsh: Open wetlands along the coast that are flooded during high tide. The combination of brackish to saline water and saturated soil severely restricts the plant species that can live in salt marsh habitats.

saturated: Soil in which all the spaces between soil particles are filled with water. Saturated soil has very little oxygen (it is anaerobic). Oxygen is needed to support the life of plant roots.

scrub: A plant community dominated by shrubs and other low woody and herbaceous vegetation. Scrub usually succeeds to forest unless subject to frequent disturbances such as storms which kill back-dune scrub by blow-outs or inundation from salt spray.

secondary species: A common but not dominant plant in a habitat restoration.

spine: A sharp, pointed, projection that is a modified leaf. The stems of *Ribes cynosbati* are spiny at nodes but often prickly on stems between nodes (*see* prickle).

spring ephemeral: Forest herbs that grow, bloom, and set fruit before the leaf canopy closes. They are not shade tolerant but squeeze their life cycle into the time between freezing weather and deep shade of the summer forest floor after the trees leaf out. Most go dormant and disappear by July. Examples are trout lily, spring beauty.

submerged (submersed): Plants that grow with their leaves underwater (Submerged Aquatic Vegetation, SAV), such as pondweeds (*Potamogeton* spp.).

succession: The sequential change in vegetation over time after a disturbance such as farming, fire, wind throw, or logging (see Introduction).

swamp: Occasionally flooded wetlands, dominated by woody vegetation adapted to periodically inundated soil. Shrub swamp or swamp forest.

thorn: Stiff, sharply pointed projection that is a modified stem, such as branches of *Crataegus pruinosa*.

tidal: Habitats influenced by fluctuating water levels caused by tides. Salinity of estuaries and rivers can be saline, brackish, or fresh water depending on the inflow of fresh water from upstream.

understory: Habitat below the tree canopy of a forest. Tree saplings, shrubs, and herbs that can live in shade or part shade. Many of these plants leaf out before the tree canopy closes and do most of their growing during that time (e.g., Canada mayflower).

vegetative: Not involving sexual reproduction or reproductive organs (i.e., flowers, sporangia, cones, sex cells). Tissues such as leaves, stems, bark, roots are vegetative.

vegetative reproduction: Asexual reproduction, as with runners, rhizomes, bulb offshoots, layering. Reproduction resulting in clonal (colonial) plants, with identical genetic makeup of the parent. Sexual reproduction results in daughter plants with genetic makeup that is altered (remixed) from that of two parents.

wetland: An area that is "inundated or saturated by surface water or ground water at a frequency and duration sufficient to support vegetation typically adapted for life in saturated soil. Wetlands generally include swamps, marshes, bogs and similar areas." (Reed 1988) The defining characteristic of wetland plants is that they can tolerate soil with little oxygen because the air spaces are filled with water (saturated) (see Introduction).

wetland mitigation: The attempted creation or enlargement of a wetland to offset the destruction of a natural wetland during a construction project.

Bibliography

Allaby, M. (ed.). 1998. *A Dictionary of Plant Sciences.* 2nd ed. Oxford University Press, New York.

Anella, L. B., and T. H. Whitlow. 2000. Photosynthetic response to flooding of *Acer rubrum* seedlings from wet and dry sites. *Am. Midl. Nat.* 143:330–341.

Anonymous. 2002. Glossary of statistical terms. OECD (Organization for Economic Cooperation and Development). cs3-hq.oecd.org/scripts/stats/glossary/detail.asp?ID=55.

Anonymous. 2005. *Plymouth Geography.* GGX1007, Skills for Geographers. www.geog.plym.ac.uk/labskills/bdpg.htm.

Borman, F. H., and G. E. Likens. 1976. *Pattern and Process in a Forested Ecosystem.* Springer-Verlag, New York.

Brady, N. C., and R. R. Weil. 1996. *The Nature and Properties of Soils.* 11th ed. Macmillan, New York.

Brown, L. 1979. *Grasses: An Identification Guide.* Houghton Mifflin, Boston.

Burns, R. M., and B. H. Honkala. 1990. *Silvics of North America.* Vol. 2: *Hardwoods.* Agriculture Handbook 654. Forest Service, USDA, Washington, DC. www.na.fs.fed.us/spfo/pubs/silvics_manual/volume_2/.

Clemants, S. E. Unpublished. New York City Checklist, New York Metropolitan Flora. Brooklyn Botanic Garden.

Collins, B. R., and K. H. Anderson. 1994. *Plant Communities of New Jersey.* Rutgers University Press, New Brunswick, NJ.

Connecticut Botanical Society. 2006. http://www.ct-botanical-society.org/index.html.

Dave's Garden Network: www.plantsdatabase.com/go/54337/.

DeJong-Hughes, J., J. F. Moncrief, W. B. Voorhees, and J. B. Swan. 2001. Soil compaction causes, effects and control. University of Minnesota Extension Service FO-03115. www.extension.umn.edu/distribution/ cropsystems/DC3115.html.

Fernald, M. L. 1950. *Gray's Manual of Botany.* 8th ed. Dioscorides Press, Portland, OR.

Gleason, H. A. 1952. *The New Britton and Brown Illustrated Flora of the United States and Adjacent Canada.* Hafner Press for the New York Botanical Garden, New York.

Gleason, H. A., and A. Cronquist. 1991. *Manual of Vascular Plants of Northeastern United States and Adjacent Canada.* New York Botanical Garden, Bronx, NY.

Graham, S. A. 1954. Scoring tolerance of forest trees. University of Michigan School of Natural Resources, *Michigan For.* 4.

Greller, A. M., D. C. Locke, V. Kilanowski, and G. E. Lotowycz. 1990. Changes in vegetation composition and soil acidity between 1922 and 1985 at a site on the North Shore of Long Island, New York. *Bull. Torrey Bot. Club* 117(4): 450–458.

Grime, J. P. 1965. Shade tolerance in flowering plants. *Nature* 208: 161–163.

Gundale, M. J. 2002. Influence of exotic earthworms on the soil organic horizon and the rare fern *Botrychium mormo*. *Conservation Biology* 16(6): 1555–1561.

Hanlon, E. A., B. L. McNeal, and G. Kidder. 2002. Soil and container media electrical conductivity interpretations. University of Florida Cooperative Extension Service Circular 1092. http://edis.ifas.ufl.edu/BODY_SS117.

Hightshoe, G. L. 1988. *Native Trees, Shrubs, and Vines for Urban and Rural America: A Planting Design Manual for Environmental Designers.* Van Nostrand Reinhold, New York.

Holmgren, N. H. 1998. *Illustrated Companion to Gleason and Cronquist's Manual: Illustrations of the Vascular Plants of Northeastern United States and Adjacent Canada.* New York Botanical Garden Press, Bronx, NY.

Hough, M. Y. 1983. *New Jersey Wild Plants.* Harmony Press, Harmony, NJ.

Houston, D. R., and J. T. O'Brien. 1983. Beech Bark Disease. Forest Insect and Disease Leaflet 75. U.S.D.A. Forest Service. www.na.fs.fed.us/spfo/pubs/fidls/beechbark/fidl-beech.htm.

Killham, K. 1994. *Soil Ecology.* Cambridge University Press, New York.

Kortebein, P., T. Wenskus, and M. Matsil. 2002. Restoration of closed canopy forest in a mugwort dominated fill site (New York). *Ecological Restoration* 20(2): 130–131.

Larson, Gary E. 1993. Aquatic and wetland vascular plants of the northern Great Plains. Gen. Tech. Rep. RM-238. Fort Collins, CO: U.S. Department of Agriculture, Forest Service, Rocky Mountain Forest and Range Experiment Station. Jamestown, ND: Northern Prairie Wildlife Research Center Online. http://www.npwrc.usgs.gov/resource/plants/vascplnt/index.htm (Version 02FEB99).

Lincoln, R. J., G. A. Boxshall, and P. F. Clark. 1982. *A Dictionary of Ecology, Evolution and Systematics.* Cambridge University Press, New York.

Mitchell, R. S. 1986. A Checklist of New York State Plants. Bulletin No. 458. New York State Museum, the University of the State of New York.

Morris, M., D. E. Eveleigh, S. C. Riggs, and W. N. Tiffney, Jr. 1974. Nitrogen fixation in the bayberry (*Myrica pensylvanica*) and its role in coastal succession. *Amer. J. Bot.* 61(8): 867–870.

National List of Plant Species That Occur in Wetlands: New York. 1988. U.S. Fish and Wildlife Service, St. Petersburg, FL.

Newcomb, L. 1977. *Newcomb's Wildflower Guide.* Little, Brown and Co., Boston.

Nolte, B. H., and N. R. Fausey. 2005. Soil compaction and drainage. The Ohio State University AEX-301. ohioline.osu.edu/b301/.

Northern Prairie Wildlife Research Center. 2006. U.S. Geological Survey. http://www.npwrc.usgs.gov/resource/plants/vascplnt/species/gtri.htm

Petrides, G. A. 1972. *A Field Guide to Trees and Shrubs.* Peterson Field Guide Series. Houghton Mifflin, Boston.

Petrides, G. A. 1988. *Eastern Trees*. Peterson Field Guide Series. Houghton Mifflin, Boston.

Pokorny, J. D., and W. A. Sinclair. 1994. How to Identify and Manage Ash Yellows in Forest Stands and Home Landscapes. USDA Forest Service Northeast Area, State and Private Forestry. NA-FR-03-94. www.na.fs.fed.us/spfo/pubs/howtos/ht_ash/ht_ash.htm.

Pouyat, R. V., R. W. Parmelee, and M. M. Carreiro.1994. Environmental effects of forest soil–invertebrate and fungal densities in oak stands along an urban-rural land use gradient. *Pedobiologia* 38: 385–399.

Reschke, C. 1990. Ecological Communities of New York State. New York Natural Heritage Program, N.Y. State Dept. Environmental Conservation, Latham, NY.

Rice, E. L. 1972. Allelopathic effects of *Andropogon virginicus* and its persistence in old fields. *Amer. J. Bot.* 59(7): 752–755.

Runesson, U. T. 2005. Borealforest.org. Faculty of Forestry and the Forest Enviornment, Lakehead University, Ontario, Canada. http://www.borealforest.org.

Saltonstall, K. 2002. Cryptic invasion by a non-native genotype of the common reed, *Phragmites australis*, into North America. *Proc. Nat. Acad. Sci.* 99(4): 2445–2449. www.pnas.org, or www.invasiveplants.net.

Sauer, L. J., and Andropogon Associates. 1998. *The Once and Future Forest: A Guide to Forest Restoration Strategies*. Island Press, Washington, DC.

Schemske, D. W., M. F. Willson, M. N. Melampy, L. J. Miller, L. Verner, K. M. Schemske, and L. B. Best. 1978. Flowering ecology of some spring woodland herbs. *Ecology* 59(2): 351–366.

Schultz, K., J. Zasada, and E. Nauertz. 2005. Annual, local, and individual variation in the inflorescence and fruit production of eastern leatherwood (*Dirca palustris* L. Thymelaeaceae). *J. Torrey Bot. Soc.* 131(4): 292–304.

Sinclair, W. A., H. H. Lyon, and W. T. Johnson. 1987. *Diseases of Trees and Shrubs*. Comstock Publishing Associates, Cornell University Press, Ithaca, NY. www.na.fs.fed.us/spfo/pubs/silvics_manual/volume_2/.

Skinner, M. W. 2005. USDA, NRCS. The PLANTS Database, Version 3.5 (http://plants.usda.gov). National Plant Data Center, Baton Rouge, LA 70874-4490 USA.

Sotir, R. B., and D. H. Gray. 1992. *Engineering Field Handbook*. Chapter 18: Soil bioengineering for upland slope protection and erosion reduction. USDA, Soil Conservation Service, Washington, DC.

Steyermark, J. 1963. Flora of Missouri. http://www.missouriplants.com/.

Thunhorst, G. A. 1993. *Wetland Planting Guide for the Northeastern United States: Plants for Wetland Creation, Restoration and Enhancement*. Environmental Concern, Inc., St. Michaels, MD.

Young, J. A., and C. G. Young. 1992. *Seeds of Woody Plants in North America*. Dioscorides Press, Portland, OR.

Young, S. M. 2002. *New York State Rare Plant List*. New York Natural Heritage Program. N.Y. State Dept. Environmental Conservation, Latham, NY. www.dec.state.ny.us/website/dfwmr/heritage/plants.htm.

Young, J. A., and C. G. Young. 1992. *Seeds of Woody Plants in North America*. Dioscorides Press, Portland, OR.

Index

About the Author

Margaret Gargiullo has a Ph.D. in plant ecology. She worked as a plant ecologist for the New York City Parks Natural Resources Group from 1994 to 2006. She was involved in many projects inventorying and identifying plants, evaluating land for potential preservation, planning restorations of natural areas, and teaching plant ecology.